The Food Lover's Guide to Paris

The Food Lover's Guide to Paris

PATRICIA WELLS

Assisted by SUSAN HERRMANN LOOMIS
Photographs by PETER TURNLEY
Front Cover photographs by ROBERT FRESON

Methuen

To Walter, with gratitude
for his unwavering love,
trust, and support

First published in the United States of America 1984
by Workman Publishing Company, New York

. First published in Great Britain 1984
by Methuen London Ltd
11 New Fetter Lane, London EC4P 4EE

Reprinted 1985

Copyright © 1984 by Patricia Wells
Photographs copyright © 1984 by Peter Turnley
Front cover photographs © 1984 by Robert Freson

Art Director: Paul Hanson
Designer: Susan Aronson Stirling
Front cover photographs: Robert Freson
Book photographs: Peter Turnley

ISBN 0 413 56720 6

First printing March, 1984

Printed in Great Britain by
Redwood Burn Limited, Trowbridge, Wiltshire
and Bound by Pegasus Bookbinding, Melksham, Wiltshire

Acknowledgments

Thanks to the generosity, enthusiasm, and encouragement of so many fine people, much of the work on this book was transformed into sheer pleasure. I am deeply grateful to Susan Herrmann Loomis, whose friendship and fidelity, energy and inspiration sustained me throughout; to Jane Sigal, who in the midst of chaos always managed to hold the office together; to Nihal Goonesekera, who kept my world scrubbed and polished as I drowned in a sea of clips and files.

I was touched by the generosity of the French chefs, bakers, restaurateurs, and shopkeepers who gave so freely of their time and expertise, and shared their recipes. Special thanks to Jean-Claude Vrinat of Taillevent, Joël Robuchon of Jamin, Gilbert and Maguy Le Coze of Le Bernardin, Paul Blache of La Coquille, and bakers Bernard Ganachaud, Lionel and Max Poilâne, and Jean-Luc Poujauran.

None of this would have been possible without the remarkable confidence of Peter Workman and the expert attention of my editor, Suzanne Rafer, who believed in both me and the book when others remained doubtful. Thanks also go to Kim Honig and Amy Gateff for their careful checking of information, and to Paul Hanson and Susan Aronson Stirling for the beautiful design of the book.

Throughout my career, dozens of friends and colleagues have advised, assisted, steered me in the proper direction, and I am delighted to acknowledge them here. Special thanks to all those at the *New York Times,* particularly Craig Claiborne, Arthur Gelb, Annette Grant, and Mike Leahy, who allowed me to combine my love for journalism with my passion for food; to Sam Abt and Vicky Elliott at the *International Herald Tribune,* for their careful and diligent editing of my restaurant reviews; to Berna Huebner and Vivian Cruise, for their companionship and healthy appetites.

I want to offer special thanks to our dearest friends, Rita and Yale Kramer and Lydie and Wayne Marshall, with whom we have shared so many fine feasts on both sides of the ocean, for their encouragement and special friendship. Finally, I thank my parents, Vera and Joseph Kleiber, who instilled in me without fuss or fanfare a natural love and respect for the world's gastronomic bounties.

A Taste for Paris

From the moment I set foot in France one chilly, grey January morning in 1973, I knew that Paris was a city I would love the rest of my life. More than ten years later, after spending four of those years in this gentle city, each day I am moved by Paris's elegance and beauty, its coquettish appeal. The quality of life here is better than in any other place I know, and eating well has much to do with it.

This is the book I came to Paris to write. Equal only to my passion for food is my love for reporting. I have always thought that one of the most enjoyable aspects of journalism is that you get to know people on their own turf, and you get to poke around, asking the questions that any curious person wants answers to. In researching this book, I—along with Susan Herrmann Loomis as assistant and companion—walked just about every street in Paris in search of the gastronomic best the city has to offer, talking, chatting, interviewing, meeting with the city's men and women who are responsible for all things great and edible. We set out to find the crispest *baguette,* the thickest cup of steaming hot chocolate; to spot the most romantic site for a warm morning *croissant* or a sun-kissed summer lunch; to track down the trustiest cheese or chocolate shop; to uncover the happiest place to sip wine on a brisk winter's day. We quickly gave up counting the number of times we got lost or rained out as we checked off addresses and discovered back streets and sleepy neighbourhoods. We toured the markets and tea salons, sparred with butchers, laughed with the owners of a favorite bistro, and shared the incomparable aroma of a great loaf of bread as it came crackling from the oven. We rose eagerly at dawn to catch a pastry chef as he pulled the first batch of steaming *croissants* from his wood-fired oven; climbed down rickety ladders into warm and cosy baking cellars to discuss the state of the French *baguette* with a skilled baker; shivered as we toured aromatic, humid, spotless rooms stacked with aging Brie and Camembert, Vacherin and Roquefort. Each day we lunched and dined, sometimes at modest neighbourhood bistros, sometimes in fine restaurants. We gathered recipes from pastry chefs, cooks, bakers, and tea shop owners, and tested, tested, tested until my apartment took on the same irresistible mixture of aromas as in the food streets and shops of Paris. Throughout, it was an exhilarating labour of love, one from which I hope you will profit, the joy of which I hope you will share.

This is a personal guide, and whenever I had to decide whether to include or delete a shop, a restaurant, a market, I asked myself one question: Would I want to go back there again? If the answer was no, the address was tossed into the ever-growing reject file.

In choosing restaurants, I have tried to be comprehensive but selective. I have tried as best I know how to tell you exactly what I think you will want to know about a restaurant: why you should go, where it is, how to get there, what you'll find when you arrive, and what it will cost. I intentionally did not rate restaurants, for I find personal restaurant ratings clumsy, arbitrary, and generally unreliable. Besides, they make a burdensome science out of what should, essentially, be joyful discovery.

No doubt, some places you will love less than I. Some you will love more. I hope this book will stimulate every reader to explore, look around, and ask questions, and will help everyone to understand just a bit more clearly the history, daily customs, and rich texture of Paris, the great gastronomic capital of the world.

HOW TO USE THIS BOOK

Alphabetizing

Within each chapter (with the exception of the chapter on markets), establishments are grouped by the neighborhoods in which they are located, then listed in alphabetical order. Following French style, any articles such as *au, la,* or *le* and words such as *bistro, brasserie, café,* or *chez* that appear before the proper name of the establishment are ignored in the alphabetizing. For example, Chez Pauline, Le Petit Montmorency, and Au Pied de Cochon are all listed under the letter *P*. Likewise, when the name of a restaurant is also the full name of a person, such as Jacqueline Fénix, Michel Rostang, or Guy Savoy, the last name (Fénix, Rostang, Savoy) is used for purposes of alphabetizing.

What's an arrondissement?

While many major cities are divided into variously named quarters for easy identification and organization, Paris is divided into twenty *arrondissements*. The *arrondissements* are arranged numerically in a spiral, beginning in the centre of the city on the Right Bank (with the 1st *arrondissement* at the Louvre and Les Halles) and moving clockwise, making two complete spirals until reaching the central eastern edge of the city (at the 20th *arrondissement,* at Père Lachaise cemetery).

In organizing the book, we have listed establishments by *arrondissement,* also noting the popular quarter—the Madeleine, Montmartre, Invalides—in which they are located. Because of the spiral arrangement, *arrondissements* that adjoin one another—such as the 3rd, 4th, and 11th at the Marais and the Bastille—are generally listed together, since they overlap within a specific neighbourhood, even though *arrondissement* numbers are not consecutive. For convenience, *arrondissements* may be grouped together differently from one chapter to another.

Listings

Each listing presented in *The Food Lover's Guide to Paris* includes the following information: the name of the establishment; its address; its phone number (in parentheses); the closest Métro stop; when it is open and closed.

If applicable, any or all of the following information is also included: whether the establishment is air-conditioned; whether it has a terrace, outdoor dining, or private dining facilities; what the specialities include; and what you can expect to spend.

Abbreviations

The following abbreviations are used for credit cards in the listings:

AE: American Express
DC: Diners Club
EC: Eurocard or MasterCard
V: Visa or Carte Bleue

The following abbreviations are used in the recipes to indicate weights and measures:

cm: centimetre
g: gram
kg: kilogram
ml: millilitre

Contents

Marchés
MARKETS
124

Pâtisseries
PASTRY SHOPS
136

Boulangeries
BAKERIES
152

Fromageries
CHEESE SHOPS
170

Charcuteries
PREPARED FOODS TO GO
186

Chocolateries
CHOCOLATE SHOPS
198

Spécialités Gastronomiques
SPECIALITY SHOPS
207

Vin, Bière, Alcool
WINE, BEER, AND SPIRITS
221

Librairies Spécialisées: Gastronomie
FOOD AND WINE BOOK SHOPS
229

Pour la Maison
KITCHEN AND TABLEWARE SHOPS
235

Recipe Contents

Cafés
CAFES

Salons de Thé
TEA SALONS

Pâtisseries
PASTRY SHOPS

Boulangeries
BAKERIES

Fromageries
CHEESE SHOPS

Chocolateries
CHOCOLATE SHOPS

Spécialités Gastronomiques
SPECIALITY SHOPS

FRENCH/ENGLISH
FOOD GLOSSARY

The Food Lover's Guide to Paris

Restaurants
RESTAURANTS

Studying the menu in elegant restaurant surroundings.

I am constantly being asked to name my favourite Paris restaurant. For me, that is akin to trying to name my best friend, favourite piece of music, film, or classic novel. The answer depends on the hour, the season, my mood, the company.

This is a personal guide representing a cross section of Paris restaurants, including only those I enjoy returning to, those I recommend to others. I hope they will serve simply as a starting point, enabling you to begin exploring and sorting out until you discover the kind of restaurants you like. You should not have a bad meal at any listed here. But this doesn't mean you can't.

I dine out in Paris four or five times each week. I always make a reservation and always arrive hungry, for that's one of the best compliments one can pay a chef. I dine anonymously and so am known at few of these restaurants. What do I look for? Final judgment rests on the quality of ingredients, the chef's creativity, and overall service. In menus, I look for a healthy balance of dishes. In wine lists, value and variety are essential. A good restaurant is like good theatre: One leaves in a good frame of mind, physically and psychologically satisfied, with a feeling that both the time and the money have been well spent.

Likewise, your restaurants and meals should be chosen according to your own mood and appetite, the time of year, and of course, the time of day.

WHERE AM I, ANYWAY?

An American traveller once related this story: She was stopped on a street in Paris by another American visitor, who asked, in a state of sheer frustration, "What I don't understand here is with all these restaurants, how do you tell which ones are French? You know, the ones that serve soufflés." Slightly less complicated, but equally frustrating for visitors, is the distinction between bistro, brasserie, and restaurant. Although the lines between bistro and restaurant are often blurred, here are a few definitions that should clear the matter.

Bistro

A bistro is a rather small restaurant, traditionally a mom and pop establishment with mom at the cash register and pop at the stove. Bistro menus are usually handwritten or mimeographed, and dishes are limited to a small selection of traditional, home-style dishes. Wine is generally offered by the carafe, while wines available by the bottle are listed on the single-page menu. Bistro decor is usually simple, not fancy (though Paris's *Belle Epoque* bistros have some of the city's most beautiful interiors), often with a long zinc bar, tile floors, paper tablecloths, and sturdy, serviceable tableware. At some of the most modest establishments, diners may share long tables.

Brasserie

Brasserie is French for brewery, and almost all of Paris's large and lively brasseries have an Alsatian connection: That means lots of beer, Alsatian white wines such as Riesling and Gewürztraminer, and usually *choucroute*, that hearty blend of sauerkraut and assorted sausages. Brasseries tend to be brightly lit and full of the sounds of good times, fine places for going with a large group. Generally, snacks or full meals are available whenever the restaurant is open. Brasseries tend to keep late hours, and while a reservation is recommended, one can usually get a table without one.

Restaurants

Beyond bistros and brasseries, Paris offers numerous sorts of full-fledged restaurants, some offering elegant and classic cuisine, some specializing in creative, inventive, modern cooking. As well, there are restaurants that specialize in fish or grilled meats, in the cooking of specific regions of France, or in dishes from countries outside of France. Classifications for all restaurants listed in the guide appear on page 275.

Reservations

Almost without exception, reservations are necessary. For the grand restaurants, such as Taillevent, reserve weeks to months in advance. For others, reservations can be made several days ahead for popular weekend dinners, though for a weekday lunch, reserving the same day is often sufficient. If you are unable to keep a reservation, phone to cancel. Many restaurants now require that advance reservations be confirmed by telephone, the day you plan to dine there. Another good reason for reserving: Restaurants freely, and without warning, change opening and closing times and vacation plans, particularly during summer months and holiday periods. So it is always safest to call ahead to make sure the restaurant will be open when you plan to visit.

Dining Hours

Set aside plenty of time for a Paris restaurant meal. In general, expect to spend anywhere from one and a half to three hours at table for a substantial lunch or dinner. If you want to be in and out within thirty minutes to an hour, visit a café, tea salon, wine bar or brasserie, but don't attempt to rush through a meal at a serious restaurant. Currently, most Parisians begin lunch at 12:30 or 1 P.M. (although one can begin at noon), and most dine starting at 8:30 or 9 P.M. (although some restaurants will accept reservations for any time after 7:30 P.M.). Despite the later hours, most kitchens close early, so a 2 P.M. lunch or 10 P.M. dinner reservation would be stretching it. On the other hand, the majority of cafés and brasseries serve at almost any hour. A few restaurants continue taking orders until 11 P.M. or later, and a list of those can be found on page 271.

Prices

The price range of restaurants listed here goes from low to high. I have made no attempt to include restaurants serving mediocre food simply because they are inexpensive. Bargains can be found everywhere, and there are always ways to cut costs, even in the most expensive restaurants. Forego the before-dinner drink, after-dinner Cognac or cigar, and if you smoke, buy cigarettes at a neighbourhood *tabac,* where they will be cheaper than in the restaurant. Share dishes, if you like. You are not obliged to order either cheese or dessert, and if they do not suit your budget or appetite, forget them. You can often cut costs by ordering from a fixed-price menu (though it is not always cheaper than ordering *à la carte*), or by opting for a carafe of wine or an inexpensive house wine.

In all cases, the average price noted with each restaurant listing represents a meal for one person that includes a first course, main course, cheese or dessert, and half a bottle of moderately priced wine, as well as the service charge. Generally, a good inexpensive meal can be had for 100 francs, a good moderately priced meal for 200 francs, while a luxury meal, in a higher class of restaurant with more expensive wines, will range from 300 up to 500 francs. Almost without exception, prices are the same for lunch and dinner.

Advice on Paying the Bill and Tipping

No subject is more confusing to visitors than French restaurant bills. You need remember only one fact: You are never required to pay more than the final total on the bill. Service, which ranges from twelve to fifteen percent, depending upon the class of the restaurant, may or may not be included in the price of individual dishes, but it will always be added to the final bill. When a menu says *service compris*, that means the twelve to fifteen percent service charge has been built into the price of each dish. When the menu says *service non compris*, the service will be added to the total, after the food and wine have been added up. Either way, the bottom line is what you pay. Etiquette does not require you to pay more. If you have particularly enjoyed the meal, if you feel that the *maître d'hôtel* or *sommelier* has offered exceptional service, if you are in a particularly generous mood, then you might leave anywhere from a few francs to five percent of the total bill as an additional tip.

Credit Cards

The majority of Paris restaurants now accept credit cards, and almost all will accept traveller's cheques. Although every attempt has been made to insure the accuracy of credit card information in this guide, policies change rapidly. When reserving, it is a good idea to confirm credit card information. If you are sharing the bill with another person or couple, and you both wish to pay by credit card, most restaurants will oblige by dividing the bill between the two credit cards. Out of kindness to the waiters and *sommelier*, any tips (beyond the obligatory twelve to fifteen percent service charge) should be left in cash.

A Private Room

Many restaurants, including such establishments as Taillevent, Jamin, and Le Grand Véfour, offer private dining rooms for anywhere from eight to several hundred people. Some rooms, such as those at Taillevent, are particularly elegant and well appointed. Others may be drab, uncomfortable, and less appealing than the restaurant's main dining room, so it is a good idea to see the room before making plans.

There are advantages and disadvantages in reserving a private room. One advantage is privacy, and it makes it easier to organize a special feast, discussing and preparing beforehand the complete menu, including wines. The main disadvantage is that you must plan several weeks ahead and in most cases will need a French-speaking person to make arrangements. Also keep in mind that since your group will be set apart from the main dining room, you will miss much of the "theatre" and ambience that goes with the dining experience. There is no extra charge for the private rooms, and in many cases the total bill will be less expensive than if the group chose from the regular menu. Where private rooms are available, such facilities are noted with each restaurant description, and a separate listing can be found on page 274.

WHAT TO EXPECT AT THE TABLE

Suggestions on Ordering

There are four simple things to keep in mind when ordering in a Paris restaurant. First, think about what foods are likely to be fresh and in season. Thank goodness the French are still fanatical about freshness, and about eating only what is naturally in season. When dining out in Paris, I often go on seasonal "binges," eating asparagus, melon, scallops, oysters, or game, day after day when they are at their peak. If you see melon on the menu in January, or scallops during the month of July, beware.

Second, take the time to learn about the restaurant's specialities. Every restaurant has at least one or two dishes of which it is particularly proud, and the majority of restaurants either offer a *plat du jour* or underline or boldface its specialities. These dishes, assuming they are to your liking, will usually be a good buy, and generally fresh. Note that the fish is usually freshest on Fridays (when the demand is greatest) and least fresh on Mondays, when the wholesale market is closed.

Third, stick to your guns and order the kind of food you really like to eat. This is a caveat to those diners who will blindly accept a critic's or a waiter's suggestion, then all too late realize that they hate tripe, or duck, or whatever it was that was recommended.

Finally, today many restaurants offer a tasting menu, or *menu dégustation,* which allows diners to sample small portions of from four to eight different dishes. I am generally opposed to such menus, for in the end they are rarely good buys, and inevitably provide more food than it is humanly (and healthily) possible to eat. Because a tasting menu offers so many different dishes, it is difficult, if not impossible, to take with you a memorable impression of the meal or the restaurant. While the *menu dégustation* is often easier on the kitchen, you just may get the feeling that the dishes you are eating came off of an assembly line.

Butter

Most, but not all restaurants offer butter at the table. If you don't see butter, just ask for it. Only at the smallest cafés will a supplement be charged. Since the French do not ordinarily butter their bread, restaurants do not systematically offer it, unless you order a dish that generally calls for buttered bread—*charcuterie,* oysters served with rye bread, sardines, or radishes, or the cheese course. Almost all French butter is unsalted.

Coffee

The French have very specific coffee-drinking habits. Many Frenchmen begin their day with a *café au lait*—usually lots of hot milk with a little bit of coffee. During the rest of the day they drink either black coffee or *café crème* (coffee with steamed milk). But in restaurants, the coffee taken after meals is always black coffee, never coffee with added milk. Some restaurants will provide cream or milk if requested, some will not. In France coffee is always taken at the very end of the meal, almost served as a course of its own. In finer restaurants, chocolates and/or *petits fours* might also be served.

Fish, Meat, and Poultry

Almost all fish, meat, and poultry taste better when cooked on the bone. If you have problems boning fish, ask if the dish you are ordering is boned *(sans arêtes),* and if not, ask the waiter to debone it before serving *(enlevez les arêtes).*

The French prefer their meat and some poultry (particularly duck) cooked quite rare. But if rare meat or poultry really bother you, be insistent, and ask for it *bien cuit* (well done). Be prepared for the waiter to wince. (For rare meat, order it *saignant,* for medium, *à point.*)

Salt and Pepper

Some chefs are insulted if diners alter their creations with additional seasonings, and so do not offer salt and pepper at the table. If you don't see salt or pepper, just ask for it. But do be sure to taste the food before reaching for the mill or shaker.

Water

I am always shocked when, in this day and age, people ask "Is it safe to drink the water in Paris?" Of course it is. Perhaps visitors assume that because the French are so passionate about bottled water—a table of eight diners might include four different preferred brands of mineral water—that tap water is unsafe. Either tap water (ask for *une carafe d'eau*) or mineral water (*plate* is flat bottled water, *gazeuse* is bubbly mineral water) may be ordered with all meals. If ordering Perrier brand mineral water, don't be surprised if only small bottles are available. The French consider Perrier too gaseous to drink with meals, so most restaurants stock only small bottles, for drinking as an *apéritif* or with mixed drinks.

Wine and Spirits

This is one area where I firmly advise you to follow the rule "When in Paris, do as the Parisians do." Most Frenchmen do not drink hard spirits before meals and few restaurants are equipped with a full bar. If you are accustomed to drinking hard spirits before meals, try to change your habits during a Paris visit. The spirits will numb your palate for the pleasures to follow, and requests for a martini or whiskey before a meal will not put you in good stead with the waiter or with management. Almost all restaurants offer a house cocktail—most often a Kir, a blend of either white wine or champagne mixed with *crème de cassis* (black currant liqueur). I personally dislike most of these concoctions (which can be expensive and run up the bill) and always ask for the wine list when requesting the menu. Then, I usually order as an *apéritif* a white wine that will be drunk with the meal, or at least with the first course.

Selecting Wines

I have learned almost all I know about wines by tasting, tasting, tasting in restaurants: I study wine lists, keep track of average prices and favorite food and wine combinations, and am always eager to sample a wine that's new or unfamiliar to me.

Although I have found some *sommeliers,* or wine waiters, to be outrageously sexist (I was once refused even a simple glance at a wine list, and a few *sommeliers* still bristle when I insist on ordering the wine), generally I haven't found them to be unfair or unwilling to help when I sought information or assistance. If you don't know a lot about wine, ask the *sommelier's* advice. Give him a rough idea of your tastes and the price you would like to pay. This assumes, of course, that you share a common language. If you do not, ask simply whether there is a *vin de la maison* (house wine).

If you are knowledgeable about wine, you will want to study the wine list. Don't allow yourself to be pressured or bullied into making a quick decision (this isn't always easy) and if pressed, simply explain that you are fascinated by the restaurant's wonderful selection, and would like a few minutes to examine and fully appreciate the list of offerings.

Prices for the same wines vary drastically from restaurant to restaurant: some have large, long-standing wine cellars, others are just getting started. I love wine, consider it an essential part of any good meal, and probably tend to spend slightly more than the average diner on a good bottle. When dining in a bistro or brasserie, I often order the house wine, either by the carafe or by the bottle. When ordering from a wine list, I follow one simple rule: I rarely pay more than 150 to 200 francs for a bottle of wine, and that is usually a six- to fourteen-year-old Bordeaux. In Paris restaurants, the general rule of thumb is that one-third of the final bill should be for wine. That is, if you are paying, say 400 francs for a meal for two, about 135 francs of that will be spent on wine.

PALAIS-ROYAL, LES HALLES, OPERA, BOURSE
1st and 2nd arrondissements

AU COCHON D'OR,
31 Rue du Jour, Paris 1.
(236.38.31).
Métro: Les Halles.
Closed Saturday lunch
and Sunday.
Credit cards: AE, V.
82-franc menu, including
wine but not service. *A
la carte,* 150 to 200
francs.

SPECIALITIES:
*Grilled meats, andouillettes
(chitterling sausages),
Beaujolais.*

For a good, reasonably priced meal near Les Halles, one can hardly do better than the reputable Au Cochon d'Or, a small, friendly restaurant specializing in great cuts of beef, grilled *andouillettes* and other classic bistro fare. Begin with the *fricassée d'escargots aux girolles,* a full-flavoured dish that combines deliciously rich snails with wild mushrooms in a buttery sauce that's perfect for dipping the crusty *baguettes.* Then move on to the famed grilled beef served with a pleasant shallot butter. Or, if you prefer, kidneys, or grilled pork with garlic. On one occasion the *tarte Tatin* arrived swimming in butter and not up to par, but after such fare as this, who has room anyway? The house Beaujolais is delicious, and there's also a nice, small selection of Bordeaux.

A calm exterior at La Ferme Irlandaise.

LA FERME IRLANDAISE,
30 Place du Marché-Saint-
  Honoré, Paris 1.
(296.02.99).
Métro: Pyramides.
Closed Sunday evening and
  Monday lunch.
Credit cards: AE, V.
150 francs.

SPECIALITIES:
Irish salmon, Irish stew,
oysters, breads, and beer.

L a Ferme Irlandaise is an unpretentious, homespun
spot, offering honest Irish fare. Everything here
is Irish, from the sturdy, handmade earthenware pottery and rustic antique tables to the pungent farm
cheese. There's also velvety Irish smoked salmon, superb homemade brown bread, fresh scones on Sunday,
and yeasty whole-grain breads through the week. From
time to time, they also have fresh, home-smoked herring from Shanagarry. The menu changes frequently,
but there is usually Irish stew, a roast stuffed loin of
lamb chops with mint sauce, soups, and various fish
and shellfish. There's a wonderful Sunday brunch, from
10 A.M. to 1 P.M., featuring smoked salmon, poached,
scrambled, or fried eggs surrounded by black pudding, a rasher of thick Irish bacon, slender pork sausages, and a pork-based white pudding. With this,
there is all the homemade bread, Irish salted butter,
jam, and honey you can eat, followed by a warming
pot of Irish tea. Service is a bit helter-skelter, and
some of the young Irish waiters act as though they're
on holiday, but they are generally pleasant and respon-
sive, so nobody gets upset. Ask to sit on the main
floor: The downstairs is damp, dark, and cavelike.
English spoken, of course.

CHEZ GEORGES,
1 Rue du Mail, Paris 2.
(260.07.11).
Métro: Sentier.
Closed Sunday and
  holidays.
Credit cards: AE, DC, V.
150 to 200 francs.

SPECIALITIES:
Boeuf, rognons de veau (veal
kidneys), Beaujolais by the
carafe.

C hez Georges is one of that dying breed of old-time
bistros where the food may never be great but is
good enough to keep the place filled day and night.
The handwritten menu changes little from day to day,
but one can always go assured of finding giant and
generous bowls of silvery Baltic herring, *foie de veau*
(calf's liver), *steak de canard* (pan-fried duck breast),
kidneys and sweetbreads, and generally, hot and crunchy *frites*. The restaurant is small and alleylike, with
rows of banquettes and giant arched mirrors, and an
aging cadre of waitresses in black dresses protected by
frilly white aprons. At lunchtime, men come from the
nearby Bourse, while on week nights and Saturdays
bourgeois French couples gather for their grilled *pavé*
du Mail—a fine platter of beefsteak in mustard sauce
with fries. There's a nice and fruity Brouilly served
from little pewter-colored pitchers, as well as an impressive assortment of Burgundies and Bordeaux. The
steak de canard is generally good—beefy, rosy red, and
often accompanied by garlicky *cèpes,* fresh and perfectly
sautéed wild mushrooms. Desserts tend to be traditional and banal.

GERARD,
4 Rue du Mail, Paris 2.
(296.24.36).
Métro: Sentier.
Dinner served until
    11 P.M. Closed Saturday
    lunch, Sunday, and the
    month of August.
No credit cards.
100 francs.

SPECIALITIES:
Pot-au-feu, grilled beef, ris de
veau (sweetbreads), foie de
veau (calf's liver), potato
gratin, tarte Tatin.

A popular neighbourhood spot just off the Place des Victoires. Each day they serve a good, fresh *pot-au-feu,* a hearty soup-type dish composed of various cuts of beef gently simmered along with bone marrow, turnips, leeks, cabbage, and carrots. There's a superb house salad that, in the winter at least, includes a colourful mixture of greens, Belgian endive, fresh walnuts, and beets in a light vinaigrette. If *pot-au-feu* is not to your liking, sample the grilled beef, served with a deliciously fresh potato *gratin.* The wine list here is short and rather boring, though it does offer some good Burgundy from the reputable Prosper Maufoux. The *tarte Tatin* is flaky and authentic, and a nice ending to a fine, filling meal.

LE GLOBE D'OR,
158 Rue Saint-Honoré,
    Paris 1.
(260.23.37).
Métro: Louvre.
Closed Saturday and
    Sunday.
Credit cards: AE, V.
150 to 200 francs.

SPECIALITIES:
Southwestern, including
cassoulet (Thursdays), foie de
veau (calf's liver), petit salé
(poached, lightly salted pork).

The cuisine here has the accent of France's southwest, and the decor has a touch of grandmother's attic, with its lace curtains and mismatched plates. On Thursdays, businessmen gather for the duck, pork, lamb, and white bean *cassoulet,* served in gigantic portions out of orange enamel casseroles. If it's on the menu, order the *foie de veau rôti,* roasted calf's liver smothered in pungent, coarsely ground black pepper. English spoken.

LE GRAND VEFOUR,
17 Rue de Beaujolais,
    Paris 1.
(296.56.27).
Métro: Bourse.
Closed Saturday, Sunday
    and the month of
    August.
Credit card: AE.
Private dining room for 14.
400 francs.

SPECIALITIES:
Sole Grand Véfour, côtes
d'agneau (lamb chops),
rognons à la moutarde (veal
kidneys with mustard).

Le Grand Véfour typifies the lively gaiety of the old Paris world of writers, artists, politicians, and historians. Here, in an elegant, red, white, and black 1760s café, Napoleon is said to have dined with Josephine. Later diners included Victor Hugo, Colette, and Jean Cocteau, whose drawing still graces the menu cover of one of Paris's most charming restaurants. (Among the sixteen tables, there are several with brass plaques commemorating many of the famous who've dined here, and these tables can be requested when making reservations.) Go when there's an occasion to celebrate a special event—dress fit to kill and imagine the year is 1900. This is a romantic spot for lunch on a sunny summer afternoon, when you can dine looking out onto the bright pink rose garden of the Palais-Royal. The food here is classic and correct, not intended to astonish or surprise. But it is one of the grand Paris restaurants where you can feel perfectly comfortable ordering just a mixed salad and grilled steak with a solid bottle of old Bordeaux from the exceptional wine list. Try the *foie gras de canard* salad, the *soufflé de grenouilles* (frog's legs soufflé), or *côtes d'agneau Albarine*, perfectly rosy lamb chops served with a potato *gratin*. There are always seasonal fresh fruits and delicious desserts from pastry chef Gaston Lenôtre.

The dining room of Le Grand Véfour.

ISSE,
56 Rue Sainte-Anne,
  Paris 2.
(296.67.76).
Métro: Pyramides.
Closed Sunday, and Monday
  at lunch.
Air-conditioned.
No credit cards.
100 to 150 francs at lunch,
  250 to 300 francs at
  dinner.

SPECIALITIES:
Japanese, including Sushi bar.

If the Japanese had bistros, they would do well to model them after Issé, which serves the best *sushi, sashimi, chirashi,* and *tempura* in town. The tiny upstairs dining room is always filled with waiters weaving past, carrying trays full of steaming *tofu,* giant boats of fresh, multi-toned *sushi,* and tiny bamboo plates of crispy *tempura.* Go with at least three or four people, so you can order the giant *sushi* platter, an impressive selection of neat little rounds and rectangles of raw fish fillets in vinegared rice. The assortment includes chunks of silvery-skinned mackerel, mounds of bright red caviar, and little slabs of chewy, snow-white squid. There's also bright red fatty tuna, perfect pink crab meat, remarkably fresh salmon, as well as giant scallops and shrimp—all set on little beds of rice, with a dab of *wasabi,* a fiery green horseradish. For a change from *sushi,* try Issé's *chirashi*—loose rice mounded in a large lacquered bowl and covered with a variety of fish and shellfish. Asian diners here always start with a steaming bowl of *tofu,* or *yudofu,* cubes of custardlike soybean curd in boiling water. The *tofu* is scooped out with a miniature strainer then dipped in a mixture of soy sauce, minced scallion, and dried bonito flakes. There is a good selection of Japanese beer, and a *sushi* bar on the main floor.

Conviviality at Chez Georges (see entry, page 11).

LOUIS XIV,
1 bis Place des Victoires,
   Paris 1.
(261.39.44).
Métro: Bourse.
Closed Saturday, Sunday,
   and the month
   of August.
No credit cards.
Pavement terrace.
150 francs.

SPECIALITIES:
Burgundian, including escargots (snails), fromage de tête (head cheese), boeuf bourguignon (beef stew), and Beaujolais by the carafe.

A classic bistro, where the food is never great but the service and atmosphere are gay and friendly, and everyone seems to be having a wonderful time. At lunch, the much-prized pavement tables overlooking the Place des Victoires are filled with the chic fashion crowd from the boutiques on the square, and at night couples wander in from every part of town to enjoy the city views and often spectacular sunsets. This is the place to drink Beaujolais by the carafe and eat *lapin à la moutarde* (rabbit with mustard sauce), but fish eaters will want to order the fine grilled turbot, classic *sole meunière* (sole sautéed in butter), or a popular daily spring and summer special, salmon with sorrel. Unfortunately, their famous *friture d'éperlans*—fried smelt—can be disastrous. On one occasion, the tiny fish were far from fresh and the oil in which they were fried had seen better days. For those who never get enough butter in French restaurants, this is the place to go: The waiter moves a giant, three-pound block from table to table, and everyone helps himself. If it happens to rain, the best table is upstairs, just in front of the arched windows that overlook the square.

CHEZ PAULINE,

5 Rue Villedo, Paris 1.
(296.20.70).
Métro: Pyramides.
Closed Saturday evening
and Sunday.
Credit card: V.
Private dining room for 16.
200 francs.

SPECIALITIES:
Foie gras, filet de boeuf à la
moelle et au vin de Chiroubles
(beef with marrow), gâteau de
riz Madame Ducottet (rice
pudding). Also, daily
specialties. Good selection of
Beaujolais.

PHARAMOND,

24 Rue de la Grande-
Truanderie, Paris 1.
(233.06.72).
Métro: Les Halles.
Closed Sunday, Monday
lunch, and the month of
July.
Credit cards: AE, DC, V.
Small pavement terrace.
Private dining room for 18.
150 to 200 francs.

SPECIALITIES:
Normand, including tripes à
la mode de Caen (tripe cooked
in cider), pied de porc (pig's
foot), andouillettes (chitterling
sausages), cider.

AU PIED DE COCHON,

6 Rue Coquillière, Paris 1.
(236.11.75).
Métro: Les Halles.
Open daily, 24 hours a day.
Credit cards: AE, DC, V.
Pavement terrace.
Private dining room for 40.
150 francs.

SPECIALITIES:
Pied de cochon (pig's foot), fish
and shellfish, onion soup.

Chez Pauline is the restaurant you would choose if you were selecting a stage set for a classically Parisian bistro. Red banquettes, sprays of fresh flowers, well-worn chairs, dignified waiters, and great home cooking. Chez Pauline appeals to the young and the old, folks who love classics such as *blanquette de veau,* beef with marrow, and *boeuf Bourguignon.* The *jambon persillé*—ham that's cubed, jellied, and colourfully blended with parsley—is nicely seasoned, and when wild mushrooms are in season, sample the *cèpes à la Bordelaise,* meaty wild mushrooms sautéed with a good hit of garlic. Desserts are simple and classic, including the sweet and succulent rice pudding. Service is swift, professional, and it comes with a smile.

If all your life you've wanted to sample *tripe à la mode de Caen*—the classic Normandy speciality of tripe cooked in apple cider and served in old-fashioned brass braziers—this is the place to find it in Paris. Reserve a table on the main floor dining room, with its *fin de siècle* glazed tile decor and accompany your tripe with a bottle of delicious Normandy apple cider. If you're not inclined toward tripe, you might sample the grilled lamb chops, served with delicately souffléed potatoes. With it, drink some of Pharamond's bargain-priced Bordeaux. Unfortunately, many wonderful regional specialties once offered here—cheese from Normandy, apple desserts—have been replaced by ordinary, banal selections found everywhere. And, service can be extremely rude.

Authentic, or simply a tourist trap? It all depends on how you look at it. For those—like most of us—who missed the old Les Halles, Au Pied de Co-

Au Pied de Cochon.

chon is one of the few authentic eateries remaining. The food is decent, service slow and abominable, but this is where to go at three in the morning, when you have a sudden craving for onion soup or fresh and briny oysters.

PIERRE TRAITEUR,
10 Rue de Richelieu,
   Paris 1.
(296.09.17).
Métro: Palais-Royal.
Closed Saturday, Sunday,
   holidays, and the month
   of August.
Credit cards: AE, DC, V.
200 francs.

SPECIALITIES:
Foie gras, filets de rougets
vigneronne (mullet filets),
rognons de veau à l'échalote
(veal kidneys with shallots).

A classic and wonderful neighbourhood spot, situated right behind the Comédie Française. This welcoming little restaurant is filled with regulars day and night, Frenchmen who come by themselves or with large groups to enjoy the hearty bistro fare. Ingredients here are first-rate, and care is taken in preparation. Best bets are the first course *maquereaux au cidre,* silvery little mackerel cooked in cider and cider vinegar and garnished with apples (see recipe below); the fresh terrine of *foie gras;* perfectly cooked veal kidneys served with superb *gratin dauphinois* (see recipe opposite), and a simple but delicious pan-fried *côte de boeuf* (rib of beef).

MAQUEREAUX AU CIDRE PIERRE TRAITEUR
PIERRE TRAITEUR'S MACKEREL IN CIDER

Marinated or lightly cooked mackerel is popular bistro fare, appearing on dozens and dozens of Paris menus in many different variations. It is the sort of dish that can be delicious or disastrous, depending on the freshness of the fish and the quality of vinegar used. At its best, it is a light and satisfying, full-flavoured first course. The finest version I've ever tasted was at Pierre Traiteur. Here, mackerel and apples come together, combining the meaty flavor of the bright and silvery fish with the apple's mild fruitiness. In preparing the dish, they use French cider, which tends to be mild and not too acidic. A good, fresh, apple juice could be substituted.

2 large onions, finely
   chopped
2 pounds (900 g)
   mackerel, gutted,
   cleaned, with heads
   removed
1 teaspoon salt
Freshly ground black
   pepper to taste
2 firm cooking apples,
   peeled, cut in half,
   and cored
1 quart (1 litre) French
   cider, or substitute
   pure apple juice
1 cup (250 ml) cider
   vinegar
3 tablespoons fresh
   chopped chives

1. In a large, heavy-bottomed skillet that has a cover, evenly spread the chopped onions. Generously season the insides of the mackerel with the salt and pepper and place the fish on top of the onions. Top with the apple halves.

2. Add the cider or apple juice and the vinegar, cover, and bring to a boil over high heat. Reduce the heat to medium and simmer, covered, for 10 minutes. Remove the skillet from the heat, gently lift the mackerel with a slotted spatula, and set the fish aside to cool. Reserve the cooking liquid, apples, and onions. (The dish can be prepared several hours ahead up to this point.)

3. To serve the mackerel, remove the filets from each fish, being careful to keep them intact. Remove as many bones as possible. Arrange the filets on a serving platter. Cut the apples halves into very thin slices and arrange on top of the mackerel. Moisten with the cooled cooking liquid and onions. Sprinkle with fresh chives and serve at room temperature.

Yield: 4 to 6 servings.

GRATIN DAUPHINOIS PIERRE TRAITEUR
PIERRE TRAITEUR'S POTATO GRATIN

Is there a French potato dish more classic, and welcoming, than gratin dauphinois? This delicious version is bathed in cream and Gruyère cheese with just a hint of garlic. Traditionally, the potatoes are cut very thin, the thickness of a 5-franc piece—about one-sixteenth of an inch. Pierre Traiteur serves these homey potatoes with their famous roast kidneys. Be sure not to wash them after they've been sliced or you won't have the wonderful cheese flavour that develops as the potatoes cook.

1 clove garlic, peeled
2 pounds (900 g)
   potatoes, peeled and
   sliced very thin
1 cup (100 g) grated
   Gruyère cheese
2 cups (500 ml) milk
½ cup (125 g) *crème fraîche*
   (see recipe, page 182)
   or heavy cream,
   preferably not ultra-
   pasteurized
1 teaspoon salt
Freshly ground black
   pepper to taste

1. Preheat the oven to 375° F (190° C).

2. Rub the inside of an oval porcelain gratin dish (about 14 × 9 × 2 inches or 35.5 × 23 × 5 cm) with garlic.

3. In a large mixing bowl combine the potatoes, ¾ cup (75 g) of the cheese, the milk, *crème fraîche* or cream, salt and pepper. Mix well, then spoon the potatoes into the baking dish, pouring the liquid over the slices. Sprinkle with the remaining cheese and bake for 1 hour and 15 minutes, or until the top is crisp and golden.

Yield: 4 to 6 servings.

PILE OU FACE,
52 bis Rue Notre-Dame-
   des-Victoires, Paris 2.
(233.64.33).
Métro: Bourse.
Closed Saturday and
   Sunday.
No credit cards.
Pavement terrace.
130 to 150 francs.

SPECIALITIES:
Changing variety of fresh and simple dishes.

Pile ou Face—heads or tails—is an elegant little restaurant near the Bourse recently transformed from a grubby corner café. It has quickly attracted the solidly hungry stock exchange crowd by day and loyal local residents by night.

It's the kind of place to go for a serious business meeting or a romantic dinner for two: The decor is refined and intimate, service attentively correct, and the classical music soothing. Reserve one of the tables on the main floor or in the tiny upstairs dining room, where fresh, appealing desserts are set out on a sideboard so you can spend your dinner hour deciding which one you'll give in to.

The food here borders on *nouvelle cuisine* but is neither exotic nor contrived, and the menu is based on high quality, inexpensive meats, fish, and poultry.

The best dishes sampled here include a salad of the freshest mushrooms, thinly sliced, and tossed in a good vinaigrette showered with fresh herbs; a green *salade frisée* served with extraordinarily good grilled Saint-Marcellin cheese; and a subtly seasoned rabbit with fresh rosemary (see recipe, page 18). Desserts are above average, and on a given day may include a respectable *marquise au chocolat* and mouth-puckering lemon pie. For wine, try the dry white Doisy-Daëne.

RITZ-ESPADON,
15 Place Vendôme, Paris 1.
(260.38.30).
Métro: Opéra.
Open daily.
Credit cards: AE, DC,
    EC, V.
Garden dining.
350 to 400 francs.

SPECIALITIES:
Turbotin grillé à la moutarde
(grilled turbot with mustard),
bar grillé au fenouil (grilled
sea bass with fennel),
Wednesday: rack of lamb,
Friday: fish.

Some sunny summer afternoon when you want to feel special, get all dressed up and reserve an outdoor table on the lovely pink and green, flower-filled terrace at the Ritz-Espadon. Service here is attentive and professional and the crowd always interesting (eavesdropping is permitted). The food is not spectacular, but if you order simple grilled dishes, you shouldn't be disappointed. Best bets are the grilled bar, a sea bass which arrives accompanied by flaming, aromatic stalks of dried fennel, and the grilled turbot with mustard sauce. The Ritz offers nice, elegant touches one rarely finds these days: If you go during asparagus season in the spring, you'll be served tiny individual silver asparagus tongs, to assist in your enjoyment. (See page 66 for chef Guy Legay's flavourful recipe for a gratin of fennel, zucchini, and fresh tomatoes.)

MARMELADE DE LAPIN AU ROMARIN PILE OU FACE
PILE OU FACE'S RABBIT WITH ROSEMARY

Four and a half cups of rosemary? Yes. This is a remarkably delicious and simple dish to prepare, and a favorite of diners at Pile ou Face (see entry, page 17). I sampled it the first time I lunched at Pile ou Face (French for "heads or tails"), and now it's become a favourite at home, made with either rabbit or chicken and served with rice or fresh, homemade pasta. The dish can easily be prepared ahead of time, then reheated.

1 fresh rabbit or chicken,
    2½ to 3 pounds (1 kg
    125 g to 1 kg 350 g),
    cut into serving pieces
1 cup (250 ml) dry white
    wine
1 quart (1 litre) water
1 onion, halved
2 carrots, sliced into
    rounds
2 bay leaves
1 teaspoon dried thyme
Salt and freshly ground
    black pepper to taste
4½ cups (100 g) fresh
    rosemary on the stem,
    or 1 cup (40 g) dried
1 cup (250 ml) crème
    fraîche (see recipe, page
    182) or heavy cream,
    preferably not ultra-
    pasteurized
½ teaspoon whole black
    peppercorns

1. In a large skillet combine the rabbit (or chicken), wine, water, onion, carrots, bay leaves, thyme, salt and pepper, and 4 cups (90 g) of fresh rosemary. If you are using dried rosemary, add the entire amount. Cover and cook over medium heat for 45 minutes.

2. Remove the rabbit pieces and set them aside to cool. Strain the liquid into a medium-size saucepan, discarding the vegetables and herbs, and, over high heat, reduce to 2 cups (500 ml).

3. Meanwhile, remove the rabbit meat from the bones, cutting the meat into bite-size chunks. (The dish may be prepared several hours ahead to this stage.)

4. Stem the remaining ½ cup of rosemary, if using fresh.

5. In a large skillet combine the reduced stock with the crème fraîche or heavy cream and peppercorns and heat through. Add the stemmed rosemary and the rabbit pieces.

6. Cook over medium heat until the flavours have blended and the meat is thoroughly heated. Adjust seasoning, if necessary. Serve hot, with rice or fresh pasta.

Yield: 4 servings.

LE RUBAN BLEU,
29 Rue d'Argenteuil,
   Paris 1.
(261.47.53).
Métro: Pyramides.
Closed Monday and Tuesday
   evenings, Saturday,
   Sunday, and the month
   of August.
Credit card: V.
150 francs.

SPECIALITIES:
_T-bone steaks, confit de canard
(duck cooked and preserved in
duck fat)._

LA TABLE DE
JEANNETTE,
12 Rue Duphot, Paris 1.
(260.05.64).
Métro: Madeleine.
Closed Saturday and Sunday
   and three weeks in
   August.
Credit cards: AE, DC, V.
200 francs.

SPECIALITIES:
_Southwestern, including confit
d'oie (goose cooked and
preserved in goose fat), foie
gras, ris de veau
(sweetbreads), garbure (meat
and vegetable stew)._

VAUDEVILLE,
29 Rue Vivienne, Paris 2.
(233.39.31).
Métro: Bourse.
Open daily; last orders
   taken at 2 A.M.
Credit cards: AE, DC, V.
Pavement terrace.
150 francs.

SPECIALITIES:
Fish and shellfish.

Everything about Le Ruban Bleu is neat, tidy, and welcoming—from the very simple, no-nonsense menu to the bright blue plaster ribbon (_ruban bleu_) that floats along the crisp white walls. The friendly _patron,_ Roger Simon, recently took over this 1940s bistro, originally decorated by a man with a passion for ships. The restaurant was named in honour of the famed Normandie, which won a blue ribbon for making the fastest trip across the Atlantic. Specialities include a fine _salade frisée,_ a curly endive salad with hot sautéed chicken livers; roast rack of lamb; _confit de canard;_ and an American-style T-bone steak, served with marrow. And with each cup of coffee, they offer a little cube of delicious Lindt chocolate.

Hidden inside a little courtyard not far from the Concorde and the Place de la Madeleine, this elegant, pleasant restaurant is the place to go on a cold wintry day, when the huge stone fireplace and soft classical music offer diners warmth and a touch of the country. The decor is simple and refreshing, service is friendly and attentive, the hearty southwestern French cuisine served in copious portions worthy of a serious gourmand. Innovative dishes at La Table de Jeannette—transformed a few years ago from an old neighbourhood bar—include a salad that cleverly combines steaming hot, sliced turnips with fresh _foie gras;_ superb _confit d'oie,_ served with delicious _pommes à la Sarladaise,_ a garlicky potato _gratin;_ and _lapin aux aromates,_ rabbit with an herb and mustard sauce. At times, the food is oversalted, the fish items are not always fresh, and desserts not particularly exciting. But do go when you're in the mood for a southwestern meal and a warming fire, and you shouldn't be disappointed. The red house Graves, Château de l'Etoile, is pleasant and reasonably priced.

A lively 1925 brasserie full of mirrors and marble and the sounds of great times. Go with a large group, order up carafes of the house Riesling, and feast on oysters, scallops, mussels, or sole. Meatier specialties, such as pork knuckle with lentils, calf's liver, and a duck and white bean _cassoulet,_ are also part of the huge brasserie menu that changes from day to day. In warm weather, opt for a table on the pavement terrace, facing the imposing Bourse, or stock exchange.

In 1765 the first full-fledged restaurant—not simply a hotel serving meals—was opened by a Monsieur Boulanger. He wanted to offer more than just soups, but since he wasn't a licensed traiteur he couldn't offer sauces or stews. He decided to offer pieds de mouton (sheep's feet), with a thick white bechamel sauce, and the society of traiteurs took him to court over it. The whole affair, which Monsieur Boulanger won, brought his pieds de mouton so much notoriety that tout Paris rushed to the restaurant to taste the delectable dish that had been declared "not a stew" by the court. Even Louis XV had the dish served to him at Versailles, though he wasn't, apparently, terribly enthusiastic.

CHEZ LA VIEILLE,
37 Rue de l'Arbre-Sec,
Paris 1.
(260.15.78).
Métro: Pont-Neuf.
Open for lunch only. Closed
Saturday and Sunday
and the month of
August.
No credit cards.
180 to 200 francs.

SPECIALITIES:

*Terrine maison (house terrine),
pot-au-feu, boeuf aux carottes
(beef with carrots), mousse au
chocolat.*

Adrienne Biasin has been serving up her famous *pot-au-feu* for several decades, and if you can secure a lunchtime table (reservations seem to be dispensed with a great deal of subjectivity) it's worth the journey. Everything here is served up family-style, with a menu that's delivered brusquely and orally by the all-female, matronly staff. A typical lunch will begin with a procession of hearty, homey appetizers: an excellent *museau de boeuf* (beef head cheese), a well-seasoned pork liver pâté, and hot, sautéed chicken livers. The *pot-au-feu* is copious and filling, and includes moist, flavorful chunks of beef, carrots, nicely cooked leeks and turnips. There is more quantity than quality in the dessert assortment, which on a given day will include traditional sweets such as chocolate mousse, floating island, and chocolate cake.

REPUBLIQUE, BASTILLE, LES HALLES, ILE SAINT-LOUIS
3rd, 4th, and 11th arrondissements

AMBASSADE D'AUVERGNE,
22 Rue du Grenier-Saint-Lazare, Paris 3.
(272.31.22).
Métro: Rambuteau.
Closed Sunday.
Credit cards: AE, DC, EC, V.
Air-conditioned.
Private dining room for 16.
150 francs.

SPECIALITIES:
Auvergnat, including daily specialties. Monday: pot-au-feu; Tuesday: daube de canard (duck stew); Wednesday: potée (meat and vegetable soup in an earthenware casserole); Thursday: cassoulet des lentilles du Puy (casserole of lamb, duck, sausage, and lentils); Friday: estofinado (codfish casserole); Saturday: chou farci (stuffed cabbage).

Yes, one could eat here three nights in a row—as one friend recently did—and not tire of the cuisine. This warm, folkloric spot is still one of Paris's most solid and consistent regional restaurants, serving a medley of specialties from the Auvergne region in south central France. Good first courses include the *salade de cabécous rôtis* (grilled goat cheese on a bed of greens), and the *émincé de choux verts aux lardons* (a salad of freshly chopped cabbage covered with chunks of bacon and vinegar; see recipe, page 72). Don't miss the well-seasoned *boudin noir* (blood sausage), served here with a mound of wonderful chestnuts; the country pork sausage served with *aligot* (a blend of potatoes and fresh, melted Cantal cheese), and their own version of the traditional *pot-au-feu*, which includes beef, poultry, and vegetables. While the menu changes little from season to season, there is a different speciality each day of the week, to add to the temptation. Ambassade d'Auvergne offers a good selection of inexpensive, and drinkable, regional wines, including a fruity Saint-Pourçain and a dark and vigorous Madiran. (See page 77 for the Ambassade d'Auvergne recipe for stuffed cabbage.)

L'AMI LOUIS,
32 Rue du Vertbois, Paris 3.
(887.77.48).
Métro: Temple.
Closed Monday, Tuesday, and the months of July and August.
Credit cards: AE, DC, V.
250 francs.

SPECIALITIES:
Foie gras, roast chicken, frog's legs, gigot rôti (roast lamb), coquilles Saint-Jacques (scallops) from October to April, game from October to February.

This great, historic bistro looks a bit dilapidated, but that doesn't keep a Rolls-Royce or two from lining up outside. Chef Antoine Magnin, now well past eighty, still serves some of the best *foie gras* in town (cut into slabs, not slivers), he roasts a chicken better than anyone's grandmother ever did, and his giant mounds of *pommes allumettes* (fresh shoestring potatoes) still cause eyes to open wide as they come sizzling from his cramped, copper-filled kitchen.

Whoever it was that said snails are simply a vehicle for butter and garlic never tasted the snails at L'Ami Louis. Here you'll find some of the biggest, most flavourful *escargots* in Paris. The snails are earthy, not rubbery, and they're allowed to hold their own, not being camouflaged by an overdose of garlic, parsley, and butter. Mr. Magnin is a master at roasting, and fall or winter is the time to come for his simple roast pheasant, partridge, or wild duck, all cooked in an ancient,

L'Ami Louis.

wood-fired oven. Best forgotten are the thin and greasy *côtes de mouton*, or mutton chops; the tasteless *baguettes*; and dessert, which you won't have room for anyway. So order up a bottle of their Fleurie, and enjoy.

BENOIT,
20 Rue Saint-Martin,
  Paris 4. (272.25.76).
Métro: Châtelet.
Closed Saturday, Sunday,
  and the first and last
  week in August.
No credit cards.
200 francs.

SPECIALITIES:
Lyonnais, including saucisson chaud de Lyon, salade croquante au lardons chauds (warm sausage salad with bacon), boeuf mode (braised beef with carrots).

A fresh, sparkling plant-filled 1900s bistro, still offering traditional *boudin noir*, blood sausage, served with roast potatoes and apples; their famous *boeuf mode* (braised beef with carrots); duck with turnips; and a variety of modern-day specials that vary from day to day. A favourite with businessmen at lunch, and families in the evening.

BOFINGER,
5 Rue de la Bastille,
  Paris 4. (272.87.82).
Métro: Bastille.
Open daily; last orders
  taken at 1 A.M.
Credit cards: AE, V.
Pavement terrace.
Air-conditioned.
Private dining room for 250.
150 francs.

SPECIALITIES:
Alsatian, including choucroute (sauerkraut and sausages).

One of the prettiest brasseries in Paris, festive and classy, with attentive service and a varied menu. Try the famous *choucroute* (sauerkraut served with *boudin noir*, or blood sausage, spicy pork sausage, and excellent frankfurters) or the *brandade*—a full-flavored purée of salt cod and olive oil—which is light, creamy, and full of garlic. The house Riesling is just fine.

CARTET,
62 Rue de Malte, Paris 11.
(805.17.65).
Métro: République.
Closed Saturday, Sunday,
   and the month of
   August.
No credit cards.
150 to 200 francs.

SPECIALITIES:
Lyonnais, including salade au
lard (warm curly endive and
bacon salad), saucisson chaud
(warm pork sausage), gigot
d'agneau aux herbes de
Provence (leg of lamb with
herbs).

Madame Cartet no longer holds court here, urging, coaxing the handful of diners who, since 1932, have filled her minuscule, six-table restaurant. But her replacement, the unflappable Marie-Thérèse, and her husband, Raymond Nouaille, have tried to keep things as they were. They've succeeded about as well as anyone might: The decor is still 1930s, with green plastic banquettes full of cigarette holes and wooden walls covered with mirrors and dime store paintings. People still flock here for *la grande bouffe*, filling up on dishes that don't stop coming until you waddle out the door. Sample the *brandade de morue*, a silken purée of salt cod, garlic, and olive oil, smooth as mashed potatoes and even more filling, and the *gigot d'agneau aux herbes de Provence*, pink, soft, and fragrant leg of lamb accompanied by a casserole of tiny dried *flageolets*. The *salade au lard* is a classic: crispy *frisée* (chicory) with copious chunks of bacon and a perfectly pungent vinegary dressing. The *pâté de campagne* is simple and honest, and the *saucisson chaud de Lyon* is pure pork and large enough to feed an army. I'm not a fan of the famous *soufflé de tourteau*, a crab meat soufflé that is often limp, deflated, and bitter. The bread is dreadful and the desserts are more copious than satisfying. But I go anyway, and I eat.

FIGUES CHAUDES A LA MOUSSE D'AMANDES CHARDENOUX
CHARDENOUX'S WARM FIGS WITH ALMOND MOUSSE

A delicious, imaginative dish, these warm figs filled with almond mousse are served in the fall at Chardenoux. Chef Alain Morel serves the shiny purple figs warm, set in a pool of thin, light crème anglaise, but they also taste wonderful with vanilla ice cream.

12 fresh purple figs,
   washed
1 tablespoon unsalted
   butter, at room
   temperature
1 tablespoon sugar
¼ cup (35 g) almonds,
   ground to a fine
   powder
1 quart (1 litre) vanilla ice
   cream

1. Preheat the oven to 400°F (205°C).

2. Cut the top from each fig and reserve. With a teaspoon, scoop out just the red pulp, being careful not to break through the skin. Reserve the fig pulp. Keeping the tops with the fig shells, set them aside.

3. Prepare the *mousse:* In a medium-size bowl, cream the butter and sugar, stir in the powdered almonds, then the fig pulp, mixing well after each addition.

4. Fill each fig with a teaspoon of the almond *mousse,* then replace the top of each fig. Arrange the figs in a shallow baking dish and bake for 10 minutes, or just until the *mousse* begins to melt and the figs are heated through.

5. Serve immediately, with vanilla ice cream.

Yield: 4 to 6 servings.

CHARDENOUX,
1 Rue Jules-Vallès,
    Paris 11.
(371.49.52).
Métro: Charonne.
Closed Saturday, Sunday,
    holidays, and the month
    of August.
No credit cards.
Menu dégustation, 200
    francs. *A la carte,* 250
    francs.

SPECIALITIES:
Pudding de moëlle de boeuf
(bone marrow pudding), foie
gras, tarte fine aux pommes
(apple tart).

A bright, impeccable, 1900s bistro, complete with an undulating zinc-top bar, etched-glass windows and *Art Nouveau* murals on the walls. Chef Alain Morel is a dedicated, creative sort who has found it slow going in this charming but quiet part of town. Yet Chardenoux merits a visit, for Mr. Morel is ambitious and, one suspects, has the talent to make this tiny, plant-filled bistro a success. His food is subtle, simple, and unadorned: He roasts a leg of lamb, deglazes the pan juices with a little wine, then at the last minute tosses in freshly chopped tarragon, giving the sauce a wonderfully meaty, herby essence. He carves out a fig, then fills it with powdered almonds, a touch of butter and sugar, roasts it ever so quickly (see recipe page 23), then serves the delicate fruit hot from the oven with a thin, thin *crème anglaise.* Service is professional, and the welcome warm. And in such a lovely setting, who could ask for more?

**BRASSERIE DE
L'ILE SAINT-LOUIS,**
55 Quai de Bourbon,
    Paris 4.
(354.02.59).
Métro: Pont-Marie.
Open until 1 A.M. Closed
    Wednesday and the
    month of August.
No credit cards.
100 francs.

SPECIALITIES:
Alsatian, including choucroute
(sauerkraut and sausages),
Munster cheese, beer.

T his lively, always crowded brasserie serves as the neighborhood gathering spot for all of Ile Saint-Louis. Go with the entire family on a Sunday afternoon after visiting Notre-Dame, sit down at one of the long, communal tables and order the sauerkraut and sausages, a mug of beer, and a slice of Alsatian Munster. You won't dine like a king, but you won't spend a fortune, either.

What could be more typical of a Parisian bistro than a checkered tablecloth?

The specials are posted daily at Chez Jenny.

CHEZ JENNY,
39 Boulevard du Temple,
   Paris 3.
(274.75.75).
Métro: République.
Open daily; last orders
   taken at 1 A.M.
Credit cards: DC, V.
Private dining room for
   150.
75-franc menu. *A la carte*,
   about 100 francs.

SPECIALITIES:
Alsatian, including choucroute
(sauerkraut and sausages),
grilled meats, beer and
Alsatian wines.

This huge Alsatian brasserie just off Place de la République may not serve the best *choucroute* in town, but it is certainly in the running for first place. From the outside, Chez Jenny looks like any ordinary brasserie, but step inside the gigantic, wood-panelled dining room and you'll instantly be transported to Alsace, land of chilled white Riesling, pork and *choucroute*. Matronly waitresses dressed in regional costumes serve the hearty fare off of giant copper platters, and they're swift, open, and friendly. Perhaps best of all, you can dine well here for less than 100 francs a person, selecting the copious *choucroute paysanne* (which includes expertly cured, grilled slab bacon, well-seasoned bratwurst, frankfurters, and fresh *palette* of pork; see recipe, page 33), washed down with a dependable house Riesling. Other specialities, all moderately priced, include grilled saddle of lamb, *coq au vin*, and a hefty *jarret de porc,* or pork knuckle, garnished with sauerkraut. Forget about the waterlogged, tasteless *choucroute aux trois boudins de poisson*, a bizarre trio of fish sausages served with sauerkraut.

MONTECRISTO,
81 Rue Saint-Louis-en-l'Ile,
   Paris 4.
(633.35.46).
Métro: Pont-Marie.
Closed Sunday and the
   month of August.
Credit cards: AE, DC, V.
Private dining room for 8.
150 francs.

SPECIALITIES:
Italian. Excellent choice of
Italian wines.

Montecristo is a casual Italian restaurant in the middle of Ile Saint-Louis, the sort of spot where you won't feel out of place if you go alone. Each meal begins with fresh, hot little pizza appetizers, flavoured with fresh tomato sauce, herbs, and cheese. The pastas are professional, with a fine herb and spinach ravioli and fresh fettucine flecked with basil. Sample the salad of greens, walnuts, and Gorgonzola, a refreshing, satisfying first course. The wine list includes some unusual offerings, including Venegazzù, a high-alcohol, Bordeaux-style red produced near Treviso.

**CHEZ PHILIPPE/
AUBERGE PYRENEES-
CEVENNES,**
106 Rue de la Folie-
   Méricourt, Paris 11.
(357.33.78).
Métro: République.
Closed Saturday, Sunday,
   holidays, Christmas
   week, and the month of
   August.
No credit cards.
Air-conditioned.
200 francs.

SPECIALITIES:
*Foie gras, cassoulet, pipérade
(scrambled eggs with peppers,
onions, and ham).*

Auberge Pyrénées-Cévennes, or more simply, Chez
Philippe, is so unpretentious from the outside
that one is tempted to go no further than the front
door. But give it a chance. Inside, you'll find a quiet,
private Parisian world, filled with French journalists,
businessmen, and neighbourhood regulars. It's a world
where people come to eat well and eat a lot.

   The stone walls, shining beamed ceilings, red tile
floors, and crisp white linens all make for cosy surroundings, and the menu includes both the hearty
Gascon food of the southwest and the more spicy,
peppered foods of the Basque region of the Pyrénées,
bordering Spain. Order *crudités* (raw vegetables), and
the outgoing Burgundian owner, Philippe Serbource,
will frown, saying "that sounds awfully sad," then
bring along a gigantic salad of carrots, tomatoes, lettuce, and cucumbers in a big white terrine. What he
really wants you to order—and swoon over—is the
rich and silky *foie gras* (they make it fresh every day),
the *cochonnailles de pays*, huge baskets of country sausages (eat as much as you like), and the *cassoulet d'oie
Toulousain,* an authentic combination of sausage, goose,
pork, and white beans. Equally good are the fresh,
grilled *rougets*, or mullet, served with anchovy butter.
Mr. Serbource does all the marketing and selects the
wines himself: There's a small but good selection of
wines representing all the major regions of France.

AU QUAI DES ORMES,
72 Quai de l'Hôtel-de-
   Ville, Paris 4.
(274.72.22).
Métro: Hôtel-de-Ville.
Closed Saturday, Sunday,
   holidays, and the month
   of August.
No credit cards.
Small outdoor terrace.
Air-conditioned.
110- and 125-franc menus
   at lunch and dinner. *A
   la carte,* 180 francs.

SPECIALITIES:
*Poêlée d'artichauts et
langoustines (sauté of
artichokes and small spiny
lobster), râble de lapereau aux
morilles (rabbit with morel
mushrooms).*

This cool, open restaurant—marred by an overbearing mural on the wall—is run by the young
Egyptian-born chef, Georges Masraff, and his wife,
Marianne. Mr. Masraff started out to be a doctor, but
soon found food more appealing, and went on to work
in the kitchens of Troisgros, Taillevent, and L'Auberge
de l'Ill.

   The cuisine here is inventive but uneven; sometimes
it misses the mark, sometimes it hits the high notes.
Service can be downright unpleasant, unbearably slow,
or both; but if you happen to hit it on a good day, you
should dine well, particularly if the day's offerings
include Masraff's superb *raviolis de champignons des bois*
(little pockets of pasta filled with fresh wild mushrooms, tarragon, and sweetbreads). It's one of the most
memorable dishes I've ever tasted—a complex, satisfying preparation full of simple, understated flavours.

   In the winter, Masraff can do wonders with game,
roasting a wild duck perfectly rare, embellishing it

with assorted wild mushrooms. He loves rabbit, too, pairing it with wild morel mushrooms set on a bed of pasta.

Desserts tend to be on the sweet side, and the wine list offers no bargains. Although noise can be a problem, the small upstairs terrace overlooking the Seine can be quite lovely on a summer's evening.

A SOUSCEYRAC,
35 Rue Faidherbe,
Paris 11.
(371.65.30).
Métro: Faidherbe-Chaligny.
Closed Saturday, Sunday,
Easter week, and the
month of August.
Credit card: V.
150 to 200 francs.

SPECIALITIES:
Foie gras, saucisson chaud aux morilles (hot sausage with wild morel mushrooms), lièvre à la royale (wild hare stew), served Fridays only, October 8 through December 15.

If you're looking for a real, honest, neighbourhood restaurant full of faithful Parisian diners, this is it. Situated in the out-of-the-way 11th *arrondissement*, the home of cabinetmakers and artisans, A Sousceyrac is a typical, traditional bistro where the chef-owner—Gabriel Asfaux—tends to the marketing and wine buying, and keeps careful tabs on the dining room to be sure everyone's satisfied. The old-fashioned, mimeographed menu tips you off right away: You're in the land of plenty. Plenty of fresh *foie gras,* plenty of sturdy pistachio-studded *saucisson chaud*, good hot sausage served with a sauce of cream and wild morel mushrooms. If you love game, do come on a Friday night in the fall to sample their famous *lièvre à la royale*, a mahogany-hued wild hare stew that is long on execution and, when properly prepared, a unique gastronomic experience. The hare is marinated for at least ten hours in a heady blend of red wine, shallots, onions, carrots, cinnamon, and herbs, stewed for hours, and finally compacted into a coarse, chunky, pâté-like roll filled with both *foie gras* and truffles. All this makes for a dark, dense, and gamey dish that, one must admit, is not to everyone's taste. The small wine list offers some exceptional buys.

LATIN QUARTER, LUXEMBOURG, SEVRES-BABYLONE
5th and 6th arrondissements

CHEZ AISSA FILS,
5 Rue Sainte-Beuve,
    Paris 6.
(548.07.22).
Métro: Vavin.
Open for dinner only; last
    orders taken at 11:30
    P.M. Closed Sunday,
    Monday, and the month
    of August.
Credit card: V.
Private dining room for 25.
100 francs.

SPECIALITIES:
Moroccan, including couscous,
tajine de mouton (mutton
stew).

Paris has scores of cafés and restaurants serving North African *couscous*, and this is one of the best. Open for dinner only, the brilliantly decorated Moroccan-style dining room doesn't really get going until 10:30 or so, when the *patron* races around taking orders, flirting with the customers, and generally inspiring a good time. Go with a group so you can sample a variety of dishes, including the spicy lamb sausage known as *merguez* and the heavenly *tajines*, or stews, one of mutton and pickled lemons, and another of chicken and plump prunes. Everything comes with unlimited servings of *couscous*, offered from a platter piled high with the fine, delicate and tender grains of hand-rolled semolina that have been steamed over a savoury broth. With the couscous comes the delicious broth, containing chick peas and raisins, and with it, as much fiery *harissa* pepper sauce as your palate will tolerate. Aissa Fils is always crowded, lively and noisy, as everyone gets happy on heady Moroccan red wine.

ALLARD,
41 Rue Saint-André-des-
    Arts, Paris 6.
(326.48.23).
Métros: Saint-Michel or
    Odéon.
Closed Saturday, Sunday,
    holidays, and the month
    of August.
Credit cards: DC, V.
Air-conditioned.
225 francs.

SPECIALITIES:
Burgundian, including
escargots (snails), canard aux
olives (duck with olives),
poissons au beurre blanc (fish
in white butter sauce). Daily
specials offered.

For some years, it's been fashionable to whisper "Allard has slipped," much as catty women might whisper about someone's needing a face-lift or putting on a pound or two. We all age, and so do bistros like Allard, and with age comes change. Madame Allard no longer tends the stove, and Monsieur Allard is no more. Yet Allard remains a lively, authentic bistro with its long zinc bar and tiny, open kitchen, still drawing crowds, and serving up the internationally

famous duck with olives, duck with turnips (soggy on the last visit), sizzling snails, and turbot with *beurre blanc,* all washed down with their popular Sancerre, Fleurie, or Gevrey-Chambertin.

L'AMBROISIE,
65 Quai de la Tournelle, Paris 5.
(633.18.65).
Métro: Maubert-Mutualité.
Closed Sunday evening, Monday, and August 15 to September 15.
Credit cards: AE, V.
140-franc menu, including service, but not wine, available at lunch only.
A la carte, about 250 francs.

SPECIALITIES:
Mousse de poivrons doux au coulis de tomates (red pepper mousse), effeuillée de raie aux choux (skate with cabbage), mille-feuilles (puff pastry desserts with seasonal fruit).

B ernard Pacaud remains one of Paris's most talented young chefs, and each visit reveals new growth, new horizons. The tiny, contemporary nine-table restaurant is always filled, and often noisy, so note this is not the place for a quiet romance. But go to pay attention to the food: Chef Pacaud magically manages to take the most basic, simple ingredients, and transform them into something elegant and grand yet totally uncomplicated. His *foie gras* is a delight; the red pepper mousse (see recipe, page 74) so smooth it's almost ethereal; the skate with cabbage is bright-flavoured and refreshing; and his puff pastry desserts are generally fresh and authoritative. The wine list is brief but well chosen, and the welcome always warm.

A cheerful presentation of l'addition.

AUX CHARPENTIERS,
10 Rue Mabillon, Paris 6.
(326.30.05).
Métro: Mabillon.
Last orders taken at 11:30 P.M. Closed Sunday.
No credit cards.
125 francs.

SPECIALITIES:
Petit salé aux lentilles (lightly salted pork with lentils), chou farci campagnarde (stuffed cabbage), pied de porc (pig's foot).

A n authentic bistro, serving solid, uncomplicated food at reasonable prices. The restaurant takes its name and decor from the *compagnons charpentiers*—master carpenters and cabinetmakers whose organization stemmed from the medieval guilds. The museum that housed their work used to be next door and this was their hangout. The carpenters and the museum are gone, leaving a simple, friendly place to eat right across from the Saint-Germain market. Try the roast duck with olives, the stuffed cabbage, or the pork with lentils.

DODIN-BOUFFANT,
25 Rue Frédéric-Sauton,
   Paris 5.
(325.25.14).
Métro: Maubert-Mutualité.
Last orders taken at 12:45
   A.M. Closed Saturday,
   Sunday, the month of
   August, and two weeks
   at Christmas.
Credit cards: DC, V.
Sidewalk terrace.
Air-conditioned.
180 to 220 francs.

SPECIALITIES:
Plateau de fruits de mer (fresh
seafood platter), harengs frais
marinés (marinated fresh
herring), soufflés chaud aux
fruits (warm fruit soufflés).

A good meal always deserves a
bit of concentration.

JOSEPHINE,
(Chez Dumonet),
117 Rue du Cherche-Midi,
   Paris 6.
(548.52.40).
Métro: Sèvres-Babylone.
Closed Saturday, Sunday,
   December 24 and 25,
   and the month of July.
Credit card: V.
120-franc menu. *A la carte,*
   200 francs.

SPECIALITIES:
Foie gras, ris de veau aux
morilles (sweetbreads with
wild morel mushrooms), confit
de canard (seasoned duck
cooked and preserved in
duck fat).

Casual and unpretentious, Dodin-Bouffant is one of Paris's most popular fish restaurants. Service is pleasant and swift and the crowd totally Parisian, and the large, rather classic menu should please those in the mood for fish and shellfish, meat, and game. The food is light and original, and the menu offers a refreshing variety of appetizers, including a *salade folle* (a mound of matchstick-size vegetables, seasonal seafood, and a touch of *foie gras*) and the house-smoked herring, sliced paper thin, and served with a small potato salad tossed with whole grain mustard. The *fricassée de morue à la Provençale* is a welcoming, well-seasoned blend of fresh salt cod, onions, tomatoes, zucchini, and potatoes showered with fresh basil and parsley.

A bright and popular neighbourhood bistro with an outstanding wine list. Service can be insufferably slow and/or unpleasant, but if you're after some wine bargains, take a deep breath and go anyway. The red Bordeaux date back to 1898, the Burgundies to 1929. If you're looking for something more recent and affordable, sample a great 1970 Margaux or a fine 1976 Pauillac. (A cautionary note: If ordering an older wine, ask to see the bottle first. On one occasion, we ordered a bottle of 1945 Château Latour and were not shown the bottle until after it was decanted.) The food is uneven, but some good bets include the sweetbreads with morels, the grilled *chateaubriand* (served only blood rare or rare), and the *foie gras.*

LA LOZERE,
4 Rue Hautefeuille,
   Paris 6.
(354.26.64).
Métro: Saint-Michel.
Closed Sunday, Monday,
   and the month of
   August.
No credit cards.
51- and 61-franc menus,
   not including wine and
   service, and 78-franc
   menu, including wine
   and service.

S P E C I A L I T I E S :
Lozérien, including country
hams, sausages, omelets.
Thursday only: aligot (creamy
mashed potatoes with fresh
Cantal cheese).

CHEZ MAITRE PAUL,
12 Rue Monsieur-le-Prince,
   Paris 6.
(354.74.59).
Métro: Odéon or
   Luxembourg.
Closed Sunday, Monday,
   and the month of
   August.
Credit cards: AE, DC, V.
Private dining room for 25.
125-franc menu, including
   wine but not service.
   A la carte, about 125
   francs.

S P E C I A L I T I E S :
From the Jura and Franche-
Comté, including charcuterie
(cold cuts), coq au Vin Jaune
(chicken cooked in white wine),
foie de veau (calf's liver).

L a Lozère, half restaurant, half tourist office, represents the hearty cuisine of the Lozère region in
central France. The decor is simple and rustic, and
diners sit elbow to elbow at the five bare wooden
tables, slicing their own bread from hefty loaves of
pain de campagne that are brought straight from the
region twice a week. (You can buy the same bread at
the Produits d'Auvergne market at 32 Rue de Buci. It
arrives there fresh on Tuesday, Thursday, and Saturday.) The clientele is a mix of young workers looking
for a bargain, and well-fed, old-time Parisians who
bring their newspapers or invite their wives to feast on
omelets, salty country cured ham (*jambon cru*), and
filling, meaty *plats du jour*. There is always soup, salad,
and good regional cheese, such as the nutty, smooth-
textured Cantal and the sharp, farm-ripened Bleu
d'Auvergne. Good bets here are the *salade aux lardons*
et au Cantal (wilted greens tossed with chunks of crispy
bacon and Cantal) and the daily special such as the
côtes d'agneau, lamb chops, served with good, pan-fried
potatoes.

T iny, tidy, and friendly, Chez Maître Paul is a refreshing family-run restaurant offering the rustic
cuisine of the Jura/Franche-Comté region of eastern
France. There are just seven little tables in the cot-
tagelike main floor dining room, from which diners
can watch the activity in the small corner kitchen.
Start with the absolutely delicious smoked garlic sausage, served warm with potatoes bathed in vinegar and
parsley. Then move on to the *coq au vin jaune* (this
version with tomatoes, meaty mushrooms, and white
wine is better than the one with cream), a light and

A staff luncheon at Chez
Maître Paul.

pleasant dish that's prepared with the regional white Arbois wine and is definitely worth sampling. The *baguettes* are delicious, desserts forgettable, and the choice of regional wines appealing.

MOISSONNIER,
28 Rue des Fossés-Saint-
   Bernard, Paris 5.
(329.87.65).
Métro: Jussieu or Cardinal
   Lemoine.
Closed Sunday evening,
   Monday, and the month
   of August.
No credit cards.
125 to 150 francs.

SPECIALITIES:
Lyonnais and Franche-
Comtois, including carré
d'agneau rôti persillé (roast
rack of lamb), assorted
charcuterie.

Solid, substantial and old-fashioned, Moissonnier is the sort of homey place where giant *saladiers*— glass salad bowls—laden with assorted charcuterie seem to appear out of nowhere. Portions are copious, copious, copious, and service could not be friendlier. Ask them to cook the roast lamb chops any other way than *rosé*, and the matronly waitress explains, "This is fragile lamb, not old mutton, and if we overcook it, we ruin it." A gentle way of suggesting things be done their way. The menu is large, offering starters of *terrines*, salads with bacon or cheese, Lyonnais sausages, and mackerel marinated in white wine. Popular main courses include roast kidneys, *boudin noir* (blood sausage), duck with turnips, and the superb roast rack of lamb. A single complaint: The food generally lacks seasoning. Cheese lovers should make room for the fine assortment of regional cheese, including the nutty Swiss Tête de Moine, creamy Vacherin and hearty Comté. This is a popular gathering spot for winemakers and wine merchants; thus the wine list offers some fine choices, ranging from inexpensive Beaujolais to well-priced Burgundies and Bordeaux.

POLIDOR,
41 Rue Monsieur-le-Prince,
   Paris 6. (326.95.34).
Métro: Odéon or
   Luxembourg.
Closed Sunday, Monday, and
   the month of August.
No credit cards, no
   reservations.
Private dining room for 60.
33-franc menu at lunch
   only, not including wine
   and service. *A la carte*,
   about 70 francs.

SPECIALITIES:
Escargots (snails), pintadeau
aux choux verts (young guinea
fowl with green cabbage),
dessert tarts.

With its little lace curtains, *Art Déco* light fixtures, and fresh home cooking, Polidor is a lively old bistro that's aged with grace and charm. A meal here should not cost any more than 80 francs a person, and those on a tight budget can get by for even less.

Order the piping hot garlicky and buttery snails and the waitress breaks into a wide grin of approval and tells you that they are *fait maison*—not plucked from a plastic freezer bag—so you'll have to wait a few minutes. Here, a few minutes means two, maybe three.

Regulars—well-dressed businessmen who come alone and doodle on the paper tablecloths—don't even bother with the menu. They just wait for the waitress to tell them what's good that day.

There is steak and *frites*, pumpkin soup, and a generous serving of well-spiced marinated *champignons à la grecque*. Do try the moist and succulent *pintadeau* served with fresh curly green cabbage, or the saddle of lamb with deliciously warming white *flageolet* beans. The bread is crisp, the wine selection decent, and the *tarte Tatin* is prepared authentically, with huge chunks of apples, though at times it may be overcaramelized and slightly bitter. If you go at noontime, profit from the location by taking an afternoon walk through the Luxembourg gardens.

CHOUCROUTE CHEZ JENNY
CHEZ JENNY'S SAUERKRAUT, SAUSAGES, AND BACON

I've yet to find better choucroute in Paris than the variation served at Chez Jenny, a giant Alsatian brasserie (see entry, page 25). Here the hearty platters of sauerkraut, sausages, bacon, and potatoes arrive in perfect order: The sauerkraut is ultimately digestible (not too bland, acidic, fatty, or greasy) and it is neither dried out from overcooking nor swimming in watery juices, as is too often the case. The sausages are first-rate, and fresh, and the crisply grilled slab bacon is a wonderful touch. You know the platter is at its best when it complements, as well as compliments, chilled Alsatian Riesling. Here is a home version of Chez Jenny's house speciality.

3 pounds (1 kg, 350 g) sauerkraut, preferably fresh bulk sauerkraut, not canned
3 tablespoons lard or goose or chicken fat
2 onions, coarsely chopped
2 cups (500 ml) Riesling wine
1 cup (250 ml) fresh chicken stock or water
2 pounds (900 g) pork chops
Freshly ground black pepper to taste
2 cloves
6 juniper berries
2 bay leaves
2 cloves garlic
6 knackwurst
6 fresh German frankfurters
1 pound (450 g) smoked pork sausage such as Polish Kielbasa
2 pounds (900 g) new potatoes
1 pound (450 g) slab bacon, cut into large chunks

1. Preheat the oven to 350°F (175°C).

2. Rinse the sauerkraut in a colander under cold running water. If it is very acidic or very salty, repeat several times. Drain well.

3. In a large casserole over low heat, melt the fat and add the onions. Sauté until the onions are wilted, then add the wine and stock or water.

4. Add the pork chops. Cover with the sauerkraut. Add the pepper, cloves, juniper berries, bay leaves, and garlic. Cover and bake in the oven for 1 to 1½ hours.

5. In separate saucepans cook each variety of sausage in gently simmering water for about 20 minutes. Do not allow the water to boil or the sausages will burst. Drain all the sausages, slice the kielbasa, and keep all warm until serving time.

6. Meanwhile, steam or boil the potatoes. Allow them to cool just enough to handle, then peel. Keep warm.

7. Just before serving, grill the slab bacon until very crisp.

8. To serve, drain the sauerkraut (removing the herbs and spices) and mound it in the center of a large, heated platter. Surround the sauerkraut with the pork chops, the sausages, including the sliced kielbasa, the potatoes, and the grilled bacon. Serve with several kinds of mustard and plenty of chilled white Riesling wine.

Yield: 8 to 10 servings.

Stop in at Polidor for Art Déco atmosphere and delicious home cooking (see entry, page 32).

LA PORTE FAUSSE,
72 Rue du Cherche-Midi,
  Paris 6.
(222.20.17).
Métro: Sèvres-Babylone.
Open until 11 P.M. Closed
  Sunday, Monday, one
  week at Easter, the
  month of August, and
  first week of September.
No credit cards.
Pavement terrace.
100 francs.

SPECIALITIES:
*Niçois, including polenta
(cornmeal pudding), sardines
à la sauge (sardines in sage),
beignets (doughnuts).*

Good Niçoise food is hard enough to find in Nice, much less in Paris. La Porte Fausse, set along the chic and well-travelled Rue du Cherche-Midi, not far from the Bon Marché department store, fits the bill here. The food is authentic and generally fresh, though service is haphazard and terribly distracted. The crowd is young and casual, and on warm days a few tables stretch out onto the pavement for those who want sunshine and a chance to observe the passing scene. This is the perfect place to go when you're in the mood for nothing but vegetables, imaginatively prepared. There's a good crunchy *ratatouille*, a nice blend of eggplant, tomatoes, and zucchini, that is served cold as an appetizer or warm as a main course; delicious roasted red peppers sprinkled with olive oil; and an enormous *salade mesclun*, a colorful toss of mixed greens. The *pissaladière*—a thick-crusted sort of pizza topped with onions and tomatoes—is good but not great, though the Swiss chard filled *terrine de blettes* is nicely seasoned and refreshing. Other good offerings include a first-course preparation of sardines smothered in sage, and cornmeal *polenta* topped with a sauce of cheese and tomatoes. (A lovely variation of this recipe appears on page 61.)

The breads—crisp *baguettes* and thinly sliced *pain Poilâne*—are fresh and excellent. And there is a small selection of regional wines, including Nice's local wine, Bellet, in red and white. For dessert, sample their freshly made doughnuts, or *beignets*, some twisted into bow ties, others filled with jam.

CHEZ RENE,
14 Boulevard Saint-
  Germain, Paris 5.
(354.30.23).
Métro: Cardinal Lemoine.
Closed Saturday, Sunday,
  and the month of
  August.
No credit cards.
104-franc menu, not
  including wine and
  service. *A la carte*, about
  150 francs.

SPECIALITIES:
*Monday: pot-au-feu; Tuesday:
haricot mouton (lamb with
white beans); Wednesday: gras
double (tripe); Thursday: boeuf
mode carottes (braised beef with
carrots); Friday: blanquette de
veau (veal in white sauce).*

A simple, honest bistro with a menu that's as steady as its clientele. The line-up of daily specials has barely changed for three decades, though many of the young, chic diners who populate the large, unadorned dining room, have not been around that long. The daily special is inevitably the best dish on the menu— precede it with seasonal *pleurotes provençales*, fresh wild mushrooms bathed in garlic and oil; a simple salad; or a dish of country sausages. Wash it down with the house Beaujolais and enjoy the fresh *baguettes* from André Lerch, the pastry shop right next door. (See page 258 for Chez René's classic recipe for mutton with white beans.)

RESTAURANT TIEPOLO,
7 Rue des Ecoles, Paris 5.
(326.83.59).
Métro: Maubert-Mutualité.
Closed Sunday.
No credit cards.
85-franc menu at lunch
  only, including wine,
  coffee, and service. *A la
  carte*, about 150 francs.

SPECIALITIES:
*Italian, including regional
hams, pastas.*

Tiepolo is one of Paris's few authentic and casual Italian restaurants, much like the sort of *trattoria* found all over Italy. Here, you can feast on half a dozen different varieties of Italian ham (including the rarely found Sauris, lightly wood-smoked with a touch of juniper), more than a dozen pasta variations, soups, and of course fish, shellfish, and meat. Tiepolo serves some of the best *risotto* I've tasted outside of Italy— tooth tender, not too dry, and delicately seasoned with a quartet of Italian cheeses. Portions here are gigantic, so sharing is in order. The wine list is detailed and nicely presented, the service slow but friendly.

An enclosed terrace provides a meal with plenty of natural lighting.

LA TOUR D'ARGENT,
15 Quai de la Tournelle,
　　Paris 5.
(354.23.31).
Métro: Maubert-Mutualité.
Closed Monday.
Credit cards: AE, DC.
Private dining room for 40.
195-franc menu Tuesday
　　through Saturday at
　　lunch only, not including
　　wine and service.
A la carte, 500 francs.

SPECIALITIES:
Caneton de la Tour d'Argent
(duckling), quenelles de brochet
(pike dumplings).

CHEZ TOUTOUNE,
5 Rue de Pontoise, Paris 5.
(326.56.81).
Métro: Maubert-Mutualité.
Closed Sunday, Monday,
　　and August 15 to
　　September 15.
Credit card: V.
Sidewalk terrace.
85-franc menu, not
　　including wine and
　　service.

SPECIALITIES:
Home-style cooking with a
Provençal accent. Daily
specials vary with the season.

VILLARS PALACE,
8 Rue Descartes, Paris 5.
(326.39.08).
Métro: Monge.
Closed Saturday lunch.
Credit cards: AE, DC,
　　EC, V.
Private dining room for 50.
145-franc menu, service
　　included. *A la carte,* 300
　　francs.

SPECIALITIES:
Fish and shellfish.

Paris's best-known restaurant, and still one of the most theatrical. One can argue about whether or not it's worth a visit, but everyone who loves Paris and food should go at least once, if only for the record. The wine list is superb, the food's getting a bit more attention than it once did, and the view of the flying buttresses of Notre-Dame knows no equal. Service can be overbearing, and you may not hear a word of French spoken in the dining room. Best bets here are the scallop and artichoke salad, the famous Tour d'Argent duck, and a solid yet light, bitter chocolate cake. The restaurant is less crowded at lunchtime, when a window table allows diners to observe the daily Paris scene from on high. If there's time later, ask to see the vaulted underground wine cellar.

One wonders how "Toutoune," Colette Dejean—blonde, petite, and businesslike—does it. Day after day, night after night, Parisians crowd into her tiny, homey restaurant to feast on her fresh, lively ever-changing repertoire and take part in one of Paris's best bargain meals. Copious portions of soup, a first course, a main course, cheese or dessert are served for a fantastically inexpensive price of 85 francs. The entire menu is changed nearly every day, following Toutoune's whim, and always offers enough choice so that no one need go away disappointed. A typical meal might include an excellent red pepper mousse or a salad of fresh pasta with shellfish (see recipe, page 41), grilled leg of lamb with delicious French fries and a fresh red currant tart. The soup course is often a disappointment, and could easily be deleted from the menu. Service can be slow, so order up a bottle of the good house Sancerre and relax.

Diners who love fresh fish and bright, crisp, contemporary surroundings will want to pay a visit to Villars Palace, set in an out-of-the-way corner of the 5th *arrondissement* near Rue Mouffetard. I love the restaurant's decor and ambience: spotless, blue and white tile on the walls, muted gray carpeting, soothing classical music. The food is fresh, flavourful, and straightforward, showing sparks of creativity and signs that the chef and management care. Here, you can order a simple platter of fresh, briny oysters, served with toast and a sauce of good quality wine vinegar and shallots, then move on to one of the restaurant's specialities, fresh salmon grilled on just one side, so its texture varies from crisp to buttery to soft. Other good selections include a first-course platter of raw, marinated *daurade* (sea bream), served with a delicious *timbale* of watercress, followed by a superb main course combination of *brochet* (pike), set on a bed of sorrel. Desserts are above average, and include a fine lemon tart and a respectable chocolate cake. The wine list offers a wide selection of white Burgundies. Service can be so attentive, in fact, it errs on the side of overattentiveness.

LAPIN A LA MOUTARDE
RABBIT WITH MUSTARD

Rabbit with mustard sauce is a classic bistro dish, and a year-round favorite. Traditionally, lapin à la moutarde is served with rice, but I love it with fresh, homemade pasta, which absorbs the wonderfully delicious sauce. Do use top-quality French whole-grain mustard; fresh, not frozen rabbit, and a solid, full-bodied white wine. An Alsatian Riesling is an excellent wine for this dish, but I've also prepared it with Gewürztraminer, as well as with a white Hermitage. You can also experiment by adding various herbs to the sauce just before serving: Fresh rosemary, summer savoury, or thyme would be lovely. If you can't find fresh rabbit, chicken makes an excellent substitute.

1 fresh rabbit (or chicken), 2½ to 3 pounds (1 kg 125 g to 1 kg 350 g), cut into serving pieces
⅓ cup (80 ml) peanut oil
1 tablespoon unsalted butter
½ cup (125 ml) whole-grain mustard
3 cups (750 ml) dry white wine
1 cup (250 ml) *crème fraîche* (see recipe, page 182) or sour cream
Salt to taste
¼ cup (5 g) fresh parsley, minced

1. Preheat the oven to 350° F (175° C).

2. In a Dutch oven or large, ovenproof skillet, heat the oil and butter over medium-high heat. When hot, quickly brown the rabbit. Do not crowd the pan, and turn the pieces, making sure that each is thoroughly browned. Discard the excess oil.

3. Brush the rabbit pieces evenly with mustard, reserving 3 tablespoons for the sauce. Place the rabbit in the oven, covered, and bake for 20 minutes. Pour the wine over the rabbit, making sure all pieces are moistened, and continue cooking, covered, another 25 minutes.

4. Remove from the oven and reserving the cooking liquid, place the rabbit pieces on an ovenproof dish. Lower the oven heat to 200° F (90° C). Cover the rabbit with foil and keep warm in the very low oven.

5. Prepare the sauce: Over high heat reduce the reserved cooking liquid by half. This should take 8 to 10 minutes. Whisk in the *crème fraîche* or sour cream, the reserved mustard, and salt. Reduce the heat and continue cooking for 3 to 4 minutes.

6. To serve, arrange the rabbit pieces on a platter, and cover with the sauce. Alternately, fill a platter with fresh, cooked pasta, toss with the sauce, and arrange the rabbit pieces on top of the pasta. Sprinkle with the minced parsley.

Yield: 4 to 6 servings.

Freshly-opened briny oysters.

OYSTERS

He was, indeed, a brave man who first ate an oyster. But, from the moment that intrepid gentleman slid it down his throat, this pale, glistening, meaty shellfish was destined for stardom, and one can be certain that Frenchmen eagerly shouldered their gastronomic responsibilities.

Up until the 1850s oysters were so plentiful in Paris they were considered poor man's food, even though the journey from the Brittany shores to Paris was never a simple one. Oysters travelled in wooden carts laden with ice and snow, and as it melted it was regularly replenished at ice houses set along the route.

During the 18th century, oyster criers filled the streets of Paris, carrying wicker hampers on their backs filled with their inexpensive fare. Although the colourful hawkers are gone, today France remains a major oyster producer—cultivating some 1,400 tons of precious shallow, round, flat-shelled Belon-style *plates* oysters and more than 81,000 tons of deep, elongated, crinkle-shelled *creuses* oysters. From Cherbourg in the north to Toulon along the Mediterranean, French fishermen in high rubber boots and thick blue jerseys carry out their battle with nature. Each oyster is nursed from infancy to maturity, a labour of three to four years, and along the way, the filmy, fragile creature, always prey to disease, pollution, and numerable sea-borne predators, may be moved from one coastline to another.

Baby oyster larvae begin life floating in the sea with plankton, searching about for something to grip onto. Their survival rate is low: Out of a batch of 100,000 larvae, only a dozen survive.

Six to seven months later the larvae have grown to spats—now about the size of a fingernail—and are detached and moved along to another *parc* (oyster bed) where they remain from 1 to 2½ years.

Then, the flat-shelled *plates* are often dispatched to river estuaries, where the shallow, warmish blend of salt water and fresh water helps them develop their distinctly sweet, creamy flavour.

The more common, crinkle-shelled *creuses*—which grow twice as fast as the *plates*—might be transferred several times before they swing into their final stage of development. They spend the last few months of their lives in swampy, shallow, slightly alkaline fattening beds known as *claires,* where they pick up their unusual green tinge by feasting on certain flourishing microscopic blue algae. The longer the oysters remain in the fattening beds, the greener, more richly flavoured, and more valuable they become.

Just before oysters are ready for the market, they spend a few days being purified in reservoirs. There they are dipped in and out of water so they learn to keep their shells shut. As long as the oyster remains chilled and the shell stays closed during transport, the oyster can survive on its own store of saline solution. Once out of the water, it will easily stay alive for eight days in winter, two days in warmer summer months.

Today's Parisians remain oyster enthusiasts. The shellfish is still plentiful, but the best are a rather expensive luxury. A prized, distinctive flat *Belon* oyster—from beds at the mouth of Brittany's small, coastal Belon river—can cost fifteen francs each at the market, twenty francs each at a restaurant, a price that adds up if one plans a proper feast of a dozen or more. In Paris, oysters are sold year-round, most often from a *banc d'huîtres,* an outside oyster bar attached to a restaurant or brasserie, where swift oystermen open more than ten a minute.

Oysters are sold by the half dozen or dozen, and are generally available in a number of sizes. The larger are more expensive, though not necessarily better. They are best eaten raw, on the half shell from a bed of crushed ice, without lemon or vinegar. They need no further embellishment than a glass of Muscadet or Sancerre, and a slice of buttered rye bread.

Although Parisian restaurants offer numerous varieties of oysters, there is no reason to be intimidated by the sometimes confusing assortment. Visually, it is easy to distinguish the *plates* from the *creuses.*

Plates: The two most popular types of flat French oyster are the prized *Belon,* a small, elegant oyster that is slightly salty, faintly oily, with a hint of hazelnut; and the fringy, green tinged *Marennes. Plates* are calibrated according to their weight; the smallest, and least expensive, no. 5, offers about about 1 ounce (30 grams) of meat, while the largest, and most expensive, no. 0000, called the *pied de cheval,* or horse's hoof, about 3 ounces (100 grams).

Creuses: France's most common oyster—deep, elongated and crinkle-shelled. The *creuse* is sometimes called the *Portugaise,* even though this variety of oyster was essentially replaced by the *Japonaise,* after the Portuguese oyster was struck by a gill disease in 1967.

The three common sub-categories of *creuse* relate to the method of final aging, or fattening. The smallest are the *huîtres de parc;* the medium-size is known as *fines de claires,* oysters which have spent about two months aging in the fattening beds or *claires,* with forty to fifty oysters to the square metre; and the *spéciales,* the largest, aged in fattening beds for up to six months, just three to five oysters to the square metre.

Creuses are calibrated according to weight, from the smallest, and least expensive, *petite,* which weighs a bit over 1 ounce (50 grams) to the largest, and most expensive *très grosse,* about 3 ounces (100 grams).

A *glistening platter of shellfish.*

FAUBOURG SAINT-GERMAIN, INVALIDES, ECOLE MILITAIRE
7th arrondissement

CHEZ LES ANGES,
54 Boulevard La Tour-
   Maubourg, Paris 7.
(705.89.86).
Métro: La Tour-Maubourg.
Closed Sunday evening,
   Monday, and holidays.
Credit cards: AE, DC,
   EC, V.
Air-conditioned.
Private dining room for 15.
200 francs.

SPECIALITIES:
Oeufs en meurette (eggs poached
in red wine), filet de turbot au
fenouil (filet of turbot with
fennel), foie de veau (calf's
liver).

R eserve here for Sunday lunch and join a thoroughly traditional, bourgeois crowd—in couples, families, and groups—for a serious Sunday afternoon of dining. Both food and service in this large,
fifties-style dining room are classic and correct. The
menu includes their thinly sliced and perfectly seasoned *jambon persillé,* thick slices of grilled calf's liver,
and an eye-opening, rolling dessert cart laden with
about a dozen pristine, classic fruit tarts.

Beginning dinner with a toast
at L'Archestrate.

L'ARCHESTRATE,
84 Rue de Varenne,
   Paris 7.
(551.47.33).
Métro: Varenne.
Closed Saturday, Sunday,
   first three weeks in
   August, and Christmas
   week.
Credit card: AE.
Air-conditioned.
380- and 420-franc menus.
   A la carte, about 450
   francs.

SPECIALITIES:
Change with the season.

F ew Paris restaurants are as controversial as L'Archestrate. The food can be stunning, service often
querulous and pretentious, and prices exorbitant. But
it's good to go just to see what chef Alain Senderens
is up to—if he's there and not jetting around the
world promoting his own name. He does go to the
trouble of making his own fresh bread, his own superb
chocolates, and when his imagination is in high gear,
you'll leave with good memories of a creative meal.
The cheese tray is superb, the wine list appealing, if
you don't get into an argument with the *sommelier.*

LE DIVELLEC,
107 Rue de l'Université,
   Paris 7.
(551.91.96).
Métro: Invalides.
Closed Sunday, Monday,
   Christmas week, and the
   month of August.
Credit cards: AE, DC, V.
Air-conditioned.
Private dining room for 15.
300 francs.

SPECIALITIES:
Fish and seafood: oysters,
turbot aux pâtes noires (turbot
with black pasta), soufflé
chaud au chocolat amer (bitter
chocolate soufflé).

Oysters so huge you can make a meal out of one. Fish so remarkably fresh it makes your teeth squeak. A stunning, shimmering black pasta prepared with the ocean-flavoured squid ink. Not to mention a sparkling, contemporary blue and white decor that puts you right in the mood for a trip to the sea. Much of the fish is brought in fresh direct from the coast, where the Le Divellec family ran the famous La Pacha restaurant in La Rochelle. Everything here is imaginative, original, and professional. Le Divellec was the best new Paris restaurant of 1983 and already counts as one of Paris's top fish restaurants.

SALADE DE PATES FRAICHES AUX FRUITS DE MER
FRESH PASTA AND SEAFOOD SALAD

Delicate and satisfying, this colourful salad of fresh pasta, seafood, and herbs is typical of the varied offerings at Chez Toutoune, a little Left Bank bistro (see entry, page 36). The friendly, blonde chef, Colette Dejean, serves this dish with several kinds of fresh pasta: She might blend thin, fresh strands of beet, spinach, and white fettuccine together, making for a spectacularly brilliant first course. Strips of roasted red pepper could be added for even more colour and flavour.

½ cup (125 ml) dry white
   wine
1½ pounds (1 litre)
   mussels, thoroughly
   scrubbed in several
   changes of water and
   bearded
1½ pounds (1 litre) small
   clams, thoroughly
   scrubbed in several
   changes of water
10 ounces (280 g) fresh
   fettuccine
¼ cup (60 ml) olive oil
3 tablespoons red wine
   vinegar
1 clove garlic, minced
Salt and freshly ground
   black pepper to taste
½ cup (10 g) or 1 bunch
   fresh basil leaves,
   washed and dried
½ cup (10 g) or 1 bunch
   fresh parsley leaves,
   washed and dried

1. In a 6-quart (6-litre) Dutch oven, add the white wine, mussels, and clams and bring the wine to a boil over high heat. Cover and cook for about 5 minutes, or just until the mussels and clams open. Do not overcook. Remove from the heat, strain, and discard the liquid and any mussels or clams that do not open.

2. Cool slightly and when they are not too hot to touch remove the mussels and clams from their shells and set aside.

3. Bring a large pot of salted water to a rolling boil. Add the pasta and cook just until tender, but not soft. Drain.

4. In a large salad bowl combine the warm pasta, oil and vinegar, mussels, clams, minced garlic, salt, and pepper. Let marinate for about 20 minutes before serving.

5. Just before serving, coarsely chop the basil and parsley and add to the pasta. Toss gently and serve immediately.

Yield: 4 to 6 servings.

**LA FONTAINE
DE MARS,**
129 Rue Saint Dominique,
    Paris 7.
(705.46.44).
Métro: Ecole Militaire.
Closed Saturday evening,
    Sunday, and the month
    of August.
Credit card: V.
50-franc menu, includes
    service but not wine. *A
    la carte,* 100 francs.

SPECIALITIES:
*Foie gras frais (fresh duck
liver), changing plat du jour,
wines of Cahors.*

This family bistro with its almost illegible mimeographed menu, is inexpensive, bright, and airy.
The windows overlook the gentle arches leading to the
tiny Rue de l'Exposition, service is friendly, the food
simple. Good dishes include grilled sardines, thick
slabs of country ham, and a rich *mystère* ice cream dessert with chocolate sauce and meringue.

LES GLENAN,
54 Rue de Bourgogne,
    Paris 7. (551.61.09).
Métro: Varenne.
Closed Saturday, Sunday,
    holidays, the month of
    August, and January 1
    to 10.
No credit cards.
200 francs.

SPECIALITIES:
*Fish and seafood, white
chocolate marquise.*

A most pleasant, honest little Left Bank restaurant
devoted to imaginative fish preparations. The
young chef, an American named Mark Singer, offers a
lively first-course salad of marinated sardines flavoured
with green peppercorns, perfectly grilled salmon served
with a *timbale* of fresh spinach, and an unusually delicious white chocolate *marquise* with a bitter chocolate
sauce. The bread may not always be very fresh, and
the wine list needs attention.

PANTAGRUEL,
20 Rue de l'Exposition,
    Paris 7. (551.79.96).
Métro: Ecole Militaire.
Closed Saturday lunch,
    Sunday, and the month
    of August.
Credit cards: AE, DC, V.
200 francs.

SPECIALITIES:
*Soufflé aux oursins (sea urchin
soufflé) from November to
March, foie chaud de canard
(warm fattened duck liver),
noisettes de chevreuil grand
veneur (venison in wine sauce)
from October to March.*

A tiny, charming family-run restaurant tucked away
on the hidden Rue de l'Exposition, near the
Champ de Mars. A good place to go during game
season, between October and February, when chef Alfred
Israël serves a variety of game, including an aromatic
civet de chevreuil, a very correct and classic venison stew,
with huge, manly chunks of bacon, whole baby onions, and good-size cubes of moist and rosy deer. Also
try the wild *cèpe* mushrooms sautéed with garlic, and
enjoy a good bottle of Burgundy.

AU QUAI D'ORSAY,
49 Quai d'Orsay, Paris 7.
(551.58.58).
Métro: Invalides.
Closed Sunday, and the
    month of August.
Credit cards: AE, DC,
    EC, V.
Air-conditioned.
Pavement terrace.
250 francs.

SPECIALITIES:
Change with the season.

A very Parisian, very animated restaurant with a bustling staff and a steady clientele that arrives with huge appetites. Portions are enormous, but this is one restaurant that allows you to order half portions of many of the dishes listed on the long, imaginative, and ever-changing menu. During the fall and winter months, sample the delightful *pissenlit* salad (dandelion greens tossed with freshly grilled chunks of fresh tuna), the satisfying sauté of fresh wild mushrooms laden with garlic and sprinkled with fresh chervil, or any of the roast game specialities. Meat and poultry are better bets than the fish, which tends to be overcooked. The thick slices of country bread are delicious, the thin almond *tuiles* perfectly fresh, service rushed but friendly.

LA SOLOGNE,
8 Rue de Bellechasse,
    Paris 7.
(705.98.66).
Métro: Solférino.
Closed Saturday, Sunday,
    and the month of
    August.
Credit cards: AE, DC, V.
Air-conditioned.
200 francs.

SPECIALITIES:
Game from October to
February, local river fish the
rest of the year.

A cosy, countrylike spot in the city, where chef-owner Christian Guillerand and his wife, Jeannine, treat diners as though they're being entertained in a private home. In fall and winter months, the restaurant devotes itself to game, offering crisp-skinned *sauvagine* —young wild duck, grilled simply over an open fire nurtured with grape vines. There's also a nourishing *pot-au-feu de gibiers,* a large, old-fashioned soup plate laden with huge joints of partridge, pheasant, and duck, strips of leek, and chunks of carrot. In the spring and summer, Guillerand turns his attention to local river fish, including *brochet* (pike), *sandre* (pikeperch), and *lotte* (monkfish).

MADELEINE, SAINT-LAZARE, CHAMPS-ELYSEES
8th arrondissement

ANDROUET,
41 Rue d'Amsterdam,
    Paris 8.
(874.26.93).
Métro: Liège.
Closed Sunday and
    holidays.
Credit cards: AE, DC, V.
Private dining room for 26.
Cheese *dégustation* (tasting),
    120 francs. *A la carte,*
    about 150 francs.

SPECIALITIES:
Cheese.

A nyone who loves cheese owes himself at least one visit to the rustic, vaulted dining room at Androuët. The multi-course feast of tray upon tray of cheese is like taking a mind-boggling cheese tour of France while sitting still. The friendly, fatherly waiters are pleased to offer advice as they wheel past with more than 100 varieties of cheese, most of them made from raw milk and aged in the cellars beneath the shop. The tasting begins with high-fat triple cream cheese (Lucullus, Grand Vatel, La Butte), moves on to pressed varieties (Tête de Moine, Reblochon, Tomme de Savoie), then to the soft Brie and Camembert. Next come the spiced cheeses and those aged in ash (try the refined Soumaintrain or rustic Feuille de Dreux); a stunning assortment of *chèvres* (goat cheeses); the *fromages forts* (pungent Pont l'Evêque and Livarot); and finally the blue varieties, the best being Roquefort and Fourme d'Ambert. If the budget permits order a good bottle of Bordeaux and plan to make an afternoon or evening of it. (See also Fromageries)

L'ARTOIS,
13 Rue d'Artois, Paris 8.
(225.01.10).
Métro: Saint-Philippe-du-Roule.
Closed Saturday, Sunday, and July 14 to September 15.
No credit cards.
Private dining room for 12.
100 to 150 francs.

SPECIALITIES:
Coq au vin (chicken cooked in red wine), cailles rôties aux raisins frais (roast quail with fresh grapes).

A bustling, popular businessman's bistro off the Champs-Elysées, L'Artois features a hearty line-up of solid fare, including filets of herring with warm, sliced potatoes, superb Auvergne sausages served with sautéed *cèpe* mushrooms, grilled *boudin noir* (blood sausage), and *coq au vin* prepared with the dark red wine of Cahors. There's a good selection of regional wines, and though service can be slow, the lively atmosphere puts everyone in a willing mood.

CAVIAR KASPIA,
17 Place de la Madeleine, Paris 8.
(265.33.52).
Métro: Madeleine.
Last orders taken at 11:30 P.M. Closed Sunday.
Credit cards: AE, DC.
Private dining room for 20.
100 to 150 francs.

SPECIALITIES:
Caviar, salmon, smoked fish.

E legant but informal, this little restaurant above Caviar Kaspia—a neat shop devoted to a handful of food fantasies—is the perfect spot for a quick lunch in the Madeleine/Opéra neighbourhood. Try for one of the window tables overlooking the church, and settle into the luxurious world of caviar, salmon, and icy vodka. You can make a fine meal out of the fresh, plump blinis served with a few thin slices of tender smoked salmon. Or, if the budget allows, sample 30 grams (about an ounce) of caviar, either Beluga, Sevruga, Oscietra, or pressed caviar, just enough to tease the palate and fill you full of fine food memories for the day.

CHIBERTA,
3 Rue Arsène-Houssaye,
  Paris 8.
(563.77.90).
Métro: Charles-de-Gaulle/
  Etoile.
Closed Saturday, Sunday,
  holidays, the month of
  August, and Christmas
  week.
Credit cards: AE, DC, V.
Air-conditioned.
300 francs.

SPECIALITIES:
Change with the season.

This streamlined *Art Déco*-style restaurant just off the Champs-Elysées is one of Paris's most popular *nouvelle cuisine* restaurants. Chef Jean-Michel Bédier offers an ever-changing, original menu that follows the seasons, and a chic, upscale crowd enjoys following his progress. In the fall, there are generally wonderful combinations of wild mushrooms, or a terrine of rabbit surrounded with sweet and sour figs, or fresh fig desserts, while spring and summer find a menu showered with dishes of salmon, artichokes, or sweet white turbot. The food can vary from stunning (see the recipe for chef Bédier's refreshing summer soup, below) to just plain boring, the wine list needs work, and service can be terribly uneven.

Soupe d'Oranges et Fraises a la Menthe Fraiche
ORANGE AND STRAWBERRY SOUP WITH FRESH MINT

A light, refreshing, and beautiful early summer dessert, this lovely blend of candied orange zest, fresh strawberries, and mint is reminiscent of a formal garden party set on a bright green lawn. The dessert takes a bit of time to prepare, but requires little last-minute attention.

4 navel oranges
6 tablespoons grenadine
¼ cup (50 g) sugar
1 pound (450 g)
  strawberries
½ cup (10 g) loosely
  packed fresh mint
  leaves

1. Carefully remove the zest (the orange portion of the peel) from each orange, being sure not to get any of the white inner peel. Cut the zest into fine julienne strips.

2. Fill a small saucepan with water and bring it to a boil. Add the zest, and as soon as the water boils again, remove the zest. Repeat this one more time with a fresh pan of water. Drain zest on paper towels.

3. In a small saucepan over medium heat, combine the grenadine and zest, and cook, stirring constantly, until all the grenadine has evaporated, leaving the zest candylike and bright red. Do not prepare the candied zest more than several hours in advance, as it will lose its crispness.

4. Remove the white pith from the oranges and discard. Divide the oranges into neat sections, being careful to reserve the juice. Set the juice aside and put the orange sections in a bowl. Add 2 tablespoons of the sugar to the sections, cover with plastic wrap and refrigerate.

5. Hull and quarter the strawberries, and add them to the reserved orange juice with the remaining sugar. Reserve 8 whole mint leaves and chop the rest very fine. Add the chopped mint to the strawberry mixture, cover with plastic wrap, and marinate in the refrigerator for no longer than 15 minutes.

6. To serve: Arrange the orange sections around the edges of very shallow bowls or plates and place the strawberries in the center. Sprinkle with the candied orange zest and the whole mint leaves.

Yield: 4 servings.

COPENHAGUE,
142 Avenue des Champs-
　Elysées, Paris 8.
(359.20.41).
Métro: Charles-de-Gaulle/
　Etoile.
Closed Sunday, holidays,
　August, and the first
　week in January.
Credit cards: AE, DC,
　EC, V.
200 francs.

SPECIALITIES:
Danish, including salmon,
herring, eel, various breads,
and pastries.

At lunchtime, a well-heeled international business crowd makes this upstairs dining room their watering hole: Fresh, cured, or smoked salmon and assorted varieties of Dutch herring find their way into many dishes, while Danish beer and tiny fluted glasses of aquavit fill in the gaps. Try the delicious platter of four kinds of herring, then move on to the sumptuous, barely grilled salmon—crispy skin on one side, buttery rich and smooth on the other. The Danish rye bread can arrive stale; if it does, ask for a fresh basket. Service is swift and professional, the decor cosy, subdued, and authentically Danish.

FLORA DANICA,
142 Avenue des Champs-
　Elysées, Paris 8.
(359.20.41).
Métro: Charles-de-Gaulle/
　Etoile.
Open daily until 11 P.M.
Credit cards: AE, DC,
　EC, V.
Garden dining.
50 to 200 francs.

SPECIALITIES:
Danish, including salmon,
herring, eel, various breads,
and pastries.

In the summertime, the entire city competes for the umbrella-shaded tables set back on the pleasant little terrace behind Flora Danica, a casual main floor boutique (downstairs from the Copenhague restaurant) serving simple Danish fare. Best bets are the *gravlax*—thin slices of dilled salmon marinated in sugar, salt, and spices—or any of the assorted herrings.

LA MAREE,
1 Rue Daru, Paris 8.
(763.52.42 and
　227.59.32).
Métro: Ternes.
Closed Saturday, Sunday,
　the month of August,
　and during holiday
　periods.
Credit cards: AE, DC.
Private dining room for 30.
350 francs.

SPECIALITIES:
Fish and seafood.

You can spot the restaurant by the chauffeured limousines and shiny new Rolls-Royces that wait patiently outside while the elegant, wealthy, totally Parisian crowd dines inside. Fish and seafood are the specialties here year-round, but in the fall and winter months roast game birds and venison compete for attention. The wine list, and the *sommelier,* Jean-Luc Pouteau, who in an international competition was named the world's best wine waiter in 1983, are worth a bit of attention.

Oysters to go.

Scallops and boudin are the specialities at La Coquille (see entry, page 68).

LE PETIT MONTMORENCY,

5 Rue Rabelais, Paris 8.
(225.11.19).
Métro: Saint-Philippe-de-Roule.
Closed Saturday, Sunday, and the month of August.
Credit card: V.
Air-conditioned.
300 francs.

S P E C I A L I T I E S :
Foie gras de canard au naturel à la cuillère (fresh fattened duck liver), tendron de veau aux nouilles (veal stew with noodles), changing dessert menu.

A bright, cheery little bistro that exudes good will and generosity. The fourteen-table restaurant is so cozy, and so filled with decorative, personal mementos, you feel as though the Bouché family is inviting you into their home to sample the latest dish. But, you'd have to make several visits if you wanted to wend your way through chef Daniel Bouché's imaginative and highly personal menu. Year-round, you can find fresh and well-seasoned *foie gras de canard,* while in fall and winter months opt for the truffle salad—a generous toss of warm sliced potatoes and thick black truffle slices. Main dishes are copious and filling, including a good mix of meat and fish specialities. Chef Bouché's desserts are equally good: Imagine a blend of fresh *mûres* (blackberries), chopped pears, and pale mint ice cream, topped with a sweet, creamy custard *gratiné.* The breads and *petits fours* may be stale, but the service is warm and professional, and the wine list worth more than a cursory glance.

LA POULARDE LANDAISE,

4 Rue Saint-Philippe-de-Roule, Paris 8.
(359.20.25).
Métro: Saint-Philippe-de-Roule.
Closed Saturday, Sunday, and holidays.
Credit cards: AE, V.
145-franc menu, not including wine and service; also 130-franc menu at night, includes wine and service. *A la carte,* 175 francs.

S P E C I A L I T I E S :
Southwestern, good regional wines.

A cosy little *auberge*—complete with a roaring fire and bossy, but friendly, owner—lost in the centre of the city. Authentically Parisian, this dark, beamed dining room overflows at lunchtime, serving hearty southwestern dishes such as *confit de canard* (duck cooked and preserved in its own fat), breast of fattened goose, or *magret d'oie* (ask them to just grill it and leave off the sauce), platters of seductive, garlicky *pleurote* mushrooms, fresh Poilâne bread, and simple regional wines. The staff seems a bit harried, but service is friendly, just the same. Do save room for the warm, nicely caramelized tarte Tatin.

TAILLEVENT,
15 Rue Lamennais, Paris 8.
(561.12.90 and
   563.39.94).
Métro: George V.
Closed Saturday, Sunday,
   holidays, two weeks at
   Easter, last week in July
   to last week in August.
No credit cards.
Air-conditioned.
Private dining room for 32.
300 francs.

SPECIALITIES:
Cervelas de fruits de mer aux
truffes et aux pistaches (seafood
sausage with truffles and
pistachios), turbotin grillé
(grilled turbot), marquise au
chocolat à la pistache (chocolate
cake with pistachio sauce).

I always flinch a bit when pressed to name the best restaurant in Paris. Restaurant ratings and criticism often elevate dining out to such sober and serious heights that people tend to forget that restaurants are there for simple enjoyment. But yes, I do believe Taillevent is the best in Paris. Impeccable, serious, welcoming, and genuine, Taillevent embodies the qualities I look for in a grand restaurant. The well-appointed *hôtel particulier* has the air of a private club, providing wonderful food and great theatre, not just glitter and pomp. Service within warm, panelled rooms, decorated with crystal chandeliers and silver goblets filled with fresh flowers, is gracious, discreet, and unselfconscious. A great restaurant is one that provides rich, rewarding, pleasant memories years after that fleeting lunch or romantic dinner. I can play back in careful detail every meal I've had at Taillevent, can almost taste certain dishes when I think of them, remember how each wine tasted, and where I sat. Every restaurateur could

---

MARQUISE AU CHOCOLAT TAILLEVENT
TAILLEVENT'S CHOCOLATE CAKE

This is the dessert I order almost every time I dine at Taillevent, the finest restaurant in Paris. The cake is rich and classic, rather like a ripened chocolate mousse. A marquise is easy to make and requires no baking. Taillevent adds its signature by serving it with a rich pistachio sauce, actually a crème anglaise flavoured with ground pistachio nuts. The sauce is a bit time-consuming, but not difficult. The cake may, of course, be served without a sauce, or with a plain crème anglaise. Both the cake and the sauce should be made twenty-four hours before serving.

9 ounces (250 g)
   bittersweet chocolate
   (preferably Lindt or
   Tobler brand)
¾ cup (100 g)
   confectioner's sugar
¾ cup (6 ounces; 170 g)
   unsalted butter, at
   room temperature
5 eggs, separated
Pinch of salt
Pistachio sauce, optional
   (see recipe below)

1. Melt the chocolate in a small saucepan over very low heat. Add these ingredients in the following order, mixing well after each addition: ½ cup (70 g) sugar, all the butter, and the egg yolks. Leave pan on low heat.

2. In a small mixing bowl, beat the egg whites with a pinch of salt until stiff, then add the remaining sugar and beat another 20 seconds, or until glossy.

3. Remove the chocolate batter from the heat, and add one third of the egg white mixture, folding in gently but thoroughly. Then gently fold in the remaining whites. Don't overmix, but be sure that the mixture is well blended.

4. Rinse an 8½-inch (22-cm) springform pan with water. Leave the pan wet and fill it with the mixture. Refrigerate for 24 hours. Remove from the refrigerator about 30 minutes before serving. To serve, pour several tablespoons of the pistachio sauce onto a dessert plate. Place a thin slice of the *marquise* in the centre of the plate and serve.

Yield: One 8½-inch (22-cm) cake.

SAUCE A LA PISTACHE
PISTACHIO SAUCE

⅓ cup (100 g) pistachio
   paste (see recipe below)
1 quart (1 litre) milk
8 egg yolks
1¼ cups (250 g) sugar

1. Prepare the pistachio paste.

2. In a medium-size saucepan combine the pistachio paste with the milk and bring the mixture to a boil over medium heat. Remove from the heat and allow it to steep for 5 minutes, then strain through cheesecloth or a fine-mesh sieve into another medium-size saucepan. Set aside.

3. In a medium-size mixing bowl combine the egg yolks and sugar, and beat until thick and light. Whisk in half the warm strained milk, then whisk the mixture back into the remaining milk.

4. Warm the sauce gently over medium heat, stirring constantly, until it thickens. Do not allow the sauce to boil or it will curdle. You can prepare this 24 hours in advance and refrigerate, removing from refrigerator 1 hour in advance.

Yield: 1 quart (1 liter).

PATE DE PISTACHE
PISTACHIO PASTE

A generous ½ cup (60 g)
   shelled raw, unsalted
   pistachio nuts
⅓ cup (65 g) sugar
1 small egg white

1. Preheat the oven to 300°F (150°C).

2. Toast the nuts on a baking sheet in the oven for 5 minutes. Allow them to cool, then, squeezing them between your thumb and forefinger, remove as much skin as possible from the nuts. (If using already roasted, salted nuts, remove as much skin as possible from the shelled nuts, then rinse quickly under boiling water. Drain, then remove as much remaining skin as possible.)

3. Place the nuts in a food processor or nut grinder, and grind the nuts to a paste.

4. In a small bowl mix the nut paste with the sugar, then add the egg white to give it a sticky quality. The pistachio paste will keep in the refrigerator for a week in a tightly sealed container.

Yield: ½ cup (150 g).

learn a lesson from Taillevent's owner, Jean-Claude Vrinat. He is the perfect gentleman, a wise man who is willing to pay attention to the little details others can't be bothered with. The restaurant is both democratic and generous, and it's certain that most people leave feeling as though their money was well spent. Chef Claude Deligne skilfully manages to retain elements of classic cuisine, picking up some of the more positive influences of *nouvelle cuisine*. Sauces have their role, but not at the expense of fresh, perfectly cooked

*Taillevent chef, Claude
Deligne.*

ingredients. Some of the most memorable dishes here
include the *cervelas de fruits de mer aux truffes et aux
pistaches,* a feather-light, pistachio-studded sausage of
lobster, crayfish, pike, and truffles in *beurre blanc;* an
unforgettable perfectly grilled turbot; and a brilliant
marquise au chocolat à la pistache (see recipes, pages 48
and 49).

There may be people who leave Taillevent disappointed—asking "Is that all there is?"—and I can
understand why. The food doesn't slap you in the face
or make you turn somersaults. It succeeds with quiet
refinement, subtlety, an uncompromising dedication
to quality. Taillevent offers one of the finest—and most
reasonably priced—wine lists in Paris. Take your time
examining it, and don't be bashful about asking Mr.
Vrinat's educated opinion when organizing the meal.

AU VIEUX BERLIN,
32 Avenue George V,
    Paris 8.
(720.88.96).
Métro: George V.
Closed Saturday and
    Sunday.
Credit cards: AE, DC, V.
Air-conditioned.
Private dining room for 40.
50 to 100 francs.

SPECIALITIES:
*German, including assorted
sausages, pork filet with
cumin, sauerkraut, beer.*

When I'm in the mood for the food of my childhood—fresh grilled German bratwurst smothered in sauerkraut—I head straight for the little res-
taurant/boutique at Au Vieux Berlin. Deliciously
warming is the platter of *weisswürste*—white pork and
veal sausage properly simmered, not boiled, in beer
and caraway—which goes down well with a chilled
stein of German beer. Just adjacent, there is also a
more classic German dining room with a full-scale
menu.

GRANDS BOULEVARDS, PLACE DE CLICHY, GARE DU NORD
9th and 10th arrondissements

CHARLOT, LE ROI DES COQUILLAGES,
12 Place de Clichy, Paris 9.
(874.49.64).
Métro: Place de Clichy.
Open daily. Last orders
taken at 12:45 A.M.
Closed in June, July,
and August.
Credit cards: AE, DC, V.
Air-conditioned.
120-franc menu, not
including wine or
service. *A la carte,* 200
francs.

SPECIALITIES:
Fish and seafood.

When I want a casual lunch of oysters, mussels, little clams, tiny shrimp, and crab, I go to Charlot, the "King of Shellfish." During the "R" months from September to April, when shellfish is in season, memorable Paris meals are made of a refreshing *plateau de fruits de mer* (a platter of mixed shellfish), served with slices of fresh rye bread, butter, and glasses of chilled, flinty Sancerre. The bright, friendly upstairs dining room overlooks the active Place de Clichy, a lively setting for a long weekend lunch with a group of three or four. Ask for a table near the window, order a *plateau,* a bottle of wine, and enjoy.

AU CHATEAUBRIANT,
23 Rue de Chabrol,
Paris 10.
(824.58.94).
Métro: Gare de l'Est.
Closed Sunday, Monday,
and the month of
August.
No credit cards.
Air-conditioned.
200 francs.

SPECIALITIES:
Italian.

With so much good food in his own front yard, the Frenchman does not take other cuisines very seriously. Still, a recent poll found that they do consider Italian their favourite foreign cuisine. For decades, the best place for Italian food in Paris has been Au Châteaubriant. Anyone used to the "real thing" in Italy will likely be a little disappointed, but understanding that, this elegant, classic little restaurant merits a visit. Try the superb pastas (the *paglia e fieno,* or straw and hay, is extraordinary), the simple grilled *scampi,* fresh asparagus in season, and the nicely aged wines. Service in this flower-filled dining room is friendly, outgoing, and ultra-efficient.

LES DIAMANTAIRES,
60 Rue La Fayette, Paris 9.
(770.78.14)
Métro: Cadet.
Closed Monday evening,
Tuesday, the month of
August, and the first
week of September.
No credit cards.
About 100 francs.

SPECIALITIES:
Greek, including moussaka,
kebabs, stuffed grape leaves.

Paris is full of "made up" Greek restaurants, serving unappetizing, gargantuan kebabs and over-roasted lamb. But Diamantaires is different, and authentic. The diamond dealers who used to frequent this pale blue, no-nonsense dining hall are less of a presence today, but Diamantaires is always roguish and lively; a fine place for sampling flaky spinach and cheese pies, lamb and eggplant *moussaka,* hearty lamb-based meatballs, delicious homemade yogurt, and potent Greek wine.

BRASSERIE FLO,
7 Cour Petites-Ecuries,
    Paris 10.
(770.13.59).
Métro: Château d'Eau.
Open daily. Last orders
    taken at 1:30 A.M.
Credit cards: AE, DC, V.
100 francs.

SPECIALITIES:
Choucroute (sauerkraut and
sausages), foie gras, fresh
oysters year-round.

An honest 1900s Alsatian brasserie, with a faithful and flashy Parisian clientele. Flo is often too crowded, too noisy, too hectic, but for many regulars, that is part of its charm. The standard fare here is accompanied by very drinkable wines by the pitcher. Don't attempt a visit without reservations.

JULIEN,
16 Rue du Faubourg Saint-
    Denis, Paris 10.
(770.12.06).
Métro: Strasbourg-Saint-
    Denis.
Open daily. Last orders
    taken at 1:30 AM.
    Closed in July.
Credit cards: AE, DC, V.
103-franc menu. *A la carte,*
    about 120 francs.

SPECIALITIES:
Saumon en rillettes (fresh and
smoked salmon pâté), cassoulet
d'oie (casserole of goose and
white beans), foie gras,
changing fish and seafood
specialties.

Despite its rather seedy location, Julien remains one of the city's most chic, most popular nighttime addresses. One look inside this bright, stunning 1890s dining hall and you understand: Who could not love the stained-glass skylights, the mahogany bar, the *Art Nouveau* mirrors and murals, the noisy brasserie charm? Service can be slow or too rushed, depending on the waiter and the time of day, but the menu offers enough variety to please the most finicky crowd. I generally opt for the restaurant's classics: *saumon en rillettes* (see recipe, page 58), their famous Riesling-laced *foie gras,* or *cassoulet d'oie,* a warming casserole of goose and white beans. Dessert lovers should try the *profiteroles au chocolat,* little rounds of *chou* pastry filled with ice cream and served with a steaming hot pitcher of chocolate sauce.

AU PETIT RICHE,

25 Rue Le Peletier, Paris 9.
(770.68.68).
Métro: Le Peletier.
Last orders taken at 12:15
A.M. Closed Sunday, and
the month of August.
Credit card: V.
Private dining room for 45.
95- and 122-franc menus,
include service but not
wine. *A la carte,* 100 to
150 francs.

SPECIALITIES:
Terrine de haddock au coulis de
tomates (haddock terrine with
fresh tomato sauce), sauté de
veau aux poireaux (sautéed
veal with leeks), tarte fine aux
pommes chaudes (warm apple
tart), good Loire Valley wines.

For more than 100 years the gracious, well-preserved Au Petit Riche has served as a favourite gathering spot for Parisian journalists and businessmen. The welcome here is still gracious and friendly, and the decor remains warmly authentic. At lunchtime, the various little wood-panelled and mirror-lined dining rooms are packed with businessmen in search of a solid lunch, while at dinnertime the men come back with their wives to sample a pleasant cuisine that combines classics and *nouvelle*-inspired specialties. Good bets are the marinated octopus, or *poulpe,* salad; the mustard-seasoned roast rabbit, *lapin au four, sauce moutarde;* and a warm and delicious apple tart, *tarte fine aux pommes chaudes.* Do try the fine Sauvignon, Chablis, Gamay, or Bourgueil by the carafe.

LE ROI DU POT-AU-FEU,

34 Rue Vignon, Paris 9.
(742.37.10).
Métro: Madeleine.
Continuous service noon to
9 P.M. Closed Sunday,
holidays, and the month
of July.
Credit card: V.
Pavement terrace.
75 francs.

SPECIALITY:
Pot-au-feu.

This funky little bistro off the Place de la Madeleine is great on a chilly fall or winter afternoon, when a nourishing dish of boiled beef, bone marrow, and vegetables is what's needed to warm the soul. The decor here is a bit kitschy but humorous just the same—cartoons paper the walls, an old piano stands beside the zinc bar, and the chatty staff make a *fête* of even the simplest lunch. Here, the *pot-au-feu* begins with the traditional bouillon, steaming beef broth ladled from the stockpot in which the meat and vegetables have simmered. Next comes the enormous platter of beef, vegetables, and fresh, fragrant marrow, served with puckery cornichons, plenty of mustard, and coarse salt. The bistro serves a young Côtes-du-Rhône from Lucien Legrand, one of the city's better wine merchants.

The fare at Le Roi du Pot-au-Feu.

POT-AU-FEU
BEEF SIMMERED WITH VEGETABLES

"Eating pot-au-feu is an act that gives significance to life," wrote one French critic. A bit precious, to be sure, but few peasant dishes are as healthfully nourishing, fragrant, or satisfying as a superb pot-au-feu—various cuts of beef simmered gently along with bone marrow and earthy vegetables such as turnips, leeks, cabbage, carrots, onions, and potatoes. It is served in two or three courses, usually during a long, unhurried Sunday afternoon.

In its most classic form, the dish begins with a shallow, steaming bowl of bouillon, ladled from the pot in which the meat, marrow, and vegetables have been slowly simmering. To the bowl one might add garlic-touched croutons, freshly grated Parmesan or Gruyère cheese, a few grains of coarsely ground black pepper. The second course is made up of the meat, vegetables, and accompaniments, a procession of condiments that might include fiery horseradish, three or four varieties of mustard, coarse salt, puckery cornichons and tiny white pickled onions. This recipe is based on the one shared with us by Le Roi du Pot-au-Feu (see entry, page 53).

2 pounds (900 g) short
    ribs of beef
2 pounds (900 g) boned
    beef shank
2 pounds oxtail (900 g),
    cut into 2-inch (5-cm)
    lengths
Coarse (kosher) salt and
    freshly ground black
    pepper
6 small onions, each
    peeled and studded
    with a clove
4 leeks, cleaned of sand
1 fennel bulb, trimmed,
    washed, and quartered
4 cloves garlic, unpeeled
6 whole carrots, peeled
Bouquet garni: 2 bay
    leaves, 2 sprigs fresh
    parsley, and 1 teaspoon
    dried thyme, tied in a
    piece of cheesecloth
1 whole apple, washed
Approximately 1½
    pounds (675 g) beef
    marrow bones, cut into
    2-inch (5-cm) lengths,
    and each length
    wrapped in green
    portion of leek (to seal
    in the marrow)

**Garnishes and
    condiments:**
Toast rubbed with garlic
Freshly grated Parmesan
    cheese
Horseradish
Several kinds of mustard
Cornichons

1. Using household string, tie in two separate bundles the ribs of beef and the boned shank, so they retain their shape and fit compactly into a large stockpot. Place the oxtail on top of the other meat. Cover the meat completely with cold water and cook, uncovered, over medium-high heat. The water should barely simmer, never boil.

2. After about 20 minutes, skim the stock very carefully, removing all traces of impurities or grease. Careful skimming is essential to producing a fine *pot-au-feu.*

3. When the impurities have turned to foam, skim again and move the pot to halfway off the heat so that the foam rises on one side only, making it easier to skim. Continue cooking for another 20 minutes.

4. Season the liquid lightly with coarse salt (about 1 tablespoon should finely season this dish) and pepper. Add the vegetables, using only the white portions of the leeks; the *bouquet garni;* and the apple, which will help absorb some of the fat. Skim again and cook another 40 minutes. Skim frequently, and after about 30 minutes, test the vegetables to see if they are cooked.

5. Once the vegetables have cooked, remove them to a heatproof dish and moisten with bouillon. Cover with aluminum foil and keep warm in a low oven.

6. Continue cooking the meat, skimming if necessary, for 1 hour more. About 15 minutes before serving, add the marrow bones.

7. To serve the first course, place a slice of toast rubbed with garlic in a warmed soup bowl, cover with bouillon, and sprinkle with freshly grated Parmesan cheese.

8. To serve the second course, remove the twine from the meat and cut it into chunks. Place it on a warmed platter, surrounded by the marrow bones and the vegetables, discarding the *bouquet garni* and the apple. Serve with the horseradish, a variety of mustards, *cornichons,* coarse salt, and pepper. The dish can easily be reheated.

Yield: 4 to 6 servings.

TERMINUS NORD,
23 Rue de Dunkerque,
    Paris 10. (285.05.15).
Métro: Gare du Nord.
Open daily. Last orders
    taken at midnight.
Credit cards: DC, V.
Pavement terrace.
Private dining room for 10.
100 to 150 francs.

SPECIALITIES:
Fish and seafood, choucroute
(sauerkraut and sausages).

Terminus Nord is a rambling, authentic 1925 brasserie just outside the Gare du Nord train station,
but you don't have to wait until a journey brings you
to this end of town. The year-round *banc* of fresh
oysters and shellfish is enough to. lure most diners,
along with excellent grilled Mediterranean *rouget* (red
mullet), grilled sliced leg of lamb, and inexpensive
wines that go down so easily amid the lively old-time
atmosphere.

GARE DE LYON, BOIS DE VINCENNES
12th arrondissement

AU PRESSOIR,
257 Avenue Daumesnil,
    Paris 12. (344.38.21).
Métro: Porte Dorée.
Closed Saturday lunch from
    October to March, all
    day Saturday from April
    to September, Sunday,
    two weeks in February,
    three weeks in August.
Credit card: V.
265-franc *menu dégustation,*
    including service but
    not wine. *A la carte,*
    250 francs.

SPECIALITIES:
Brandade de morue aux asperges
(codfish purée with asparagus).

My only regret with Au Pressoir is that it is so far
off the beaten track, basically on the way to
nowhere. But those in search of a highly inventive
though rarely bizarre cuisine, won't regret the journey. Chef Henri Seguin changes his menu often, and
you can usually be assured of finding a fine medley of
seasonal salads, lovely warm sautéed *foie gras,* and seasonal roast game. Au Pressoir is worth a trip just on
the merit of its wine list and helpful *sommelier.* Show a
little enthusiasm for wine, and he may just run down
to the cellar and dig out a special bottle, just for you
to taste. In all, a place that's solid, serious, and authentically warm.

LE TRAIN BLEU,
20 Boulevard Diderot,
Gare de Lyon (one flight
    up), Paris 12.
(343.09.06).
Métro: Gare de Lyon.
Open daily.
Credit cards: AE, DC, V.
160-franc menu, including
    wine and service (lunch
    only). *A la carte,* 200
    francs.

SPECIALITIES:
Lyonnais, including quenelles
de brochet (pike dumplings).

One of the grandest *Belle Epoque* decors in all of
Paris, Le Train Bleu is a classic that should not
be missed. Everything from the starched white linens
to the stiff but friendly old waiters, from the sculpted
ceilings to the portrait of Sarah Bernhardt makes this
spot quintessentially Parisian. It's the kind of place
that's fun to go alone to at odd hours, just to people-
watch and enjoy a leisurely meal. The old-fashioned
tableside service is friendly and attentive, but remember that you're not here principally for the food. If it
happens to be good that day, so much the better.
Order the simplest, least complicated dishes, and you
should have a pleasant meal. Recommended: the platter of Niçois appetizers, the garlicky *anchoïade* served

with raw vegetables, the grilled salmon and a chilled white Arbois wine.

AU TROU GASCON,
40 Rue Taine, Paris 12.
(344.34.26).
Métro: Daumesnil.
Closed Saturday, Sunday,
   and the month of
   September.
Credit card: V.
Air-conditioned.
260-franc *menu dégustation,*
   including service but
   not wine. *A la carte,*
   220 to 250 francs.

SPECIALITIES:
Foie gras de canard (fattened duck liver), raviolis de foie gras aux truffes (ravioli of foie gras and truffles), cassoulet (casserole of white beans, homemade sausages, mutton, pork, duck, and tomatoes).

Alain Dutournier is, unquestionably, one of Paris's most talented young chefs. Season after season, he continues to astonish and surprise, for he's always growing, always creating, always coming up with dishes that are original and appealing. By combining elements of regional southwestern cuisine with hints of *nouvelle cuisine,* the Au Trou Gascon menu always manages to offer a fine mix of the old and the new. Depending on your mood, you can go country or city: Feast on a hearty Gascon *cassoulet,* washed down with a vigorous Corbières from the Pyrénées; or follow chef Dutournier's fantasies of the day, which might just include a simple but refined salad of marinated salmon, lamb's lettuce, and watercress, showered with a thick layer of fresh truffle shavings, a perfect companion for a mellow, golden Meursault. There is always a variety of new and seasonal specialities, and chef Dutournier

Au Trou Gascon.

handles wild mushrooms, salmon, poultry, and game with a touch of genius. This is a former *Belle Epoque* bistro, and as such, the noise level tends to be too high for some diners' pleasure. So go with a group, plan to make a night of it, sharing food, good times, and some fine wines from the extensive cellar. Whether you want a simple *vin de pays* or a grand cru Bordeaux, the *sommelier* will graciously oblige. Do save room for dessert, particularly the fine bitter chocolate cake and the *tourtière chaude et glace à l'Armagnac,* an updated version of the popular southwestern French prune and apple strudel. Chef Dutournier also offers one of the city's largest collections of rare Armagnacs.

R.I.P.

Throughout history, France has known true gourmets—the connoisseurs and epicures—and true gourmands—the ravenous and gluttonous. From time to time, eaters big and small take just one bite too many. May these people, most of whom died of excesses at the table, rest in peace.

Docteur Julien Offray de Lamettrie: while attempting to consume an entire pheasant after having already "dined excellently," on November 11, 1751.

Docteur Gastaldy: member of Grimod de la Reynière's famous "tasting jury," and the man considered the biggest glutton of the gluttonous set of Parisian doctors, of indigestion after embarking on his fourth helping of salmon, in 1805.

Fragonard: the painter, eating an ice cream, in 1806.

Général Andache Junot: who generally ate 300 oysters as an appetizer, died insane in 1813.

Duc of Escars: a table companion of Louis XVIII, while dining on truffles and ortolan purée, in 1822.

Pierrette: the youngest of Brillat-Savarin's three sisters, at the dinner table after having said to her servant, "And now, my dear, bring me dessert." She was 99 years and 10 months old. Sometime in the latter half of the 19th century.

Léon Gambetta: celebrated French leader, of wound complications . . . or of *cassoulet,* on December 31, 1882. Gambetta had been advised to take exercise after a tedious recovery from a gunshot wound. He was so hungry that on his return his cooks served up his favorite dish, *cassoulet,* a rich, hearty blend of meats and white beans. He took three generous helpings, and died later that night.

GOBELINS, VAUGIRARD, MONTPARNASSE, GRENELLE, DENFERT-ROCHEREAU
13th, 14th, and 15th arrondissements

CHEZ ALBERT,
122 Avenue du Maine,
 Paris 14.
(320.21.69).
Métro: Gaîté.
Closed Monday and last
 three weeks of August.
Credit cards: AE, DC, EC,
 V.
250 francs.

SPECIALITIES:
*Foie gras de canard (fattened
duck liver), côtes d'agneau
(lamb chops), wines from the
Arbois.*

Talk about service with a smile. There's Monsieur Beaumont, an elderly, outgoing wisp of a man, attending to every detail in this minuscule, old-fashioned restaurant. Each day, Chez Albert is filled with beefy businessmen who appear to have passed many an hour here, enjoying the moist and rosy lamb chops, the fine Arbois wines, and a fabulous raspberry sorbet. This is an example of a dying breed of restaurant that should not die out, with its pampered, professional tableside service, its menu made up of the freshest ingredients, and its cluttered, amusing decor that speaks of one's *grand-mère* and the good old days.

SAUMON EN RILLETTES JULIEN
JULIEN'S SALMON PATE

Julien, a huge and popular brasserie, is one of Paris's prettiest restaurants (see entry, page 52), and this is one of Julien's most pleasant first courses. Generally, the pâté-like rillettes are made of goose, duck, pork, or a combination of those meats. This recipe combines smoked and fresh salmon, butter, and Cognac, and it's melt-in-your-mouth delicious, especially served on wedges of toasted, homemade rye bread, with a glass of champagne before a festive meal. Sometimes, I serve it as a first course, also with toast, and a crisp Pouilly Fumé from the Loire Valley, the same wine I use in preparing the rillettes.

4 ounces (115 g) skinned
 fresh salmon fillets
½ cup (125 ml) dry white
 wine
1 tablespoon olive oil
2 tablespoons Cognac
Salt and freshly ground
 black pepper to taste
4 ounces (115 g) smoked
 salmon
6 tablespoons (3 ounces;
 85 g) unsalted butter

1. Cut the fresh salmon into bite-size pieces. In a small saucepan combine the salmon and wine, and bring slowly to a boil over medium heat. Remove from the heat and drain the salmon, discarding the wine.

2. In a small saucepan heat the olive oil and add the salmon. Cook gently over medium heat for about 5 minutes. Do not let it brown. Add the Cognac, salt and pepper. Remove from the heat and set aside.

3. Cut the smoked salmon into bite-size pieces. In a small saucepan over medium heat sauté the smoked salmon in half the butter for 3 to 5 minutes. Cool, then blend the smoked salmon in a food processor, adding the remaining butter.

4. Working by hand, combine the fresh salmon and smoked salmon mixtures with a fork until well blended. Check for seasoning. Refrigerate at least 12 hours before serving.

5. To serve, remove from the refrigerator about 30 minutes before serving. Serve on thin slices of warm toast.

Yield: 4 to 6 servings.

L'AQUITAINE,
54 Rue de Dantzig,
   Paris 15.
(828.67.38).
Métro: Convention.
Closed Sunday and Monday.
Credit cards: AE, DC, V.
Terrace dining in summer.
210-franc menu, including
   wine and service. *A la
   carte,* 240 francs.

SPECIALITIES:
*Panaché de poissons au beurre
blanc (an assortment of fish in
white butter sauce), confit de
canard (duck cooked and
preserved in its own fat),
beignets de fromage de chèvre
(deep-fried goat cheese).*

LA COUPOLE,
102 Boulevard du
   Montparnasse, Paris 14.
(320.14.20).
Métro: Vavin.
Open daily, noon to 2 A.M.
   Closed the month of
   August.
Credit card: V.
95-franc menu, including
   service but not wine;
   111-franc menu,
   including wine and
   service. *A la carte,* 150
   francs.

SPECIALITIES:
*Oysters, grilled meats, curry
d'agneau (lamb curry).*

LE DUC,
243 Boulevard Raspail,
   Paris 14.
(322.59.59).
Métro: Raspail.
Closed Saturday, Sunday,
   Monday, and holidays.
No credit cards.
250 francs.

SPECIALITIES:
*Fish and shellfish, including
plateau de fruits de mer (fish
and seafood platter).*

From the outside, you would never imagine that L'Aquitaine boasts a pleasant little terrace upstairs, next to the homey first floor dining room. Do stop by on a sunny afternoon to sit at one of the casual, umbrella-covered tables and sample some of the superbly fresh and imaginative fish preparations, or other items nicely woven into the southwestern French menu such as duck *confit,* veal kidneys, and various beef dishes. Christine Massia offers a pleasant medley of salads, including the refreshing smoked salmon served with a paprika-showered lettuce *chiffonade,* (see recipe, page 62); a fine *fricassée de lotte* (monkfish paired with delicate wild *mousseron* mushrooms); and the strudel-like southwestern dessert, *tourtière,* delicious when fresh, filled with a combination of sautéed apples and prunes and served with prune ice cream. Also sample the fine white Graves, Château Bouscaut.

After nearly five decades, La Coupole remains one of the most authentically Parisian scenes, with its bustling and solidly professional waiters, young families, old couples, and singles, all there to enjoy the lively atmosphere. You can pop in any time of day or night, for people-watching, a platter of oysters, a chilled Muscadet.

Chic, chic, and *tout* Paris. Despite high praise from many critics, Le Duc is really a place to see and be seen, not one in which to pay too much attention to the food (it is totally uneven), or to anticipate attentive service (which can be downright condescending). Enjoy a bottle of chilled Muscadet-sur-Lie, and if the chef is in form that night, you should be pleased with the peppery, marinated bass, or *loup cru,* and the *fricassée de lotte,* a lively, meaty sauté of cubed monkfish, fresh zucchini slices, and mountains of wild mushrooms.

LE JARDIN DE LA PARESSE,

20 Rue Gazan, Paris 14.
(588.38.52).
Métro: Cité Universitaire.
Open daily from May to
   October. Closed Sunday
   evening and Monday
   from October 1 to April
   30 and from December
   15 to January 15.
Credit cards: AE, DC, V.
Private dining room for 30.
30-franc menu for children;
   also 98- and 120-franc
   menus, not including
   wine and service. A la
   carte, 200 francs.

SPECIALITIES:
Raie aux choux (skate with
cabbage), filet de rouget aux
cèpes (red mullet with cèpe
mushrooms).

A Sunday afternoon lunch and a stroll in the Parc de Montsouris can easily take the place of a day trip to the country. This airy, well-tended park has been a Paris favourite since 1878, when Baron Haussmann transformed the unsightly quarries at the southern edge of the city into a fifty-acre (twenty-hectare) stretch of ordered greenery. And the park's rambling restaurant, Le Jardin de la Paresse—"The Garden of Leisure"—is just that, a not-too-serious eating spot in an incomparable, countrylike setting. The casual restaurant, with its covered porch and umbrella-topped tables, overlooks the park's bandstand and a man-made lake that serves as the park's centrepiece and home to flocks of ducks and swans. (Unfortunately, the man who designed and constructed the lagoon was never able to enjoy it. He reportedly committed suicide when it dried up on opening day.) The food is fresh and simple, service a bit scattered. Sample the fine selection of Georges Duboeuf wines.

SABLES DE POMMES CHAUDES, CONFITURE DU TEMPS
SHORTBREAD COOKIES WITH WARM APPLES AND SEASONAL FRUIT JAM

Many Paris restaurants are returning to simpler, homey desserts such as this one of warm shortbread, topped with sautéed apple slices and a dollop of homemade apricot jam. This version comes from Michel Rubod, chef at Jacqueline Fénix, a refreshing little restaurant in Neuilly (see entry, page 63). Note that the dough must be prepared the day before it is being served.

Shortbread:
⅓ cup (50 g) almonds,
   ground to a fine
   powder
¼ cup (50 g) sugar
2 egg yolks
⅓ cup (3 ounces; 80 g)
   unsalted butter,
   softened
1 cup (130 g) flour (do
   not use unbleached
   flour)

Apple slices:
1 tablespoon unsalted
   butter
4 tart cooking apples,
   peeled, cored, cut into
   thin slices
1 tablespoon sugar

Fruit jam

1. Prepare the shortbread dough: In the bowl of a food processor, blend the ground almonds, sugar, and egg yolks. Add the butter and flour and process until well blended. Remove the dough from the bowl and shape it into a 6 × 2 inch (15 × 5 cm) roll, wrap in plastic wrap, and refrigerate for 24 hours.

2. Preheat the oven to 375°F (190°C).

3. Roll the cookie dough to a ¼-inch (7 mm) thickness, then cut into 18 2½-inch (6-cm) rounds. Place on a baking sheet and bake for 10 minutes, or until golden.

4. Prepare the apple slices: While the cookies are baking, melt the tablespoon butter in a medium-size skillet over moderate heat. Add the apples and sugar, and cook, stirring occasionally, just until the apple slices are cooked through, about 10 minutes.

5. To serve, place 3 warm cookies on each plate, top a portion of apples, and serve immediately with a pot of jam.

Yield: 6 servings.

SARDINES A LA SAUGE LA PORTE FAUSSE
LA PORTE FAUSSE'S SARDINES WITH SAGE

Sardines are one of the most popular and inexpensive varieties of fish found in Paris. They appear on many menus, most often simply grilled over an open fire. This version, from La Porte Fausse (see entry, page 34), is lively, full-flavoured and particularly quick and easy to make. If you can't find fresh sardines, fresh or frozen smelt are a milder though tasty substitute.

24 to 28 fresh sardines (2 pounds; 900 g), heads removed, cleaned, and patted dry
¼ cup (35 g) unbleached flour
½ cup (125 ml) olive oil, approximately
2 large onions, finely chopped
4 cloves garlic, minced
½ cup (10 g) whole dried sage leaves
1 cup (250 ml) red wine vinegar
Salt and freshly ground black pepper to taste

1. Preheat the oven to 375°F (190°C).

2. Roll the sardines in flour, shaking off any excess. In a large skillet over medium-high heat, heat ¼ cup (60 ml) of the olive oil until hot. Add as many sardines as will fit easily into the pan without crowding and cook for 2 to 3 minutes on each side, or until fish are golden. Remove the sardines from the pan and drain on paper towels. Repeat the process until all the sardines are cooked, adding additional oil as necessary.

3. Using the same oil, sauté the onion and garlic for 10 minutes, or until golden, stirring constantly. Add the sage, cook for 2 to 3 minutes, then add the vinegar. Stir, and continue cooking for 5 minutes. Add the salt and pepper, stir, then remove pan from the heat and set aside.

4. Layer the sardines in a shallow ovenproof dish and cover with the vinegar sauce. Bake, uncovered, for 25 minutes, or until heated through. Serve either warm or at room temperature, with plenty of crusty bread and a dry white wine, such as Muscadet.

Yield: 4 to 6 servings.

RESTAURANT L'OLYMPE,
8 Rue Nicolas-Charlet, Paris 15.
(734.86.08).
Métro: Pasteur.
Open for dinner only; also open for lunch on Thursday. Last orders taken at midnight. Closed Monday and the first three weeks of August and two weeks at Christmas.
Credit cards: AE, DC, V.
Air-conditioned.
200-franc menu, including service but not wine. *A la carte,* 300 francs.

SPECIALITIES:
Ravioli, pigeon au miel (pigeon with honey), foie gras d'oie (liver of fattened goose).

Although L'Olympe is decorated like a cosy, 1930s luxury liner, this bouncing, noisy little restaurant could not be more up-to-date. Every evening L'Olympe fills up with a Marlboro haze and a crowd that's authentically Parisian, young and chic. The food and service are totally uneven—even for regulars—but that deters no one. Nothing happens here until 9 or 10 P.M., when the curtain goes up and chef Dominique Nahmias and her husband, Albert, provide their own brand of culinary entertainment. The menu changes from season to season, but good bets include her ravioli (on one visit stuffed with meaty chunks of well-seasoned duck), the perfectly poached *turbotin,* and absolutely irresistible dinner rolls. The wine list, which includes the white Graves, Château Carbonnieux, is pricey, but worth a glance.

LE PETIT MARGUERY,
9 Boulevard de Port-Royal,
   Paris 13.
(331.58.59).
Métro: Gobelins.
Closed Sunday evening and
   Monday.
Credit cards: AE, DC, V.
Private dining room for 25.
175 to 200 francs.

SPECIALITIES:
*Terrine chaude de Saint-Jacques
beurre blanc (warm scallop
terrine with butter sauce), civet
de marcassin vieille France aux
pâtes fraîches (wild boar stew
with fresh pasta).*

A lively, bright, and generous 1900s neighbourhood bistro, offering food that's completely original and refreshing. This is the kind of place that really hits the spot when one's had one's fill of *nouvelle cuisine.* And I can't imagine not having a good time here: The waiters are friendly and jolly and the totally Parisian clientele helps fill the air with the unmistakably French sound of good times. The handwritten menu is barely legible, but you should be able to decipher such treasures as *poireaux aux truffes fraîches* (nicely cooked, marinated leeks sprinkled with fresh slivers of truffle); *noisettes de biche* (perfectly cooked nuggets of venison, served with a sumptuous portion of celery root purée); and a totally drinkable Bourgueil. The chef makes his own walnut rye bread (a bit dry, but three cheers for the effort), served with the small but well-aged selection of cheese.

LA TOISON D'OR,
29 Rue Castagnary,
   Paris 15.
(531.52.44).
Métro: Volontaires.
Closed Tuesday, last two
   weeks in July, and
   month of August.
No credit cards.
130 francs.

SPECIALITIES:
*Russian, including goulash de
mouton (lamb goulash), gâteau
au fromage*

You'll need to make your reservation at least two weeks in advance (if you can ever get one of the aging Antadze brothers on the telephone), but the dining experience will be unique. This humble duo from Georgia runs what's probably the only authentic Russian bistro in Paris. The greeting may be cool, but by the end of the evening most clients are embracing the chef or his brother, in thanks for a great old time and some tasty Georgian food: grilled *brebis* (sheep's milk cheese); a spicy mutton stew; marinated, skewered meatballs; and glass after glass of rough Georgian wine or chilled Russian vodka.

CHIFFONNADE DE SAUMON
SALAD OF SHREDDED GREENS AND SMOKED SALMON

This dish is the creation of Christiane Massia, the imaginative chef at L'Aquitaine (see entry, page 59). The dressing can be made a day in advance then refrigerated, but prepare the rest of the ingredients just before serving.

½ cup (125 ml) *crème
   fraîche* (see recipe, page
   182) or sour cream
1 tablespoon lemon juice
¼ teaspoon hot paprika
1 head Boston lettuce,
   rinsed and dried
4 thin slices smoked
   salmon, cut into wide
   strips

1. In a small bowl, combine the *crème fraîche* or sour cream, lemon juice, and paprika.

2. Stack several lettuce leaves on top of one another, and, using a long chef's knife, cut the lettuce into very fine strips, almost as if you were slicing cabbage for cole slaw. Place in a large salad bowl and toss with the dressing.

3. Distribute the lettuce among four salad plates and cover each with several strips of salmon. Serve immediately.

Yield: 4 servings.

ARC DE TRIOMPHE, TROCADERO, BOIS DE BOULOGNE, NEUILLY
16th arrondissement and Neuilly

LA BOUTARDE,
4 Rue Boutard, Neuilly.
(745.34.55).
Métro: Pont de Neuilly.
Closed Saturday lunch and
Sunday.
Credit cards: DC, V.
72-franc menu, including
wine and service. *A la
carte*, 75 to 100 francs.

SPECIALITIES:
*Changing bistro fare,
including lapin à la moutarde
(rabbit with mustard sauce),
foie de veau (calf's liver),
blanquette de veau (veal in
white sauce).*

This is one of Paris's fine and solid bistros, set off on a quiet side street in Neuilly, at the western edge of the city. La Boutarde is always impeccably clean, friendly, and bustling with well-heeled Neuilly residents and office workers. The tables are covered with red-checkered oilcloths, and the daily wine specials and *plats du jour* (such as *boeuf Bourguignon* and *blanquette de veau*) are scribbled on mirrors that line the walls. Favourite dishes here include the smoky *tarama* appetizer, thick and perfectly grilled *foie de veau, lapin à la moutarde*, good *frites* (French-fried potatoes), and delicious honey ice cream served with raspberry sauce. If ordering *à la carte*, do sample the house Chinon, a delicate, fruity Loire Valley red wine.

JACQUELINE FENIX,
42 Avenue Charles-de-
Gaulle, Neuilly.
(624.42.61).
Métro: Les Sablons.
Closed Saturday, Sunday,
the month of August,
and Christmas week.
Credit card: V.
Air-conditioned.
250 francs.

SPECIALITIES:
*Change with the seasons and
include: foie gras de canard
(liver of fattened duck),
feuillantines de poires
caramélisées (caramelized,
pear-filled puff pastry dessert).*

Jacqueline Fénix—a warm, cosy, and elegant little restaurant just beyond the Arc de Triomphe—continues to provide the sort of care and consistency that keep diners coming back. The blonde and serious Jacqueline Fénix (who ran the dining room at Michel Guérard's renowned Pot-au-Feu) watches over the newly decorated dining room with riveting attention, while chef Michel Rubod continues to turn out ever-imaginative, solid fare. He's my kind of cook—someone who understands that some people don't just tolerate vegetables, they love them. So the mild-mannered chef continues to garnish and embellish a wide variety of salads and main courses with substantial portions of herbs and real, live greens. And he practices what so many *nouvelle* chefs only preach, understanding that freshness is where it all starts. Always worth sampling: the carefully seasoned *foie gras;* the copious first-course quail salad—a perfectly fresh, meaty roast quail served with a blend of dressed greens and a warm, poached quail egg; and the *confit de saumon* (actually a spiral of salmon poached in oil, then grilled) served with fresh tomatoes. The *feuillantines de poires caramélisées,* puff pastry filled with fresh poached pears and caramelized to a shiny brown, is as good as ever. (See page 60 for chef Rubod's recipe for Shortbread Cookies with Warm Apples and Seasonal Fruit Jam.)

JAMIN/JOEL ROBUCHON,
32 Rue de Longchamp, Paris 16.
(727.12.27).
Métro: Trocadéro.
Closed Saturday, Sunday, and the month of July.
Credit cards: AE, DC, EC, V.
Air-conditioned.
Private dining room for 24.
135- and 340-franc menus, not including wine or service. *A la carte,* 300 to 400 francs.

SPECIALITIES:
Raviolis de langoustines au chou (ravioli filled with langoustines, dressed with cabbage), ragout d'huîtres et de noix de Saint-Jacques au caviar (scallops wrapped in spinach, dressed with oysters and caviar), rôti d'agneau aux herbes en croûte de sel (roasted lamb with herbs cooked in a salt crust).

Joël Robuchon—at the peak of his career—is one of the top chefs working in France today. Even the toughest critics whisper "genius," when they speak of this shy and dedicated young man. There's no question that, when one talks of Robuchon and his well-conceived, personal cuisine, it is hard not to speak in superlatives. Because he is so talented, because he has slowly and patiently climbed the ladder to success, he has accomplished what many chefs only dream of. He has redefined modern dining in France, understanding that the classic concept of "eating well" no longer applies. So he offers luxury, but never excess. He provides imaginative, original food that is never bizarre. Each dish is a well-conceived, well-constructed work of art, as pleasing to the eye as it is to the palate. His dining room is perfectly elegant, modern and welcoming, neither overbearing nor self-conscious. Robuchon does so little to the food and yet he does so much. He alternates the most simple of dishes like a moist, thyme-flecked roast lamb (see recipe opposite) or a blend of perfect greens showered with fresh truffles with dishes of daring complexity such as scallops wrapped in spinach leaves, dressed with poached oysters and a dollop of caviar (see recipe, page 215), or giant ravioli filled with *langoustines* and paired with fresh cabbage. Only the finest ingredients come into his kitchen, where he and his young, ambitious staff turn truffles, salmon, poultry, and game into authoritative gastronomic treasures. Robuchon makes his own bread and rolls (see recipe, page 169), twice a day, and offers a stunning selection of cheese and desserts. (A recipe for his Puff Pastry Pineapple Tart appears on page 151.) The *sommelier* is most helpful, while the *maître d'hôtel,* Jean-Jacques Caimaint, is a breath of fresh air. The 135-franc menu, available at both lunch and dinner, is one of the city's gastronomic bargains.

LE PETIT BEDON,
38 Rue Pergolèse, Paris 16.
(500.23.66).
Métro: Argentine.
Closed Saturday, Sunday,
  holidays, and the month
  of August.
Credit cards: DC, V.
Air-conditioned.
250 to 275 francs.

SPECIALITIES:
Méli-mélo de queues de
langoustines au xérès (salad of
small spiny lobster, capers, and
lettuce in vinegar dressing).

After working five years as a pastry chef with Gaston Lenôtre and six years at Le Grand Véfour, chef Christian Ignace is flying on his own. He offers a young, imaginative, and generally successful cuisine. Some of chef Ignace's best dishes include an unusually seasoned smoked salmon, a seldom-found milk-fed lamb, and a fresh and satisfying caramelized pear dessert. The salmon is smoked by the chef himself, after being cured first in salt, sugar, and an almost flowery, aromatic Brazilian black pepper. Most of his desserts are worth a detour on their own. Two complaints: Ingredients are not always fresh, and some creations are unnecessarily complicated.

ROTI D'AGNEAU AUX HERBES EN CROUTE DE SEL JAMIN
JAMIN'S ROASTED LAMB WITH HERBS COOKED IN A SALT CRUST

This remarkably simple and flavourful dish is the item ordered most often at chef Joël Robuchon's restaurant, Jamin. The lamb roasts in a thyme-infused salt crust, which actually serves as a hermetic, flavourful roasting shell. The crust is discarded after cooking.

Salt Crust:
½ cup (150 g) salt
1 cup (240 g) coarse
  (kosher) salt
1 egg, separated
3¾ cups (525 g)
  unbleached flour
2 tablespoons dried
  thyme, mixed with 1¼
  cups (310 ml) water

Lamb:
2 pounds (900 g) boneless
  roasting lamb (a
  portion of leg of lamb
  works very well)
Freshly ground black
  pepper
½ teaspoon dried thyme
Pinch of salt
1 teaspoon coarse (kosher)
  salt

1. Preheat the oven to 400° F (205°C).

2. Prepare the salt crust: In a large bowl, blend together the two salts, the egg white, flour, and thyme and water mixture. Knead until well blended. It is essential that the dough be firm, not too moist or sticky, or the lamb will steam, not roast. If necessary, knead in additional flour for a firm dough. Roll out the dough so it is large enough to wrap the lamb.

3. Season the lamb with the pepper and thyme. Completely wrap the lamb in the salt crust, checking to make sure it is well sealed, and place on a baking sheet. (This can be done several hours ahead of time.)

4. Just before roasting, combine the egg yolk with the pinch of salt and ½ teaspoon water and, with a pastry brush, brush the mixture over the surface of the crust. Sprinkle all over with coarse salt.

5. Place the lamb on a baking sheet in the oven and roast for 25 to 30 minutes for rare (or until the interior of the lamb is cooked to 112°F, or 45°C, when measured with a meat thermometer). For well-done lamb, cook an additional 5 or 10 minutes. The crust should be a deep, golden brown. Let the lamb rest in the crust for 1 hour before serving. (The lamb will remain warm.)

6. To serve, cut open the crust at one end, remove the lamb, and cut the meat on the diagonal, into very fine slices. Discard the crust. Serve with buttered fresh pasta or a potato gratin.

Yield: 4 servings.

GRATIN DE FENOUIL, COURGETTES, ET TOMATES FRAICHES
GRATIN OF FENNEL, ZUCCHINI, AND FRESH TOMATOES

A simple and appealing vegetable gratin, this combination of fennel, zucchini, and tomatoes can be served as a main luncheon course or as a side dish to accompany grilled fish, fowl, or meat. The recipe comes from chef Guy Legay of the Ritz-Espadon (see entry, page 18), who serves it with grilled bar (sea bass), which arrives surrounded by flaming, aromatic stalks of dried fennel. The long, slow cooking of the fennel in this gratin gives it a particularly elegant flavour. The fennel and zucchini portion of the gratin can be made several hours ahead, then thoroughly heated just before serving. Make the tomato sauce at the last minute, to really profit from its freshness.

3 to 4 medium-size bulbs fennel, about 2 pounds (900 g), trimmed and finely chopped

1 large onion, finely chopped

3 tablespoons olive oil

Salt and freshly ground black pepper to taste

2 medium-size zucchini, about 1 pound (450 g), thinly sliced

2 pounds (900 g) tomatoes, peeled, cored, seeded, and finely chopped

1. In a large skillet combine the fennel, onion, and 1 tablespoon olive oil. Season with salt and freshly ground black pepper and cook, uncovered, over very low heat for 1 hour, stirring frequently.

2. In another large skillet heat 1 tablespoon olive oil over high heat, add the zucchini and sauté for 3 to 4 minutes, or just until cooked through. Remove the zucchini and drain.

3. In the skillet in which you cooked the zucchini, heat the remaining 1 tablespoon oil, add the tomatoes and cook over medium-high heat for about 15 minutes, or until the pieces cook down and the sauce is quite thick. Season to taste.

4. Spoon the fennel and onion mixture into an oval gratin dish (about 7 × 12 inches, or 18 × 30½ cm), and decoratively arrange the zucchini on top of the fennel. Season lightly with salt and freshly ground pepper and place under a broiler for 2 to 3 minutes. Remove from oven and mound the tomato sauce in the centre of the gratin.

Yield: 4 to 6 servings.

LE PRE CATELAN,
Route de Suresnes, Bois de Boulogne, Paris 16.
(524.55.58).
Not accessible by Métro.
Closed Sunday evening, Monday, and two weeks in February.
Credit cards: AE, DC, V.
Terrace and garden dining.
Private dining for up to 440.
250- and 350-franc menus, not including wine or service. *A la carte,* 350 to 400 francs.

SPECIALITIES:
Change with the seasons.

In the summer, this is one of the city's most pleasant outdoor settings: Diners can sit beneath broad chestnut trees, protected by crisp white canvas umbrellas, enjoying the ever-inventive cuisine of chef Patrick Lenôtre, nephew of pastry chef Gaston Lenôtre. In the colder months, secure a table near the fireplace, and you will feel equally pampered and at home. Chef Lenôtre's repertoire continues to grow, and the *sommelier,* Didier Bordas, is always ready to offer expert advice on wine selections. In the winter months, opt for game, some of which comes from Lenôtre's private reserve in the Sologne, south of Paris. Year-round, there is always fresh and smoked salmon, fine duck preparations, and often superb fruit tarts. Do save room for the irresistible chocolates. Service, unfortunately, can be uneven, and lackadaisical.

GUY SAVOY,
28 Rue Duret, Paris 16.
(500.17.67).
Métro: Argentine.
Closed Saturday, Sunday,
and the first two weeks
in January.
Credit card: V.
Air-conditioned.
230- and 300-franc menus,
not including wine or
service. *A la carte,* 350
francs.

SPECIALITIES:
Aiguillettes et foie de canard en
salade (salad of strips of duck
breast and fattened duck
liver), mille-feuille (fruit-
filled puff pastry dessert),
rolling dessert cart.

Guy Savoy remains one of France's most creative young chefs, and despite the fact that he is splitting his time between his restaurants in Paris and Connecticut, neither the food nor the service seems to be suffering. The elegant, salmon-coloured dining room is as discreet and well thought out as his cuisine. The *sommelier* could not be more obliging and helpful, and diners should always leave this intimate restaurant with a sense of well-being. Chef Savoy (pronounced sa-vwah) offers a very personal cuisine which is light, aesthetically appealing, and fashioned from ingredients he loves best: simple cuts of meat and poultry, kidneys, and sweetbreads, mounds of lightly cooked spinach, lots of herbs, and always side dishes of parchment-thin, pan-roasted potatoes cooked in just the right amount of butter.

ARC DE TRIOMPHE, PLACE DES TERNES, PORTE MAILLOT
17th arrondissement

LE BERNARDIN,
18 Rue Troyon, Paris 17.
(380.40.61).
Métro: Charles-de-Gaulle/
Etoile.
Last orders taken at 11:30
P.M. Closed Sunday,
Monday, and the month
of August.
Credit cards: AE, V.
300 to 375 francs.

SPECIALITIES:
Fish and seafood, including
oursins chauds au beurre
d'oursins (sea urchins with sea
urchin butter), fricassée de
coquillages (shellfish stew),
escalope de saumon aux truffes
(salmon with truffles).

Le Bernardin—comfortable, refined, consistent—is one of my favourite Paris restaurants. Gilbert and Maguy le Coze have devoted their lives to creating one of the finest fish restaurants in the world, and their efforts have not been in vain. Here, fish and shellfish are treated with utmost respect. Chef Gilbert's secret:

Gilbert le Coze stands by a portrait of his grandfather, a Brittany fisherman, which hangs at Le Bernardin.

Begin with the freshest ingredients, add maybe a little butter or cream, herbs or oil, but don't tamper. The *plateau de fruits de mer* is one of the most sumptuous in town, a true Pantagruelian feast. There are more than a dozen exceptional dishes here, including Le Bernardin's trademark *fricassée de coquillages,* a rich first course that's a generous blend of clams, mussels, and oysters in a stunning, sea-salty broth of butter, *crème fraîche,* tomato and shallots (see recipe, page 251). When *escalope de saumon aux truffes* is on the menu (usually from February to September, when the Scottish salmon is most flavourful), don't pass up this ethereal blend of fresh truffles and just-cooked salmon touched with butter and cream (see recipe, page 217). Other favourites include *Saint-Pierre aux poireaux,* white chunks of St. Peter's fish (John Dory), poached for seconds in a rich fish fumet, and served on buttery slivers of leeks, lightly cooked and still crunchy; *saumon à la menthe,* salmon infused with the essence of fresh mint and tomatoes; and anything Gilbert does with his fresh, gigantic *coquilles Saint-Jacques* (scallops). Add to this an ever-impressive list of white wines, Berthillon's reliable and unforgettable ice creams, Le Bernardin's own pastry offerings, and you have the makings of a memorable evening. I have complained, to no avail, of the often-stale bread; other diners have complained of less than attentive service.

LA COQUILLE,
6 Rue du Débarcadère,
  Paris 17.
(574.25.95).
Métro: Porte Maillot.
Closed Sunday, Monday,
  holidays, and the month
  of August.
Credit card: V.
Air-conditioned.
250 to 300 francs.

S P E C I A L I T I E S :
Coquilles Saint-Jacques au naturel (scallops baked in their shells) from October to May, boudin noir grillé (grilled blood sausage), soufflé au praslin de noisettes (hazelnut soufflé).

I embrace this friendly, lively neighbourhood bistro. From my first visit several years ago, I've felt at home with the outgoing owners, Paul and Catherine Blache, the surroundings, menu, wine list, and the efficient, caring staff. I know the menu and wine list almost by heart, and when I'm going to dine at La Coquille, I think all day about just what I'll choose. One never goes wrong with their unadorned, quickly baked *coquilles Saint-Jacques,* served only from October to May; the finely spiced *boudin noir;* perfectly roasted game available from October to February; the plumpest springtime asparagus; nicely grilled lamb chops or steak, plus, of course, their signature dessert: *soufflé au praslin de noisettes* (see recipe opposite). The wine list is particularly well priced and includes some well-chosen bargains. One won't go wrong with the *maître d'hôtel's* suggestions, which might include a fine Sancerre, the seldom-found white Hermitage, Chante-Alouette, and a fine array of red Bordeaux.

SOUFFLE AU PRASLIN DE NOISETTES LA COQUILLE
LA COQUILLE'S HAZELNUT SOUFFLE

La Coquille is my favourite neighbourhood bistro, and this is its signature dessert. I sampled the soufflé the first time I dined there one cold wintry evening. As my love for La Coquille grew, so did my fondness for this light, hazelnut-filled dessert.

Praline powder:
¾ cup (100 g) hazelnuts
½ cup (100 g) sugar
1 teaspoon unsalted butter
   for buttering a cookie
   sheet

Pastry cream:
1 cup (250 ml) milk
½ vanilla bean
6 eggs, separated
3 tablespoons sugar
¼ cup (30 g) flour (do not
   use unbleached flour)
Pinch of salt
1 tablespoon unsalted
   butter, for buttering a
   4-cup (1-litre) soufflé
   mould

¼ cup (60 ml) kirsch

1. Preheat the oven to 300°F (150°C).

2. Toast the hazelnuts on a baking sheet in the oven for 5 minutes. While they are still warm, rub them in a dishtowel to remove as much skin as possible. Cool, then chop coarsely by hand.

3. In a medium-size saucepan over low heat melt the sugar until it dissolves and becomes slightly rust-coloured. Add the nuts and stir until they are thoroughly coated with sugar. This is now your praline.

4. Turn the praline out onto a cool buttered cookie sheet and allow to harden, about 5 minutes. When hard, place the praline in a food processor and grind to a powder. Set aside. (The praline powder can be made in advance and stored in an airtight container. It can be refrigerated for a week or frozen indefinitely.)

5. Prepare the pastry cream: In a medium-size saucepan over medium heat, bring the milk and vanilla bean to a boil. Remove from the heat and allow to steep for 5 minutes.

6. In a medium-size mixing bowl combine 4 of the egg yolks with the sugar, then the flour. Remove the vanilla bean from the milk and whisk the milk into the egg mixture. Place the mixture in a medium-size saucepan and cook over medium heat, stirring constantly until it begins to boil. Continue cooking for 2 minutes, stirring constantly. Remove from the heat and add the 2 additional egg yolks, whisking until well blended. (The soufflé can be prepared ahead up to this point.)

7. Preheat the oven to 325°F (165°C).

8. To finish the soufflé, in a large bowl add half the praline powder to the pastry cream and mix until well blended.

9. In another large bowl beat the egg whites with a pinch of salt until stiff but not dry. Add one third of the egg white mixture to the pastry cream mixture and fold in gently but thoroughly. Then gently fold in the remaining whites. Don't overmix, but be sure that the mixture is well blended.

10. Butter the soufflé mould. Gently pour the soufflé mixture into the mould and sprinkle the remaining praline powder on top of the soufflé. This will form a golden crust when the soufflé is baked. Bake for 12 to 15 minutes.

11. Remove the soufflé from the oven, sprinkle with the kirsch, and serve immediately.

Yield: 4 servings.

**LES GOURMETS
DES TERNES,**
97 Boulevard de Courcelles,
   Paris 17.
(227.43.04).
Métro: Ternes.
Closed Saturday, Sunday,
   and the month of
   August.
No credit cards.
Pavement terrace dining in
   summer.
100 francs.

SPECIALITIES:
Grilled meats, garnished with
French fries.

MICHEL ROSTANG,
20 Rue Rennequin,
   Paris 17.
(763.40.77).
Métro: Ternes.
Closed Saturday lunch,
   October to March; all
   day Saturday, April to
   September; Sunday;
   holidays; and the last
   week in July to the last
   week in August,
   Christmas week, and
   one week in February.
Credit card: V.
Air-conditioned.
Private dining room for 20.
135-franc menu, not
   including wine or
   service, available at
   lunch only; 235- and
   280-franc *menu*
   dégustation, not
   including wine or
   service, available at
   lunch and dinner. *A la*
   carte, about 350 francs.

SPECIALITIES:
Raviolis de fromage de chèvre
frais au bouillon de poule
(ravioli filled with fresh goat
cheese), canette au sang
(pressed duck), poulette de
Bresse en pot-au-feu (chicken
with vegetables).

Anyone looking for a superb grilled steak or lamb chops in totally unpretentious surroundings should reserve at Les Gourmets des Ternes, a modest bistro near the Place des Ternes. The *complet* sign appears in the window around eleven each morning, meaning that all tables are already reserved. The neighbourhood businessmen know a good deal when they find it. This is a well-worn spot, recently improved with a coat of paint, and although none of the chairs or light fixtures match and the waitresses lost interest a long time ago, the regulars keep returning, enjoying the chic and lively crowd, the solid, simple fare. In the summertime, you can enjoy a meal on the small pavement terrace.

Over the past few years Michel Rostang's talent has grown so that today he can certainly be counted among Paris's most creative and conscientious young chefs. You could not possibly be disappointed in his feather-light ravioli filled with fresh goat cheese and floating in a rich chicken broth (see recipe opposite); the unforgettable *canette au sang,* a pressed roast duck served in two courses; or the utterly simple and exquisite *poulette de Bresse en pot-au-feu,* a light and modern stewlike blend of chicken and tiny vegetables. Years later, I can still taste Rostang's heavenly salad of warm sliced potatoes tossed with fresh black truffles, or a similar first-course marriage of potatoes, sour cream, and caviar. The bread (from Monsieur Pain, just across the way) is irresistible, the cheese tray well selected, and the wine list quite respectable, with some good buys on regional wines. Try the red Domaine Tempier Bandol from Provence, or one of the fine Châteauneuf-du-Pape wines. For those who want a touch of the modern, from a man with a fine palate and solid respect for the classics, Michel Rostang is the place.

RAVIOLIS DE FROMAGE DE CHEVRE FRAIS
AU BOUILLON DE POULE
RAVIOLI FILLED WITH FRESH GOAT CHEESE

This is a such wonderful first course, I rarely order anything else when visiting Michel Rostang's warm, elegant restaurant in the 17th arrondissement. Although many nouvelle-inspired French chefs have added pasta to their repertoire, Rostang's is authentically regional. His family comes from the Savoie, the area of France that borders on Switzerland. Here, farm women often prepare ravioli filled with their own homemade goat cheese, then cook the pasta in a stock made from their farm-fresh poultry. Although the dish is time-consuming, it is irresistible and I make it often at home, varying the filling according to my mood and what's on hand. The pasta is delicious filled with goat cheese and rosemary, or in lieu of chèvre, a sharp Swiss Tête de Moine. The purchase of a little tin tooth-edged tray for shaping ravioli (available in Italian speciality shops as well as professional cookware shops in Paris) will simplify the preparation, though instructions are given for forming the ravioli by hand. This pasta, prepared quickly in the food processor, is made with cream, rather than oil, so it will be softer and easier to seal.

Pasta:
2 cups (280 g) unbleached
    flour, plus additional as
    needed
2 eggs
2 tablespoons heavy cream
1 teaspoon salt

Filling:
7 ounces (200 g) mild
    goat cheese, cubed
5 ounces (145 g) Gruyère
    cheese, cubed
2 tablespoons heavy cream
1 egg, beaten
2 tablespoons finely
    chopped fresh chervil,
    rosemary, or chives
Salt and freshly ground
    black pepper to taste
2 quarts (2 litres)
    homemade chicken
    stock
1 tablespoon additional
    chervil or parsley, to
    garnish

1. Prepare the pasta: In the bowl of a food processor fitted with the metal blade, combine all the ingredients in the pasta listing and process until the mixture forms a ball. If the dough is very sticky, add more flour tablespoon by tablespoon and process after each addition until you have a smooth dough. Remove the dough from the processor and knead it for 1 minute, then cut it into four equal sections. Cover with a floured cloth and let rest while preparing the filling.

2. Prepare the filling: In the bowl of a food processor fitted with the metal blade, combine the goat cheese, Gruyère cheese, cream, and egg, and process until well blended. Add herbs, salt and pepper, blend again and check for seasoning.

3. Prepare the ravioli: Take one section of dough and using a pasta machine, roll the dough very thin. Trim the strip into a 5- × 11-inch (13- × 28-cm) length. Using a teaspoon, place a small mound of filling about ½ inch (1½ cm) from the edge of one long side of the strip of pasta. Continue down the strip, spacing the mounds of filling about 1 inch apart. Fold the other half of the dough over the mounds of filling and press the edges together firmly. Using a ravioli cutter or pastry trimmer, trim excess dough from the edges. Now cut between the mounds, pressing the edges firmly together with the tips of your fingers. Make certain that the squares are well closed, or they will leak while cooking. Continue until all the pasta and filling have been used.

4. To cook the pasta, bring the stock to a simmer, drop in about half a dozen ravioli and cook for just 2 or 3 minutes. As the ravioli cook, remove them to a warm, covered bowl. To serve, spoon several ravioli into a soup bowl and pour in the broth. Sprinkle with fresh chervil or parsley.

Yield: 4 servings.

LE TIMGAD,
21 Rue Brunel, Paris 17.
(574.23.70).
Métro: Porte Maillot.
Closed Sunday, and the
    month of August.
Credit cards: DC, V.
Air-conditioned.
150 to 200 francs.

SPECIALITIES:
Couscous, tajines (meat and
poultry stews), méchoui (whole
grilled lamb).

Combining the rich gastronomic traditions of Morocco, Algeria, and Tunisia, Le Timgad offers some of the most refined and elegant *couscous* in Paris, the best spicy *merguez* lamb sausage, along with impeccably seasoned *tajines,* meat and poultry stews cooked over a wood-fired stove. Timgad's fantasy interior—decorative white walls of intricately carved plaster, brightened with sprays of fresh fruit and a flowing fountain—puts everyone in a festive mood, eager to enjoy plate after plate of buttery *couscous*, garnished with vegetables, raisins, chick peas, and a luscious broth. As in most Parisian restaurants, the staff is all male, save for one important employee: the *couscous* lady. As chef Ahmad Laasri insists, only women have the patience for rolling the delicate grains of *couscous*, or semolina. So each morning a young Moroccan woman rolls some thirty pounds (about fifteen kilos) of the delicate grain, enough to feed the restaurant's customers for the day. Favourites here—along with the *couscous* and mandatory second helpings of their homemade *merguez*—include the coriander-laced chicken with olives and any version of their full-flavoured lamb, grilled over an open wood fire.

EMINCE DE CHOUX VERTS AUX LARDONS CHAUDS
HOT CABBAGE AND BACON SALAD

This is such a simple and delicious dish, I'm surprised more Paris restaurants don't offer it. The salad is generally on the menu at Ambassade D'Auvergne, a solid restaurant with hearty fare (see entry, page 21). Here, it's served as a first course, but I make the salad often at home, as part of a light meal that might also include a cheese tray, fresh homemade bread, and a favourite red wine from Provence. Do use the best-quality slab bacon or side pork and red wine vinegar you can find. I like to add lots and lots of coarsely ground black pepper.

½ medium-size cabbage
Salt and freshly ground
    black pepper to taste
6 ounces (170 g) slab
    bacon or side pork, cut
    into bite-size cubes
½ cup (125 ml) red wine
    vinegar

1. Cut the cabbage by hand into fine slivers. Do not use a food processor or the cabbage is likely to be too fine and will release too much liquid. Place in a large salad bowl and sprinkle lightly with salt and pepper.

2. In a large skillet, cook the bacon over medium-high heat, stirring frequently. Cook until very crisp. Leaving the bacon and the rendered fat in the pan, deglaze it with the red wine vinegar, stirring constantly. There will be a lot of smoke, but don't be concerned.

3. Add the cabbage, stir, then reduce the heat to low. Cover the pan to allow the cabbage to sweat a bit, and to allow the flavours to blend. Let sit for about 5 minutes, stir, then taste for seasoning. The cabbage should be just slightly wilted, but still crisp. Serve immediately.

Yield: 4 to 6 servings.

SAINT-OUEN, LA VILLETTE, BELLEVILLE, PERE LACHAISE
19th and 20th arrondissements and Saint-Ouen

AU COCHON D'OR,
192 Avenue Jean-Jaurès,
  Paris 19.
(607.23.13).
Métro: Porte de Pantin.
Open daily.
Credit cards: AE, DC, V.
Air-conditioned.
Private dining room for 18.
200 francs.

SPECIALITIES:
Grilled meats, shellfish.

The old stockyards that made this and other bistros along Avenue Jean-Jaurès so famous are no more, but that doesn't stop the crowds from filling this old-fashioned, two-story restaurant. Go on a Sunday afternoon, order a steak and a bottle of Bordeaux, and sit back to watch the happy Parisian families feasting with *grand-mère* on snails, oysters, grilled meats, and plenty of wine. Note that service, for foreigners at least, can be rather inattentive.

COQ DE LA MAISON BLANCHE,
37 Boulevard Jean-Jaurès,
  Saint-Ouen.
(254.01.23).
Métro: Mairie de Saint-
  Ouen.
Closed Wednesday
  evenings, Sunday
  evenings, and the week
  of August 15.
Credit cards: DC, V.
About 150 to 200 francs.

SPECIALITIES:
Coq au vin (chicken in red
wine), jambon persillé
(parsleyed ham).

Just across the Paris city line north of town sits the rambling Coq de la Maison Blanche, a bustling place that gives you the feeling of dining in a popular country restaurant, not a corner bistro near Paris. The house specialty is *coq au vin,* here prepared with an honest curmudgeonly bird and served up in a good, thick red wine sauce from a huge copper vessel. Other dishes worth sampling include the *salade folle,* made with fresh *foie gras,* crayfish, and green beans; *escargots aux noisettes,* a hearty platter of snails seasoned with parsley and hazelnuts; and a classically good *jambon persillé.* The wine list is small but well chosen. There's always a carefully selected Beaujolais, along with inexpensive, little-known wines, such as Ménétou-Salon, from the Loire Valley.

MERE-GRAND,
20 Rue Orfila, Paris 20.
(636.03.29).
Metró: Gambetta.
Closed Friday and Saturday
  evening, Sunday, and
  the month of September.
No credit cards.
38- and 50-franc menus,
  not including wine and
  service.

SPECIALITIES:
Changing bistro fare,
including pâtés, and grilled
meats.

This homey neighborhood restaurant may not merit a detour on its own, but anyone looking for a place to eat before or after a visit to the historic Père Lachaise cemetery will want to make plans to lunch at Mère-Grand, a charming spot decorated in shades of mauve, with little copper saucepans hanging from the walls. Everyone here orders from one of the two simple menus, which include such classic bistro fare as *lapin à la moutarde* and grilled *tournedos* of beef. There's a varied assortment of fresh-flavoured first courses, among them a rugged country *pâté du Périgord,* and better than average *fromage de tête* (head cheese). The house wine is drinkable and service is friendly. Reservations are not accepted, so if you plan on lunch get there at noon. By 12:05, every table is taken.

RELAIS DES PYRENEES,
1 Rue du Jourdain,
Paris 20.
(636.65.81).
Métro: Jourdain.
Closed Saturday and the
month of August.
Credit cards: AE, DC,
EC, V.
200 to 250 francs.

SPECIALITIES:
*Pipérade (scrambled eggs,
peppers, tomatoes, and ham),
foie gras frais de canard
(fattened duck liver), confit
d'oie (goose cooked and
preserved in goose fat).*

Like something out of the 1950s, this tranquil, modest neighbourhood bistro seems to have ignored the past three decades as it continues along on its classical course. Bravo for chef Jean Marty, who knows when to leave well enough alone. The professional, well-trained waiters are a delight to watch, as they prepare, slice, heat, and serve many dishes tableside, off spotless copper and silver platters. The cuisine here is southwestern French, with a menu that includes a bright and creamy *pipérade* (see recipe opposite), a fine, fresh *foie gras*, and a formidable *confit d'oie* paired with sautéed potatoes that anyone would be proud to serve. The homemade desserts are more copious than professional, but the creamy, classic Grand Marnier soufflé is a real eye-opener.

MOUSSE DE POIVRONS DOUX AU COULIS DE TOMATES
RED PEPPER PUREE WITH FRESH TOMATO SAUCE

This is one of the specialties at L'Ambroisie (see entry, page 29). Chef Bernard Pacaud created the sublime red pepper mousse when he worked at Paris's Vivarois restaurant, then added the dish to his small but imaginative menu when he opened L'Ambroisie in 1981. There are no tricks to this recipe; just be certain that the red peppers are cooked to a thick paste and that the cream and whipping utensils are very cold.

Mousse:
4 red bell peppers
Pinch of salt
½ cup (125 ml) *crème
  fraîche* (see recipe, page
  182) or heavy cream,
  preferably not ultra-
  pasteurized

Tomato Sauce:
4 medium tomatoes
½ teaspoon salt
½ teaspoon sugar
½ teaspoon sherry wine
  vinegar

1. Preheat the broiler with the rack about 2 inches (5 cm) from the heat, then broil the whole peppers for approximately 10 minutes, turning them as their skins blister and turn black. Remove the peppers from the broiler and, when they are cool enough to handle, peel and seed them.

2. Purée the peppers in a food processor until smooth. For an extra-fine purée, force it through a fine-mesh sieve.

3. In a small saucepan over medium heat cook the purée with a pinch of salt until it is very thick. Remove to a bowl, cover and chill.

4. Put a whisk or electric beaters and a mixing bowl in the freezer for at least 1 hour, so they will be very cold and will whip the cream very stiff.

5. Meanwhile, prepare the sauce. Peel, seed, and core the tomatoes and chop them very fine. Season with the salt, sugar, and vinegar, place in a fine strainer that is resting in a bowl, and drain in the refrigerator for at least 1 hour.

6. To assemble the mousse, whip the *crème fraîche* or heavy cream until very stiff, and carefully fold in the cooled pepper purée.

7. To serve, place a scoop of the *mousse* in the centre of a plate and surround with the tomato sauce.

Yield: 4 servings.

PIPERADE
SCRAMBLED EGGS WITH PEPPERS, ONIONS, AND TOMATOES

Pipérade, a bright and lively egg and vegetable dish from the Basque region of France bordering Spain, is served in just about every Basque-related café or bistro in Paris. There are many versions of pipérade, but good unsmoked ham is essential, as are fresh, fresh eggs. This version is from Relais des Pyrénées. The 1½-hour cooking time for the vegetable mixture may seem excessive, but it is worthwhile, for it produces a thick, full-flavoured blend.

2 green bell peppers
6 thin slices unsmoked
    ham, such as
    prosciutto (6 ounces;
    170 g)
3 medium onions, minced
4 tomatoes, coarsely
    chopped
1 clove garlic, minced
1 bay leaf
1½ teaspoons fresh
    thyme, or ½ teaspoon
    dried
Sprig of fresh parsley,
    minced
3 tablespoons unsalted
    butter
8 eggs, slightly beaten
Salt and freshly ground
    black pepper to taste

1. Preheat the broiler with the broiler rack about 2 inches (5 cm) from the heat. Broil the peppers for about 10 minutes. Turn them as their skins blister and turn black. Remove the peppers and when they are cool enough to handle, carefully peel and seed them, discarding skins and seeds. Cut the peppers into thin strips.

2. Cut 2 slices of the ham into thin strips, reserving the other 4 slices.

3. In a large skillet, using no butter or oil, combine the peppers, strips of ham, onions, tomatoes, garlic, and herbs and cook, covered, over low heat for 1½ hours, stirring occasionally. The mixture should be quite thick.

4. When the vegetables are just about finished cooking, preheat the broiler again, then broil the remaining ham slices until they are crispy around the edges. Keep them warm while you cook the eggs.

5. In another large skillet, melt the butter over medium heat. When melted, reduce the heat to low, add the eggs, salt, and pepper, and cook, stirring constantly with a wooden spoon, just until the eggs set. The eggs should be very creamy.

6. At the last minute, combine the vegetable mixture with the scrambled eggs, divide among four plates and cover each portion with a slice of grilled ham. Serve immediately.

Yield: 4 servings.

LES TROIS PILOUX,
61 Rue de Meaux,
    Paris 19. (208.08.48).
Métro: Laumière.
Closed Sunday, Monday,
    and the month of August.
Credit cards: AE, EC, V.
70-franc menu, including
    service but not wine. *A
    la carte,* 150 to 175 francs.

SPECIALITIES:

Corrézien, including magret de canard (grilled breast of fattened duck), beef and lamb from the Limousin.

A corner café where the chef comes out wearing a white *toque* as he makes the rounds of the handful of tables? No joke. Everything here—including chef René Sourdeix, the menu, and the beefy lunchtime clientele—has a strong accent of the Corrèze, in southwestern France. Try the gigantic, perfectly grilled *magret de canard* (breast of fattened duck); the local ham, *jambon cru,* thinly sliced and attractively arranged like overlapping petals; or, if it's on the menu, a remarkable, full-flavoured salad of fresh cod (*morue fraîche),* tomatoes, and a variety of greens served with a medley of sauces.

PARIS ENVIRONS: ENGHIEN-LES-BAINS, SAINT-GERMAIN-EN-LAYE, VERSAILLES

CAZAUDEHORE,
1 Avenue du Président-Kennedy,
Saint-Germain-en-Laye.
(451.93.80).
Métro: RER A line, Saint-Germain-en-Laye.
Closed Monday and holidays.
No credit cards.
Terrace and garden dining.
Private dining room for 30.
250 francs.

SPECIALITIES:
Foie gras de canard (fattened duck liver), saumon cru mariné (marinated raw salmon), canard sauce rognon (duck with kidney sauce).

DUC D'ENGHIEN,
3 Avenue de Ceinture,
Enghien-les-Bains.
(412.90.00).
Not accessible by Métro.
Closed Sunday evening, Monday, holidays, and last three weeks in January.
Credit cards: AE, DC, V.
Terrace dining.
300 to 350 francs.

SPECIALITIES:
Huîtres au champagne (oysters in champagne), marinade de Saint-Jacques (marinated scallops), fresh homemade rolls.

The bright, flower-filled terrace of Cazaudehore, on the edge of the Saint-Germain forest in the historic little town of Saint-Germain-en-Laye, is ideal for a leisurely summer lunch. Energetic travellers may want to walk from the train station—it's a vigorous, thirty-minute walk along the edge of a forest full of songbirds and wildflowers. Otherwise taxis are readily available. In addition to the terrace—one of the prettier outdoor dining spots in the Paris region—there is a rustically elegant, well-appointed dining room, where service is accommodating and professional. Cazaudehore offers a few specialities of the Basque region, including _pipérade_ (a hearty blend of scrambled eggs mixed with tomatoes, peppers, and country ham), and the cuisine here is generally classic and correct. Good dishes to sample are a mixed salad tossed with apples and walnuts and a superb poached salmon set on a bed of spinach. The cheese tray is thoughtfully selected. For dessert, sample the lively _cassis sorbet,_ served with elegant butter cookies. For wine, the crisp, dry white Graves, Château Olivier, is a good choice.

Enghien-les-Bains—a quick twenty-minute drive from the city—is the once highly fashionable resort and spa town. The gambling casino and spas remain, along with a bright, contemporary restaurant offering well-considered, well-executed modern cuisine. The large and spacious restaurant provides a fine view of the lagoon, dotted with stunning white and black swans, and serves as an ideal spot for a leisurely summer Sunday lunch. Chef Alain Passart is a talented man, offering a fine medley of light, refreshing fare. Try the perfectly poached _bar_ (sea bass) infused with thyme and served with tiny _palourdes_ (clams); or the elegant _salade tiède,_ a toss of greens, oysters, tiny red _rouget_ (mullet), and _langoustines_ (small spiny lobster). The chef also offers many pasta-based dishes, such as ravioli stuffed with _langoustines_ or with crab meat. He makes his own deliciously fresh rolls each day, offers a nicely chosen cheese tray with each selection carefully labeled, and a wine list with a few bargains. Although the modern decor is quite distracting, service is swift and accommodating, and puts everyone at ease.

CHOU FARCI AMBASSADE D'AUVERGNE
AMBASSADE D'AUVERGNE'S STUFFED CABBAGE

This is a "Sunday-night supper" dish; it's easy to make and popular with those who love hearty, one-dish meals. I also find it fun to make. The Ambassade D'Auvergne (see entry, page 21) features the cuisine of the Auvergne region in central France, where cabbage, sausage, and smoked bacon are daily fare. The restaurant's version is stuffed with well-seasoned pork sausage, prunes, and Swiss chard, the popular green and white ribbed vegetable known in France as blette. Chopped fresh spinach can be substituted, but when I could find neither Swiss chard nor spinach in the market, I made the dish anyway, and it was a big hit. Be sure to cook the bacon just before serving, so it offers a crispy contrast in color and texture. Bring the whole cabbage to the table on a platter, and slice it in front of the family or guests, for it forms a pretty, mosaic pattern.

1 cabbage
1 cup (250 ml) dry white wine
1 quart (1 litre) meat or poultry stock
6 ounces (170 g) slab bacon, cut into bite-size pieces

Stuffing:
6 ounces (170 g) fresh Swiss chard or spinach, rinsed, dried, and coarsely chopped
1 large bunch parsley, minced
1 large onion, minced
1 clove garlic, minced
10 ounces (280 g) pork sausage meat
1 egg
1 slice white bread, soaked in 2 tablespoons milk
6 ounces (170 g) prunes, pitted
Salt and freshly ground black pepper to taste

1. Preheat the oven to 475°F (245°C).

2. Bring a large pot of water to boil. Separate the leaves of the cabbage and blanch them in the boiling water for 5 minutes. Rinse under cold water until cool, then drain.

3. In a large bowl, combine the stuffing ingredients and mix until well blended. Season to taste.

4. Lay a dampened 24 × 24-inch (60 × 60-cm) piece of cheesecloth on a work surface. "Reconstruct" the cabbage, beginning with the largest leaves, arranging the leaves with the ribs pointing toward the centre. Season with salt and freshly ground black pepper between the layers. Continue until all the leaves have been used.

5. Form the stuffing into a ball, pushing 4 pitted prunes into the center. Place the ball of stuffing in the centre of the cabbage and bring the leaves up to envelop the stuffing. Bring the cheesecloth up around the rounded cabbage and tie securely. Place the cabbage in a deep baking dish Add the remaining prunes and the wine, season to taste, and cover with the stock.

6. Bake for 1½ to 2 hours. Just before serving, sauté the slab bacon in a small skillet until very crisp. Unwrap the cabbage and place on a serving platter. Garnish with the prunes and grilled bacon. Serve immediately.

Yield: 4 servings.

LES TROIS MARCHES,
3 Rue Colbert, Versailles.
(950.13.21).
Métro: RER C line,
Versailles Rive Gauche.
Closed Sunday, Monday,
and holidays.
Credit cards: AE, DC,
EC, V.
Terrace dining.
Private dining room for 40.
130-franc menu at lunch
only; 195- and 265-
franc *menu dégustation*. A
la carte, 400 francs.

SPECIALITIES:
*Flan chaud de foie gras aux
huîtres et écrevisses, canette de
Barbarie au cidre et miel
(Barbary duck with cider
and honey).*

This theatrical, elegant, and newly restored private mansion literally *trois marches,* or three steps, from the Versailles palace, is an ideal spot for a spring or summer lunch outdoors or a fall or winter dinner indoors. Chef Gérard Vié spreads himself a bit thin with other business affairs, and at times, Les Trois Marches suffers in his absence. But certain dishes here are beyond reproach: The complex flan of warm *foie gras,* oysters, and crayfish is full-flavoured and refined, while his first-course platter of lightly marinated haddock served with an abundance of green peppercorns and a soothing poached pear is both stimulating and satisfying. In fall and winter months there is a fine assortment of game, and year-round, the stunning cheese tray merits a visit all on its own. The wine list is expertly chosen, and the staff is extraordinarily knowledgeable.(See opposite page for chef Vié's recipe for Tea Ice Cream.)

RESTAURANTS: AN ALPHABETICAL LISTING
(WITH ARRONDISSEMENTS)

Jenny (Chez), Paris 3

Joséphine, Paris 6

Julien, Paris 10

Louis XIV, Paris 1

Lozère (La), Paris 6

Maître Paul (Chez), Paris 6

Marée (La), Paris 8

Mère-Grand, Paris 20

Moissonnier, Paris 5

Montecristo, Paris 4

Olympe (Restaurant l'), Paris 15

Pantagruel, Paris 7

Pauline (Chez), Paris 1

Petit Bedon (Le), Paris 16

Petit Marguery (Le), Paris 13

Petit Montmorency (Le), Paris 8

Petit Riche (Au), Paris 9

Pharamond, Paris 1

Philippe/Auberge Pyrénées-Cévennes (Chez), Paris 11

Pied de Cochon (Au), Paris 1

Pierre Traiteur, Paris 1

Pile on Face, Paris 2

Polidor, Paris 6

Porte Fausse (La), Paris 6

Poularde Landaise (La), Paris 8

Pré Catelan (Le), Paris 16

Pressoir (Au), Paris 12

Quai des Ormes (Au), Paris 4

Quai d'Orsay (Au), Paris 7

Relais des Pyrénées, Paris 20

René (Chez), Paris 5

Ritz-Espadon, Paris 1

Roi du Pot-au-Feu (Le), Paris 9

Rostang (Michel), Paris 17

Ruban Bleu (Le), Paris 1

Savoy (Guy), Paris 16

Sologne (La), Paris 7

Sousceyrac (A), Paris 11

Table de Jeannette (La), Paris 1

Taillevent, Paris 8

Terminus Nord, Paris 10

Tiepolo (Restaurant), Paris 5

Timgad (Le), Paris 17

Toison d'Or (La), Paris 15

Tour d'Argent (La), Paris 5

Toutoune (Chez), Paris 5

Train Bleu (Le), Paris 12

Trois Marches (Les), Versailles

Trois Piloux (Les), Paris 19

Trou Gascon (Au), Paris 12

Vaudeville, Paris 2

Vieille (Chez la), Paris 1

Vieux Berlin (Au), Paris 8

Villars Palace, Paris 5

GLACE AU THE
TEA ICE CREAM

This is a rich and refined dessert, a recipe given to us by Gérard Vié, chef at Les Trois Marches. Gérard Vié is passionate about both coffee and tea, and in fact offers a separate tea and coffee menu at this elegant restaurant. Monsieur Vié varies the flavours of his tea ice cream, sometimes using a delicate orange pekoe, other times an infusion of herbs, such as the citruslike tilleul. I love it made with a good quality Earl Grey. Monsieur Vié suggests sprinkling the ice cream with Armagnac, or, if you like, prunes soaked in Armagnac.

1 quart (1 litre) milk
1 heaping tablespoon best-quality tea
1½ cups (300 g) sugar
12 egg yolks, lightly beaten

1. In a medium-size saucepan over medium-high heat, bring the milk, tea, and sugar to a boil. Remove from the heat and let steep for 15 minutes. Strain through cheesecloth into a bowl, discarding the tea leaves.

2. Whisk the hot milk mixture into the egg yolks, then return the mixture to the saucepan. Cook over low heat just until the mixture begins to thicken. Do not let it boil. Remove from the heat and transfer to a bowl.

3. Allow the mixture to cool to room temperature, then transfer it to an ice cream maker and freeze according to the manufacturer's directions.

Yield: 1 quart (1 litre)

Cafés
CAFES

Au Petit Fer à Cheval (see entry, page 87).

It is impossible to imagine Paris without its cafés. Parisians are sun-worshippers, and the attraction of an outdoor pavement stopping place perfectly suits their inclination. Around the first week of February, sunshine or not, café doors open, chairs and tables tumble out, and the season begins.

The city has some 12,000 cafés varying in size, grandeur, and significance. As diverse as Parisians themselves, the café serves as an extension of the French living room, a place to start and end the day, to gossip and debate, a place for seeing and being seen.

No book on Paris literary, artistic, or social life is complete without details of café life noting who sat where, when, and with whom; and what they drank. One wonders how writers and artists accomplished all they did if they really whiled away all those hours at pavement tables sipping *café au lait*, Vichy water and *ballons* of Beaujolais.

When did it start? The café billed as the oldest in Paris is Le Procope, opened in 1686 by a Sicilian, Francesco Procopio dei Coltelli, the man credited with turning France into a coffee-drinking society. He was one of the first men granted the privilege of distilling and selling wines, liqueurs, *eaux-de-vie*, coffee, tea, and chocolate, with a status equal to a baker or butcher. Le Procope attracted Paris's political and literary elite, and its past is filled with history. It has been reported that it was there that Voltaire drank forty cups of his favourite brew each day: a blend of coffee and chocolate, which some credit with inspiring his spontaneous wit. When Benjamin Franklin died in 1790 and the French assembly went into mourning for three days, Le Procope was entirely draped in black in honour of France's favourite American. Even the young Napoleon Bonaparte spent time at Le Procope: When still an artillery officer, he was forced to leave his hat as security while he went out in search of money to pay for his coffee. Le Procope still exists at the original address, 13 Rue de l'Ancienne Comédie, but as a restaurant, not a café.

By the end of the 18th century, all of Paris was intoxicated with coffee and the city supported some 700 cafés. These were like all-male clubs with many serving as centres of political life and discussion. It is no surprise to find that one of the speeches that precipitated the fall of the Bastille took place outside the Café Foy at the Palais-Royal.

By the 1840s the number of Paris cafés had grown to 3,000. The men who congregated and set the tenor of the times included journalists, playwrights, and writers who became known as *boulevardiers.* Certain cafés did have special rooms reserved for women, but in 1916 a law was passed that prevented serving women sitting alone on the terraces of those along the boulevards.

Around the turn of the century, the pavement cafés along Boulevard du Montparnasse—Le Dôme, La Rotonde, and later, La Coupole— became the stronghold of artists; those along Boulevard Saint Germain—Aux Deux Magots, Flore, and Lipp—were the watering holes and meeting halls for the literary. When the "lost generation" of expatriates arrived in Paris after World War I, they established themselves along both boulevards, drinking, talking, arguing, and writing.

Cafés still serve as picture windows for observing contemporary life. The people you see today at Aux Deux Magots, Café de Flore, and Lipp may not be the great artists of the past, but faces are worth watching just the same. Linger a bit and you will see that the Paris stereotypes are alive and well: the surly waiters and red-eyed Frenchmen inhaling Gitanes; old men in navy berets; *clochardes* (bag ladies) hauling bright pink Monoprix shopping bags holding all their earthly possessions; ultra-thin, bronzed women with hair dyed bright orange; and schoolchildren decked out in blue and white seersucker, sharing an afternoon chocolate with mother.

If you know how to nurse a beer or coffee for hours, café-sitting can be one of the city's best buys. No matter how crowded a café may be, waiters will respect your graceful loafing, and won't insist that you order another round just to hold the table. Drinks are usually less expensive if you are willing to stand at the bar. At mealtime, if you see a table covered with a cloth or even a little paper placemat, that means the table is reserved for dining. If it is bare, you are welcome to sit and just have a drink. Note that the service charge is automatically added to all café bills, so you are required to pay only the final total and need not leave an additional tip, although most people leave any loose change.

The following listing offers a short glimpse of Paris café life, suggesting the grand and famous cafés, along with some lesser known neighbourhood favourites.

CHATELET, LES HALLES, PONT-NEUF
1st and 2nd arrondissements

LE COCHON A L'OREILLE,
15 Rue Montmartre,
   Paris 1.
(236.07.56).
Métro: Les Halles.
Open 4:45 A.M. to 4:30
   P.M. Closed Sunday.

This is the most beautiful working man's bar in Paris. It houses great murals, fresh flowers on the tiny bistro tables, workers in blue overalls five deep at the zinc bar, and peanut shells on the floor. If you happen to be up and about at 6 A.M., you may want to toss back a few drinks with the local merchants, who still keep this end of Les Halles busy in the early morning hours.

AUX DEUX SAULES,
91 Rue Saint-Denis,
   Paris 1.
(236.46.57).
Métro: Les Halles.
Open daily, noon to 1 A.M.

This is a popular spot for the young-and-chic-but-impoverished, and comes on as a small breath of fresh air amid a sea of sex shops and fast food eateries. Most of the action here goes on outdoors, where the trendy crowd hangs out at the large, communal picnic tables set along this busy pedestrian *passage*. There are no willows (*saules*), left here, but the café serves a

Aux Deux Saules, both outside (right) and in (facing page).

rather decent bowl of onion soup *gratinée* and drinkable red wine. Do save time for a trip inside: You can down a quick coffee at the bar, facing the fabulous ceramic murals depicting life in old Les Halles.

UN CAFE, S'IL VOUS PLAIT

Cafés are, of course, for more than just coffee. Although café fare has not changed drastically since the early days, food, like fashion, goes in and out of style. During the 19th century, one popular drink was *fond de culotte* ("seat of your pants"), so named since supposedly it could only be drunk while sitting down. It was a mixture of gentian liqueur and *crème de cassis*. During the same period, other popular drinks included the *mêle-cassis*, half cassis and half Cognac; the *bicyclette*, a blend of champagne and vermouth; and the *pompier*, or "fireman," a blend of vermouth and cassis.

Today, coffee, beer, and anise-flavored *pastis* are the staple drinks, along with various fruit juices sweetened with sugar. The *croque monsieur*—a ham sandwich topped with grated cheese, then grilled—and the *sandwich mixte*—a thickly buttered *baguette* filled with Gruyère cheese and thin slices of *jambon de Paris*—are favourite café snacks. For larger meals, there are often meaty *plats du jour,* pork *rillettes,* pâtés, platters of raw vegetables known as *crudités, salade niçoise,* and even hot dogs.

Coffee and other hot drinks come in many forms. This small glossary should help you order what you want.

***Café noir* or *café express*:** plain black espresso

***Double express*:** a double espresso

***Café serré*:** extra-strong espresso, made with half the normal amount of water

***Café allongé*:** weak espresso, often served with a small pitcher of hot water so clients may thin the coffee themselves

***Café au lait* or *café crème*:** espresso with warmed or lightly steamed milk

***Grand crème*:** large or double espresso with milk

***Décaféiné* or *déca*:** decaffeinated espresso

***Café filtre*:** filtered coffee (not available at all cafés)

***Chocolat chaud*:** hot chocolate

***Infusion*:** herb tea

***Thé nature, thé citron, thé au lait*:** plain tea, tea with lemon, tea with milk

"I was often alone, but seldom lonely: I enjoyed the newspapers and books that were my usual companions at table, the exchanges with waiters, barmen, booksellers, street vendors . . . the sounds of the conversations of others around me, and finally, the talk of the girls I ended some evenings by picking up."
—A. J. Liebling

L'INNOCENT,
12 Rue Berger, Paris 1.
(236.55.31).
Métro: Les Halles.
Open daily, noon to 1 A.M.

There is no lack of sunkissed pavement cafés in the Les Halles area, but of those on the tree-lined Square des Innocents, this one offers the most charm. Indoors, the decor is total *Déco*, with walls of bevelled white Métro tile covered with posters of current art exhibitions. They still offer up newspapers—there are *Le Monde* and *Le Matin* for leisure-time reading in a choice sunny spot facing the giant Renaissance Fountain of the Holy Innocents. Or, you can retreat to the shade of umbrellas, away from the pedestrian hordes. The square, by the way, is on the site of the medieval Cimetière des Innocents, the chief burial ground in Paris until 1785, when the remains were transferred to the Catacombs.

LA SAMARITAINE CAFE,
19 Rue de la Monnaie,
   Paris 1.
(Go to Magasin 2, 5th
   floor, and follow signs.)
(508.33.33).
Métro: Pont-Neuf.
Bar open 9:30 A.M. to 6:30
   P.M. and on Wednesday
   to 10 P.M. Food service
   begins at 11:30 A.M.
   Closed Sunday.

The popular slogan of this well-known department store is *"On Trouve Tout à la Samaritaine,"* or "One Finds Everything at La Samaritaine." That everything includes one of the most spectacular views of the Paris cityscape. Visit on a sunny afternoon, order up a *citron pressé* (lemonade), or a beer, and relax before or after a visit to this mammoth, confusing department store.

A solitary café moment.

MARAIS, HOTEL-DE-VILLE, REPUBLIQUE, GARE DE L'EST, ILE SAINT-LOUIS
4th, 10th, and 11th arrondissements

MA BOURGOGNE,
19 Place des Vosges,
  Paris 4.
(278.44.64).
Métro: Saint-Paul.
Open 8 A.M. to 1 A.M.
  Closed Monday.

This is the best, and most active, café in the Marais, and it's set under the arcades of Paris's oldest square. Sit outdoors on the traditional beige and red rattan chairs, absorbing the beauty of the architecture dating back to 1407. The café is calm in the morning, and packed with local office workers at lunchtime. The *pommes frites* are not bad, just ask for them *bien cuites*—well cooked. Writer Georges Simenon's inspector Maigret spent a lot of time here, perhaps inspecting the varied clientele, which ranges from old locals to tourists to the chic young residents of one of Paris's most sought-after addresses.

Tête-à-tête at Ma Bourgogne.

LE CLOWN BAR,
114 Rue Amelot, Paris 11.
(700.51.18).
Métro: Filles-du-Calvaire.
Open 7:30 A.M. to 7:30
  P.M. Closed Saturday.

A dive, to be sure, but an honest *café du quartier*, worth visiting if you have a passion for clowns or the circus or *Belle Epoque* ceramic murals. The good part is that the place probably hasn't changed during the past fifty years. The bad part is that it probably hasn't been cleaned in as long. But along with the dirt-encrusted windows and walls papered with photographs of stars of the Cirque d'Hiver (winter circus), which is housed down the street, there's a lot of history and a rather grubby sort of charm conveyed in the red and yellow murals of circus clowns, acrobats, and other circus figures.

LE FLORE EN L'ILE,
42 Quai d'Orléans, Paris 4.
(329.88.27).
Métro: Pont-Marie.
Open daily, 11 A.M. to
  1:45 A.M.

This combination café/restaurant/tea salon on Ile Saint-Louis is nothing special on the outside, but if you can secure a seat at the open-air windows along the pavement, the view of Notre Dame, just across the bridge, is breathtaking. Settle in to read one of the French or English publications that hang from bamboo racks along the *caisse,* and enjoy one of the famous and fabulous Berthillon sorbets or ice creams sold here. Tea does not come from a tea bag but is freshly brewed and steaming hot, and the classical music in the background helps one enjoy a moment of peace and a nice breeze on a warm day.

**LE PETIT
CHATEAU D'EAU,**
34 Rue du Château
  d'Eau, Paris 10.
(208.72.81).
Métro: République.
Open 7:45 A.M. to 8:30
  P.M. Closed Saturday
  and Sunday.

This is a perfect neighbourhood café, just down the street from the old-fashioned little Château d'Eau covered market. The barrel-chested *patron* with a deep, booming voice is usually decked out in Wrangler jeans and red braces and holds court with locals as he tends his zinc-covered, half-moon bar. Le Petit Château D'Eau also offers one of the city's classic interiors: Bevelled

Au Petit Fer à Cheval (see facing page), a place for coffee and classical music.

A BIT OF PARISIAN COFFEE HISTORY

When Louis XIV first tasted coffee in 1664, he was not impressed. But Parisian high society fell in love with the intoxicating brew, enjoying it at lavish and exotic private parties arranged by the Turkish ambassador, who arrived in 1669.

By 1670, the general public got a taste of the rich, caffeinated drink when an Armenian named Pascal hawked it at the Saint-Germain fair in the spring. He hired formally dressed waiters to go out among the crowds and through the streets, crying as they went, *"Café, Café."* Later Pascal opened a little coffee boutique like those he had seen in Constantinople. It was not a smashing success, but he survived with the help of his wandering waiters, who even went door to door with jugs of the thick, black brew. Their only competition was *"le Candiot,"* a cripple who sold coffee in the streets of Paris for a meager two *sous,* sugar included.

Then, as now, doctors discussed the merits and drawbacks of coffee. Those who favoured the drink argued that it cured scurvy, relieved smallpox and gout, and was even recommended for gargling, to improve the voice. *Café au lait* was lauded for its medicinal qualities, and in 1688, Madame de Sévigné, whose letters record the life of the period, noted it as a remedy for colds and chest illness.

By the time the city's first café, Le Procope, opened in 1686, coffee was well on its way to winning the Parisian palate.

glass doors lead to the spotless and cheery little café, with its fresh coat of paint and bright bouquets of market-fresh flowers. Large mirrors rimmed in antique green and white tiles make the room even cosier, as you sit back in a brown upholstered booth to read one of the local newspapers or magazines set out for the clientele.

**AU PETIT FER
A CHEVAL,**
30 Rue Vieille-du-Temple,
Paris 4.
(272.47.47).
Métro: Hôtel-de-Ville.
Open 7:30 A.M. to
8:30 P.M. Closed
Sunday.

A tiny, popular neighbourhood café that dates back to 1903, when the Combes family opened it as the Café de Brésil. Today, the café still boasts a fabulous marble-topped horseshoe (*fer à cheval*) bar, mirrored walls, and the original patchwork tile floor. The *patron,* André Collin, has embellished the room a bit but retained a feeling of authenticity by adding another mirror, a giant chandelier, and shelves of glass and brick. Instead of bothersome pinball machines, so popular lately in cafés, Mr. Collin offers soothing classical music. The back room, always packed at lunchtime for his *plat du jour,* boasts a giant Métro map and booths made up of old wooden Métro seats.

**BRASSERIE DU PONT
LOUIS-PHILIPPE,**
66 Quai de l'Hôtel-de-
Ville, Paris 4.
(272.29.42).
Métro: Pont-Marie.
Open noon to 2:30 P.M.,
7:30 P.M. to 11:30 P.M.
Closed Monday.

This little café across from the Pont Louis-Philippe, one of the bridges leading to Ile Saint-Louis, gets the simplicity award for decor: plain white walls, giant white vases filled with bright fresh flowers, oval bevelled mirrors, and wide windows that open out onto the streets. On nice days, sit on the white folding chairs in the sun, reading whatever it is you've found at the booksellers along the *quai.* At night, it's a popular spot for an inexpensive meal.

LATIN QUARTER, LUXEMBOURG, SAINT-GERMAIN, SEVRES-BABYLONE
5th and 6th arrondissements

AUX DEUX MAGOTS,
170 Boulevard Saint-
Germain, Paris 6.
(548.55.25).
Métro: Saint-Germain-des-
Prés.
Open daily, 8 A.M. to 2
A.M. Closed in August.

The ultimate Paris café, great for observing the current fashion scene and restoring yourself with a steaming cup of good hot chocolate on a chilly afternoon. Aux Deux Magots offers more than twenty-five different whiskies, and coffee is still served in thick, white cups. Pavement entertainment varies from fire eaters to organ grinders to junior Bob Dylans. The interior is calm, and appealing, with its mahogany-red banquettes and brass-edged tables, walls of mirrors, and waiters attired in white floor-length aprons

Aux Deux Magots.

CAFE DE FLORE,
172 Boulevard Saint-
    Germain, Paris 6.
(548.55.26).
Métro: Saint-Germain-des-
    Prés.
Open daily, 8 A.M. to
    2 A.M. Closed in July.

and neat black waistcoats. You can sit under the famous wooden statues of the two Chinese dignitaries—
the *deux magots,* who gave their name to the café. (The
café's name does not, as some writers have suggested,
translate as two maggots!) The owner recalls watching
Jean-Paul Sartre indoors from 10 to 12:30 each day,
writing while smoking cigarette after cigarette. Ernest
Hemingway came, too, after World War I, for "serious
talk" and to read aloud the poetry he'd written.

The rival of Aux Deux Magots next door, this was
always more of a literary hangout, popular with
Sartre, Simone de Beauvoir, and Albert Camus. During the Occupation, the cafés in Montparnasse were
full of German soldiers, and so Parisians preferred
Flore, where not only were there no German soldiers,
there was even a small stove. After the war in the late
1940s, when most artists still gathered in Montparnasse, Picasso used to come here every night, sitting
at the second table in front of the main door, sipping
a glass of mineral water and chatting with his Spanish
friends. Little has changed since. There's still the simple and classic *Art Déco* interior: red banquettes, walls
of mahogany and mirrors, and a large sign suggesting
that, while pipe smoking is not forbidden, *"l'odeur de
certains tabacs de pipe parfumés incommode la plupart de nos
clients."* In other words, "courteous clients don't smoke
pipes here." The large sidewalk café is neither as pleasant nor as accessible as that at Aux Deux Magots, yet
it is equally popular.

Café de Flore.

CROQUE-MONSIEUR
(GRILLED HAM AND CHEESE SANDWICH)

The croque-monsieur is the most Parisian of sandwiches. It's really no more than a grilled ham sandwich topped with grated cheese, but it appears in many different guises. One could spend weeks hopping from café to café, taking notes on variations and favorites. Sometimes a croque-monsieur is topped with a thick cheese béchamel sauce, or transformed into a croque-madame with the addition of an egg, but frankly, few Parisian cafés do justice to the sandwich. All too often, a croque-monsieur is made with airy, factory-made white bread, second rate ham, and the cheese, well, it's not always Gruyère. (Parisian supermarkets even sell frozen croque-monsieur, ready for popping in the oven!) If you want a great croque-monsieur, make it yourself, with exceptional homemade pain de mie, the slightly buttery white bread that's been unjustly distorted by industrialization.

3 tablespoons unsalted butter
12 small, thin slices homemade *pain de mie* (see recipe, page 164)
7 ounces, or 6 thin slices (200 g) best-quality ham, cut to fit bread
4½ ounces (125 g) Gruyère cheese, grated

1. Preheat the broiler.

2. Butter 6 slices of bread on one side. Place one slice of ham on each of the buttered sides, and cover with the remaining bread slices.

3. Place the sandwiches under the broiler, and grill on one side until golden. Remove the sandwiches, turn, and cover each with grated Gruyère. Return to the broiler and grill until the cheese is bubbling and golden.

Yield: 6 *croque-monsieur.*

Note: To transform a *croque-monsieur* into a *croque-madame,* grill a *croque-monsieur,* until it is almost bubbling and golden, then cut a small round out of the top piece of cheese-covered bread, exposing the ham. Reserve the round. Break a small egg into the hole and place under the broiler for 2 or 3 more minutes. To serve, top the egg with the cheese-covered round.

One French cookbook even offers a recipe for a sandwich named after the food critic Curnonsky. To prepare a *croque Curnonsky,* blend equal amounts of butter and Roquefort cheese, spread on thin slices of *pain de mie,* top with ham and another slice of bread and grill on both sides.

BRASSERIE LIPP,
151 Boulevard Saint-Germain, Paris 6.
(548.53.91).
Métro: Saint-Germain-des-Prés.
Open 8 A.M. to 12:45 A.M. Closed Monday and the month of July.

One of the city's most famous café-restaurants, still a late-night spot for politicians such as François Mitterrand, designers such as Yves Saint-Laurent, and editors from houses such as Gallimard and Hachette. During the day, the rather cramped and airless terrace is filled with American, German, and English tourists drinking the delicious Alsatian beers and sharing platters of *jambon* and *fromage.* The walls of the interior are classically dark and dingy, but in a felicitous way. Colourful ceramic tiles painted with parrots and cranes give the main floor dining room a lighter feel, and the bright lights of the old-fashioned chandeliers turn night into day. Despite the fact that the food is barely edible—the famous *choucroute* is third rate, the popular *gigot* tasteless, and the pastries soggy and tired—Lipp packs them in night after night. They don't take reservations by telephone, and a good deal of fuss is made of securing a table on the main floor. Those who dine upstairs don't talk about it.

LUTETIA,
23 Rue de Sèvres, Paris 6.
(544.38.10).
Métro: Sèvres-Babylone.
Open daily, noon to
　midnight.

Although one is welcome to sit outdoors at the tiny espresso bar for a tea or coffee, I love the brilliant *Art Déco* interior, all mirrors and silver, with a horseshoe zinc bar dominating the room. Lutétia caters to an older, well-heeled crowd, which comes here for onion soup and little salads of mixed greens and smoked goose breast. This is a busy area, with the Bon Marché department store, Poilâne bakery, and numerous boutiques, as well as a lovely little nearby park at the foot of the pedestrian street, Rue Récamier.

CAFE MOUFFETARD,
116 Rue Mouffetard,
　Paris 5.
(331.42.50).
Métro: Monge.
Open 6 A.M. to 8 P.M.
　Closed Monday.

The big sign outside reads *"Brasserie"* in bold burgundy lettering, but this rather earthy little spot set right in the middle of the busy Rue Mouffetard market is one of the homier cafés in Paris. A smoky little worker's hangout, it was brought to my attention by an American colleague, Martha Rose Shulman, who was lured here by the homemade pastries, dense and buttery *croissants,* and delicious, almost creamy, *brioches.* This is probably the only café in town where the *patron* and his wife make their *croissants* and *brioches,* working through the night so the market workers will have something fresh and warm to sustain them through a long morning's labour. In wintertime, they also make little *chaussons aux pommes,* hot apple tarts, perfect for eating with a giant *café crème.*

Time for a café lunch.

SNACKS

The most popular café snacks are sandwiches, made either on the long and narrow *baguette;* on *pain de mie,* the square white bread; or *pain* Poilâne, Paris's most popular country-style loaf. Poilâne's bread is often served as a *tartine,* an open-face sandwich with various toppings.

Here are some of the most popular sandwich ingredients, followed by other popular snacking items.

Jambon de Paris: cooked ham

Jambon de pays: country ham, usually salt-cured

Saucisson sec or *saucisson à l'ail:* dried sausage, plain or with garlic

Rillettes: soft, spreadable pork or goose pâté

Pâté de campagne: pork pâté

Sandwich mixte: Gruyère cheese and ham on a *baguette*

Cornichons: small French pickles or gherkins

Oeuf dur: hard-cooked egg

Carottes rapées: grated carrot salad, usually with vinaigrette dressing

Crudités: variety of raw vegetables in a salad, usually including grated carrots, beets, and tomatoes

Assiette de charcuterie: a combination plate of dried sausage, pâté, and *rillettes*

LA PALETTE,
43 Rue de Seine, Paris 6.
(326.68.15).
Métro: Mabillon.
Open daily, 8 A.M.
 to 2 A.M.
 Closed in August.

This artist's hangout is perfect on a sunny summer's afternoon, when the tables fill as much of the pavement as law and reason will allow. Everyone is in a light mood, and seems to know everyone else, so La Palette has a particularly intimate, Parisian air. The *patron* wanders about shaking hands and chatting with the brightly dressed clientele, who come for hearty cups of coffee and to snack on open-face sandwiches made with fresh *pain Poilâne.*

**AU PETIT
CAFE CLUNY,**
20 Boulevard Saint-Michel,
 Paris 5.
(354.23.64).
Métro: Saint-Michel.
Open daily, 7 A.M. to
 2 A.M., and all night
 Saturday.

This is one of those large and rambling cafés of the main streets of the Latin Quarter, where people don't go for the decor or the food, but simply to people-watch and relax. It's a few steps from the Cluny Museum and at one of the city's busiest crossroads, the corner of Boulevard Saint-Michel and Boulevard Saint-Germain.

OPERA, CHAMPS-ELYSEES
8th and 9th arrondissements

LE FOUQUET'S,
99 Avenue des Champs-
  Elysées, Paris 8.
(723.70.60).
Métro: George V.
Open daily, 9 A.M. to
  midnight.

This is one of the most popular Right Bank cafés, perfect for observing the ever-changing scene on the Champs-Elysées. Le Fouquet's is always making society news, as starlets and journalists talk and write about their rendezvous here. James Joyce used to dine at Le Fouquet's almost every night, and today well-known French chef Paul Bocuse stops in whenever he's in town. Most don't come for the scene or the food, but to grab a snack before or after viewing one of the dozens of first-run films playing at movie houses along the avenue. Sexism lives at Le Fouquet's, where a sign warns, *"Les dames seules ne sont pas admises au bar"* ("Women who are alone are not allowed at the bar"). The management insists that the sign, which has been up at the seven-stool bar since the restaurant opened at the turn of the century, was put there to protect women, not insult them. Most women see it otherwise. Incidentally, Le Fouquet's is pronounced to rhyme with "bets" not "bays," a remnant of the fashionable fascination with English early in the century.

POPULAR APERITIFS

Absinthe, the highly alcoholic, anise-flavoured drink invented by a Frenchman in 1797, was banned in 1915 because of its harmful effects on the nerves. It was quickly replaced by two other popular though less dangerous drinks, *pastis* and *anis*. The two have much in common with absinthe, but are lower in alcohol. Wormwood, the ingredient which caused absinthe to be banned, is omitted.

Pastis: anise-flavoured alcohol that becomes cloudy when water is added (the most famous brands are Pernod and Ricard)

Suze: bitter liqueur distilled from the root of the yellow mountain gentian

Picon and *Mandarin:* bitter, orange-flavoured drink

Pineau des Charentes: sweet fortified wine from the Cognac region

Kir: dry white wine mixed with *crème de cassis* (black currant liqueur)

Kir royal: champagne mixed with *crème de cassis*

CAFE DE LA PAIX,
12 Boulevard des
    Capucines, Paris 9.
(268.12.13).
Métro: Opéra.
Open daily, 10 A.M. to
    1:30 A.M.

This open, expansive café near the Opéra represents a sort of gaiety of days past. The building has been declared a historic monument, and is not a bad place to sip your lemonade while sitting under the crisp green and white striped umbrellas that line the pavement. You should enjoy the spectacle of the passing show, including international tourists as well as Parisians.

MONTPARNASSE
14th arrondissement

An animated moment at Ma Bourgogne (see entry, page 85).

CLOSERIE DES LILAS,
171 Boulevard du
    Montparnasse, Paris 14.
(326.70.50).
Métro: Port-Royal.
Open daily, noon to 1 A.M.

The lilacs are long gone, but the romance of days when men like Henry James and Ernest Hemingway gathered here is still very much alive at this popular café-restaurant. Beneath the colourful green and white awnings amid a garden of greenery, you can sit outdoors and sip coffee, or move to the enclosed terrace for an authentic *salade niçoise,* or dine in the open-air covered garden. Try the restaurant's still famous *loup de mer flambé au fenouil* (whole grilled sea bass that arrives in a flame of dried fennel branches). Closerie des Lilas is a comfortable place for Sunday lunch in August when everything else has closed down. It is still a hangout for French film stars and chic young Frenchmen, and a spot where one can linger while reading the copies of *L'Express* and *Paris Match* provided for the clients.

LA COUPOLE,
102 Boulevard du
   Montparnasse, Paris 14.
(320.14.20).
Métro: Vavin.
Open daily, 8 A.M. to 2 P.M.
   Closed in August.

This Montparnasse café-restaurant (see also page 59) is still a favourite meeting place for artists, models, and tourists, and the haunt of young Americans since its opening in 1927. Though today few artists can afford to live in this popular district, little seems to have changed over the past five decades. Artists still come and sit at the left, under the posters of current exhibitions, while the chic set dines on the right. Sunday is for family lunches, when reservations are at a premium. During off hours, the old-timers fill the large, cavernous hall, sitting at the same tables they've occupied for decades and reading the papers that hang from bamboo frames. The food is above average for such a long-established café. Try the briny Belon oysters, grilled lamb chops, the moist pistachio-studded sausages, or the Baltic herring served with mounds of *crème fraîche* and chunks of fresh apples. This is one place you can always go for a snack or a full meal and never have a sense of being rushed.

OTHER ALCOHOLIC DRINKS

Calvados: apple brandy

Marc de Bourgogne: pronounced "mar," an *eau-de-vie* distilled from pressed grape skins and seeds

Pippermint Get: bright green alcoholic mint drink

Cidre: hard apple cider

Café de Flore, a place for being seen (see entry, page 88).

LE DOME,
108 Boulevard du
  Montparnasse, Paris 14.
(354.53.61).
Métro: Vavin.
Open 10 A.M. to 2 A.M.
  Closed Monday.

When Le Dôme first opened at the turn of the century, it was just a drinking shack and Montparnasse was a suburb of the Latin Quarter. Today, this well-populated neighbourhood is a mix of young and old, and the fern-filled terrace of Le Dôme is a fine place for lingering over coffee, a *ballon* of *rosé*, a *croque-monsieur* or a *sandwich mixte*.

POPULAR NON-ALCOHOLIC DRINKS

Orangina: carbonated orange soda, the most popular non-alcoholic café drink

Citron, orange, or *pamplemousse pressé:* lemon, orange, or grapefruit juice served with a carafe of tap water and sugar, for sweetening to taste

Gini: bitter lemon

Limonade: 7-Up style drink

Diabolo: lemonade with a variety of sweet fruit syrups

Menthe: sweet, bright green mint-flavoured syrup, drunk with water

Diabolo menthe: mint syrup and lemonade

Coca: Coca-Cola

Schweppes: tonic water

LA ROTONDE,
105 Boulevard du
  Montparnasse, Paris 14.
(326.68.84).
Métro: Vavin.
Open daily, 8 A.M. to
  2 A.M.

Lenin and Trotsky sipped their *café crème* here in 1915, along with others of the international intelligentsia who made the café famous. It has all been remodelled, and much of its charm has been lost, but in the afternoon La Rotonde gets the sun, so the Montparnasse crowd camps out here, sipping Ricard and smoking Gitanes.

Bois de Boulogne
16th arrondissement

**LA GRANDE
CASCADE,**
Near the Longchamp
  Racetrack, Bois de
  Boulogne, Paris 16.
(506.33.51).
Not accessible by Métro.
Open noon to 7:30 P.M.
  June to September,
  4 P.M. to 6 P.M.
  October to May.

This grand old *Belle Epoque* café-restaurant serves coffee and tea in the afternoons, on the open-air terrace right in the middle of the Bois de Boulogne. At one time, the restaurant probably had some of the best service in town; now the single, aging waiter makes no attempt to hide his boredom, and the rather skimpy menu of coffee, tea, and ice cream offers little imagination. But if you happen to be hiking through the Bois on a sunny day, this is the place to sit, amid bright geraniums on a pretty tiled patio, and share the moment with old French couples offering their lumps of sugar to the birds.

BEER

B eer (*bière*) comes in many sizes and can be ordered by the bottle, *bouteille*, or on tap, *à la pression*.

Demi—8 ounces (25 centilitres)

Sérieux—16 ounces (50 centilitres)

Formidable—1 quart (1 litre)

LE JARDIN DE BAGATELLE,
Parc Bagatelle, Bois de
    Boulogne, Paris 16.
(722.88.29).
Not accessible by Métro.
Open daily, noon to 7 P.M.
    Only cold plates are
    served.

T he Bagatelle is one of Paris's prettiest parks, famous for its stunning rose gardens. The café, set at the edge of the woods some distance from the gardens, is the perfect place to relax after a Sunday's stroll through the park. This is the only Paris café I know where you get to press your own lemons and oranges for *citron* or *orange pressé*. Gruff, overworked waiters bring the old-fashioned clear glass citrus press right to the table, along with the neatly halved fruit.

A daily Parisian ritual.

Salons de Thé
TEA SALONS

The Art Déco allure of Brocco (see entry, page 100).

Golden *pains au chocolat,* lush ruby strawberry tarts, and moist, dark chocolate cakes form a multi-coloured still life in the sparkling window; gazing through, one senses an air of calm, repose, contentment. The door opens, revealing a mysterious blend of jasmine tea, vanilla-scented apple tart, and Haydn. At a far table, elderly women in veiled hats sit *tête-à-tête,* immersed in gossip and frothy hot chocolate, while nearby a well-dressed businessman flirts with a slender, chic Parisienne who seems more involved in her *tarte abricot* than in his advances. This is the daily life of the Parisian *salon de thé;* cosy, intimate affairs designed to indulge France's insatiable sweet tooth and flair for guiltlessly whiling away hours at the table.

Though teatime is associated more closely with London, Paris supports some sixty or seventy fully-fledged *salons de thé,* most of them distinctly French; Parisians don't fool around with frail cucumber sandwiches and dry currant buns—they get right to the heart of the matter, dessert.

In Paris, as in London, tea salons reached the height of popularity at the turn of the century, providing matrons of standing with well-appointed surroundings for entertaining guests outside the home, and offering women a respectable career opportunity.

During the 1920s, tea and dance salons became popular along the Champs-Elysées and in restaurants in the Bois de Boulogne: Here aging *grandes dames* came alone, as did young men. They met, they danced, they drank tea, then went their separate ways.

Thanks to a renaissance during the 1970s, Paris now offers an unlimited variety of tea salons, each with a distinctive decor, menu, and ambience that follow the whim and passion of the owner. Some double as a bookshop or pastry or antique shop, and the best provide an unparalleled opportunity for sampling superbly fresh, original pastries. A cup of coffee or pot of tea will be more expensive here than in a run-of-the-mill café, but the atmosphere is usually calmer (no noisy pinball machines) and the food generally superior. Lunch, and sometimes dinner, is available at most *salons de thé,* but more often than not, the food is an afterthought. An early morning or late afternoon visit for tea and pastry will, in the end, be more rewarding. Tea salons are, by the way, places where one feels perfectly comfortable alone. Depending upon what you order, expect to pay about forty francs per person for tea or coffee and a pastry.

PALAIS-ROYAL, PLACE DES VICTOIRES, LOUVRE
1st and 2nd arrondissements

A PRIORI THE,
35 Galerie Vivienne,
   Paris 2.
(297.48.75).
Métro: Bourse.
Open 10 A.M. to 7 P.M.
   Closed Sunday and the
   first week of August.

Galerie Vivienne is Paris's prettiest turn-of-the-century *passage*—the arched, romantic forerunner of the shopping mall. Leave it to a group of Americans to turn this sleepy but elegant area into a lively meeting spot. Here, the chic set that haunts the *avant-garde* shoe and clothing shops that encircle the nearby Place des Victoires come for classical music, brownies or corn muffins, and lots of English tea. Welcoming wicker chairs spill into the brightly tiled arcade year round, no matter what the weather.

ANGELINA,
226 Rue de Rivoli, Paris 1.
(260.75.34).
Métro: Tuileries.
Open daily, 10 A.M. to
   6:30 P.M. Closed the
   first three weeks
   in August.

One almost expects a troupe of Proustian characters to wander into this turn-of-the-century salon just across the street from the Jardin des Tuileries. Up until 1948, this was the old and celebrated Rumpelmayers, where as a child A. J. Liebling downed ersatz American ice cream sodas and began his love affair with Paris. Today—with its green-veined, marble-topped tables and walls embellished with murals and mirrors—it's still snobbish, expensive, and ever-popular, and about the only place in town where they melt real chocolate bars for their lethally rich, delicious hot chocolate.

FANNY TEA,
20 Place Dauphine,
  Paris 1.
(325.83.67).
Métro: Pont-Neuf.
Open 1 P.M. to 8 P.M.
  Tuesday through Friday;
  3:30 P.M. to 8 P.M.
  Saturday and Sunday.
  Closed Monday.

The world of Fanny Tea, on the diminutive Place Dauphine near the Pont-Neuf, is so strange and mystical you almost expect a palm reader to sit down, gently, beside you. Books of poetry and old French novels vie for table space with flickering candles, giant Victorian pewter teapots and delicious, vanilla-scented warm apple tarts. There's seldom a table free, but this is the perfect place to escape the damp on a rainy Parisian afternoon, and to listen to classical music as you write your memoirs. If you're lucky, film star Yves Montand, who lives on the square, will wander by.

MUSCADE,
36 Rue de Montpensier,
  Paris 1.
(297.51.36).
Métro: Palais-Royal.
Open daily, noon to
  11 P.M.; tea, coffee, and
  desserts only from
  3 P.M. to 7 P.M.

You don't have to book a table at the costly Grand Véfour to enjoy the romantic pink rose garden of the Palais-Royal. From May to September, Muscade expands to the garden terrace, one of the city's most tranquil, elegant outdoor spots for people-watching or just resting weary bodies. The Palais-Royal garden is an honest neighbourhood park as well, filled with old ladies sharing their *baguettes* with the pigeons, maids and mothers pushing infants in pristine navy prams, and children at play in the sandbox. Stop off before or after a visit to the Louvre or the Comédie Française, ignore the less than professional service, and enjoy the fresh fruit tarts and *café crème*.

VERLET,
256 Rue Saint-Honoré,
  Paris 1.
(260.67.39).
Métro: Louvre.
Open noon to 7 P.M.
  Monday through Friday.
  Closed Saturday, Sunday,
  and the month of
  August.

The rich aroma of freshly roasted coffee mingling with teas from China, Ceylon, India, and Japan draws passersby to the door of Verlet, one of the most reputable and helpful coffee and tea merchants in Paris. Here, not far from the Place du Palais-Royal and the Louvre's Musée des Arts Décoratifs, you enter a casual, cosmopolitan world, crammed with open sacks of roast coffee from all corners of the globe, mounds of dried fruits and nuts, and colourful tins of tea blended on the spot to your liking.

There's always a line continuing outside the door for Verlet's products, but if there's some table space, settle down for a few minutes in this unadorned 1930s setting for the famous coffee, or tea served from silver-plated teapots with handles covered by bright felt mittens. There are always four or five rich cakes and pastries made on the premises, including a luscious apricot tart (see recipe, page 102) that goes so well with a warming cup of jasmine tea.

MARAIS, BASTILLE, REPUBLIQUE, BEAUBOURG
3rd and 4th arrondissements

BROCCO,
180 Rue du Temple,
   Paris 3.
(272.19.81).
Métro: République.
Open daily, 9 A.M.
   to 7 P.M. Closed
   in August.

The aromas of freshly baked *croissants* and thick black espresso lure visitors into Brocco, an impressive, impeccable *Art Déco patisserie* and *salon de thé* just off the Place de la République. Here, amid marble and mirrors and theatrical strips of fluorescent lighting, matronly waitresses often buzz about, defending themselves and *la maison,* against a client's complaint over less than perfect *pains au chocolat.* But the little cane chairs and triangular oak tables, the pretty white china and thick foam of milk atop the *café crème* allow one to ignore the pastry chef's momentary lapses.

DATTES ET NOIX,
4 Rue du Parc-Royal,
   Paris 3.
(887.88.94).
Métro: Saint-Paul.
Open noon to 2 A.M.
   Monday through
   Saturday; noon to 8 P.M.
   Sunday.

Dattes et Noix—"dates and nuts"—is one of the Marais's best *salons de thé,* situated across from the bright gardens of the Parc-Royal and the Musée Carnavalet. The decor consists of stark white tiled floors and contemporary graphics, the service is super-casual, and the *tarte Tatin* and chocolate cake definitely worth making a detour for. Just before lunchtime, French women in the neighbourhood stop in with their children for ice cream and sorbet treats to take home with them.

**LE LOIR DANS
LA THEIERE,**
3 Rue des Rosiers, Paris 4.
(272.90.61).
Métro: Saint-Paul.
Open noon to 7 P.M.
   Tuesday through
   Saturday; 11 A.M. to
   7 P.M. Sunday.
   Closed Monday.

Le Loir Dans la Théière, recalling Lewis Carroll's dormouse in the teapot, doesn't pretend to be anything more than a comfortable place to pass the time of day. The loftlike space, with huge overstuffed *Art Déco* leather chairs, long wooden tables to share

At Brocco, it's café crème.

with neighbours, and a fresh daily assortment of home-made tarts, cakes, and pastries doubles as an art and photo gallery. It's faded and slightly worn, but honest and casual, the kind of place you can take your mother or your children for a most affordable lunch or an unhurried afternoon snack. The lemon tart was deliciously lemony, perfectly fresh. So good, in fact, I asked for the recipe to include in this book.

TARTE AU CITRON LE LOIR DANS LA THEIERE
LE LOIR DANS LA THEIERE'S LEMON TART

A ritual at this cosy tea salon in the Marais is to wander over to the counter where all the pastries are displayed to see what's fresh, and what looks appealing. The only problem is that as soon as you sit down, another fresh dessert arrives from the kitchen, looking even better than the one you ordered. I love lemon (but not as much as chocolate), and this tart really hit the spot the first time I visited Le Loir Dans La Théière. It also brought back Proustian memories of a lemon cookie I used to make as a child. The pastry, with a hint of lemon and almonds, is easy and versatile. You can, if you like, make it several days ahead and refrigerate it.

Pastry:
1 cup plus 2 tablespoons
    (160 g) unbleached
    all-purpose flour
¼ cup (50 g) sugar
¼ cup (35 g) almonds,
    ground to a fine
    powder
Zest (peel) of 1 lemon,
    grated
Pinch of salt
½ cup (4 ounces; 115 g)
    unsalted butter,
    cubed, at room
    temperature
1 egg
1 teaspoon rum
1 teaspoon milk
1 teaspoon unsalted
    butter, for buttering
    tart pan

Filling:
4 eggs
1 cup (200 g) sugar
Zest (peel) of 2 lemons,
    grated
Juice of 2 lemons
1 cup (140 g) almonds,
    ground to a fine
    powder
¾ cup (6 ounces; 170 g)
    unsalted butter, melted

1. Prepare the pastry: In a medium-size bowl, combine the flour, sugar, ground almonds, lemon zest, and salt and mix until well blended. Make a well and add the butter, egg, rum, and milk. Knead until well blended. The pastry should have the consistency of a soft cookie dough. Wrap the pastry with plastic wrap and let it rest in the refrigerator at least 1 hour. Butter a 10½-inch (27 cm) tart pan. Flour your hands and use them to press the pastry into the buttered pan. Set aside.

2. Preheat the oven to 400°F (205°C).

3. Prepare the filling: In a medium-size mixing bowl, combine the eggs, sugar, lemon zest, lemon juice, and ground almonds, and mix until well blended. Add the melted butter, mix again, then pour the filling into the pastry shell.

4. Bake in the centre of the oven for 30 to 40 minutes. Serve at room temperature.

Yield: One 10½- inch (27 cm) tart.

TARTE ABRICOT VERLET
VERLET'S APRICOT TART

Verlet is a tiny tea and coffee shop that also serves good homemade pastries. Anyone who loves apricots will love this simple, homey pie, which takes about twenty minutes to make. Be sure to use fresh, not canned, apricots.

Pastry:
½ cup (4 ounces; 115 g) unsalted butter, melted
½ cup (100 g) sugar
2 cups (260 g) all-purpose flour (do not use unbleached flour)
1 teaspoon unsalted butter, for buttering tart pan

Filling:
5 tablespoons *crème fraîche* or heavy cream (see recipe, page 182), preferably not ultra-pasteurized
1 egg
¼ cup (50 g) sugar
1 tablespoon unbleached all-purpose flour
1 teaspoon vanilla
1 pound (450 g) fresh apricots, pitted and halved
1 tablespoon confectioners' sugar

1. Preheat the oven to 325°F (165°C).

2. Prepare the pastry: In a medium-size bowl mix the butter and sugar together thoroughly, then add the flour and knead by hand until well blended. The pastry will be very crumbly. Butter a 10½-inch (27 cm) tart pan. Using your hands, press the pastry into the buttered pan and bake in the preheated oven for 10 minutes.

3. Meanwhile, prepare the filling: In a small bowl combine the *crème fraîche* and egg, and mix until well blended. Add the sugar, mix well, then add the flour and vanilla. Pour the mixture into the pre-baked pastry shell and arrange the apricots, cut side down, on top of the cream mixture.

4. Bake in the centre of the oven for 30 minutes, or until a knife inserted in the cream comes out clean. Cool and serve at room temperature, preferably within an hour of baking. Sprinkle with confectioners' sugar just before serving.

Yield: One 10½-inch (27 cm) tart.

LATIN QUARTER, LUXEMBOURG, SEVRES-BABYLONE, ECOLE MILITAIRE
5th, 6th, and 7th arrondissements

LE SALON BELUSA,
86 Rue du Cherche-Midi, Paris 6.
(222.52.58).
Métro: Sèvres-Babylone.
Open noon to 6 P.M.
Closed Sunday.

Everything is for sale at La Belusa, a funky little tearoom that doubles as an antique shop, of sorts. Decorated a bit like grandmother's front parlour, with oriental rugs, an odd assortment of paintings, and an upright piano, this cosy little shop does display that special brand of Rue du Cherche-Midi snobbiness, but the homey atmosphere and selection of antique china and teatime-related bric-a-brac make it an agreeable spot for a late afternoon pause. The hot chocolate is almost as thick as chocolate *mousse,* and the chocolate Linzer torte is heartily delicious.

**A LA COUR
DE ROHAN,**
59-61 Rue Saint-André-
des-Arts, Paris 6.
(325.79.67).
Métro: Odéon.
Open noon to 7:30 P.M.
Tuesday through Friday;
3 P.M. to 7:30 P.M.
Saturday and Sunday.
Closed Monday and the
month of August.

At first glance A la Cour de Rohan, in a *passage* near the Odéon Métro, looks more like a chic decorating boutique than a tea salon. But wander inside and you'll find a superb, English country-style salon decorated in white and various shades of green. The aromas of Darjeeling and *gâteau Opéra,* and the soothing sounds of classical music, make you want to settle in for the afternoon. If it happens to be available that day, sample the fine pear tart flavoured with almonds, selected from a round table in the centre of the room. A La Cour de Rohan offers live classical music concerts on occasional Friday evenings.

**LA MOSQUEE
DE PARIS,**
1 Rue Daubenton and
39 Rue Geoffroy-Saint-
Hilaire, Paris 5.
(331.18.14).
Métro: Censier-Daubenton.
Open daily, 11 A.M. to 8 P.M.

From a brilliant tree-shaded garden move into darkness, entering a mysterious, atmospheric Moorish-style tearoom. As a single waiter makes the rounds, carrying trays filled with tiny glasses of sweet mint tea and flaky pastries, settle back on one of the fabric-covered banquettes and soak in the ambience. It doesn't pay to be in a hurry, so bring a book or a friend to help you admire the marble-tiled floors, colourful glass windows, and otherwise exotic decor. The salon is attached to the first mosque to be erected in France.

LE PETIT BOULE,
16 Avenue de la Motte-
Picquet, Paris 7.
(551.77.48).
Métro: La Tour-Maubourg.
Open 10:30 A.M. to 7 P.M.
Wednesday through
Sunday; 2:30 P.M. to
7 P.M. Tuesday. Closed
Monday.

Near the Ecole Militaire, Le Petit Boulé is one of Paris's more refreshingly original tea salons. Every detail is attended to with tasteful care, and it's no surprise to find that this Russian-accented tea and pastry shop is in the hands of the Petrossian family of salmon and caviar fame, who impart to everything they touch a flair and perfection.

Here, in a sun-kissed atmosphere peppered with Victorian wicker chairs, tiny marble-topped tables, mirrored walls, and frosted glass *Art Déco* chandeliers, pastries are displayed like jewels. Mounds of golden, glazed *croissants,* bamboo trays filled with hearty, round *piroshki* (meat and cabbage filled turnovers), and tiny fruit tarts form an inviting window display. At lunchtime, there is, of course, salmon and blinis, caviar and vodka. After relishing the house specialities and admiring the refined decor, take home one of the more than thirty varieties of tea, superb *miel de sarrasin* (buckwheat honey), or the unusual and delicious *confiture de kumquat,* just a few of the dozens of jams, vegetable purées, and rustic dishes from France's southwest prepared under the Petrossians' direction.

PONS,
2 Place Edmond-Rostand,
  Paris 6.
(329.31.10).
Métro: Luxembourg.
Open 9:15 A.M. to 7 P.M.
  Closed Sunday, the last
  week in July, and the
  first three weeks in
  August.

After a walk through the Luxembourg gardens settle in at Pons, an aristocratic, old-world tea salon with a rambling terrace facing the park greenery and the stunning fountain at Place Edmond-Rostand. The snooty young waitresses in red plaid uniforms act as though they'd rather be elsewhere, but overlook that because in the summertime this is one of the classiest people-watching spots in town. In winter, go at about 10 A.M., mount the curving stairway to the tearoom, take a table overlooking the gardens, order up a steaming cup of smoky Chinese tea, and enjoy a yeasty little *brioche* in stately silence.

GATEAU AU CHOCOLAT LA TCHAIKA
LA TCHAIKA'S CHOCOLATE CAKE

All good chocolate cakes are by their very nature "sinful." This one is more sinful than most. It's usually on the pastry tray at La Tchaïka, where the young and the old linger, unable to decide between it and vatrouchka, the Russian version of cheesecake. The chef varies the amount of chocolate in the cake according to her mood. I always make it with the full 14 ounces of bittersweet chocolate.

Cake:
10½ to 14 ounces (295 to
  395 g) bittersweet
  chocolate (preferably
  Lindt or Tobler brand)
6 eggs, separated
¾ cup (100 g)
  confectioners' sugar
1 cup (140 g) almonds,
  ground to a fine
  powder
1 tablespoon cornstarch
¾ cup (6 ounces; 170 g)
  unsalted butter at
  room temperature
Pinch of salt
1 teaspoon unsalted
  butter, for buttering
  cake pan

Icing:
3½ ounces (100 g)
  bittersweet chocolate,
  broken into small bits
½ cup (125 ml) *crème
  fraîche* (see recipe, page
  182)

1. Preheat the oven to 375°F (190°C).

2. In a small saucepan, over very low heat, melt the chocolate with 3 tablespoons water.

3. In a medium-size bowl beat the egg yolks with the sugar until pale lemon-coloured. Add the next ingredients to the egg yolk mixture in the following order, mixing well after each addition: the melted chocolate, the sugar, ground almonds, cornstarch, and butter. Set aside.

4. In a second bowl, beat the egg whites with the pinch of salt until stiff but not dry.

5. Add one third of the egg white mixture to the chocolate batter and fold in gently but thoroughly. Then gently fold in the remaining whites. Don't overmix, but be sure the mixture is well blended.

6. Butter an 8½-inch (22 cm) springform pan and fill it with the batter. Bake for 35 to 40 minutes in the oven, or until the top of the cake is firm and springy. Cool before unmolding, and when completely cooled, make the icing.

7. Prepare the icing: In a small saucepan, bring the *crème fraîche* to a boil over low heat. Reduce the heat and add the chocolate, bit by bit, stirring until it is all melted. Remove from the heat and let cool. The icing should have the consistency of a thick but spreadable frosting. (If the icing hardens before the cake is frosted, reheat gently, until it reaches the proper consistency.) Cover the top and sides with a thin layer of icing.

Yield: One 8½-inch (22 cm) cake.

Always a smile and a warm welcome at La Tchaïka.

LA TCHAIKA, ✓
9 Rue de l'Eperon, Paris 6.
(354.47.02).
Métro: Odéon.
Open 11:30 A.M. to
10:30 P.M. Closed
Sunday, Monday, and
the month of August.

This welcoming, homey little tea salon and restaurant next to the Maison du Livre Etranger is a personal favourite, for lunch or a relaxing afternoon tea. The intimate, Russian-style living room is decorated with finds from flea markets and Victorian attics and includes fabric coverings in warm shades of red. Stony portraits of Chekhov and Tolstoy hang on the walls, and a crisp white mobile of a *tchaïka* (seagull) adds a touch of whimsy.

Although one can easily drop in (with reservations) for a quick lunch or dinner, La Tchaïka has the cosy, drawing room quality that allows, even encourages lingering. The food here is good, honest, fresh, and consistent, and guests can partake of a bowl of hot soup and a glass of wine, or a full-fledged meal. There's a hot *plat du jour* each day, and La Tchaïka offers the standard repertoire of *zakouskis* (Russian appetizers), including excellent tarama, herring, sprats, and chicken liver pâté, along with salmon, caviar, and of course Russian vodka. I always order the borscht (see recipe, below), which is the best I know, consisting of a blend of rich meat stock, beets, and white cabbage, enlivened with vinegar and chopped dill. The blinis are buttermilky fresh and good served with smoked salmon from the house of Petrossian.

Desserts are irresistible. At Eastertime there's the classic *pashka,* a fruit and nut filled cheesecake, and year-round there's a remarkable flourless chocolate cake (see recipe, page 104), a rich blend of bitter chocolate, almonds, eggs, butter, and sugar. And the *vatrouchka,* the Russian torte of *fromage blanc* (better known as cheesecake) is feather light and not overly sweet.

BORSCHT LA TCHAIKA
LA TCHAIKA'S BEET AND CABBAGE SOUP

This is a tart, refreshing version of the popular Russian soup, with its blend of cabbage, broth, and beets, enlivened with fresh dill and a touch of vinegar. It's the sort of soup M.F.K. Fisher calls "a little borscht" as opposed to one that's long and complicated to prepare.

The first time I sampled this soup at La Tchaïka, I also ordered cassis, a crisp, cool white Provençal wine, and found the contrast in colours and temperature most refreshing. At home, I enjoy it with a chilled Loire Valley white, such as Sancerre or Pouilly Fumé, and crusty rye bread.

In France, the soup takes about twenty minutes to prepare, since the beets found in French markets are already cooked. The soup can be made ahead and reheated or served cold. At La Tchaïka, the chef, Maud Seligmann, prepares it with beef broth, but I've found any good meat or poultry stock will do. In a pinch, I've used goose stock and it was delicious. Traditionally, the soup is served with a dollop of crème fraîche floating in the centre of the bowl.

2 tablespoons unsalted butter
½ medium cabbage, very finely grated
2 quarts (2 litres) warm meat or poultry stock
1 large beet, cooked and julienned
3 tablespoons fresh dill, finely minced
¼ cup (60 ml) best quality red wine vinegar
Salt to taste
¼ cup (60 ml) *crème fraîche* (see recipe, page 182) or sour cream (optional)

1. In a large skillet melt the butter over low heat. Add the cabbage and cook until wilted. Do not let it brown.

2. Add the warm stock, then the beets, and cook over medium heat for 15 minutes. Add the dill, vinegar, and salt. Taste and adjust seasoning if necessary. Serve hot, with *crème fraîche*, if desired.

Yield: 4 servings.

CONCORDE, MADELEINE, PIGALLE
8th and 9th arrondissements

LADUREE,
16 Rue Royale, Paris 8.
(260.21.79).
Métro: Madeleine.
Open 8:30 A.M. to 7 P.M.
 Closed Sunday and the
 month of August.

Until I discovered the delights of Ladurée one day at ten in the morning, I could not have cared less about morning *croissants*. But after visiting some sixty *salons de thé* throughout Paris, it's the frothy cup of *café au lait* and the flaky, yeasty *croissants* of Ladurée near the Place de la Madeleine that return in my dreams.

Can there be any early morning atmosphere more elegantly Parisian in tone? There's the hushed and intimate turn-of-the-century decor, with pale olive wood-panelled walls, straightback chairs, tiny marble-topped tables, curt waitresses in frilly white aprons, and a clientele that's equally at home at Cartier and the Ritz. The air is not snobbish, just a bit blasé, and while the sandwiches wouldn't keep a bird alive, the pastries are deliciously fresh and I've not found a better cup of *café au lait* in Paris. The chewy, almondy almost marzipan *financiers* (almond cakes) are a little taste of heaven.

Before leaving, examine the ceiling mural in the main floor salon: Angels float through the pastel clouds, as one pink-faced cherub wearing a chef's white toque bakes his pastries by the intense heat of the sun.

**MARQUISE DE
SEVIGNE,**
32 Place de la Madeleine,
 Paris 8.
(265.19.47).
Métro: Madeleine,
Open 9:45 A.M. to 7 P.M.
 Closed Sunday.

Next door at Fauchon, the "tearoom" has all the atmosphere and charm of a Greyhound bus station coffee counter. In contrast, Marquise de Sévigné, a combination chocolate shop and tearoom, is subdued and tranquil, a fine spot for resting with a superb cup of coffee and one of a dozen or so different desserts, most of them chocolate. Avoid the *gâteau au chocolat*: To me it tasted of cooked milk. Have instead the outstanding chocolate praline cake or the plain macaroons, which have little competition in this pastry-filled capital.

PENY,
3 Place de la Madeleine,
 Paris 8.
(265.06.75).
Métro: Madeleine.
Open 8 A.M. to 8 P.M.
 Closed Sunday and the
 month of August.

The best tables at Peny (also known as Penny) are the ones out on the pavement facing the Place de la Madeleine. Although this popular summertime spot looks more like an ordinary café, it merits tea salon status thanks to its fresh sweet coconut cake, a nostalgic favourite among Americans transplanted to Paris.

TEA FOLLIES,
6 Place Gustave-Toudouze,
  Paris 9.
(280.08.44).
Métro: Saint-Georges.
Open noon to 7 P.M.
  Monday through
  Saturday; 12:30 P.M. to
  7 P.M. Sunday. Closed
  first two weeks in
  August.

Bright, friendly, and casual, a stop at Tea Follies is like having an impeccable afternoon tea on a front porch, strewn with stacks of local newspapers and magazines and fresh flowers. The contemporary red, white, and gray tea salon opens out onto the tree-filled Place Gustave-Toudouze in the 9th *arrondissement*, and in good weather tables spread out onto the sidewalk for sunning, gossip, and delicious lemon curd tarts. There's also a nice selection of wines, and on Sunday brunch is offered with a cuisine that suggests English and American influences.

TORAYA,
12 Rue Saint-Florentin,
  Paris 8.
(260.13.00).
Métro: Concorde.
Open 10 A.M. to 7 P.M.
  Closed Sunday.

The miniature pastries and handmade ceramics are displayed like diamonds in a jeweller's window; the spotless decor is a sober, modern blend of black, gray, and white. Toraya is an authentic, contemporary Japanese tea salon, complete with white ceramic cups used for *matcha* (the ceremonial Japanese green tea), frothy, almost bitter, and whisked to a foam. To most Western palates the pastries look much better than they taste, but the adventuresome will want to try the tiny, multi-coloured variations made of *adzuki* bean purée, or the little leaf-wrapped balls of sticky rice. It's a lot cheaper than a trip to Tokyo, and a nice exotic touch for those with little enthusiasm for pastries laden with Western cream and sugar.

TROCADERO
16th arrondissement

CARETTE,
4 Place du Trocadéro,
  Paris 16.
(727.88.56).
Métro: Trocadéro.
Open 8 A.M. to 7 P.M.
  Closed Tuesday, the last
  week of July, and the
  first three weeks of
  August.

By nine in the morning this spacious, terraced tea salon facing the Trocadéro swarms with handsome male joggers who come for a little after-run nourishment. It's not unusual to see a trim, well-muscled Frenchman down two *pains au chocolat*, a couple of glasses of freshly squeezed orange juice, and a *café au lait* in record time, as he buries his nose in the French sporting journal *l'Equipe*. The *pain au chocolat* is yeasty and fresh and the smoky Chinese tea first rate, but the *financier* is better left to someone else. Don't bother in the afternoons, unless you enjoy being asphyxiated by a cigarette-induced haze.

Bistros à Vin
WINE BARS

A toast to good times.

Enter the land of bread and Beaujolais, cheese and *charcuterie*. Known as *bistros à vin* (wine bars), most of these cosy, neighbourhood spots open about the time much of Paris is rising for breakfast. From the exterior many resemble ordinary cafés, yet once you've entered and sipped a glass of silky, scented Fleurie or fresh and fragrant Sancerre, and sampled an open-face sandwich of garlic and thyme-flecked *rillettes* (spreadable pork or goose pâté) on thick sourdough bread, you understand the difference.

There is always food and conviviality, but more important, there is wine—by the glass, the carafe, the bottle. Light and fruity Beaujolais is king, but one also finds delicate Bourgueil from Touraine; young wines from Bordeaux, Chinon, and Côtes-du-Rhône; the Loire Valley's delicious Muscadet; the Jura's white and pleasant Arbois; and the heady, vigorous Gigondas. Obviously, not every wine bar stocks every wine, but most offer from a dozen to thirty wines at from four to twenty francs a glass, along with—at the very least—cold platters of cheese or *charcuterie* designed to complement the house selection. Most are casual affairs with no printed menu, but wine selections and daily specials are usually handwritten on blackboards set behind the bar.

Is there any reason to go to a wine bar rather than a café for a glass of wine? Categorically, yes. The wine sold in most cafés is mass-produced and banal, some of it not even French in origin (though so designated), and much of it watery and undrinkable. The wine sold in wine bars is usually carefu'ly chosen by the *bistrotiers* (owners), most often dedicated men who are passionate about wine. When not behind the bar, many of them are travelling the country in search of good little wines. Usually their selections are shipped directly to the wine bar in barrels (it's cheaper that way) and the *bistrotier* bottles them himself, storing the excess in basementlike caves beneath the bar.

The food—simple and unpretentious as it may be—is chosen with the same care. Most offer platters of French cheese, several kinds of hams, sausages, and pâtés, and bread, often either Lionel or Max Poilâne's famous country loaf (see recipe, page 158), redolent of sourdough and fresh from their huge, wood-fired ovens. Sometimes, homey pâtés, *quiches,* or dessert tarts—all dishes chosen to go perfectly with the house wines—are prepared by the owner's wife. Some wine bars offer even heartier fare, such as wintry *daubes* (stews), platters of cooked sausages, and *confit d'oie* (preserved goose). As one *bistrotier* put it, "Wine is made to go with food. Tasting wine alone should be left to the experts."

Best of all, wine bars serve as a tasting and testing ground for wines yet to be discovered, as well as for familiar favourites. Since many wine bars offer little-known, small production wines by the glass, this is the time to acquaint oneself with those such as Montlouis or Quarts de Chaume, both whites from the Loire; or to sample several of the nine *cru* Beaujolais, perhaps a Moulin-à-Vent, a Juliénas, and a Chiroubles, side by side.

While years ago, most wine bars specialized in the young, inexpensive quaffing wines, today the trendier, more formal "English style," wine bars—such as Willi's, the Blue Fox Bar, and L'Ecluse—offer a wider selection, including older vintages and those from more noble vineyards.

Dozens of wine bars pepper the streets of Paris. Here are a few special ones, a choice selection for a quick lunch, a pleasant afternoon interlude, or a late-night snack. They present a good alternative to a fully-fledged meal, a sort of drinkable feast or indoor picnic. One should lunch well for 40 to 120 francs depending on selections. The most popular spots are very crowded at lunchtime, but if you go early, at noon, or late, at around 2:30, you're likely to get a seat and still enjoy the atmosphere.

LES HALLES, PALAIS-ROYAL, LOUVRE
1st arrondissement

**LA CLOCHE
DES HALLES,**
28 Rue Coquillière,
Paris 1.
(236.93.89).
Métro: Les Halles.
Open 7:30 A.M. to 10 P.M.
Closed Sunday.

WINES:
Morgon, Brouilly, Beaujolais-Villages, Côtes-du-Rhône, white and rosé Sancerre, Sauternes.

SPECIALITIES:
Charcuterie, goat cheese.

This pleasant little wine bar takes its name from the *cloche* (bronze bell) that once was used to note the opening and closing of the neighbouring Les Halles wholesale market, which was demolished in the 1970s. But the area is as lively as ever, and La Cloche des Halles still serves as the neighbourhood wine bar for the many meat, vegetable, and poultry merchants who prefer to remain in the area.

HEART OF THE MATTER

Most wine bars open early in the morning to accommodate the Frenchmen—nearly 5 percent of the population—who indulge in a spiritous breakfast, a practice known as *tuer le ver,* or "killing the worm."

According to legend, a certain madame, the wife of Monsieur de la Varende, died suddenly as a result of a worm gnawing away at her heart. An autopsy was performed, the worm was still alive, and all attempts to kill the creature failed. Finally, someone doused the worm with white wine, bringing about its quick demise. Quite logically, the moral of the story is: A glass of wine early in the day will keep the worms at bay.

**CAFE-TABAC
HENRI IV,**
13 Place du Pont-Neuf,
Paris 1.
(354.27.90).
Métro: Pont-Neuf.
Open 11:30 A.M. to 9:30
P.M. Closed Saturday,
Sunday, the month of
August, and holidays.
Reservations recommended.

WINES:
Beaujolais-Villages, Morgon, Fleurie, Loire Valley, Sancerre, Muscadet-sur-Lie.

SPECIALITIES:
Charcuterie and cheese platters.

Opposite the statue of its namesake Henri IV, this tobacco shop offers that certain grubby, old-fashioned Parisian charm, where men sit reading *Le Monde* or *France Soir* as they munch on *tartines* of goose *rillettes* and sip a glass of hearty Morgon. This is the place to stop and sample such seldom found wines as the sweet Montlouis, or golden Quarts de Chaume, both Loire Valley whites. Meilleur Pot winner in 1960.

Raising a glass with a friend.

LE RUBIS,
10 Rue du Marché-Saint-
  Honoré, Paris 1.
(261.03.34).
Métro: Tuileries.
Open 7 A.M. to 10 P.M.
  Closed Saturday, Sunday,
  and the month of
  August.
Hot meals at lunch only.

WINES:
Beaujolais, Brouilly, Morgon,
Chiroubles, Juliénas, Côtes-
du-Rhône, Bordeaux,
Muscadet, Anjou, Bourgueil.

SPECIALITIES:
Sandwiches, rillettes,
charcuterie, cheese, and ham
and cheese omelettes. Hot daily
special.

A classic, happy sort of bustling wine bar, where lunch is a free-for-all as clients stand five and six deep at the bar, dodging waiters and nudging neighbours. In good weather, you can lunch outside, standing at the huge wine barrels that serve as makeshift tables. Meilleur Pot winner in 1963.

MEILLEUR POT

The annual "Meilleur Pot" award designates the elite in Parisian wine bars. The travelling trophy—named after the traditional half-litre (about 17-ounce) Beaujolais *pot*, or jug—is awarded to *bistrotiers* who carry on the tradition of searching out and buying good French wines direct from the producer. The *bistrotier* then bottles the wines himself, and serves them over the counter, by the glass or by the bottle.

The award, begun in Paris in 1957, is given to the *bistrotier* himself, not his establishment. If he sells or moves on, the title goes with him, right into retirement. Only one award is given each year.

Judging takes place from April to December, when a jury of ten makes anonymous visits to various Parisian wine bars. At the end of December or beginning of January, a formal award ceremony is held and the current titleholder relinquishes the trophy, handing it to the new season's winner.

WILLI'S WINE BAR,
13 Rue des Petits-Champs,
  Paris 1.
(261.05.09).
Métro: Pyramides.
Bar open 11 A.M. to 10:30
  P.M.; restaurant open
  12:15 P.M. to 2:30 P.M.
  and 7:15 P.M. to 10
  P.M. Closed Saturday
  and Sunday.
Lunch reservations
  recommended.

WINES:
Excellent selection of Côtes-du-
Rhône.

SPECIALITIES:
Salads, platters of ham and
cheese, and a hot plat du jour.

The most refined and chic wine bar in Paris, with the snobbiest clientele. But if you're seeking an introduction to the delights of the many undiscovered wines of the Côtes-du-Rhône, take a deep breath and cut through the crowd of sheepdogs and bronzed and beautiful people to sample the bold, rich, well-balanced Hermitage of Gérard Chave, or Georges Bernard's dry, fruity Tavel, the rosé many consider the best in the world. Food here serves simply as a background for the wines, though some care is taken to provide an ever-changing selection of hot daily specials and a good variety of salads. The bread, unfortunately, is totally inedible. (Wine bars *should* serve good bread!) Willi himself—the Englishman Mark Williamson—will help you place your order for wines by the glass or the bottle. Willi's is bright, airy, and pleasantly decorated with a highly polished wood bar, and just a block from the tranquil, 18th-century gardens of the Palais-Royal and a few minutes walk from the Louvre and Place de l'Opéra. English is spoken.

WILLI'S WINE BAR,
18 Rue des Halles, Paris 1.
(236.81.80).
Métro: Châtelet.
Open noon to 2:30 P.M.
  and 8 P.M. to 10:30
  P.M. Closed Saturday
  and Sunday.

This is Willi's II, the younger brother of the Willi's on Rue des Petits-Champs. Same wines, same atmosphere, similar decor.

MARAIS, BASTILLE, ILE SAINT-LOUIS
4th and 11th arrondissements

AU FRANC PINOT,
1 Quai de Bourbon,
  Paris 4.
(329.46.98).
Métro: Pont-Marie.
Open 11:30 A.M. to 2:30
  P.M. and 6 P.M. to
  11:30 P.M. Closed
  Sunday and Monday.

WINES:
Beaujolais, Sancerre, Graves,
Rully, Côtes du Jura.

SPECIALITIES:
Platters of cheese, dried or
smoked meats, salmon and
salads.

This landmark wine bar, hidden behind black wrought-iron gates, is a bit dark and often deserted, but it's a nice, quiet place to rest after wandering about Ile Saint-Louis, the Marais, or Notre-Dame. Service is friendly and the daily selection of wines and luncheon items is chalked up on a big blackboard. Good choices: the simple *tartine* of Crottin de Chavignol goat cheese, or the delicious salad of sliced lamb and greens tossed with walnut oil dressing.

JACQUES MELAC,

42 Rue Léon-Frot,
Paris 11.
(370.59.27).
Métro: Charonne.
Open 8:30 A.M. to 7 P.M.
Wednesday, Friday, and
Saturday; 8:30 A.M. to
midnight Tuesday and
Thursday. Closed
Sunday, Monday, and
the month of July.
Reservations recommended.
Hot meal at lunch and on
Tuesday evenings.
Wines may be purchased to
take home.

WINES:
Beaujolais, Chinon, Saint-
Joseph, Gigondas, Cahors, red
Rully, Sancerre, Sauternes,
Côtes du Jura, Vin Jaune,
Lirac.

SPECIALITIES:
From the Auvergne region,
including hot daily specials,
and regional cheese, such as
Bleu des Causses, Saint-Nectaire,
Laguiole, and goat cheese.

The most authentic and one of the liveliest wine bars in Paris. Found just west of the Place de la Bastille, in the 11th *arrondissement,* a working man's quarter filled with cabinetmakers and artisans, this bar is run by Jacques Mélac, an outgoing, energetic *patron.* A proud Auvergnat, he could have walked right out of central casting, with his handlebar moustache, nonstop chatter, and genuine pride in the food and wine offered in his tiny, five-table establishment. He obviously has such a great time doing what he does that no one could leave this corner bar feeling sad.

If there's any question about what you're to do at Jacques Mélac's, signs that hang on the walls will tell you: "If you want water, you must place your order the day before," advises one handwritten poster. Another reminds clients that "Water is reserved for cooking potatoes." Coffee is sold reluctantly and lemonade is reserved for children under eleven years of age.

At lunchtime, the place takes on the frenzy of the stock exchange at the height of trading as workers, businessmen, and secretaries crowd about the bar, or vie for a rickety stool around one of the red oilcloth-covered tables in order to take in the day's meaty specials. One day the dish might be a rustic platter of boiled beef tongue, accompanied by tiny potatoes in a delicate mustard sauce. The omelets are creamy and

delicious, and Jacques Mélac offers several regional wines not easily found outside France, including the Jura's sherrylike Vin Jaune.

The wine bar, which won the Meilleur Pot in 1982, serves as a wine shop as well. Diners can pick a bottle right off the shelf for sampling and, if it suits their tastes, they can buy a bottle or a case as they leave. Mélac's is also the only Paris wine bar with its own "vineyard"—vines rise along the exterior walls of the bar, and a celebratory harvest is held each fall.

Jacques Mélac, a proud, outgoing patron (facing page), takes a break with the crew (right).

LA TARTINE,
24 Rue de Rivoli, Paris 4.
(272.76.85).
Métro: Saint-Paul.
Open 7:30 A.M. to 10 P.M.
  Closed Tuesday and the
  month of August.
Cold meals only.

W I N E S :
Beaujolais, Touraine, Anjou, Loire Valley, Burgundy, Côtes-du-Rhône.

S P E C I A L I T I E S :
Tartines (open-face sandwiches) of charcuterie, and Crottin de Chavignol goat cheese.

If this was in the United States, not Paris, you'd call La Tartine a luncheonette. But this is Paris and La Tartine is a wine bar in the oldest sense of the word. (In fact, La Tartine has been called a "café for wine drinkers.") It's an authentic working man's hangout— meaning men and women—and at lunchtime the crowds gather to share modest platters of wafer-thin slices of *jambon de Paris,* the pale-coloured ham that's cured in a salt brine, then cooked. It's the ham most commonly found in Paris cafés and usually goes into the *sandwich mixte,* a ham and cheese sandwich served on a French *baguette.*

Everyone here seems to know the red-haired waitress who single-handedly coordinates the orders from the twenty or so tables bunched together in this dim, antique bar. Above the general din can be heard shouts of "Suzette, Suzette," as workers call out for a *double express* before rushing back to the streets and the office. La Tartine offers a broad range of wines, with some

30,000 bottles stashed away in the downstairs *cave.* More than thirty wines are available by the glass, all noted on the little board that hangs behind the bar. Worth sampling here: firm and fragrant Crottin de Sancerre, the young goat cheese from the Loire Valley, best enjoyed with the crisp white Sancerre wine. Nice before or after a visit to the Marais: This is the neighbourhood once frequented by Eastern European refugees, and Trotsky lived right around the corner, on Rue Ferdinand Duval. Meilleur Pot winner in 1965.

LUXEMBOURG, SAINT-MICHEL, SEVRES-BABYLONE, ECOLE MILITAIRE
5th, 6th, and 7th arrondissements

L'ECLUSE,
15 Quai des Grands-
   Augustins, Paris 6.
(633.58.74).
Métro: Saint-Michel.
Open noon to 2 A.M.
   Closed Sunday.
Meals served all day.
Lunch reservations
   recommended.

WINES:
Red and white Bordeaux, from châteaux grand and small.

SPECIALITIES:
Daily plat du jour, foie gras, smoked salmon, goat cheese, chocolate cake.

If you ever wondered whether members of a food chain of any sort can remain charming, chic, and retain at least a semblance of authenticity, the answer is yes. Over the past several years, little L'Ecluses have popped up all over Paris, following the same formula that made this first L'Ecluse, on Quai des Grands-Augustins, a success.

The decor, menu, and style are the same in each, and each appeals to a largely well-heeled international business clientele. *Belle Epoque* posters, converted gas lamps, a long wooden bar and mirrored walls give L'Ecluse a turn-of-the-century atmosphere, though the food and wine are totally up-to-date. Note, however, that a meal here will not be cheap. Service tends to be slow, perhaps intentionally. The first glass of wine comes quickly, and it's likely to be consumed by the time your snack or meal arrives. So if you think you might want more than one glass, order a carafe or a bottle—it will be less expensive in the long run.

Don't come here looking for Beaujolais; this is Bordeaux country. You may choose from more than seventy château-bottled Bordeaux, with some eighteen of these wines offered by the glass on a list that changes every three weeks. Good bets: a slice of *foie gras* and a glass of either Sauternes or Barsac; a plate of *carpaccio* with a young red Bordeaux; and then a slice of fudgy *gâteau au chocolat,* with a cup of thick, black *express.* Open into the early morning hours, L'Ecluse is good for late-night snacks, especially after the theatre, opera, or cinema.

**CAFE DE LA
NOUVELLE MAIRIE,**
19 Rue des Fossés-Saint-
Jacques, Paris 5.
(326.80.18).
Métro: Luxembourg.
Open noon to 9 P.M.
Closed Saturday and
Sunday.
Cold meals only.

WINES:
*Beaujolais, Chinon, Cabernet
de Touraine, Saint-Nicolas-de-
Bourgueil, Gamay.*

SPECIALITIES:
*Tartines of pâté de foie de porc
(pork liver pâté), saucisson,
jambon cru (salt-cured ham),
and Camembert.*

This is Paris's quintessential wine bar, set on one of the prettiest neighbourhood squares on the Left Bank. A bright cream and burgundy awning—proudly announcing owner Bernard Pontonnier's 1983 Meilleur Pot award—will lure you over, and once inside you'll find a democratic blend of workers, journalists, musicians, and even the popular neighbourhood *boulanger* from right across the street. This place is real and unpretentious—all is very simple and straightforward—from the hearty, fresh *tartines* of *pâté de foie de porc* to the lively, fruity young Beaujolais. In the summertime, tables are moved onto the pavement, and though the official closing time is 9 P.M., regulars often stay on well beyond that. Be forewarned: Many come for one drink and never leave.

*A sip of Beaujolais and a
tartine—pure pleasure.*

PETIT BACCHUS,
13 Rue du Cherche-Midi,
Paris 6.
(544.01.07).
Métro: Sèvres-Babylone.
Open 9:45 A.M. to 7:30
P.M. Closed Sunday and
July 15 to August 15.
Wine bar open at lunch
only, Monday through
Friday.
Wines may be purchased to
take home.

WINES:
*Variety of young regional
French wines.*

SPECIALITIES:
Sausages, pâtés, cheese.

This is the neighbourhood of *"bon chic, bon genre,"* and each week Jean-Marie Picard, the owner of this combination wine bar and wine shop offers three different wines for lunchtime tasting. The wines, usually a choice of two reds and one white, are selected from the inexpensive assortment of good little wines from every region of France and are sold by the bottle in this tiny shop. Though Petit Bacchus is small—there are half a dozen stools at the bar—this is a fine place for sampling just a glass of wine, a platter of Auvergnat sausages or pâtés, seasonal cheese, and homemade desserts prepared by Picard's wife, when the spirit moves her. The owner travels year-round in France to select wines for the shop, and says he's visited every wine region in the country, except for Muscadet. Each Saturday afternoon in fall and winter, Petit Bacchus invites a different winemaker in to meet clients, offer free tastings, and talk about his wines. "Winemakers are often isolated," says Picard. "They need to know how their wines are received by the public. Likewise, once you've met a winemaker, you have a special link to that wine."

SANCERRE,
22 Avenue Rapp, Paris 7.
(551.75.91).
Métro: Ecole Militaire.
Open 8:30 A.M. to 8:30
P.M. Monday through
Friday; until 4:30 P.M.
Saturday. Closed Sunday.
Wines may be purchased to
take home.

WINE:
Sancerre.

SPECIALITIES:
Crottin de Chavignol goat
cheese, omelets.

This is a low-key, casual little wine bar, with the folkloric decor of the wonderful little wine village of Sancerre, about 125 miles from Paris. The dry, flinty white Sancerre wine from Domaine la Moussière is featured here, along with its perfect mate, the dry, sometimes sharp Crottin de Chavignol goat cheese. The wine bar is popular with workers from the French television studios located nearby.

AU SAUVIGNON,
80 Rue des Saints-Pères,
Paris 7.
(548.49.02).
Métro: Sèvres-Babylone.
Open 9 A.M. to 11 P.M.
Closed Sunday and the
month of August.
Cold meals only.

WINES:
Beaujolais, Burgundy, Saint-
Emilion, rosé Sancerre, Rosé
d'Anjou, Quincy, Riesling.

SPECIALITIES:
Charcuterie platters, jambon
D'Auvergne (dry-cured
country ham), dried sausages,
Cantal.

Au Sauvignon is one of the city's tiniest and most chic wine bars, just steps from the popular Bon Marché department store and Left Bank boutiques. Like many other bars, it's high on Beaujolais hype come November 15, the first day of sale of Beaujolais *primeur,* the year's new Beaujolais. Walls are plastered with maps of wine routes throughout France and posters reading "Vive le Beaujolais." Walking into the bright blue and yellow Au Sauvignon is like walking up against a stage set: The place is so narrow and small you walk four steps inside the door and you hit the back wall. In summer, there is rarely a seat available on the tiny terrace. Still, this is a good place to stop for a quick lunch or late-afternoon snack, to sample Beaujolais or wines from Alsace and Saint-Emilion with *pâté de porc* or *jambon d'Auvergne.* Meilleur Pot winner in 1961.

MADELEINE, CHAMPS-ELYSEES, GRANDS BOULEVARDS
8th arrondissement

BLUE FOX BAR,
25 Rue Royale (Cité
Berryer; enter between
23 and 25 Rue Royale)
Paris 8.
(265.10.72).
Métro: Madeleine.
Bar open 11 A.M. to 11
P.M.; restaurant open
noon to 3 P.M. and 7
P.M. to 11 P.M. Closed
Saturday evening and
Sunday.
Hot meal at lunch in
winter, otherwise cold
meals only.
No reservations.

WINES:
Fifteen different French wines,
by the glass, each day.

SPECIALITIES:
Mixed salads, cheese, desserts.

L'ECLUSE,
15 Place de la Madeleine,
Paris 8.
(265.34.69).
Métro: Madeleine.
Open noon to 2 A.M.
Closed Sunday.
(See L'Ecluse, 6th
arrondissement, page 116.)

L'ECLUSE,
64 Rue Francois-1er,
Paris 8.
(720.77.09).
Métro: Franklin-D.-
Roosevelt.
Open daily, noon to 2 A.M.
(See L'Ecluse, 6th
arrondissement, page 116.)

At Au Sauvignon, it's smiles
(right) and toasts (facing
page) when the new Beaujolais
arrives.

One of my favourite wine bars; chic without being pretentious, offering simple salads, an exciting selection of not-too-expensive wines by the glass, and always a high-fashion, international crowd, ideal for people watching. Service here is often so casual that it borders on nonexistent, but go when you're in a patient mood, and a good glass of wine will help you put on a happy face. The bar is always lively, and crowded, especially on Tuesday and Friday, when the open-air market along Cité Berryer is in full swing. English spoken.

MA BOURGOGNE,
133 Boulevard Haussmann,
    Paris 8.
(563.50.61).
Métro: Miromesnil.
Open 7 A.M. to 8:30 P.M.
    Closed Saturday and the
    month of August.
Hot meals at lunch only.
Lunch reservations
    recommended.

WINES:
Beaujolais, Chénas, Juliénas,
Fleurie, Moulin-à-Vent,
Mâcon, Sancerre, Pouilly-
Fumé, Rully.

SPECIALITIES:
Jambon du Morvan (country
ham), jambon persillé
(parsleyed ham mould), goat
cheese, daily specials, and
grilled meats, as well as
hearty Burgundian meat dishes
that change from day to day.

Well-dressed businessmen and women stand elbow to elbow at the bar at lunchtime, when you won't be able to sit down without a reservation. This is a solid, serious wine bar. Serious, that is, about wine, but not about daily cares; so the atmosphere is comfortable and happy, just the way you ought to feel when you're standing in a room filled with sausages and hams hanging from the rafters. The friendly, chatty *patron*, one Louis Prin, was a winner of the Meilleur Pot in 1962.

LE VAL D'OR,
28 Avenue Franklin-D.-
    Roosevelt, Paris 8.
(359.95.81).
Métro: Saint-Philippe-du-
    Roule.
Open 8 A.M. to 9:30 P.M.
    weekdays; until 8 P.M.
    Saturday. Closed Sunday
    and Monday.
Hot meals at lunch only.

WINES:
Beaujolais-Villages, Côte de
Brouilly, Fleurie, Morgon,
Juliénas, Côte de Nuits-
Villages, Aloxe-Corton, white
Mâcon, Sancerre, Pouilly-Fumé.

SPECIALITIES:
Jambon, terrine de foies de
volailles (chicken liver
terrine), quiche, tarte Tatin,
and Cantal, Brie, and goat
cheese, and hot plats du jour.

Géraud Rongier's bustling wine bar off the Champs-Elysées is great any time of year, but particularly fun from November 15 to the end of the year, because one generally finds some of the best Beaujolais in town. Packed at lunch, when office workers line up at the bar, it looks like any ordinary corner café, but Rongier, who won the Meilleur Pot in 1973, makes Le Val D'Or worth a detour. He can be found each morning at the Rungis wholesale market on the outskirts of Paris, shopping for ingredients for the *plats du jour* he serves to the crowds of well-dressed businessmen in his small downstairs dining room. If the sturdy *boeuf bourguignon* is on the menu, go for it, or the platter of *saucissons* cooked in the full-bodied Côte de Brouilly. The *tarte Tatin* isn't always available, but when it is, don't pass it by. This upside-down apple tart is prepared on the premises and served with a huge pot of thick, irresistible *crème fraîche*.

On the main floor, Rongier serves a hearty ham and cheese *quiche*, abundant platters of excellent *charcuterie*, and *baguettes* filled with thick slices of superb *jambon à l'os* (a flavourful ham cured with the bone intact). When you order wine, they'll bring the whole bottle to the table, and charge you only for what you consume.

GARE MONTPARNASSE, DENFERT-ROCHEREAU
14th arrondissement

LE PERE TRANQUILLE,
30 Avenue du Maine,
  Paris 14.
(222.88.12).
Métro: Montparnasse.
Open 9 A.M. to 8 P.M.
  Closed Sunday and
  Monday, and whenever
  else the owner chooses.
Lunch reservations
  recommended.

W I N E S :
*Beaujolais, Bourgueil, red and
white Graves, Touraine
Gamay, Savennières.*

S P E C I A L I T I E S :
*Daily hot plat du jour at
lunch, and "casse-croûte," or
snacks of open-face sandwiches
and charcuterie.*

This truly misnamed wine bar is for any lover of quirky behaviour, for the owner, Jean Nouyrigat, Meilleur Pot winner in 1979, is far from a "tranquil father." If he doesn't like the looks of you, he may throw you out on your ear. On the other hand, if he takes a liking to you, you may well spend the day there, drinking his wines and sampling his hearty *plat du jour* (you won't know what it is until it's set before you). The wine list behind the bar means nothing, for some of the wines haven't been available for ages. Since Mr. Nouyrigat opens and closes at his convenience, it's best to phone before setting out.

BEAUJOLAIS

In Paris, the 15th of November—the first day of sale of Beaujolais *primeur,* the new Beaujolais—signals the beginning of a season-long fête that doesn't cease until after the holiday revelry has cleared sometime in January. From November through the beginning of the new year the French are in a festive mood, and the spirit is wildly evident in wine bars all over town as Parisians down by the glass, the carafe, the bottle, that young, fruity red wine that has been in fashion here for the last three decades.

It really doesn't matter if the year's crop happens to be overabundant, short on acidity, or even lacking in that special fruitiness associated with Beaujolais. It doesn't matter that almost everyone in Paris—even those who sell and drink Beaujolais with regularity—agrees that the publicity surrounding the wine is beyond proportion to its real worth. The fact is that Beaujolais is a "happy" wine, one that is there to enjoy; you don't have to take it too seriously.

Wherever wine bars sell Beaujolais, it is available by the glass, year round. Although the terms *primeur* and *nouveau* are used interchangeably, technically *primeur* is served only from November 15 to December 15, though the first, fresh crop is served in most bars well into the new year. The term *nouveau* is technically reserved for the wines released for sale December 15, to be drunk through the next November.

LE RALLYE,
6 Rue Daguerre, Paris 14.
(322.57.05).
Métro: Denfert-Rochereau.
Open 9:30 A.M. to 8:30
   P.M. Closed Sunday,
   Monday, and July 15 to
   September 15.
Wines may be purchased to
take home.

WINES:
Beaujolais, Côtes-du-Rhône,
Sancerre, Bandol, Muscadet-
sur-Lie, Sèvre-et-Maine,
Pouilly-Fumé.

SPECIALITIES:
Charcuterie, Cantal, Bleu
d'Auvergne, goat cheese.

A plain little workers' bar, just off the lively Rue Daguerre market street. The food is simple and the wines well chosen, with a small wine shop right next door. The owner, Bernard Péret, won the 1967 Meilleur Pot award.

ARC DE TRIOMPHE
17th arrondissement

LE PAIN ET LE VIN,
1 Rue d'Armaillé, Paris 17.
(763.88.29).
Métro: Ternes.
Open 11:30 A.M. to 2 A.M.
   Closed Saturday and
   Sunday.
Hot meals all day.

WINES:
All regions of France, with
particularly good Madiran,
Gigondas, Cahors, and
various Loire Valley selections,
as well as Bordeaux and
Burgundies.

SPECIALITIES:
Open-face sandwiches and
salads, daily hot specials such
as daube de canard (duck
stew) and navarin d'agneau
(lamb stew).

With its smashing view of the Arc de Triomphe, this bustling little wine bar is run by four Parisian chefs: Alain Dutournier of Au Trou Gascon; Bernard Fournier of Le Petit Colombier; Jean-Pierre Morot-Gaudry of Restaurant Morot-Gaudry; and Henri Faugeron of Faugeron, and here they offer a wine list better than you'll find in most restaurants. There is a changing *plat du jour,* as well as salads, plates of smoked salmon or cheese, and open-face sandwiches of duck *rillettes, foie gras,* or York ham.

PETRISSANS,
30 bis Avenue Niel,
  Paris 17.
(227.83.84).
Métro: Ternes.
Open 9:30 A.M. to 1:30
  P.M., 3 P.M. to 9 P.M.
  Closed Saturday
  evening, Sunday,
  Monday, the month of
  August and first week in
  September.
Wines may be purchased to
  take home.

WINES:
Cahors, Madiran, Chinon,
Burgundies, and young
Bordeaux.

SPECIALITIES:
Open-face sandwiches, poitrine
d'oie fumée (smoked goose
breast).

This was the neighbourhood "Petit Café" of 20th-century French dramatist and novelist Tristan Bernard. Now it is a little neighbourhood bar down the street from a branch of the Printemps department store. Sometimes peaceful, sometimes animated, Petrissans is a genteel spot, with a cosy, men's club atmosphere, mirrored walls and mahogany-coloured banquettes. The menu is simple, and minimal, offering a variety of wines by the glass and small platters of hams, cheese, and sausage. On Saturdays, men are there "baby-sitting" the children, while their wives shop at the nearby Rue Poncelet open-air market.

SAINT-OUEN

CHEZ SERGE,
7 Boulevard Jean-Jaurès,
  Saint-Ouen.
(254.06.42).
Métro: Mairie de Saint-
  Ouen.
Open 7 A.M. to 9 P.M.
  Monday through Friday;
  7 A.M. to 3 P.M.
  Saturday. Closed Sunday.
Reservations recommended.
Wines may be purchased to
  take home.

WINES:
Beaujolais, Chénas, Brouilly,
red Poitou, white Graves,
Pouilly-Fuissé, Sauternes.

SPECIALITIES:
Large daily menu as well as
dégustations (tastings) of
homemade charcuterie and
trays of assorted cheese.

You have to love wine and adventure to make the trip to this workers' village just across the city line. But the active neighbourhood wine bar is authentic, the homemade *foie gras* is good, and so is the cooking done by owner Serge Cancé's wife, Michelle. Do try the delicious dry white Graves. Meilleur Pot winner in 1975.

Marchés
MARKETS

Rue Mouffetard: a daily ritual (see entry, page 129).

Most mornings, after an early jog around Paris's Parc Monceau, I extract a string bag from my sweatshirt pocket and head straight for Rue Poncelet, the lively, open-air street market a few blocks away. Marketing is best in the morning, when the vegetable man is good-tempered (and sober), the crowds thin, and the produce at its freshest.

The cluttered, colourful market—one of many scattered about Paris— opens precisely at 9 A.M., when most days the sky is thick, sombre, and a dozen shades of grey, and the city is just beginning to wake up. A tour of Paris's markets offers a rare glimpse of an immensely important French ritual—one that should even be of interest to those not particularly passionate about food—since it allows one to examine the authentic fabric and texture of contemporary Gallic society.

Parisians devote a good part of their day to marketing, and it's obvious that what many Frenchmen do between meals is make shopping lists, market, and talk about meals past and meals future. Daily marketing is still the rule in Paris, where everything from Camembert to cantaloupe is sold to be eaten that day, preferably within a few hours. I still smile appreciatively when the cheese man asks if the Camembert will be savoured that afternoon, or perhaps that evening, then shuffles through his larder, touching and pinching to come up with one that's perfectly ripe and properly creamy.

Most of the merchants are fiercely proud people, and though some may be rough and peasantlike, they display a refined sense of aesthetics. The vegetable man admirably attacks his *métier* like an artist: Each morning, beginning around seven, he painstakingly arranges the fruits and vegetables in orderly rows, paying careful attention to shapes, textures, and shading. The result is a colourful, vibrant mosaic: Fat stalks of celery rest next to snow-white cauliflower, the ruffled green leaves of Swiss chard stand beside them, followed by yellow-white Belgian endive, pale green artichokes, then—zap!—rosy tomatoes or ruby red peppers. Across the aisle, green Granny Smith apples line up alongside the sweet Italian oranges, called *sanguine* (favoured for their juice, which runs the colour of a brilliant sunset), while bananas from Martinique and walnuts from Grenoble fill out the palette.

Mastering the intricacies and etiquette of French marketing is no simpler than learning French, and easily as frustrating. And it requires patience. A serious marketing trip—which will only keep you through the next meal—can take a good hour, and often takes more, if you want to do it right.

The selection at even the smallest markets is amazing. A large *rue commerçante* (merchant street) such as Rue Poncelet, might include half a dozen *boulangeries* and *pâtisseries;* two supermarkets; a good dozen fruit and vegetable merchants; a coffee, tea, and spice shop; three fishmongers; four or five cafés; two wine shops; three flower shops; four poultrymen; two *triperies* for tripe, kidneys, sweetbreads, and liver; three *fromageries;* one butcher for horsemeat; five other *boucheries;* four *charcuteries* for cold cuts; two or three regional or foreign speciality shops; and half a dozen restaurants. Depending on the length of the lines and the merchants' chatter, each individual purchase can take five to ten minutes.

French merchants, it must be noted, are not just merchants. They're philosophers, songsters, comics, tutors, and culinary counsellors. Parisian housewives don't need cookbooks. The butcher, poultryman, and fishmonger all willingly dispense verbal recipes with each purchase. (Otherwise, merchants are not known for their generosity. The concept of a baker's dozen doesn't exist in France, though the fishmonger will, on occasion, throw in a bunch of dill with the salmon.)

Booming voices and shrill cries fill the air throughout the day, as merchants hawk their finest produce, selling from rickety wooden pushcarts or narrow stalls. One piercing voice boasts of *"la très belle salade"* (very beautiful lettuce), while another shouts *"Jetez un petit coup d'oeil"* (take a little look) at the *"canette de Barbarie extra,"* (extra-special duckling). Another ruddy-faced butcher holds out a fresh, plump *boudin* (blood sausage) for a shopper to inhale, announcing that it offers *"une véritable symphonie"* of lively aromas.

Meanwhile, at one corner, you may trip over a donkey tended by a trader selling an exotic array of herbs and essences, while nearby a jazzy brass band plays on.

The chatter is often amusing. One fall, I looked on as a shopper requested a kilo of *raisins de Hambourg,* France's popular muscat grape. Then, by accident, she noticed that the plump, purple grapes came from Provence, in the south of France. "But I thought they came from Germany," she said in confusion. "But Madame," the merchant replied with a serious wink and a broad smile, "you know that in France, agriculture is very, very complicated."

I always begin at one end of the street—flanked by indoor and outdoor stalls—and tour the entire market before buying a thing, making mental notes of what's fresh, stopping to wave at the flower lady (who, due to my affinity for red tulips, calls me "Madame Tulipe"), reading the price and origin of each item chalked on little blackboards that dangle above the stalls.

Lots of things here work on what one friend calls the *"pas possible"* principle, meaning "it isn't done this way here, so tough luck for you if you want it otherwise." Merchants bristle at any atypical request, particularly from foreigners. One friend worked for weeks to get her pork butcher to cut the *poitrine fumée* or smoked slab bacon, thin enough to fry, American-style. The butcher finally won, insisting that if he sliced the bacon any thinner, she'd end up with lace.

Once I ordered two kilos of fresh jalapeño peppers for pickling and the vegetable merchant looked as though he'd seen a mirage. He asked, "How do you eat them?" "Just like this," I responded, pretending to bite into a fiery, raw pepper. The merchant smiled, turned to a colleague beside him, and playfully whispered, "She comes by every other morning, buys two kilos at a time!"

And it took a long time to wean myself of the democratic, American form of marketing: self-service. Here, the law is *ne touchez pas*—don't touch—and anyone caught selecting his own pears and peaches will be forcefully admonished.

The full flavour of the market varies according to the time of day. It's as much fun to tour markets at morning's close, promptly at 1 P.M., as it is when they first open. One o'clock is the hour when a sudden hush falls over all of Paris. Shoppers scurry home to lunch while merchants sing, chant, and shout like schoolchildren let free for recess. A few minutes later, the streets are deserted, save for a few *clochardes,* rifling through the rejected produce that tumbles to the gutters.

Sometimes, the population density in markets can be just too much. On a rainy Saturday around six in the afternoon, Poncelet is a veritable obstacle course. Families with strollers, slow-moving old ladies pulling metal shopping carts, dogs, and long queues make passage all but impossible.

But no matter the time of day, the season, or the market, Paris is ever a moveable feast.

The city's markets, like its neighbourhoods, reflect a variety of cultures and classes, and a tour of one or several will tell you much about the daily life of the city, and the habits of those who live in each neighbourhood.

There are three basic sorts of markets: The *rues commerçantes* or merchant streets, are stationary indoor-outdoor street markets, generally large, rambling, and open six days a week. Paris has fourteen *marchés couverts,* or covered food markets, large, open affairs with a total of 740 merchants; while the fifty-seven *marchés volants,* or roving markets, include more than 5,000 independent merchants moving from neighbourhood to neighbourhood on given days.

The following markets are grouped together according to type, then listed alphabetically.

Rues Commerçantes
MERCHANT STREETS

Standard hours are 8 A.M. to 1 P.M. and 4 P.M. to 7:30 P.M. Tuesday through Saturday. Many of these markets have lost merchants and clients over the years, and so tend to be quieter and more subdued than either the merchant streets or roving markets. They're great for visiting on a rainy day.

RUE DES BELLES-FEUILLES,
Beginning at Avenue
   Victor-Hugo, Paris 16.
Métro: Victor-Hugo.

What the street lacks in character is made up for in the quality of produce—among the best in Paris—attracting some of the wealthiest customers. Shops to look into include Lillo Fromagerie (No. 35), a spotless, friendly store with an exceptionally beautiful assortment of cheese; and Herrier (No. 39), one of the city's finest fish markets, with superb Loire River salmon.

RUE CLER, ·
Beginning at Avenue de la
  Motte-Picquet, Paris 7.
Métro: Ecole Militaire.

This is one of Paris's tidiest high-class markets, with a broad pedestrian street that makes for comfortable browsing. Since many Americans live in the quarter, merchants are used to curious stares and constant questioning about unusual items. Take a look at Charcuterie Gonin (No. 40), a brilliantly spotless corner shop with a huge assortment of carryout items, including *moussaka, coulibiac* of salmon, and tarts; and Davoli (No. 34), one of the city's few real Italian markets, all mirrors and black marble, with an amusing clutter of hams and sausages. Off Rue Cler on Rue du Champ-de-Mars, one of the newer shops, Marie-Anne Cantin (No. 12), offers a remarkable selection of goat cheese, as well as extraordinary Camembert.

RUE LEVIS,
Beginning at Boulevard des
  Batignolles, Paris 17.
Métro: Villiers.

A lively market street not far from the tiny, elegant Parc Monceau, where you can picnic on the market's offerings. Begin at No. 21, the Couasnon Bou-

---

RUNGIS WHOLESALE MARKET

France's largest food market—south of Paris, near Orly airport—covers some 440 acres of black-topped surface, with 864 wholesalers and 1,050 producers selling everything from fresh fruits and vegetables to whole sides of rosy beef, to basket upon basket of fresh Brittany coast oysters. To feed the city's ten million Parisians, the Rungis wholesale market annually processes some 700,000 tons of potatoes, 500 million eggs, 560,000 tons of meat, and 750 million liters of wine.

There's no question that Rungis, open since 1969, lacks the romantic, grubby charm of the old Les Halles market it replaced. The modern-day wholesale market is spacious and sanitary, with hangar upon hangar of sober gray buildings. Fishmongers open the market at 3 A.M. and action continues until about 11 A.M. when the flower merchants move into the scene.

Rungis is open only to professionals, and casual onlookers are not welcomed openly. There are, however, two public tours. Each Thursday at 11 A.M. the Rungis market offers a 24-franc tour, in French, which can be arranged in advance for individuals or groups by calling 687.35.35. Rungis is accessible via Paris bus numbers 183, 185, 285, and 131.

Robert Noah, an American who runs the Paris en Cuisine cooking school, conducts guided tours, in English, beginning at 5:30 A.M. and ending around 9 A.M. The 150-franc tour takes visitors through all of the major markets and Noah offers a chatty, well-informed commentary. Write Paris en Cuisine, 78 Rue de la Croix-Nivert, 75015 Paris. Telephone 250.04.23.

"The air was laden with the various smells of the city and its markets: The strong smell of leeks mingled with the faint but persistent scent of lilacs, all carried along by the pungent breeze which is truly the air of Paris."—Jean Renoir

langerie, where Louis Couasnon, a dedicated young baker, offers superb Belle Epoque brand *baguettes,* made with a touch of rye flour, and *pain paillasse,* a rustic sourdough country loaf. Further along, at No. 23, the Jean Carmes et Fils *fromagerie* offers more than 100 varieties of French cheese, all aged in its own cellars.

RUE MONTORGUEIL,
Beginning at Rue
  Rambuteau, Paris 1.
Métro: Les Halles.

L es Halles, Paris's most famous market, is no more, but Rue Montorgueil remains. It is authentic, grubby, and run-down, but many of the city's finest chefs still do their marketing here, sharing chores as one chef markets for fish, another goes after the meat, still another for the produce, then all meeting for coffee before heading back to their restaurants. While in the neighbourhood, visit the majestic 16th-century Saint-Eustache church.

Taking time for the news
between sales.

RUE MOUFFETARD,
Beginning at Rue de
  l'Epée-de-Bois, Paris 5.
Métro: Monge.

P arisians complain of high prices, poor quality produce and too many tourists, but Rue Mouffetard remains one of the city's classic and most popular merchant streets. Begin at the top of the market just before noon to get a feel of the spirit and texture of the street, which has an honest sort of beaten-down charm. There's a lot of hawking and jostling here as tough merchants sell out of wooden crates balanced on tattered wooden sawhorses.

A detour to Passage Passé Simple leads into a tiny flower market and two exceptional Auvergnat shops, selling every cut of pork imaginable, along with dried beans and nuts sold from overflowing gunnysacks. Further down, off Rue de l'Arbalète, there's a lively African market, selling all sorts of dried fish, baskets, and sandals. Back on Rue Mouffetard at No. 116 stop in at Café Mouffetard for the dense and buttery croissants, and rich brioche. Also take a quick look at the Facchetti Italian market, No. 134, with its four-story mural of animals wandering through the forest.

RUE PONCELET,
Beginning at Avenue des
Ternes, Paris 17.
Métro: Ternes.

Highlights include Aux Fermes d'Auvergne (No. 13), with chubby, smiling traders from the Auvergne region who sell homemade *foie gras, boudin,* fifteen kinds of ham and twenty pâtés, regional cheese, fresh nuts and dried fruits; and Le Moule à Gateau (No. 10), with delicious *chaussons aux pruneaux* (prune turnovers) and other pastries. If you're in the market on Tuesday, Saturday, or Sunday, peek in the little alley between Nos. 25 and 29 Rue Poncelet. No doubt there will be a queue, and at the front of it you'll find a lively *maraîcher,* a market gardener, who trucks in the freshest local farm produce. Around the corner on

Flowers, anyone?

LES MARCHES BIOLOGIQUES
(ORGANIC MARKETS)

These are food markets unlike others in Paris—more like old-fashioned country farmer's markets. On the first and third Saturday of each month, from thirty to fifty independent "organic" farmers set up stalls along one of the main streets of Boulogne and Joinville, two Parisian suburbs. They sell organically grown fruits and vegetables; homemade breads; dried fruits and nuts; *charcuterie*; farm-raised chickens, ducks, and geese; and even wine that's guaranteed to be "natural." The organic, or *biologique,* movement in France is active and well organized, and this market is a shining example of its success. On a given Saturday you might also find one stand selling freshly made pizza, and another rustic, whole-wheat breads. There is also homemade apple or pear cider, a huge variety of artisanal goat cheeses, sausages, and beer, and even one merchant offering bright and glorious sprays of dried flowers. For both markets, it is best to go early in the day for a good selection.

Le Marché Biologique, 140 Route de la Reine, 92 Boulogne-sur-Seine. Métro: Boulogne-Porte de Saint-Cloud or accessible via Paris's No. 72 bus. Open 9 A.M. to 5 P.M. first Saturday of each month.

Le Marché Biologique, Place de Verdun, 94 Joinville. Métro: RER Line A2 to Joinville or accessible via the suburban No. 106 and 108 buses. Open 8 A.M. to 1 P.M. third Saturday of each month.

For further information on both markets, call Nature et Progrès, 222.89.99.

Avenue des Ternes (No. 16), the glass front of Maison Pou shields one of the neatest neighbourhood *charcuteries*.

RUE DU POTEAU,
Beginning at Place Jules-
Joffrin, Paris 18.
Métro: Jules-Joffrin.

One of the prettiest and most pristine markets in Paris, set high above Sacré-Coeur along a series of charming, winding streets. The market's worth a detour simply to get an idea of what a real Paris neighborhood might have looked like a few decades ago. Start out early in the morning at Place Jules-Joffrin, then go to No. 81, Rue du Mont-Cenis, where, at Patisserie Hellegouarch, you'll find some of the best *croissants* and *pains au chocolat* in Paris. Take your time peeking into the shops along Rue du Poteau, where the spotless turn-of-the-century storefronts will amaze you. A real find is the Fromagerie de Montmartre, at No. 9, where you'll be certain to find something appealing among the forty varieties of goat cheese and 100 other cow and sheep's milk varieties.

RUE DE SEINE/BUCI,
Beginning at Boulevard
Saint-Germain, Paris 6.
Métro: Odéon.

This is considered Paris's most expensive market street, and certainly one of the most densely populated. The vendors are a close-knit group, changing stations from day to day. One morning the diminutive blond-haired lady with the husky voice might try to sell you a kilo of *mandarines,* while the next day she's positioned behind a pile of leafy greens. It's a bit disconcerting: Just when you've got a standing joke with the orange merchant he gets transferred to the tomatoes. At No. 81, note the Barthélémy cheese shop, offering some of the best goat cheese in the neighbourhood. It's also one of the few Paris *fromageries* to sell

A Mouffetard medley (see entry, page 129).

A Poncelet merchant (see entry, page 130).

fromage frais bien égoutté, a fresh curd cheese and key ingredient in traditional cheesecake. A big stall on the corner of Rue de Seine and Rue de Buci offers a variety of exotic produce, including mounds of fresh wild mushrooms. At the adjoining stall, there's a gruff old merchant who prides himself on his beautiful celery, black radishes, and fresh herbs. Take a right onto Rue de Buci and at No. 6 the Boudin *boulangerie* offers an unusual puff pastry *fougasse,* a flaky, satisfying lacy bread. It's available on Wednesdays only, and can be specially ordered—perfect for a Sunday brunch or an afternoon snack with coffee. Their other breads and pastries are best forgotten.

Marchés Couverts
COVERED MARKETS

Standard hours are 9 A.M. to 1 P.M. and 4 P.M. to 7 P.M. Tuesday through Saturday; 9 A.M. to 1 P.M. Sunday. Most are closed Monday, and the number of merchants is substantially reduced during the months of July and August.

MARCHE CHATEAU-D'EAU,
At Rue du Château-d'Eau and Rue Bouchardon, Paris 10.
Métro: Château-d'Eau.

This is the real thing: an earthy, historic, old market, with lower quality and less exotic produce, but one that certainly gives a hint of what the old Les Halles was like. You'll find butchers washing sweetbreads in the market's central fountain, while grandmotherly French women with tattered metal carts toddle by. Take the time to walk through the nearby Passage du Marché: It's reminiscent of old France.

ENFANTS ROUGES,
39 Rue de Bretagne, Paris 3.
Métro: Filles-du-Calvaire.

For Paris history buffs, this market will easily take you back in time. The produce is far from prime, but the atmosphere is thick as the Paris sky in winter. Stop and examine the old coffee merchant's shop, which looks like a stage set for a turn-of-the-century film. Two nearby spots worth noting: Boulangerie Onfroy at 34 Rue de Saintonge (with absolutely the best rye bread in town) and the lovely Square du Temple park, where you can have a nice picnic lunch.

MARCHE DE PASSY,
Corner of Rue Bois-le-Vent and Rue Duban, Paris 16.
Métro: La Muette.

A great little market with wonderful skylights, superb *charcuterie* from Lyons, a nice little Italian market, and top quality cheese at Monsieur Gay's stand. If there's time, take a walk down Rue de l'Annonciation, one of the city's fine merchant streets.

MARCHE SAINT-GERMAIN,
At Rue Mabillon and Rue
  Lobineau, Paris 5.
Métro: Mabillon.

Clean, quiet, and still full of character, this market offers lots of little stalls with fresh, fresh, produce and friendly merchants. Best days are Tuesday, Thursday, and Saturday, when new shipments of produce come in.

At No. 16, Rue Montmartre, there's a curiously named alley, the Queen of Hungary Passage (Passage Reine de Hongrie). Some time during the 18th-century reign of Marie Antoinette, the queen was passing through the alley, and was handed a petition by a woman who ran a market stall. The queen commented on the merchant's likeness to the queen of Hungary, and soon the alley was renamed.

TO MARKET, TO MARKET

Paris's first food market was established during the 5th century, on what is now the Ile de la Cité. As the city expanded, other small markets were created, first at the city gates, then beginning in the 13th century, at the old iron works between Rue Saint-Denis, Rue Saint-Honoré, and Rue Croix des Petits-Champs, the site of the present Forum des Halles shopping mall.

At the time, the big *halles,* or market, was shared by merchants, craftsmen, and pedlars offering an international array of goods. To encourage trade here, other city merchants and craftsmen were ordered to close their shops two days each week. It was not until the 16th century, when Paris had 300,000 inhabitants, that produce and other foodstuffs came to dominate the market. Dishonest merchants were not tolerated, and those caught cheating were exposed and publicly ridiculed near the Saint-Eustache church, which still stands today.

By 1546, Paris boasted of four major bread markets and one live animal market. In the 17th century, the Quai de la Mégisserie along the Seine's Right Bank—now the site of the live bird market—then known as the "valley of misery," was the chicken, wild game, lamb, goat, and milk-fed pig market; Rue de la Poissonnière was established as the fish market; and the wine market was installed on the Left Bank's Quai Saint-Bernard.

The French Revolution of 1789 put an end to the royal privilege of authorizing markets, and transferred the power to the city. By 1860, Paris had fifty-one markets, twenty-one of them covered and the rest open-air affairs.

By the mid-19th century the central Les Halles was badly in need of repair, so a new hall with iron girders and skylight roofs—reminiscent of the still existing Gare de l'Est—was built by the architect Baltard between 1854 and 1866. The design, complete with vast underground storehouses and linked by roofed passages and alleys, became a model for markets throughout France and the rest of the world. As the city's population grew the market space eventually became inadequate, and in 1969 the market was moved to Rungis, south of Paris, near Orly airport. Les Halles was torn down to make way for a major modern shopping area which is still undergoing construction.

**MARCHE
SAINT-QUENTIN,**
Corner of Boulevard de
  Magenta and Rue de
  Chabrol, Paris 10.
Métro: Gare de l'Est.

This huge, recently-renovated market is one of the most spotless and liveliest of the turn-of-the-century covered markets. Excellent offerings of cheese, wine, and *charcuterie,* perfect for a stop before taking the train from the nearby Gare du Nord or Gare de l'Est. One of the city's green Wallace Fountains stands in the centre of the market.

Marchés Volants
ROVING MARKETS

Note that these markets are open from 7 A.M. to 1:30 P.M. only on the days listed. These tend to be less expensive than the other markets, and often you'll find fresher, more unusual produce here, but sometimes less variety. Open two or three days each week, mornings only, they are usually set up on sidewalks or along the islands of major boulevards and include a full range of products, including fruits and vegetables, meats, poultry, fish, cheese, and fresh flowers.

BERCY,
Boulevard de Reuilly,
  between Rue de
  Charenton and Place
  Félix-Eboué, Paris 12.
Métro: Daumesnil.
Tuesday and Friday.

CITE BERRYER,
Beginning at Rue Royale,
  (enter between 23 and
  25 Rue Royale) Paris 8.
Métro: Madeleine.
Tuesday and Friday.

BRETEUIL,
Avenue de Saxe, from
  Avenue de Ségur to
  Place Breteuil, Paris 7.
Métro: Ségur.
Thursday and Saturday.

Busy merchants, broad smiles.

COURS LA REINE,
On the island between
Avenue Président-
Wilson and between
Rue Debrousse and
Place Iéna, Paris 16.
Métro: Alma Marceau.
Wednesday and Saturday.

EDGAR-QUINET,
Along Boulevard Edgar-
Quinet, beginning at
Rue Delambre, Paris 14.
Métro: Edgar-Quinet.
Wednesday and Saturday.

PLACE MONGE,
On Place Monge, Paris 5.
Métro: Monge.
Wednesday, Friday, and
Sunday.

RASPAIL,
Boulevard Raspail, between
Rue du Cherche-Midi
and Rue de Rennes,
Paris 6.
Métro: Raspail.
Tuesday and Friday.

ALLO, MENU (HELLO, MENU)

What do Parisians do when they can't decide what to fix for dinner? They dial 255.66.77, and a proper, grandmotherly French voice (on tape) at the other end offers a suggested daily menu, along with a detailed recipe for one of the key dishes. Madame *"Allô Menu,"* "Hello, Menu," offers traditional *bourgeois* dishes, ranging from a cheese soufflé to *lapin à la Solognote,* rabbit with anchovy and caper sauce. None of the recipes are so exotic that the average person can't stop in at the market on the way home from the office and pick up the ingredients.

Heavy load for a Rue Poncelet merchant (see entry, page 130).

Pâtisseries
PASTRY SHOPS

Demonstrating appropriate madeleine technique.

The Parisian pastry chef is truly a man to be admired. Imagine his responsibility. Day in and day out, season after season, he must attend to the care and feeding of the formidable Parisian sweet tooth.

Everywhere you turn in Paris, someone—man, woman, or child—seems either to be munching on a *pain au chocolat,* peering wide-eyed into the window of a pristine, wondrous pastry shop, savouring the last lick on an ice cream cone, or carrying, with admirable agility, a beribboned white box filled with the day's dessert.

Perhaps the city's per capita consumption of butter, sugar, cream, and eggs is not the highest in the world, but if a population won prizes simply on its level of enthusiasm for all things sweet and satisfying, I think that Parisians would win. I have watched reed-thin women heartily down three and four dessert helpings in a row— unashamedly, unabashedly with no remorse. I have eavesdropped as a pair of businessmen huddled at lunchtime, talking in hushed, animated tones. The subject was not politics, not Euromissiles, not racing cars, but chocolates. Chocolates! I have listened as one enthusiastic *pâtissier* explained what went on when several of Paris's pastry chefs gathered together: "I love éclairs, but I don't make them in my shop. So when I visit my friends, I have an éclair feast. Seven is my limit. And I usually meet my limit."

French regional and ethnic pastries, of course, are important in

Paris. The cheese-filled Alsatian *gâteau au fromage blanc* and the just-sweet-and-buttery-enough *kougelhopf* are everywhere; from Basque country in the southwest comes the cream-filled *gâteau basque;* from Normandy, the simply perfect apple tart. Don't miss at least a visual tour of Rue des Rosiers, the main street of the Jewish quarter, where there are almost as many pastry shops as street numbers, or a peek inside one of Gaston Lenôtre's several elegant shops, where a look is just about (but not quite) as good as a taste.

Everywhere, one finds *croissants* (along with the chocolate-filled version known as *pain au chocolat*); *brioche* (the *mousseline* variety is more buttery and typically Parisian); the *madeleine,* a lemony tea cake that Proust made famous; and the *financier* (a personal favourite), the almondy rectangle that is part cake, part cookie, and absolutely satisfying when fresh and carefully made.

For many—Parisians as well as those passing through—a day in this town without a pastry is a day not worth living. Why this is so would be the subject of a major treatise, but suffice it to say that they climb the sweet mountain because it is there.

LES HALLES, BASTILLE
2nd and 4th arrondissements

FINKELSZTAJN,
27 Rue des Rosiers,
Paris 4.
(272.78.91).
Métro: Saint-Paul.
Open 9 A.M. to 1:30 P.M.
and 2:30 P.M. to 7:30
P.M. Closed Wednesday,
the months of July and
August, and one week
in winter.

This is the best of the many pastry shops that line Rue des Rosiers, the heart of Paris's Jewish quarter. Finkelsztajn's cheesecake (better known as *vatrouchka*) rivals anything you'll find anywhere, especially when it comes fresh and warm from the oven in the afternoon. Their *gâteau aux figues* helps you understand where the fig newton began, and the assortment of poppy seed cakes and hazelnut cakes, stru-

French fruit tarts: always luscious.

dels filled with apples and raisins, honey and citrus peel, even dates, are enough to make one weep real tears. Throw discipline to the winds for a day, and enjoy.

PATISSERIE SAINT-PAUL,
4 Rue de Rivoli, Paris 4.
(887.87.16).
Métro: Saint-Paul.
Open 8 A.M. to 1:30 P.M. and 3 P.M. to 7:30 P.M. Closed Monday, Tuesday (except in December), the month of August, and one week in winter.

The windows of this pristine, jewellike shop not far from the Places des Vosges is filled with minor masterpieces. Talented, ambitious young Christian Pottier is in love with his work, and it shows: His cakes and pastries are always pure, fresh, sparkling, and authoritative. All are worth trying: the shiny, buttery *brioche* that's made with only the best *beurre des Charentes;* the moist *quatre-quarts* pound cake filled with Golden Delicious apples or enhanced with a twist of lemon; and the chocolate *étoile* cake, a blend of chocolate meringue and chocolate mousse. Monsieur Pottier, who works in the neatly organized bake shop beneath the store, also prepares some 800 pure-butter *croissants* each day, brushing them lightly with a sugar syrup that gives them a hint of almonds and hazelnuts. They come out of the oven at 8:15 each morning, so get in line.

STOHRER,
51 Rue Montorgueil, Paris 2.
(233.38.20).
Métro: Les Halles.
Open daily, 7:30 A.M. to 8 P.M.

One of Louis XV's pastry chefs opened this shop in 1730, and it continues to thrill clients with its delicious individual *pithiviers*—cream-filled, flaky puff pastry decorated like a crown—little apricot or apple tarts, and superbly fresh *pains au chocolat*. Little elderly salesladies seem to swarm about the tiny shop, eager to assist in your selection. Take time to walk through the neighbouring Rue Montorgueil market, which is slightly seedy, but still retains the charm of old Les Halles.

LATIN QUARTER, LUXEMBOURG, SAINT-GERMAIN
5th and 6th arrondissements

BOUDIN,
6 Rue de Buci, Paris 6.
(326.04.13).
Métro: Saint-Germain-des-
Prés.
Open 6:30 A.M. to 8 P.M.
Closed Monday.

Thérèse and Claude Boudin have been baking breads and pastries here since the 1950s, and there is one good reason to pay them a visit. This is perhaps the only pastry shop in Paris to offer a lacy *fougasse* made of puff pastry, rather than the traditional bread dough. They make about thirty or forty large rectangles each day, mostly in the winter months, simply because Claude Boudin enjoys creating them. Made from *croissant* dough without added yeast, his *fougasse* is flaky, buttery, and irresistible when it comes out of the oven at around 10:30 A.M. (If the *fougasse* sells well that day, and there's time, he makes a second batch in the afternoon.) The Boudins' other products—particularly the breads—are less than inspiring.

LERCH,
4 Rue Cardinal-
Lemoine, Paris 5.
(326.15.80).
Métro: Cardinal Lemoine.
Open 7 A.M. to 1:15 P.M.
and 3:15 P.M. to 7 P.M.
Wednesday through
Saturday, 8 A.M. to 1:15
P.M. and 3:15 P.M. to 7
P.M. Sunday. Closed
Monday, Tuesday, the
month of August, and
one week in winter.

A jolly, super-active pastry chef/baker, André Lerch brings the best of Alsace to Paris, with his golden *kougelhopf* (see recipe, page 142), twenty different kinds of simple, family-style fruit tarts that vary with the seasons, giant rounds of fresh cheesecake (*tarte au fromage blanc*), along with whatever new creation he dreamed up overnight. (When Monsieur Lerch can't sleep, he picks up a cookbook to inspire himself to try a new recipe the next day in the shop!) He'd like nothing better than to be able to spend four or five hours decorating a single tart, but, instead, he lives realis-

*André Lerch and his
madeleines.*

tically, and feeds his creative urgings by changing his repertoire with the seasons. He's busiest from November to March, when wintry Alsatian cookies and pastries are most in demand: *springerle, quiche lorraine,* and the delicious spice bread *pain d'épices* are all there. Year-round, he sells *kougelhopf* (along with the folkloric Alsatian moulds for making them at home) and the famous plump tea cakes known as *madeleines.*

MADELEINES
LEMON TEA CAKES

While researching this book, I became fixated, absolutely fanatical about madeleines, the plump and golden tea cakes shaped like tiny scallop shells. They were something to boost spirits on days that I walked for miles sleuthing in search of culinary jewels. I tasted dozens of madeleines, but only a few that were "just right."

The best, freshest madeleine has a dry, almost dusty taste when taken on its own. One of my favourite versions is made by André Lerch, an Alsatian baker with a bread and pastry shop on the Left Bank.

To be truly appreciated—to "invade the senses with exquisite pleasure" as they did for Marcel Proust—madeleines must be dipped in tea, ideally the slightly lime-flavoured tilleul, which releases the fragrant, flavourful lemon essence of the little tea cake. Special madeleine moulds can be found in all the French restaurant supply shops, and in the housewares section of department stores. The following is a recipe I developed.

4 eggs
1 cup (200 g) sugar
Zest (grated peel) of 2
  lemons
1¾ cups (225 g) flour (do
  not use unbleached
  flour)
¾ cup (6 ounces; 170 g)
  unsalted butter, melted
  and cooled
1 tablespoon unsalted
  butter, for buttering
  madeleine tins
	1. Place the eggs and sugar in a large bowl, then using a whisk or electric mixer, beat until lemon coloured. Add the zest. Fold in flour, then butter.
	
	2. Preheat the oven to 375°F (190°C).
	
	3. Refrigerate the batter for 30 minutes.
	
	4. Butter the *madeleine* tins, spoon in the batter, filling each about three-fourths full. Bake 10 to 12 minutes, or until *madeleines* are golden brown.
	
	5. Remove the *madeleines* from their tins as soon as they're baked and cool them on a baking rack. Wash tins immediately with a stiff brush and plain water. The *madeleines* are best eaten as soon as they've cooled. They may, however, be stored for several days in an airtight container.
	
	Yield: 36, 3-inch (8-cm) *madeleines.*

LE MOULE A GATEAU,
111 Rue Mouffetard,
  Paris 5.
(331.80.47).
Métro: Censier-Daubenton.
Open 9 A.M. to 1:30 P.M.
  and 4 P.M. to 7:30 P.M.
  Tuesday through
  Saturday, 9 A.M. to 1:30
  P.M. Sunday. Closed
  Monday.

Le Moule à Gâteau's ever-changing array of French family-style and regional cakes and pastries is welcoming and refreshing. This little chain store, with several shops around Paris, uses quality ingredients, the staff is friendly and well-trained, and some of the cakes and pastries are baked right before your eyes in the small but attractive wood and glass boutique. Their idea is to make it simple, make it fresh, and the crowds will form. They're right. Best of all, you can buy just about everything by the slice, so sampling is in order. Good bets are the *chaussons aux pruneaux* (prune turnovers) and fine, moist *pensées aux myrtilles,* cakes of blueberries and almond cream set on a shortbread crust. If you're there early, around 9 or 9:30, try a *pain au chocolat* fresh from the oven: They're warm and buttery, and the two generous sticks of chocolate inside will melt in your mouth. (If they're not warm, or not obviously fresh from the oven, try something else.)

SEVRES-BABYLONE, ECOLE MILITAIRE, LA TOUR-MAUBOURG
7th arrondissement

CHRISTIAN CONSTANT,
26 Rue du Bac, Paris 7.
(296.53.53).
Métro: Rue du Bac.
Open daily, 8 A.M. to 8 P.M. Closed the month of July.

If you'd like to see how *nouvelle cuisine* has inspired French pastries, stop in at Christian Constant's all-white, contemporary shop, where exotic kiwi tarts and tiny, boutique-size chocolates fill the display window. Not all his creations inspire respect, but Christian Constant does offer a few pleasant classics: His warm, individual *tarte Tatin* goes down well in the morning with a bracing cup of thick *express,* and they can be enjoyed, in tranquillity, in the little tea salon that adjoins the shop.

LENOTRE,
44 Rue du Bac, Paris 7.
(222.39.39).
Métro: Rue du Bac.
Open 9:45 A.M. to 7:30 P.M. Tuesday through Saturday, 9:45 A.M. to 1 P.M. Sunday. Closed Monday.

A small boutique featuring a selection of Lenôtre's famous pastries and chocolates. See 16th *arrondissement.*

André Lerch's kougelhopf (for recipe, see page 142).

KOUGELHOPF ANDRE LERCH
ANDRE LERCH'S ALSATIAN COFFEE CAKE

Kougelhopf is a yeasty, crown-shaped coffee cake from the Alsace region of France, still famous for its high-quality breads and pastries. In Paris, André Lerch, an outgoing Alsatian baker, runs a popular bread and pastry shop where he bakes forty to fifty kougelhopf each day, using well-seasoned moulds a half-century old. There's a curious story behind his dark brown, glazed clay moulds: Apparently, before World War II there was an Alsatian bakery where his now is. The baker went off to war, leaving behind his moulds, buttered and prepared with whole almonds. He never returned, and when Monsieur Lerch moved in decades later he found the moulds stashed behind the ovens. He insists that well-seasoned moulds are the secret to good kougelhopf. "The mould isn't good until it's been used 200 times," he warns. Since most of us won't make 200 kougelhopf in two and a half lifetimes, Monsieur Lerch offers a shortcut: Thoroughly butter a new mould, place it in a low oven for several hours, re-buttering every fifteen minutes or so. The mould will take on a seductive essence of browned butter, and will be ready to produce fragrant loaves.

½ cup (80 g) white raisins
2 tablespoons kirsch or
   other fruit-based *eau-de-vie*
1 cup (250 ml) milk
1 tablespoon or 1 package
   dry yeast
3¾ cups (525 g)
   unbleached flour
2 eggs, beaten
½ cup (100 g) sugar
1 teaspoon salt
¾ cup (6 ounces; 170 g)
   unsalted butter, at
   room temperature
1 tablespoon unsalted
   butter, for buttering
   the *kougelhopf* mould
½ cup (70 g) whole
   almonds
1 tablespoon
   confectioners' sugar

1. In a small bowl combine the raisins and kirsch.

2. Heat the milk to lukewarm, add the yeast, stir well, and set aside for 5 minutes until the yeast has proofed.

3. Place the flour in a large bowl and make a well in the centre. Add the dissolved yeast and milk, the eggs, sugar, and salt, mixing well after each addition. The dough will be quite sticky. Knead by hand for 10 minutes by slapping the dough against the side of the bowl, or knead by machine for 5 minutes. Add the butter, bit by bit, and knead until the dough is smooth or until the dough comes cleanly off the sides of the bowl. Drain the raisins and knead them into the dough.

4. Place the dough in a large clean bowl and cover securely with plastic wrap. Let rise at room temperature for 1 hour or until double in bulk.

5. Punch down, knead gently, cover, and let rise again until double in bulk (about 1 hour).

6. Preheat the oven to 350°F (175°C).

7. Heavily butter a 2-quart (2-liter) *kougelhopf* mould or bundt pan and place an almond in the well of each of the mould's indentations. Place the dough in the mould and let rise about 1 hour, or until it reaches the top of the mould.

8. Bake 1 hour, or until *kougelhopf* is golden brown.

9. Unmould and when cool, sprinkle with confectioners' sugar. *Kougelhopf* tastes best the day after it's baked, when it's been allowed to "ripen." Alternatively, once baked, the *kougelhopf* may be frozen.

Yield: 1 *kougelhopf*.

LA MAISON CHAVINIER,
39 Avenue Rapp, Paris 7.
(705.41.48).
Métro: Ecole Militaire.
Open 7 A.M. to 8 P.M.
  Closed Sunday.

If you're wandering about the neighbourhood, stop in for a good, lemony *madeleine*, or their fresh and famous *gâteau basque*, filled with delicious almond cream. Breads here are cooked in a wood-fired oven: Try the *pain de seigle aux raisins*, hearty rye and raisin.

> "*Make your pastry; when it is ready and you have added whatever you please, give it whatever shape and name you consider suitable.*"
>
> —*Advice to French pastry cooks*

Irresistible, buttery croissants.

MILLET,
103 Rue Saint-Dominique, Paris 7.
(551.49.80).
Métro: La Tour-Maubourg.
Open 9 A.M. to 7 P.M.
Tuesday through Saturday, 9 A.M. to 1 P.M. Sunday. Closed Monday and the month of August.

A classic, spotless pastry shop offering pure honey *madeleines;* almond-flavoured *financiers;* buttery, egg-rich *brioche mousseline* (see recipe, page 150); some twenty different varieties of cakes and tarts; and twenty flavours of ice cream. Their *croissants* are some of the best in town, and Denis Ruffel, Millet's energetic pastry chef, tucks two delicious sticks of chocolate into his remarkable *pain au chocolat.* Upstairs, behind the scenes, there's a good-size chocolate "factory," while on the main floor a small tea salon provides the perfect spot for sampling everything that tempts the palate.

PELTIER,
66 Rue de Sèvres, Paris 7.
(734.06.62).
Métro: Vaneau.
Open 9:30 A.M. to 6:30 P.M. Closed Monday.

Since 1961, the Peltier name has stood for quality pastry in Paris. Today, the family's spacious, pristine shop offers some of the most beautiful tarts and cakes in Paris, along with superb *croissants* and lovely frozen fruit soufflés. Sample their special cakes and tarts—one covered with seven different fresh fruits, another a mango-flavored *charlotte*—at the counter in the corner of the shop. Then take home a *princesse,* a meringue cake with almonds, vanilla cream, and grains of *nougatine,* all wrapped with a pretty satin bow.

POUJAURAN,
20 Rue Jean Nicot, Paris 7.
(705.80.88).
Métro: La Tour-Maubourg.
Open 8:30 A.M. to 8 P.M.
Closed Saturday, Sunday, and the month of August.

You can't help but love Jean-Luc Poujauran—he's young, feisty, ambitious, and sure to succeed. His charming shop tucked away on a nowhere street in the 7th *arrondissement* is chock-a-block full of goodies: a regional *gâteau basque,* pizzas, heady spice cake, fresh *financiers* (see recipe, page 145), and coffee- and nut-flavoured pound cakes. (See also Boulangeries.)

SAFFRAY,
18 Rue du Bac, Paris 7.
(261.27.63).
Métro: Rue du Bac.
Open 7 A.M. to 8 P.M.
  Tuesday through
  Saturday, 7:30 A.M. to 7
  P.M. Sunday. Closed
  Monday and the month
  of August.

For the person who has everything: a made-to-order, detailed, ice cream bust in the flavour of your choice. For a mere 7,000 to 8,000 francs, Jean Saffray will make a life-size mould of your head, then fill it with ice cream surrounded by white chocolate. For a bit less—about 150 francs—you can order an ice cream likeness of François Mitterrand. (His bust is already in stock.) If you've only a few francs to spend, and aren't interested in celebrity-studded ice cream, console yourself with Monsieur Saffray's delicious and almondy *financiers*.

MADELEINE, SAINT-PHILIPPE-DU-ROULE
8th arrondissement

DALLOYAU,
101 Rue Faubourg Saint-
  Honoré, Paris 8.
(359.18.10).
Métro: Saint-Philippe-du-
  Roule.
Open 9:30 A.M. to 7 P.M.
  Monday through
  Saturday, 9:30 A.M. to
  1 P.M. and 3 P.M. to
  6:30 P.M. Sunday.

Since 1802, when Napoleon ruled the republic, Dalloyau has done its best to satisfy the Parisian palate. Today, the company's activities are incredibly diverse, offering pastries, chocolates, *charcuterie,* and fully-

Strawberry tarts to make your mouth water.

catered meals and banquets. Best bets, thóugh, are the coffee macaroons, and the cake *mogador,* composed of chocolate cake, chocolate *mousse,* and a fine layer of raspberry jam. (See also Chocolateries.)

FINANCIERS
ALMOND CAKES

The little rectangular almond cakes known as financiers are sold in many of the best pastry shops in Paris. Perfect financiers are about as addictive as chocolate, and I'd walk a mile or two for a good one. The finest have a firm, crusty exterior and a moist, almondy interior, tasting almost as if they were filled with almond paste. Next to the madeleine, the financier is probably the most popular little French cake, common street food for morning or afternoon snacking. The cake's name probably comes from the fact that a financier resembles a solid gold brick. Curiously, as popular as they are, financiers seldom appear in recipe books or in French literature.

The secret to a good financier is in the baking: For a good crust, they must begin baking in a very hot oven. Then, the temperature is reduced to keep the interior moist. Placing the tins on a thick baking sheet while they are in the oven is an important baking hint from the Left Bank pastry chef Jean-Luc Poujauran, who worked for months to perfect his financiers, among the best in Paris. The special tin financier moulds, each measuring 2 × 4 inches (5 × 10 cm), can be found at restaurant supply shops. Small oval barquette moulds or even muffin tins could also be used.

1⅔ cups (210 g) confectioners' sugar

1 cup (140 g) almonds, toasted, then ground to a fine powder

½ cup (70 g) unbleached flour

¾ cup (185 ml) egg whites (approximately 5 to 6)

¾ cup (6 ounces; 170 g) unsalted butter, melted and cooled

1 tablespoon unsalted butter, for buttering 18 *financier* moulds

1. Preheat the oven to 450°F (230°C).

2. In a medium-size bowl, combine the sugar, ground almonds, and flour, then sift or force the mixture through a fine mesh sieve into a second bowl. The mixture should be very fine. Stir in the unbeaten egg whites until thoroughly blended, then stir in butter until well blended.

3. Butter the *financier* moulds (or *barquette* moulds), then fill each mold almost to the rim. Place the tins on a thick baking sheet (or a broiler pan) and place in the centre of the oven. Bake for 7 minutes, then reduce heat to 400°F (205°C) and bake another 7 minutes. Turn off the heat and let the *financiers* rest in the oven another 7 minutes.

4. Remove the *financiers* from the oven and unmould as soon as they've cooled. Serve with tea, coffee, ice cream, or *sorbet.* (Note: Wash moulds immediately after unmoulding with cold water but no detergent, so they retain their seasoning.) The *financiers* may be stored in an airtight container for several days.

Yield: 18, 2 × 4 inch (5 × 10 cm) *financiers.*

LADUREE,
16 Rue Royale, Paris 8.
(260.21.79).
Métro: Madeleine.
Open 8:30 A.M. to 7 P.M.
 Closed Sunday and the
 month of August.

Ladurée is one of Paris's most elegant and traditional shops—a tea salon and pastry shop of note. Press your nose against the window and dream on. The choice is not a simple one. Shall it be a buttery early morning *croissant,* a lunchtime strawberry tart, or a mid-afternoon chocolate macaroon? If there's time— and a table free—also stop for a cup of *café au lait,* one of the best in the city. On your way out, buy a delicate *brioche mousseline* or a raisin-filled *brioche* called *cramique,* to lure you out of bed the next morning. (See also Salons de Thé.)

PASTEUR
15th arrondissement

HELLEGOUARCH,
185 Rue de Vaugirard, Paris 15.
(783.29.72).
Métro: Pasteur.
Open 8:30 A.M. to 7:30 P.M. Closed Monday and the month of August.

Several years ago I conducted a blind tasting, in search of the best of Paris's *croissants.* Hellegouarch won hands down, and their *croissants*—when fresh from the oven around 9 A.M.—are still among the best in town. Their *pain au chocolat* is equally appealing: everything the buttery, flaky, chocolate-filled pastry should be, and even a little more.

VICTOR-HUGO, PASSY, AUTEUIL
16th arrondissement

C. BROCARD,
91 Avenue Raymond-Poincaré, Paris 16.
(500.56.55).
Métro: Victor-Hugo.
Open 8 A.M. to 7:30 P.M. Closed Monday and the month of August.

A fine little shop just off Place Victor-Hugo, for sampling superb Alsatian pastries, including a fresh and buttery *kougelhopf, quiche lorraine,* onion tarts, Christmas *stollen,* and anise bread.

COQUELIN AINE,
1 Place de Passy, Paris 16.
(288.21.74).
Métro: Muette.
Open 9 A.M. to 7 P.M. Tuesday through Saturday; 9 A.M. to 1 P.M. Sunday. Closed Monday and the month of August.

Take a break while visiting the Rue de l'Annonciation market and queue up with all the genteel ladies of this very chic *quartier.* They know where the good things are, like fresh and yeasty *brioche,* almond-rich *financiers,* and dozens of other sweets to excite even the stoic. The few tables in back are almost always taken, but if it's a warm and sunny day, take your snacks out to a park bench on the square, and enjoy.

LENOTRE,
44 Rue d'Auteuil, Paris 16.
(524.52.52).
Métro: Michel Ange/
Auteuil.
Open daily, 9:15 A.M. to
7:15 P.M.

LENOTRE,
49 Avenue Victor-Hugo,
Paris 16.
(501.71.71).
Métro: Victor-Hugo.
Open 9:30 A.M. to 7:15
P.M. Tuesday through
Saturday, 9 A.M. to 1
P.M. Sunday. Closed
Monday.

One wonders how Gaston Lenôtre does it. He and his band of pastry chefs are all over the world, turning out cakes and pastries, chocolates and ice creams, full-course meals and light snacks by the thousands. Yet throughout, everything stamped "Lenôtre" has that certain incomparable quality that can't be beat. His chocolates are still among the best in town, and no one makes a *gâteau Opéra* or meringue and chocolate mousse-filled *concorde* like Lenôtre's. (See also Boulangeries and Chocolateries.)

TERNES, WAGRAM
17th arrondissement

LENOTRE,
121 Avenue de Wagram,
Paris 17.
(763.70.30 and 766.16.37).
Métro: Ternes or Wagram.
Open 9:30 A.M. to 7:15
P.M. Tuesday through
Saturday, 9 A.M. to 1
P.M. Sunday. Closed
Monday.
See Lenôtre, 16th
arrondissement.

LE MOULE A GATEAU,
10 Rue Poncelet, Paris 17.
(763.06.49).
Métro: Ternes.
Open 9 A.M. to 1:30 P.M.
and 4 P.M. to 7:30 P.M.
Tuesday through
Saturday, 9 A.M. to 1:30
P.M. Sunday. Closed
Monday.
See Le Moule à Gâteau, 5th
arrondissement, page 140.

Warm bread, at any hour.

ICE CREAM WORTH WAITING FOR

The queue stretches right around the corner, and neither sub-zero temperatures nor pouring rain can deter the hearty souls who queue up for a taste of Berthillon, Paris's finest ice cream. There's always a lot of good-natured grumbling about the wait (it can easily stretch into half an hour), while perfect strangers trade tales of past visits, or argue passionately about which of the thirty rich and creamy Berthillon flavours is best, purest, most authentic, most decadent. It is best to use the time to make serious decisions: which flavour? how many scoops?

There's always a lot of "place saving" as customers race up to the front of the queue to check the list of current seasonal offerings. Once you reach the window you'd better have your choice well in mind—there is no time for hemming, hawing, asking advice or questions. Will it be *glace au chocolat amer,* bitter chocolate ice cream rich with cream and eggs, and so profoundly chocolatey it tastes like a cold bar of Lindt chocolate; or maybe *nougat miel,* a crunchy, heavenly blend of nuts and smooth, smooth honey? Or, perhaps, the glistening red currant *sorbet (cassis),* that tastes so much like the real thing you can't believe you're not nibbling from a handful of lusciously tart, red berries.

Berthillon, 31 Rue Saint-Louis-en-l'Ile, Paris 4. (354.31.61). Métro: Pont-Marie. Open 10 A.M. to 8 P.M. Closed Monday, Tuesday, the month of August, and during school holidays.

If the thought of having to queue is discouraging, don't despair. Berthillon ice cream and *sorbets* are sold in many Paris cafés:

Restaurant Cadmios, 17 Rue des Deux-Ponts, Paris 4. (325.50.93). (cones only)

Le Flore en l'Ile, 42 Quai d'Orléans, Paris 4. (329.88.27).

Lady Jane, 4 Quai d'Orléans, Paris 4. (633.08.36).

Le Mandarin, 148 Boulevard Saint-Germain, Paris 6. (633.98.35).

Le Petit Châtelet, 39 Rue de la Bûcherie, Paris 5. (633.53.40).

Le Reveille, 29 Boulevard Henri-IV, Paris 4. (272.73.26).

Rostand, 6 Place Edmond-Rostand, Paris 6. (354.61.58).

La Rotonde, 105 Boulevard Montparnasse, Paris 6. (326.68.84 and 326.68.86).

Always a crowd at Berthillon.

**LA PATISSERIE
VIENNOISE,**
11 Rue Poncelet, Paris 17.
(227.81.86).
Métro: Ternes.
Open 9 A.M. to 7 P.M.
Tuesday through
Saturday, 9 A.M. to 1
P.M. Sunday. Closed
Monday.

A very special shop on one of Paris's most lively market streets. Like taking a trip to old Vienna, La Pâtisserie Viennoise is sheer fantasy. At Christmastime, every inch of this tiny shop (and a few feet outdoors) is filled with marzipan snowmen and chocolate Santas, neatly packaged assortments of spice cookies, sugar cookies, anise cookies, and fruit-studded, frosted *stollen.* All year round, the window tempts shoppers with flaky apple or cherry strudels, dark, lattice-top *Linzer tortes,* and the thick, walnut-packed *engadine,* Europe's answer to the pecan pie. There's a coffee bar along the side of the shop, so pull up a stool, order a *petit crème,* and indulge.

MONTMARTRE
17th and 18th arrondissements

**HELLEGOUARCH/
PATISSERIE
MONTMARTRE,**
81 Rue du Mont-Cenis,
Paris 18.
(606.39.28).
Métro: Jules-Joffrin.
Open daily, 9 A.M. to
7:30 P.M.

A large and spotless pastry shop dedicated to quality and simplicity at affordable prices. Vaudron has been around since 1931, catering to its faithful Parisian clientele and their births, their baptisms, and weddings, generation after generation. Since 1969, Roland Indrière, now assisted by his son, has continued the tradition, aspiring to offer simple, unfussy, appealing cakes and pastries made with the highest quality ingredients. Try their chocolates, their honey-sweetened *financiers,* and deliciously fresh buttercream-filled caramel macaroons. They prepare giant apple turnovers (*chaussons aux pommes*) each Wednesday and pear-filled pound cakes (*quatre-quarts aux poires*) each Thursday, not to mention beautiful *brioches, madeleines,* twenty flavours of ice cream, and other cakes and tarts.

VAUDRON,
4 Rue de la Jonquière,
  Paris 17.
(627.96.97).
Métro: Guy-Môquet.
Open 7:30 A.M. to 1 P.M.
  and 2 P.M. to 7:15 P.M.
  Closed Monday and the
  month of August.

Take a walk along the charming Rue du Poteau market street, then stop in for a crisp and buttery *croissant,* a fine *pain au chocolat,* superb *brioche* or hazelnut-scented *financier.* There's a small tea salon in back, where a light lunch can also be had.

BRIOCHE MOUSSELINE DENIS RUFFEL

Paris bakeries offer many variations on the classic brioche, a buttery, egg-rich yeast bread that's enjoyed for luxurious breakfasts or snacks, appearing in various forms and sizes. This brioche, known as brioche mousseline because it is richer in butter than brioche ordinaire, is incredibly golden and delicious. Brioche mousseline is typically Parisian, and the light and sticky dough is often baked in tin coffee cans. Denis Ruffel, from the Left Bank pastry shop Pâtisserie Millet (see entry, page 143), offers his personal version, baked in a rectangular loaf pan. Ruffel's special glaze gives all sweet breads a certain glow.

Brioche:
1 tablespoon or 1 package
  dry yeast
¼ cup (60 ml) lukewarm
  milk
⅓ cup (65 g) sugar
1 teaspoon salt
4 cups (560 g) unbleached
  flour
8 eggs
1¼ cups (10 ounces;
  280 g)
  unsalted butter at
  room temperature,
  plus 2 teaspoons
  unsalted butter, for
  buttering the loaf pans

Glaze:
1 egg
1 egg yolk
Pinch of salt
Pinch of sugar
1 teaspoon milk

1. In the bowl of an electric mixer combine the yeast, milk, and sugar, stir by hand and set aside for 5 minutes until the yeast has proofed.

2. Stir in the salt, then with the mixer at low speed add the flour, cup by cup, then the eggs, one by one, mixing well after each addition.

3. Add the butter, bit by bit, incorporating it smoothly into the dough. The dough will be very soft and sticky. Cover securely with plastic wrap and let rise, at room temperature, for 1 hour.

4. With a wooden spoon, stir the dough to deflate it, cover again, refrigerate, and let rise 1½ to 3 hours.

5. Preheat the oven to 350°F (175°C).

6. Stir down the dough again and pour equal portions of the dough into two well-buttered 6-cup (1.5-liter) loaf pans. The dough will remain very soft and sticky. Cover and let rise 1 hour. Don't worry if it doesn't double in bulk. It will rise more during the baking.

7. Combine the ingredients for the glaze and brush all over the top of the *brioche.* Bake 35 minutes, or until golden brown. Unmold immediately and cool on a rack. The *brioche* can easily be frozen.

Yield: 2 loaves.

TARTE FEUILLETEE A L'ANANAS JAMIN
JAMIN'S PUFF PASTRY PINEAPPLE TART

Pineapple is an often-ignored fruit in France, although it has been around since the 18th century. Louis XIV pricked his tongue the first time he tried pineapple (not knowing it should be peeled), but Louis XV loved the sweet fruit. At Jamin (see entry, page 64), chef Joël Robuchon found that, at first, he had a hard time convincing diners that a simple little pineapple tart could be so delicious. Until, of course, they tasted it. It's especially easy to make if you've a stash of tart shells in the freezer. The tart must be assembled at absolutely the last minute, or it turns soggy and you lose the wonderfully fresh and fruity flavour of the pineapple. Monsieur Robuchon uses a very thin puff pastry base for this tart, but any good homemade pastry crust may be used.

1 cup (250 ml) milk
2 egg yolks
¼ cup (50 g) sugar
3 tablespoons unbleached flour
1 tablespoon cornstarch
2 teaspoons kirsch or other fruit-based *eau-de-vie*
1 pre-baked 10½-inch (27-cm) pastry shell, cooled
6 slices fresh pineapple, each ½ inch (1½ cm) thick
2 tablespoons quince or red currant jelly

1. Place the milk in a small saucepan and bring it to a boil.

2. Meanwhile, in the bowl of an electric mixer, combine the egg yolks and sugar, and beat until thick and pale yellow. Slowly incorporate the flour and cornstarch. When the milk has boiled, slowly blend it into the egg mixture.

3. Return the mixture to the pan and stir constantly for 3 to 4 minutes over medium heat. Remove from heat and whisk in the kirsch. Spread the warm pastry cream over the pastry shell.

4. Cut the pineapple slices into wedges. Arrange the wedges in a sunburst pattern over the pastry cream, starting from the outside and working in.

5. In a small saucepan melt the jelly over low heat. Strain. Brush the warm jelly over the pineapple and serve the tart immediately.

Yield: One 10½-inch (27-cm) tart.

MENILMONTANT
20th arrondissement

GANACHAUD,
150 Rue Ménilmontant, Paris 20.
(636.13.82).
Métro: Pelleport.
Open 2:30 P.M. to 8 P.M. Tuesday, 7:30 A.M. to 8 P.M. Wednesday through Saturday, 7:30 A.M. to 1:30 P.M. Sunday. Closed Monday.

I can't imagine that anyone who has made the voyage to Ganachaud has gone away disappointed. Even before you get inside the shop, you're impressed. Most mornings, the pastry chef is there in the window, folding his *croissant* dough in a neat, orderly fashion. Later, he forms *croissant* after *croissant* as your tummy rumbles. Once inside, you need to decide: Shall you wait for the moist, wheaty *croissant* to be fetched on a paddle from the wood-fired oven, or will you go for the prune turnovers or a slice of *bostock* (a recycled slice of *brioche*, miraculously given new life with a touch of almonds and a sprinkling of kirsch), or, like me, give in to the ever-irresistible *pain au chocolat*? (See also Boulangeries.)

Boulangeries
BAKERIES

Fresh bread daily—in France it's a must.

Of the hundreds of Parisians I've interviewed over the years, I love the bakers best. Most often they are roly-poly men in worn white T-shirts, who came to Paris from little French towns and villages to make their way; they are men who love their wives, who never seem to have enough time to sleep, and who are passionate — almost crazily, over-the-edge, off-the-wall passionate—about bread. So am I.

One of my greatest gastronomic Parisian treats is to walk into a favorite *boulangerie* around noon, my stomach growling with hunger. I order a crusty *baguette "bien cuite,"* and before I've set down my two francs and forty centimes I've bitten off the heel. Chewy, yeasty ecstasy. Bread *is* life. It's food that makes you feel good, feel healthy; food that goes with everything, and goes especially well with the things we love most about France—fine cheese, great wine.

Bread baking is hard, tedious, lonely work and unfortunately few young Frenchmen still aspire to be bakers when they grow up. Working through the night in a suffocatingly hot basement holds little glamour. The truth is, the romantic notion of the frail French baker slaving through the night to provide breakfast fare is basically a memory these days, though there are still a few diligent souls who do labour through the darkest hours.

How does one tell the good loaf from the bad, and what makes the difference? The good French loaf is made with a respect for the simple nature of the ingredients: wholesome stone-milled wheat or rye flour; fresh yeast (*levure*) or a fresh sourdough starter (*levain*); pure water and a minimum of salt. This is true whether it's a thin, crisp, and golden *baguette* or *ficelle;* a plump round country-style *pain de campagne;* or a made-to-eat-with-cheese loaf studded with hazelnuts, walnuts, or raisins. In the best bakeries, ovens are fired all day long, assuring that customers can purchase fresh loaves just minutes old throughout the day. Most French bread contains no fat and thus quickly goes stale. All dough is now kneaded mechanically, but the best is done slowly, so the flavour is not killed by overkneading. Good dough is allowed to rise slowly, several times, with plenty of rest between kneadings. At the finest bakeries every loaf is formed by hand. Good bread has a thick crust, a dense and golden interior with lots of irregular air holes, and a fresh wheaty aroma and flavour.

During the past few years, many bakers have joined the "good bread campaign," a nationwide, loosely organized attempt to bring back the kind of bread made before World War II brought modernization to the corner bakery. At the same time, there is a renewed interest in all things natural, and *biologique* (organic) breads are popping up all over. The back-to-the-country movement is strong here, today, and the words *campagne* (country) and *paysanne* (peasant) appear everywhere.

The French loaf is still one of the city's best buys. "There used to be a saying that the daily newspaper, a litre of milk, and the *baguette* all had equal value and importance in French daily life, and all should cost the same," explained Didier Vacher, a young Paris baker committed to making an honest *baguette*. While it may have been true at one time, the *baguette* is today an incredible bargain when you consider that daily newspapers cost three francs seventy centimes and a litre of fresh, whole milk costs three francs fifty centimes.

BOURSE, REPUBLIQUE, ILE SAINT-LOUIS
2nd, 3rd, and 4th arrondissements

ONFROY,
34 Rue de Saintonge,
   Paris 3. (277.56.46).
Métro: Filles du Calvaire.
Open 7:45 A.M. to 1:30
   P.M. and 3 P.M. to 8
   P.M. Monday through
   Friday, 7:45 A.M. to
   1:30 P.M. Saturday.
Closed Sunday.

This is one baker I almost thought of keeping a secret. I am wild about rich, sour rye bread, the sort of hearty Eastern European loaf on which you could survive forever. And this is what comes out of Fernand Onfroy's old-fashioned, wood-fired oven. This unflappable Normandy baker—whose first childhood memory is of the Americans landing on Omaha beach—works quietly and diligently, also producing a fine *baguette biologique,* from organically grown flour, a whole wheat *baguette complète,* as well as the everyday *baguette.* When Monsieur Onfroy opened his modest little shop not far from Place de la République in 1965, he discovered the remains of an old underground Roman oven, then a more recent, though still ancient oven, at another level. Rue de Saintonge was first opened in 1628, and most likely, there's been a bakery at No. 34 for several centuries.

AU PANETIER LEBON,
10 Place des Petits-Pères,
   Paris 2.
(260.90.23).
Métro: Bourse.
Open 8 A.M. to 7 P.M.
   Closed Saturday and
   Sunday.

By eight most mornings there's a line of customers streaming in to buy Bernard Lebon's *baguette au levain* (sourdough *baguette*), still baked in a sturdy, oak-fired, brick-lined oven built around the turn of the century. Up at five each day, he travels just a few stories from his apartment above the shop to a flour-dusted, but impeccably tidy cellar, where his assistant has been working since midnight. Monsieur Lebon gets right to work, ready to greet the first crackling batch of bread as it comes from the oven at 6 A.M. Working steadily, he continues to mix, knead, and form additional loaves for later bakings at 9 A.M. and noon. The 250 *baguettes* they form each day are crisp and chewy, and like the baker, authentic and honest. But Monsieur Lebon and his wife, Yvette, don't stop there: They offer some fifty different shapes of bread (not all of them available each day), including giant *couronnes* (rings) of wheat and rye, special *baguettes moulées* baked in moulds to yield even crisper crusts, in all preparing eight different kinds of dough. What's the hardest thing about his job? "Getting the various breads to rise evenly, so they're ready for baking at the same time," says the agile, square-jawed baker. Does he love his own bread? He eats it three meals a day. Plus, every afternoon he enjoys one of his pastry chef's apple tarts, warm from the oven. Decorated breads can be made to order. The shop's recently restored *Belle Epoque* interior is worth a detour.

LES PANETONS,
47 Rue Saint-Louis-
   en-l'Ile, Paris 4.
(326.77.11).
Métro: Pont-Marie.
Open 10 A.M. to 2 P.M.
   and 4 P.M. to 8 P.M.
   Closed Monday.

This bright, cheery contemporary bake shop right in the middle of Ile Saint-Louis offers appealing displays of fine, fresh breads in a variety of sizes and shapes, including gluten bread, giant round *boules biologiques,* good rye breads flavored with nuts or raisins, and tiny, delicate sesame rolls.

SAINT-GERMAIN, LATIN QUARTER, PLACE D'ITALIE
5th and 13th arrondissements

R. CLEMENT,
123 Rue L. M. Nordmann,
    Paris 13.
(707.12.78).
Métro: Glacière.
Open 7:30 A.M. to 1 P.M.
    and 2 P.M. to 7:30 P.M.
Closed Sunday.

A near-perfect *baguette:* with a wonderfully crunchy, almost nutty crust, and a dense, moist, golden *mie,* or interior. It stays fresh for hours—that is, if you can keep it that long.

**BOULANGERIE
MODERNE,**
16 Rue des Fossés Saint-
    Jacques, Paris 5.
(354.12.22).
Métro: Luxembourg.
Open 7:15 A.M. to 2 P.M.
    and 3:45 P.M. to 7:30
    P.M. Closed Saturday
    and Sunday.

There's nothing modern about the *Belle Epoque* storefront of this tiny neighbourhood *boulangerie* set on the active Place de l'Estrapade near the Panthéon. They sell an "American-style" *baguette* that tastes as though it's made with gluten-rich American flour. It's a neighbourhood favourite, with a crisp crust and denser than average, chewy interior.

LES PANETONS,
113 Rue Mouffetard,
    Paris 5.
(707.12.08).
Métro: Censier-Daubenton.
Open 7:30 A.M. to 7:30
    P.M. Tuesday through
    Saturday, 7:30 A.M. to
    1 P.M. Sunday. Closed
    Monday.
See Les Panetons, 4th
    arrondissement.

**BOULANGERIE
PERRUCHE,**
68 Rue du Cardinal-
    Lemoine, Paris 5.
(326.34.62).
Métro: Cardinal Lemoine.
Open 7:15 A.M. to 1:15
    P.M. and 4 P.M. to 7:30
    P.M. Closed Sunday and
    Monday.

At one time, Michel Perruche had the largest wood-fired oven in Paris, built near the Place de la Contrescarpe on the Left Bank. Even a documentary film, "La Boulangerie de la Contrescarpe," was made about his modest *Art Déco boulangerie.* Monsieur Perruche has newer gas-fired ovens now, but his country-style *baguette de campagne*—made from regular *baguette* dough but dusted with flour—remains a delight. The calm, quiet little baker is up at three each morning, and with the help of a single assistant, produces some 800 loaves of bread a day, with the first batch ready just after seven in the morning.

**PLACE MONGE
MARKET,**
Stall at 61 Place Monge,
Paris 5.
Métro: Monge.
Open Wednesday, Friday,
and Sunday 7 A.M. to
1 P.M.

Three mornings each week, when the Place Monge open-air market is in full swing, you can find these truly classic big, round sourdough rye loaves carefully stacked on wooden tables. Buy this dense and chewy *pain de seigle* on Friday and it will still show plenty of spunk on Tuesday. The loaves are baked in wood-fired ovens in the outskirts of Paris.

ROUILLON,
53 bis Boulevard Arago,
Paris 13.
(707.14.58).
Métro: Glacière.
Open 7:30 A.M. to 8:30
P.M. Closed Thursday
and Friday.

Try to get here right about lunchtime, when the crisp and crunchy *petits pains* are fresh from the oven. This little neighbourhood *boulangerie* also offers a nice variety of unusual, decorative breads, beautiful *kougelhopf,* and delicious, tangy sourdough *pain au levain.*

J. C. VANDERSTICHEL,
31 Boulevard Arago,
Paris 13.
(707.26.75).
Métro: Gobelins.
Open 6 A.M. to 8 P.M.
Closed Sunday and
Monday.

Wonderful, organic loaves that come from the oven around eleven in the morning. Try the hearty, crusty *baguette biologique*—you won't regret it. This is a simple, straightforward bakery, which also offers beautiful classic *baguettes* and *ficelles.*

SEVRES-BABYLONE, LA TOUR-MAUBOURG
6th and 7th arrondissements

**AVENUE DE BRETEUIL
MARKET,**
Stall at 5 Avenue de
Breteuil, Paris 7.
Métro: Sèvres-Babylone.
Open 7 A.M. to 1 P.M.
Saturday.

Each Saturday, when the Avenue de Breteuil market attracts thousands of local shoppers, you can find big, hearty rounds of country sourdough rye. Ask for the *pain de seigle* that is baked in wood-fired ovens in Vincennes, outside of Paris.

DUBUS,
175 Rue de Grenelle,
   Paris 7.
(551.94.71).
Métro: La Tour-Maubourg.
Open 7 A.M. to 7:30 P.M.
   Closed Sunday.

If you wander in on a day they've got crisp and lacy *fougasse* fresh from the oven, go for it! Covered with a sheer egg glaze, the crust of this beautiful rectangular white bread is both crisp and chewy at the same time. The pastries here are also quite respectable.

The line flows out the door at Poilâne.

LIONEL POILANE,
8 Rue du Cherche-Midi,
   Paris 6.
(548.42.59).
Métro: Sèvres-Babylone.
Open 7 A.M. to 8 P.M.
   Closed Sunday.

Pain Poilâne . . . need one say more? There is no question that Lionel Poilâne makes the most famous bread in France, perhaps the world. Thousands of Parisians buy his moist sourdough loaf each day. It's sold at more than 600 shops around Paris, more than 300 restaurants. Each day, airplanes take off for Manhattan and Tokyo, delivering fresh-baked loaves for those willing to pay a very steep price. Each giant, round, wholesome loaf is made with a pungent sourdough starter, all-French flour, and fragrant sea salt. Each is formed by hand, rising in rustic—yet practical—fabric-lined wicker baskets. The loaves are baked in wood-fired ovens, one of which was built by the *patron* himself. But Poilâne bread is far from perfect, as Monsieur Poilâne readily admits. "People complain that it is uneven," he notes, suggesting that "with *levain,* that's the name of the game. No two batches are ever the same; a simple storm can ruin an entire baking."

And he's right. There are days Poilâne bread is so dry, so lacking in authority and flavour, you know something's gone wrong. I've also tasted the bread so rich, dense, so properly acidic and authoritative, that every other loaf, before or after, is pale in comparison. Criticism aside, no one's yet attempted to meet the Poilâne challenge. Rarely imitated—never successfully—he remains *"le roi du pain."* The Poilâne loaf has set the contemporary standard for bread, the loaf against which almost all others are judged.

Visitors to the family shop on Rue du Cherche-Midi are almost always welcome to visit the wonderfully fragrant, flour-dusted cellar, to watch the famous bread being mixed, kneaded, and baked in the ancient wood-fired oven set beneath the street. Large, personalized *pain décoré* can be ordered several days in advance.

The hearty Poilâne loaf.

PAIN POILANE AU LEVAIN NATUREL
POILANE'S NATURAL SOURDOUGH BREAD

This is the recipe that Paris's most famous baker, Lionel Poilâne, created for the French housewife, and the closest I've come to recreating his superb and popular loaf at home. I also call it "Patience Bread," because it takes almost a week to make the first batch of this natural, slightly sour loaf. Anyone who loves bread-baking should try it at least once, for it is really rather miraculous that such wonderful flavours can come from the simple blend of salt, water, and flour, and not a touch of yeast.

To bakers accustomed to the fast-acting whoosh one gets from yeast doughs, Poilâne's dough is a real sleeper. This dough really takes its time expanding, but the reward for your patience is a very fine-grained, mildly acidic, gentle loaf. It's the most subtle and delicious bread I know, at the same time sophisticated and countryish. When you bite into it, you'll say "Now, this is bread!" A great crust, with a moist, chewy, wheaty-brown interior.

In developing this recipe, Susan Herrmann Loomis, who is my associate, and I baked at least 100 loaves, no two of which turned out exactly alike, nearly all of which offered a vibrantly acidic interior, and an irresistible, chewy crust. We worked with different kinds of flours, rising times, and water proportions, and found the following combination the most foolproof. If you don't bake bread regularly, you may not want to bother saving the starter, or chef, and may prefer to start from scratch each time.

5½ to 6 cups (770 to 840 g) unbleached flour

2⅓ cups (580 ml) lukewarm water

1 tablespoon sea salt

1. To make the starter, or *chef*: In a small bowl combine 1 cup (140 g) flour with ⅓ cup (80 ml) water. Stir until well blended, then transfer the dough to a floured work surface and knead and form into a smooth ball. It should be fairly soft and sticky. Return the starter to the bowl, cover with a damp cloth and let sit at room temperature for 72 hours. It should rise slightly and take on a fresh, acidic aroma.

2. After 72 hours, uncover the starter and in a medium-size mixing bowl add ½ cup (125 ml) lukewarm water to

the starter and stir. Add an additional 1½ cups (210 g) flour and stir to blend. Transfer the dough to a floured work surface and knead into a smooth ball. It should be firm but not stiff. Return the dough to the bowl, cover with a damp cloth and let sit in a warm place for 24 to 48 hours. (The length of time really depends on your schedule. A longer rise will produce a slightly more acidic bread.)

3. To complete the dough: In a very large, shallow bowl, combine the dough with 1½ cups (375 ml) water and the sea salt. Stir until the mixture is fairly well blended, then begin adding the remaining 3 to 3½ cups (420 to 490 g) flour cup by cup, mixing well after each addition. Continue folding the dough over itself to incorporate air—it may actually be too soft to knead—for 10 minutes, adding additional flour as necessary to keep the dough from being too sticky. The final dough should be rather soft, but not so soft it sticks to your fingers. Cover with a damp cloth and let sit in a warm place for 8 to 12 hours. The dough should rise slightly.

4. To form the loaf: Cut off a handful of dough, about 1 cup (250 g) to set aside for the next loaf. Transfer the dough to a very heavily floured work surface. Shape it into a tight ball by folding it over itself. Do not be disturbed if the dough is softer than ordinary bread dough. Place a large, floured towel in a round, shallow bowl or basket— one about 9½ inches (24 cm) wide and 4 inches (10 cm) deep works well—and place the dough in the towel-lined bowl or basket. Fold the towel over the dough, covering it loosely. Let sit in a warm place for 8 to 12 hours.

5. Preheat the oven to 375°F (190°C).

6. Turn the loaf upside-down onto a flour-dusted baking sheet. Slash the bread several times with a razor blade to a depth of about ¼ inch (7 mm), so it can expand regularly during baking. Bake for 1 to 1½ hours, or until golden brown. The loaf should have a very hard crust and sound hollow when the bottom is tapped. Remove to a baking rack to cool. The dough may not rise substantially—a normal loaf will rise to about 2 to 3 inches (5 to 8 cm) in the center. The ideal loaf should have an interior with large, irregular air holes throughout, and should be very moist and taste slightly acidic. The crust should be very crisp and dense. Although this bread should stay fresh for a week, it is so delicious I find it rarely lasts two days.

Note: After you have made your first loaf and have saved the *chef,* begin at step 2 for subsequent loaves. Proceed normally through the rest of the recipe, always remembering to save a *chef,* which can be stored at room temperature, covered with a damp cloth, for two or three days, or refrigerated for up to five days.

Yield: 1 loaf.

PAIN POILANE
SHORT VERSION

This is a shorter version of the Poilâne recipe and will produce a slightly less acidic bread. Once you have the chef (see previous page), this version can be made in one day.

1 cup (250 g) *chef*
  (starter), see above
2 cups (500 ml)
  lukewarm water
1 tablespoon sea salt
4½ to 5 cups (630 to 700
  g) unbleached flour

1. In a very large, shallow bowl, combine the *chef* with 2 cups (500 ml) lukewarm water, and the sea salt. Stir until the mixture is fairly well blended, then begin adding 4½ to 5 cups (630 to 700 g) of flour, cup by cup, mixing well after each addition. Continue folding the dough over itself—it may actually be too soft to knead—for 10 minutes, adding additional flour as necessary to keep the dough from being too sticky. The final dough should be rather soft, but not so soft it sticks to your fingers. Cover the bowl with a damp cloth and let sit for 1 hour.

2. To form the loaf: Cut off a handful of the dough, about 1 cup (250 g) to set aside for the next loaf. Transfer the rest of the dough to a very heavily floured work surface. Shape it into a tight ball by folding it over itself. Don't be disturbed if the dough is softer than ordinary bread dough. Place a large, floured towel in a round, shallow bowl or basket—about 9½ inches (24 cm) wide and 4 inches (10 cm) deep—and place the dough in the towel-lined bowl or basket. Fold the towel over the dough, covering it loosely. Let sit in a warm place for 8 to 12 hours.

3. Preheat the oven to 375°F (190°C).

4. Turn the loaf upside-down onto a flour-dusted baking sheet. Slash the bread several times with a razor blade, to a depth of about ¼ inch (7mm), so it can expand regularly during baking. Bake for 1 to 1½ hours, or until golden brown. The loaf should have a very hard crust and sound hollow when the bottom is tapped. Remove to a baking rack to cool.

Yield: 1 loaf.

POUJAURAN,
20 Rue Jean Nicot, Paris 7.
(705.80.88).
Métro: La Tour-Maubourg.
Open 8:30 A.M. to 8:30
  P.M. Closed Saturday
  and Sunday.

Young Jean-Luc Poujauran, an energetic, idealistic baker from France's southwest, claims he was the first in Paris to turn out a *baguette biologique,* made with organically grown, stone-ground, all-French flour. That was more than seven years ago, and his honey-colored, dense, and chewy *baguette* is unquestionably one of the best in Paris. A native of the rich and rustic southwest, Monsieur Poujauran is always trying new ideas: He once made a totally *biologique croissant,* using organic eggs, butter, and flour, in memory of his grandmother, who brought him up on pure and healthy foods. He's the sort of young man who inspires confidence: When he was first starting out and had little money, faithful customers chipped in to help him buy his first bread mixer. Try his earthy sourdough *pain de campagne,* along with delightful and delicious pastries that fill this charming turn-of-the-century *boulangerie.* High-quality French pastry and bread flour can also be purchased in the shop. (See also Pâtisseries.)

GRANDS BOULEVARDS, GARE SAINT-LAZARE
8th and 9th arrondissements

LENOTRE,
5 Rue du Havre, Paris 9.
(522.22.59).
Métro: Gare Saint-Lazare.
Open 9 A.M. to 7:30 P.M.
    Tuesday through Friday,
    9:45 A.M. to 7:45 P.M.
    Saturday and Monday.
    Closed Sunday.

Not content to reign as the king of pastries, Gaston Lenôtre with the help of his professional crew has greatly improved and increased his bread selection to include a remarkable *baguette,* along with a dozen different shapes and varieties of old-time regional breads and decorated, rustic country loaves to be personalized and ordered in advance. (See also Chocolateries and Pâtisseries.)

RENE SAINT-OUEN,
111 Boulevard Haussmann,
    Paris 8.
(265.06.25).
Métro: Miromesnil.
Open 8 A.M. to 7 P.M.
    Closed Sunday.

More like a museum devoted to *pain de fantaisie,* the windows of this rather ill-kept shop are filled with breads shaped like rabbits and bicycles, chickens and stars. The bread is inedible, but if you want a humorous souvenir to hang on your wall, this is the place to buy it.

Crusty baguettes.

BAGUETTES

The crackling crisp, slender *baguette*—the name comes from the French for wand—is not as old as most people think. And it wasn't born; it evolved essentially out of consumer demand. According to Raymond Calvel, one of France's more respected bread experts, the *baguette* came into being just before World War I, when the classic French loaf had two shapes: the round *miche,* weighing about 5 pounds (2.5 kilos), and the *pain long,* an 8-inch by 30-inch (20.5-cm by 76-cm) loaf of the same weight. The *mie,* or interior of the *pain long* was dense and heavy, the crust crisp and flavorful. Most consumers preferred the crust and bakers accommodated, making the bread thinner and thinner to obtain maximum crust, reducing the loaf's volume until they came up with the traditional 30-inch (76 cm) *baguette,* weighing about 8 ounces (250 grams).

Other historians suggest that the *baguette* evolved from the *viennois,* a long, thin Austrian-type loaf popular around the turn of the century. The loaf, still found in the majority of *boulangeries* in France, has the same slender form as the *baguette,* but the dough is sweetened with sugar and softened with milk.

BOUCICAUT, PORTE DE VANVES
15th arrondissement

LA PETITE MARQUISE,
91 Rue de la Convention,
  Paris 15.
(554.50.20).
Métro: Boucicaut.
Open 10 A.M. to 1:30 P.M.
  and 3 P.M. to 7:30 P.M.
  Tuesday through Friday,
  10 A.M. to 7:30 P.M.
  Saturday, 4 P.M. to 7:30
  P.M. Monday. Closed
  Sunday.

LIONEL POILANE,
49 Boulevard de Grenelle,
  Paris 15.
(579.11.49).
Métro: Bir-Hakeim/
  Grenelle.
Open 7 A.M. to 8 P.M.
  Closed Monday.
See Lionel Poilâne, 6th
  arrondissement, page 157.

*On January 14, 1790,
Benjamin Franklin
attended the inauguration of
the Académie de la
Boulangerie, hoping to
convince the bakers there
that the only flour worth
considering was corn flour.*

When La Petite Marquise's bread is fresh, it's chewy, pleasantly acidic, and full of flavour. They make several different shapes of bread from the same dough, including a wonderful flat *galette*.

THE DAILY LOAF

The following are just a few breads—of various sizes, flours, *fantaisie* shapes—found in the Parisian *boulangerie*.

Baguette: in Paris, this is legally a loaf weighing about 8 ounces (250 grams) and is made from flour, water, and yeast. It may also contain fava bean flour and ascorbic acid, or vitamin C. *Baguettes* dusted with flour may be sold as *baguette de campagne, baguette à l'ancienne,* or *baguette paysanne.* There are also two "brand name" *baguettes,* the Belle Epoque and the Banette, sold in various bakeries. The bakers guarantee that these are made without the addition of fava bean flour or ascorbic acid, and are made according to slower, old-fashioned methods.

Baguette au levain (also sold by other names, sometimes called **baguette à l'ancienne**): sourdough *baguette.*

Boule: ball, or round loaf, either small or large.

Chapeau: small round loaf, topped with a little *chapeau,* or hat.

Couronne: ring-shaped *baguette.*

Le fer à cheval: horseshoe-shaped *baguette.*

Ficelle: very thin, crusty *baguette.*

Fougasse: generally, a crusty, flat, rectangular-shaped, lacy bread made of *baguette* dough; can be filled with onions, herbs, spices, or anchovies, or can be made of puff pastry dough.

Miche: large round country-style loaf.

Pain de campagne: there is no legal definition for the country loaf, which can vary from a white bread simply dusted with flour to give it a rustic look (and fetch a higher price) to a truly hearty loaf that may be a blend of white, whole wheat, and perhaps rye flour with added bran. It comes in every shape, from a small round individual roll to a large family loaf.

Pain complet: bread made partially or entirely from

*A Ganachaud arrangement
(see entry, page 168).*

whole wheat flour, with bakers varying proportions according to their personal tastes.

Pain de fantaisie: generally, any odd or imaginatively-shaped bread. Even *baguette de campagne* falls into the *fantaisie* category.

Pain de mie: the rectangular white sandwich loaf that is nearly all *mie* (interior crumb), and very little crust. It is made for durability, its flavour and texture developed for use in sandwiches. Unlike most French breads, it contains milk, sugar, and butter, and may contain chemical preservatives.

Pain aux noix and pain aux noisettes: bread, most often rye or wheat, filled with walnuts or hazelnuts.

Pain polka: bread that is slashed in a criss-cross pattern; usually a large country loaf cut in this manner.

Pain aux raisins: bread, most often rye or wheat, filled with raisins.

Pain de seigle: bread made from 60 to 70 percent rye flour and 30 to 40 percent wheat flour.

Pain de son: legally, a dietetic bread which is quality-controlled, containing 20 percent bran mixed with white flour.

Pain viennois: shaped like a *baguette,* with regular horizontal slashes, this loaf usually contains white flour, sugar, powdered milk, water, and yeast.

MAX POILANE,
87 Rue Brançion, Paris 15.
(828.45.90).
Métro: Porte de Vanves.
Open 7:15 A.M. to 8 P.M.
Monday through Friday,
7:30 A.M. to 1:30 P.M.
Saturday. Closed Sunday.

One of Paris's best-kept secrets is that there is more than one Poilâne: famous brother Lionel, and less famous brother Max. Working with the same ingredients and huge, wood-fired ovens, they produce essentially the same large, round country loaf, with slight variations. Max's shop on the edge of town is worth a detour: The charming turn-of-the-century *boulangerie,* with its marble floors, glistening chandelier, and beautiful crusty loaves arranged like still lifes in wicker baskets around the room, is perhaps the most romantic little bakery in town. Lean, intense, and poetic, Max Poilâne is a fanatic about bread: "I love bread, I eat bread with bread. One day I even found myself eating bread with *sorbet*—that was too much." When he goes to restaurants, he brings a little sack of his own bread with him. Like Lionel, he has managed to keep his operation simple, artisanal, despite the fact that five huge wood-fired ovens are kept going twenty-four hours a day. Large, personalized *pain décoré* (decorated country loaf) can be ordered several days in advance.

*J. M. Callede's lacy fougasse
(see entry, page 166).*

PAIN DE MIE DENIS RUFFEL
DENIS RUFFEL'S SANDWICH LOAF

This is France's firm, fine-grained sandwich loaf: milky, just slightly sweet, and delicious when fresh and toasted. Denis Ruffel, from Pâtisserie Millet, the Left Bank pastry shop, manages to turn a single loaf of pain de mie into an entire buffet, making dozens of tiny, highly decorated, open-face sandwiches. He'll top some with caviar or smoked salmon and lemon triangles, others with a blend of Roquefort, walnuts and butter, and still others with thin slices of sausages topped with piped butter rosettes. The mie, by the way, is the crumb, or non-crusty portion of any bread, and since this bread has virtually no crust, it's called pain de mie. Some Paris bakers advertise pain de mie au beurre, to distinguish their bread from those made with margarine. The loaf is usually made in a special pan fitted with a sliding cover, which helps mold the bread into a tidy rectangle. The moulds are available at many cookware shops, although the bread can be made in any straight-sided loaf pan. To obtain a neat rectangular loaf, cover the dough-filled loaf pan with foil and a baking sheet, then weight the sheet with a brick or other heavy object and bake.

1 cup (250 ml) lukewarm milk
3 tablespoons unsalted butter, at room temperature, plus 1 tablespoon for buttering the bowl and loaf pan
1 tablespoon or 1 package dry yeast
2 tablespoons sugar
2 teaspoons salt
2¾ cups (385 g) unbleached flour

1. In a large bowl, combine the milk, 3 tablespoons butter, yeast, and sugar, stir, and set aside for 5 minutes to proof the yeast.

2. Once proofed, stir in the salt, then add the flour, cup by cup, mixing well after each addition. Knead by hand for 2 or 3 minutes, or until the dough forms a smooth ball. Place in a well-buttered, large bowl (use some of the remaining 1 tablespoon butter) and cover securely with plastic wrap. Let rise in a warm place until double in bulk, approximately 1 to 1½ hours.

3. Butter a 6-cup (1.5-liter) loaf pan, or the mould and top of a 6-cup (1.5-liter) *pain de mie* pan. If using a loaf pan, butter a piece of aluminum foil to use as a lid. Punch down the dough, knead for 1 minute, then transfer it to the pan or mould. Press down the dough smoothly, being sure it fills the corners, and cover. Let rise until double in bulk, another 1 to 1½ hours.

4. About 30 minutes before the dough is ready to be baked, preheat the oven to 375°F (190°C).

5. Bake for 45 minutes, or until the loaf is golden brown. (If using a loaf pan cover with buttered foil and a baking sheet, then weight the sheet with a brick or other heavy object.) Unmould immediately and cool on a rack. The bread will stay fresh for several days, wrapped and stored at room temperature. *Pain de mie* also freezes well.

Yield: 1 loaf.

Victor-Hugo, Auteuil
16th arrondissement

LENOTRE,
44 Rue d'Auteuil, Paris 16.
(524.52.52).
Métro: Michel Ange/
Auteuil.
Open daily, 9:15 A.M. to
7:15 P.M.
See Lenôtre, 9th
arrondissement, page 161.

LENOTRE,
49 Avenue Victor-Hugo,
Paris 16.
(501.71.71).
Métro: Victor-Hugo.
Open 9:30 A.M. to 7:15
P.M. Tuesday through
Saturday, 9 A.M. to 1
P.M. Sunday. Closed
Monday.
See Lenôtre, 9th
arrondissement, page 161.

LA PETITE MARQUISE,
3 Place Victor-Hugo,
Paris 16.
(500.77.36).
Métro: Victor-Hugo.
Open 9 A.M. to 7:30 P.M.
Closed Sunday.
See La Petite Marquise,
15th *arrondissement,* page
162.

A BREAD MUSEUM

The Musée Français du Pain, installed in the *grenier* (grain loft) of a still active flour mill just southeast of Paris at the edge of the Bois de Vincennes, is like a toy store for bread lovers. Thousands of bread-related trinkets and memorabilia line the spotless rooms that are filled with cartoons and drawings, carefully preserved bread boards and knives, wicker rising baskets and shiny copper molds—all there to celebrate the nobility of bread in history. There are façades and signs from *Belle Epoque* bakers; Saint-Honoré, the 7th-century "patron saint" of bakers, is represented paddle in hand; there are 17th-century metal moulds, designed for making hosts used for religious celebrations; fascinating tin spice-cookie moulds, ancient bread-related manuscripts as well as miniature models of brick-lined, wood-fired ovens.

Musée Français du Pain, 25 bis Rue Victor-Hugo, 94220 Charenton-le-Pont. (368.43.60). Métro: Charenton Ecoles. Open 2 P.M. to 4:30 P.M. Tuesday and Thursday, from September 8 to July 1.

Bread, by the armful, is almost a one-day supply for an enthusiastic eater.

ARC DE TRIOMPHE, PORTE MAILLOT, VILLIERS, PLACE DE CLICHY, MONTMARTRE
17th and 18th arrondissements

AUX ARMES DE NIEL,
29 Avenue Niel, Paris 17.
(763.62.01).
Métro: Ternes.
Open 6:30 A.M. to 8 P.M.
  Closed Tuesday.

BOUTIQUE DU PAIN,
11 Rue Gustave-Flaubert,
Paris 17. (763.75.68).
Métro: Ternes.
Open 7:30 A.M. to 8:30
  P.M. Closed Sunday and
  Monday.

J. M. CALLEDE,
50 Rue du Mont-Cenis,
  Paris 18. (252.25.46).
Métro: Jules-Joffrin.
Open 7:30 A.M. to 2 P.M.
  and 4 P.M. to 8 P.M.,
  7:30 A.M. to 8 P.M.
  Sunday. Closed
  Wednesday and Thursday.

LA HACQUINIERE,
25 Avenue de Clichy,
  Paris 17. (387.52.00).
Métro: Place de Clichy.
Open 8:30 A.M. to 1:30
  P.M. and 3:30 P.M. to
  8:30 P.M. Closed
  Monday.

LENOTRE,
121 Avenue de Wagram,
  Paris 17.
(763.70.30 and
  766.16.57).
Métro: Wagram.
Open 9:30 A.M. to 7:15
  P.M. Tuesday through
  Saturday, 9 A.M. to 1
  P.M. Sunday. Closed
  Monday.
See Lenôtre, 9th
  arrondissement, page 161.

For a good, solid sourdough *baguette* (ask for a *ficelle au levain*) with deep and dark brown crust, a yeasty aroma and honey-colored interior. Also huge, round, beautiful, decorative loaves made to order, for about 45 francs per loaf.

Honest, authentic breads from a friendly, dedicated baker named Marcel Pain. Both his *baguette de campagne* and *baguette biologique* are good and crusty, and the hazelnut and raisin rye is perhaps the best of its kind in Paris. Monsieur Pain and his charming wife are an ambitious pair, and each week there seems to be a new kind of bread or pastry to tempt passersby.

I don't understand why more bakers don't make *fougasse*, the lacy, elegant bread that's festive and fun to eat as well. Monsieur Callede makes a lovely assortment of *fougasse*, sprinkling some with cumin, others with sesame or poppy seeds. Take a tour of the Rue du Poteau market, then take a short walk up the hill to this modest neighbourhood *boulangerie*.

Raymond Seguy's earthy, artisanal sourdough *baguette*, made according to old-fashioned rules and standards, takes seven hours to prepare, from start to finish, and it's certain to be devoured in a matter of seconds.

Bernard Ganachaud, master baker (see entry, page 168).

BOSTOCK BERNARD GANACHAUD

Bostock is a terrific way to recycle day-old brioche, which on its own is already quite marvellous. One of my favourite Parisian bakers, Bernard Ganachaud, kindly shared the recipe for this kirsch-and almond-flavoured pastry. Superb fresh from the oven, bostock is still delicious a few days later. Eat it for breakfast or dessert. (See ganachaud entry, page 168.)

1 cup (250 ml) water
1⅜ cups sugar (275 g)
10 slices day-old *brioche*
2 large eggs
¾ cup (100 g) almonds, toasted, then ground to a fine powder, plus ½ cup almonds (70 g), coarsely chopped
3 tablespoons kirsch

1. Preheat the oven to 375°F (190°C).

2. In a medium-size saucepan over medium heat, combine the water and ⅝ cup (125 g) sugar and stir until dissolved. Remove from the heat.

3. Dip the slices of *brioche* in the syrup and drain them on a wire rack. Once drained, arrange the slices on a baking sheet.

4. In a small mixing bowl combine the eggs, finely ground almonds, and remaining ¾ cup (160 g) sugar and blend to a thick paste. Spread the mixture on the *brioche*.

5. Sprinkle the *brioche* with kirsch, then the coarsely chopped almonds. Bake for 15 minutes or until golden.

Yield: 10 servings.

BOULANGERIE QUENTIN,
21 Rue de Lévis, Paris 17. (387.28.27).
Métro: Villiers.
Open 7 A.M. to 8 P.M. Tuesday through Saturday, 7 A.M. to 1:30 P.M. and 4 P.M. to 8 P.M. Sunday. Closed Monday.

In 1982 Louis Couasnon began making the Belle Epoque, a brand-name *baguette* prepared by about eighty French bakers working to promote a return to artisanal breads. Monsieur Couasnon makes only about 100 such *baguettes* each day, using special flour. His sourdough loaf, made from 4 percent rye flour, and white flour reinforced with special gluten, is mixed at 2:30 A.M. and comes out of the oven around 9 A.M. It is fat and thick-crusted, with an almost charcoal crust and a light, airy interior.

**BOULANGERIE
VACHER,**
55 Boulevard Gouvion
   Saint-Cyr, Paris 17.
(574.04.50).
Métro: Porte Maillot.
Open 7 A.M. to 8
   P.M. Closed Thursday
   and Friday.

"I t doesn't take any longer to make good bread than bad bread, so why not make good bread?" asks young Didier Vacher, who grew up across the street, above his parents' old *boulangerie*. Now he lives above his own shop, a little corner *boulangerie* he bought at the age of 24. Since the opening, he's been making the Banette, a sort of brand-name sourdough *baguette* made according to old-fashioned methods. It's a classic, and worth a visit if you're in the neighbourhood. Also note the gigantic, rectangular country loaves.

DECORATED BREAD

O ne of the most beautiful and festive breads in Paris is the *pain decoré,* generally a large, round, decorated loaf that is personalized with one's name, a favourite symbol or saying, or most classically, a bunch of grapes or sheaves of wheat. The following *boulangeries* will prepare decorated breads to order, though all must be ordered in advance. The breads, by the way, are not simply decorative, they're edible.

Aux Armes de Niel, 29 Avenue Niel, Paris 17. (763.62.01). One day in advance.

Lenôtre, 5 Rue du Havre, Paris 9. (522.22.59); 49 Avenue Victor Hugo, Paris 16. (501.71.71); 44 Rue d'Auteuil, Paris 16. (524.52.52); 121 Avenue de Wagram, Paris 17. (763.70.30). One week in advance.

Lionel Poilâne, 8 Rue du Cherche-Midi, Paris 6. (548.42.59). One day in advance.

Max Poilâne, 87 Rue Brançion, Paris 15. (828.45.90). One day in advance.

MENILMONTANT
20th arrondissement

GANACHAUD,
150 Rue Ménilmontant,
   Paris 20.
(636.13.82).
Métro: Pelleport.
Open 2:30 P.M. to 8 P.M.
   Tuesday, 7:30 A.M. to
   8 P.M. Wednesday
   through Saturday, 7:30
   A.M. to 1:30 P.M.
   Sunday. Closed Monday.

S incere, hard-working Bernard Ganachaud is one of my favourite Paris bakers. Son of a baker, the dapper, white-haired man has been working with bread since the age of eight, when he began helping his father. Nowadays at seven each night he or one of his crew lights up the gigantic wood-fired oven that dominates his shop, and by 4 A.M. the oven is put to work, baking 1,000 or so crusty loaves each day. Monsieur Ganachaud was the first bread baker in France to win the coveted Meilleur Ouvrier de France award, and one look at his *boutique,* one bite of his bread and you understand why. He offers thirty different shapes and varieties of bread, from eight different flours, including a hearty *seigle noir,* or black rye. He also makes a wonderful *bostock* (see recipe, page 167), a pastry made from day-old *brioche.* Ganachaud is located out in the middle of nowhere, but the best things in life are always worth a detour. (See also Pâtisseries.)

PETITS PAINS PARISIENS JAMIN
JAMIN'S CRUSTY OVAL-SHAPED ROLLS

These rolls are so popular at Jamin (see entry, page 64), the nouvelle cuisine restaurant on Rue de Longchamp, that each diner consumes an average of three rolls per meal. Chef Joël Robuchon bakes them fresh for both lunch and dinner, in a small convection oven fitted with a vaporizing attachment to help develop a good crust. Equally good results can be obtained at home.

2½ cups (625 ml) lukewarm water
2 tablespoons or 2 packages dry yeast
2 teaspoons salt
6 to 7 cups (840 to 980 g) unbleached flour

1. Combine water and yeast in a large mixing bowl and set aside for 5 minutes to proof the yeast.

2. Once proofed, add the salt, then begin adding flour, cup by cup, until the dough is too stiff to stir. Place the dough on a lightly floured wooden board and begin kneading, adding additional flour as necessary. The dough should be fairly stiff and firm. Knead for 10 to 15 minutes, or until the dough is smooth and satiny. Place the dough in a bowl, cover securely with plastic wrap, and let rise at room temperature for 1 hour, or until double in bulk.

3. When dough is doubled, punch down and let rise again, covered, for about 1 hour until double in bulk.

4. Punch down again, then separate the dough into 18 equal portions, each weighing about 3 ounces (85 g). Form into neat ovals, and place on a baking sheet. Mist with water (a household flower mister works well) and let rise 45 minutes, covered with a clean cloth.

5. Preheat the oven to 450°F (230°C). Just before placing the rolls in the oven, place a shallow baking pan filled with 2 cups (500 ml) boiling water on the bottom of the oven to create a steamy atmosphere for baking, giving the rolls a good crust.

6. Bake for 20 to 25 minutes or until rolls are a rich, golden brown. Mist with cold water several times during the first 3 minutes of baking.

7. Remove the rolls from the oven to cool on a baking rack. Because there is no fat in this recipe, the rolls will not stay fresh for long. They should, ideally, be consumed within two hours of baking. (Alternatively, the rolls, once baked, may be frozen. To serve, take the rolls directly from the freezer, place unwrapped in a cold oven, set oven to 400°F/205°C and bake 15 to 20 minutes to thaw and refresh.)

Yield: 18 rolls.

Fromageries
CHEESE SHOPS

Fromagerie de Montmartre (see entry, page 184).

If all France had to offer to the world of gastronomy was bread, cheese, and wine, that would be enough for me. Of the trinity, it is cheese that links one to the other. I cannot imagine a more understated, unified French meal than one perfectly fresh *baguette,* a single Camembert, so ripe and velvety it won't last another hour, and a glass or two of young, fruity, well-balanced red wine. And I can't imagine a better place to discover French cheese than in Paris, where dozens upon dozens of *fromageries* line the streets, each shop as different and distinctive as the personality of its owner, each offering selections that vary with the seasons.

Only the French produce so many varieties of cheese, so graphically reflecting their regional landscape and the many kinds of soil, climate, and vegetation. From the milk of cows, goats, and sheep; from the green, flat lands of Normandy, the steep mountain Alps, and from the plains of Champagne east of Paris, comes a veritable symphony of aromas, textures, colours, and forms. Cheese fresh from little farms and big cooperatives, cheese to begin the day and to end it. The French consume a great deal of cheese—about forty-two pounds per capita per year, compared to the American's twenty pounds—and of all the varieties, Camembert is the undisputed favourite.

How many varieties of French cheese are there, really? The French are not a people given to simple agreement. When Winston Churchill said "A country that produces 325 varieties of cheese can't be governed," he was, undoubtedly, responding to a bit of cheese hype. The real figure, say the experts, is more like 150 to 200 serious varieties, with perhaps an additional 100 cheeses that are minor variations.

There's an old *New Yorker* magazine cartoon that describes the confusion perfectly: An elderly woman is sitting on the sofa, poring over maps of France. She looks up at her husband and says: "Has it ever occurred to you, dear, that most of the villages and towns in France seem to have been named after cheeses?"

Don't let anyone convince you that the cheese you eat in France and the French cheese you eat elsewhere are necessarily the same. For instance, in America this is caused by the United States Department of Agriculture regulations barring the importation of cheese made from unpasteurized milk that has been aged less than sixty days. Pasteurization may make cheese "safe," but in the process it kills all the microbes that give the cheese its character and flavour, that keep it a live, ever-changing organism. There is no question that pasteurized milk produces uniformly bland, "dead" cheese. The regulation rules out the importation of France's finest fresh young cheese, including raw milk Camembert and Brie, and the dozens of varieties of lively, delicate goat cheese, although there may have been occasions where a few have slipped through.

Yet even in France, cheese made from pasteurized milk is increasingly common. For instance, only 16 percent of the 500,000 pounds of Camembert produced in France each year is made from raw milk. The advantage, of course, is that cheese made with pasteurized milk can be made available year-round, and will have more stable keeping qualities. When in France, take the time to get a true taste of fresh French cheese: Specify raw milk cheese by asking for *fromage fermier* or *au lait cru*. These cheeses are produced in limited quantities, the result of traditional methods of production.

Paris has dozens of *fromageries* that specialize in raw milk cheese, with some shops offering as many as 200 different varieties. Before living in Paris I thought that cheese merchants only bought and sold cheese. Wrong. The best, most serious cheese people actually age the cheese they sell. That is, they buy the cheese ready-made from the farmer, then, following a sensitive and tricky aging process, they take the cheese from its young, raw state to full maturity, refining the cheese in underground cellars that are usually humid and cold. The process is called *affinage,* and it can last from days to months, depending on the cheese. As each cheese matures, it takes on its own personality, influenced by the person responsible for its development. Maturing cheese needs daily attention: Some varieties are washed with beer, some with a blend of salt and water, some with *eau-de-vie.* Some are turned every day, moved from one cellar to another as the aging process continues. Each merchant has his own style of aging, and there are varying opinions on how cold and how humid the cellar should be; whether the cheese should be aged on clean straw or old straw, paper, or even plastic; or whether the cheese should be turned daily or just every now and then. And, each merchant has a different opinion on when a cheese is ripe, and thus ready to be put on sale.

I adore watching the dedicated *fromagers,* whose love for cheese is totally infectious. In their cellars, they are in heaven, as they vigorously inhale the heady, pungent aromas that fill the air, and give the cheese little "love taps," the same way bakers give their unbaked loaves a tender touch before putting them in the oven. Now, having toured most of the various aging cellars that rest beneath the streets of the city, I see what a single individual can do to change the course of a cheese's life, ultimately determining taste and texture. Androuët's cheese, for instance, no matter the variety, always tastes just a bit creamier than others. Henry Voy's, from La Ferme Saint-Hubert, has a lusty, almost over-the-hill quality about it that at times can be quite appealing. Lillo's cheese is refined and elegant, always in perfect, presentable shape.

A few words on selecting cheese: Be sensitive to the seasons. For instance, don't expect to find Vacherin or the best-ever Beaufort in the middle of summer. When in doubt, ask to know the seasonal specialities in a given shop. In selecting cheese for a *dégustation* (a cheese tray or sample selection for tasting), either at home or in a restaurant, choose three to four varieties, generally including a semi-soft cheese, a goat cheese, and a blue. Eat the mild cheese first, then move on to the stronger varieties.

Generally, be wary of cheese wrapped in plastic. Like us, cheese has to breathe to maintain life and vigour. Don't be afraid of a bit of mould. Generally the bluish film is a sign that the cheese is made with raw milk, and has been ripened on fresh straw. Cheese that won't mould, and won't spoil, is already too dead to bother about.

Be open-minded and adventurous. The first months I lived in Paris I rarely bought Brie or Camembert—I'd had so many disappointing pasteurized milk varieties that I lost my enthusiasm for these wonderful cheeses. Then one day, I happened to sample a perfect Camembert and "click," I instantly understood what the fuss was all about.

PALAIS-ROYAL
1st arrondissement

TACHON,
38 Rue de Richelieu,
    Paris 1.
(296.08.66).
Métro: Palais-Royal.
Open 9:30 A.M. to 1:30
    P.M. and 4 P.M. to 7:30
    P.M. Closed Sunday and
    Monday.

A truly classic old-fashioned neighbourhood *fromagerie,* near the Louvre and the Palais-Royal. Little handwritten signs tell you about the origin and history of many cheese varieties, and there is even an advisory list noting which ones are currently at their ripest. Tachon presents some wonderful finds, including many small-production, raw milk farm cheeses: the best-ever Burgundian Epoisses, from the Laiterie de la Côte in Gevrey-Chambertin; superb Swiss Tête de Moine du Bellelay; a better than average farm-fresh Saint-Nectaire, mild, sweet, and tangy, and aged a full two months on beds of rye straw; and Livarot, from Normandy farms, strong, spicy, and elastic, the sort of cheese that sticks agreeably to your teeth. Also try the earthy, air-dried, smoked pork sausages from the French Alps.

LUXEMBOURG
5th arrondissement

**FERME SAINTE-
SUZANNE,**
4 Rue des Fossés Saint-
    Jacques, Paris 5.
(354.90.02).
Métro: Luxembourg.
Open 8 A.M. to 1 P.M. and
    4 P.M. to 7:30 P.M.
    Closed Saturday, Sunday,
    and the month of
    August.
Restaurant open noon to 2
    P.M. Monday through
    Friday, and Thursday
    evenings from 7 P.M. to
    9:30 P.M.

A pretty little shop off the active Left Bank Place de l'Estrapade, with a pleasant little cheese restaurant in back (see *Dégustation* box, page 184). This shop is typical of a good, standard, neighbourhood *fromagerie,* where there is a fine, classic selection, mostly of raw milk cheese that is carefully aged. The owners seem more interested in the little restaurant than the *fromagerie* and, from time to time, there's a slip in

---

CHEESE TO GO

If you are planning to tuck a selection of French cheese into your suitcase for your welcome-back meal be careful. Some customs authorities observe very strict government rules on foods coming into the country. Technically, no cheese, unless it is commercially sealed, can be brought by tourists into the U.S. This rules out virtually all French cheese.

---

quality. But it's worth a look inside if you're in the neighbourhood. Good bets: fresh and creamy Chabichou goat cheese; nicely aged Camembert from La Ferme d'Antignac in Normandy; and a fine Brie.

ECOLE MILITAIRE
7th arrondissement

MARIE-ANNE CANTIN,
12 Rue du Champ-de-Mars, Paris 7.
(550.43.94).
Métro: Ecole Militaire.
Open 8:30 A.M. to 1 P.M. and 3:30 P.M. to 7:30 P.M. Closed Sunday afternoon, Monday, and the month of August.

One of Paris's newest and prettiest cheese boutiques, just off the bustling Rue Cler open-air market. Marie-Anne is the daughter of Christian Cantin, whose cheese shop at 2 Rue de Lourmel, in the 15th *arrondissement,* has long been a Paris landmark. Now, along with her husband, Antoine Dias, Madamoiselle Cantin is on her own, offering 80 to 100 remarkably well-aged varieties from France, Switzerland, and the Netherlands. They're both passionate about cheese ("We never stop eating it," says Monsieur Dias), and their excitement carries over into the neatly organized, appealing little shop. Their pride and joy are the aging cellars beneath the shop, with one for goat cheese (very dry) and one for cow's milk cheese (very humid). The floor of the cow's milk cellar is lined with rocks, which are "watered" regularly to provide proper humidity. All cheese is aged on natural straw, and varieties such as Munster and Maroilles get a daily washing of beer

or salt water, to turn mild, timid little disks into strong, forceful cheese. The true cheese lover, says Monsieur Dias, is someone who invariably selects Camembert, Brie, or Livarot as part of his cheese course. The best varieties sampled here include a classic and elegant Camembert; a dusty, creamy little Bouton-de-Chèvre (farm-made goat cheese); and perhaps the best Charolais goat cheese in the world: creamy, refined, clean and full-flavored. If you're in the mood for a mercilessly pungent cheese, try the northern Vieux Lille ("old Lille")—strong and rugged, it's a cheese that almost attacks your palate. More soothing and Cheddar-like is Salers, a mild and nutty cooked cheese from the Auvergne, and Comté, France's version of the well-known Swiss Gruyère. The shop will prepare packages for travelling abroad.

GARE SAINT-LAZARE, MADELEINE
8th arrondissement

ANDROUET,
41 Rue d'Amsterdam,
   Paris 8.
(874.26.90).
Métro: Liège.
Open 8:30 A.M. to 6:30
   P.M. Closed Sunday.

Long one of Paris's most respected cheese shops, Androuët (pronounced ahn-drew-ett) sells some 10,000 pounds of cheese a month, offering 200 varieties at a given time, including a few rarely seen elsewhere, in or out of France. That's because the Androuët family has been at it longer than just about anyone else. They opened their shop on Rue d'Amsterdam in 1909, then twenty years later added a little corner for *dégustation* (tasting) of the many varieties of cheese sold in the shop. An upstairs restaurant was added in 1962 (see *Dégustation* box, page 184).

In the early days, few small-scale farmers transported their cheese to Paris, so the Androuët family went out to the farmers, travelling all over France in search of individuals who made honest, regional, raw milk cheese. Today, Androuët employees still go to local cheese fairs to search out new sources. Beneath the folkloric little shop lie five aging cellars, some of them naturally humid and cool, where cheese may rest for a few days to a few months before it is ready to be sold in the shop. When I first moved to Paris I came here every Saturday to sample new varieties, using the shop as a mini-university of cheese. This is still the place I go for a spectacular cheese tray: Androuët, more than any other shop in Paris, understands the play of flavours, colours, textures, and shapes of cheese.

Two types of Emmental, first Savoyard, then Swiss, and two types of Comté cheese from the Jura region of France, first aged, then young.

Each cheese comes with a little label, or *étiquette* (you'll have to ask for it) so you can identify it when you get home.

Year-round, Androuët offers superb Brie de Meaux and Brie de Melun, while personal favourites include the triple cream Lucullus; the smooth Soumaintrain, full of flavour as well as character; and the Arôme au Gêne from the Lyonnais region, pungent disks fermented in *marc de Bourgogne,* an *eau-de-vie* distilled from pressed grape skins and seeds. In the fall, sample the Munster, aged two or three months at large farms and given a daily splash of white wine; Pierre-Qui-Vire, an elegant, smooth Burgundian cow's milk cheese, full of character and aged two months in a cool, humid cellar; Epoisses, an autumn specialty, that's brushed with *marc de Bourgogne* to give it a rare pungency and a rind the colour of fresh fall leaves; and Rollot, the smooth and spicy cow's milk cheese from Picardy, aged two months and washed daily with a salt and water brine. Through much of the fall they also offer the rare, delicate, and subtle Brie de Melun Frais, a chalky white and delicately flavoured young Brie. Androuët's Roquefort is often disappointing, and from time to time certain varieties of goat cheese are highly oversalted.

CREPLET-BRUSSOL,
17 Place de la Madeleine,
Paris 8.
(265.34.32).
Métro: Madeleine.
Open 9 A.M. to 7 P.M.
Closed Sunday and
Monday.

Because of its location—near the famous Fauchon and Hédiard food shops—this is one of the city's best-known cheese shops. The windows are filled with a lot of processed, packaged varieties of cheese, but inside, there is a solid, classic collection, including a fine raw milk Camembert from the Isigny Cooperative in Normandy; nicely aged Brie; and a good variety of cheese from the north of France.

**LA FERME
SAINT-HUBERT,**
21 Rue Vignon, Paris 8.
(742.79.20).
Métro: Madeleine.
Open 11 A.M. to 7 P.M.
Tuesday through Friday,
8:30 A.M. to 7 P.M.
Saturday. Closed Sunday
and Monday.

Just around the corner from Fauchon, this small, compact shop offers extraordinary cheese varieties, including what's probably the best and most carefully selected Roquefort in Paris; a spectacular Beaufort, aged at least two years in special cellars; and a vigorous Maroilles, from Flanders, aged for four months and dosed daily with a sprinkling of beer. They also offer the Swiss Tête de Moine—a fabulous, fruity cylinder of cheese that resembles Gruyère, but has more punch, depth and character. It's a good travelling cheese, and will last for months, refrigerated. Also worth sampling are the delicate, pale goat's milk butter and a rather unusual goat's milk yogurt. Many varieties of cheese are somewhat rough and rustic, like the shop's owner, Henry Voy. For my taste, some cheeses have been aged too long, losing a bit of their charm. (See also the *Dégustation* box, page 184.)

VICTOR-HUGO
16th arrondissement

LILLO,
35 Rue des Belles-Feuilles,
Paris 16.
(727.69.08).
Métro: Victor-Hugo.
Open 8 A.M. to 1 P.M.
and 4 P.M. to 7:30 P.M.,
9 A.M. to 1 P.M. Sunday.
Closed Monday.

An elegant, sparkling little shop near the Place Victor-Hugo on one of Paris's most chic market streets, Rue des Belles-Feuilles. This is a neighbourhood where quality is taken for granted, and no one need worry about Monsieur Lillo letting his clients down. Though few cheeses are actually aged here, many of the 200 or so varieties are "finished" for five or six days in the neat cellars beneath the shop. Almost all are raw milk, small production cheeses, and among the best varieties sampled was a remarkable Pavin d'Auvergne, a flat disk of mildly tangy, soft, and supple cow's milk cheese from the Auvergne region. The cheese is similar to, but far better than, Saint-Nectaire. Also excellent: raw milk Brie, Munster, and Roquefort. It's no surprise that Monsieur Lillo won a civic award for the most attractive shop window on the street. The shop is happy to package a seasonal selection for foreign travellers.

FROMAGE DE CHEVRE MARINE A L'HUILE D'HERBES
GOAT CHEESE MARINATED IN OIL WITH HERBS

This is a traditional method of storing and extending the life of a goat cheese, particularly useful for chèvre that has become very firm and dry. It's great to have on hand for days when you haven't had time to market. After the cheese has been consumed, you can continue adding more cheese and herbs to the oil, or use it for cooking or for salad dressings.

6 small goat cheeses
  (Picodon, Crottin, or
  Cabécou)
1 clove garlic, peeled
½ teaspoon dried thyme
½ teaspoon dried
  rosemary
2 bay leaves
12 whole black
  peppercorns
12 whole white
  peppercorns
12 whole coriander seeds
2 cups (500 ml) olive oil

1. Cut each cheese in half horizontally. In a wide-mouth pint (500 ml) jar place the cheese, then the garlic and herbs and spices. Cover with oil. Close securely and store in a cool place for at least 1 week.

2. To serve, remove the cheese from the jar, and drain off the oil. Broil the cheese just until warm, and serve with a tossed green salad and slices of fresh bread. Use cheese within 1 month.

Yield: 12 servings.

STREET NAME MENU

It should come as no surprise to find that in Paris, a city so devoted to food, dozens of street names have a food connection. Here are a few, with the *arrondissement,* or neighbourhood, in which they are now located:

Rue des Boulangers, 5th arrondissement: When the street was named in 1844, it was lined with numerous bakeries. Today, there's not a loaf of bread for sale on "Bakers' Street."

Passage de la Brie, 19th arrondissement: named for the region east of Paris, known for its wheat, pastures, butter, and of course, cheese.

Rue Brillat-Savarin, 13th arrondissement: named in honour of the gastronome and author of the famous *Physiology of Taste.*

Rue Brise-Miche, 4th arrondissement: During the Middle Ages, it was on this street that clergymen distributed bread to the needy. *Brise-miche,* named in 1517, literally means "break bread."

Rue Curnonsky, 17th arrondissement: named in memory of the gastronome, Maurice-Edmond Sailland, who took on the Russian-sounding pseudonym around the turn of the century, when everything Russian was fashionable in Paris. The author of the multi-volume *La France Gastronomique* died in 1956, and the street was later named in his honour.

Rue des Eaux, 16th arrondissement: In 1650, when this road was opened in the Passy district, workers had discovered the area's mineral waters. (Passy is now one of the more fashionable Paris neighbourhoods.) The source dried up during the 18th century, but the name, "Street of the Waters," remained. Who knows, if the source still existed, we could all be drinking Passy water instead of Perrier.

Rue de la Faisanderie, 16th arrondissement: A pheasant preserve, or *faisanderie,* once existed here, near the château of the Muette.

Rue des Fermiers, 17th arrondissement: There are no farmers, or *fermiers,* left here today, but in the 1800s there were still a few farms in this now-citified neighbourhood not far from Parc Monceau. The street was named in 1840, when the area became part of Paris.

Rue des Jeûneurs, 2nd arrondissement: The name, perhaps, comes from a sign that hung above one of the houses in 1715, during the reign of Louis XV. It read: "Aux Déjeuners," or "Lunches Here."

Rue des Maraîchers, 20th arrondissement: During the 18th century, vegetable garden markets, or *mar-*

aîchers, bordered the region. The street was named in 1869.

Impasse Marché aux Chevaux, 5th arrondissement: There are many Paris streets named after past or still-existing markets, but this is one story I particularly enjoy. Beginning in 1687, this was a major market site. Early each Wednesday and Saturday, pigs were brought to market for sale, then later in the day, mules, donkeys, and horses (*chevaux*) were sold, giving the street its name. On Sundays, they sold wagons and dogs.

Rue des Meuniers, 12th arrondissement: The street of the millers takes its name from the flour mill that existed here during the 18th century. Today, there's no sign of a mill.

Rue des Morillons, 15th arrondissement: Morillon is the name of a grapevine that flourished in the Parisian climate, at a time when Parisians and those living on the outskirts still had room to grow grapes. The path that led from the vineyard was declared a road in 1730 and a street in 1906. Vineyards have once again been planted in the nearby Parc Georges-Brassens, but they're of the Gamay variety, not Morillon.

Impasse de la Poissonerie, 4th arrondissement: This street was built in 1783 when the Sainte-Catherine market first opened. It bordered a fish shop; thus its name.

Boulevard Poissonière, 9th and 10th arrondissements: Opened at the beginning of the 17th century, this street served as a *passage* for fish merchants coming direct from the Port of Calais, delivering their fish to the Paris central market, Les Halles. It was named in 1685.

Rue du Pressoir, 20th arrondissement: Grapevines once flourished in this outer region of Paris, and the press, or *pressoir,* was installed to press the grapes for wine. The street was named after the press in 1837.

COURCELLES, VILLIERS
17th arrondissement

JEAN CARMES ET FILS,
24 Rue de Lévis, Paris 17.
(763.88.94).
Métro: Villiers.
Open 9 A.M. to 1 P.M. and
    4 P.M. to 7 P.M. Closed
    Sunday afternoon,
    Monday, and the month
    of August.

Situated right in the middle of the hectic Rue de Lévis market, Carmès is a big, open, family-run cheese shop, with "Dad," Jean Carmès, behind the cash register while son, Patrick, rushes about with a nervous sort of vigour, keeping an eye on incoming deliveries, and checking out the progress of the 200 or so varieties of cheese aging in humid rooms, below and above the shop. These people are passionate about cheese, taking the care to label each variety, happy to help you select a single cheese or an entire platter. Eighty percent of their cheese is bought fresh from farms. Most varieties spend an average of three to four weeks in the Carmès cellars, aging on fresh, clean straw mats until the cheese is ready to be put on sale. Some specialties here: l'Ecume, a triple cream so rich

Creamy blocks of butter.

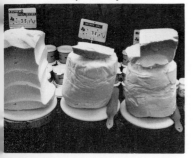

BUTTER

France produces 10 percent of the world's butter, most of it unsalted. Though Normandy, with its shining green pastures and fawn-coloured cows, produces a high-quality product, the best butter comes from Charentes, in the southwest of France. Charentes butter, sold in packets under the label *"beurre d'Echiré"* or *"beurre de Ligueil,"* is favoured by French pastry chefs, because it is firmer and less watery than other varieties and makes superior pastry.

In cheese shops you often see huge creamy blocks of butter behind the counter. They are usually labelled *"beurre des Charentes," "beurre de Normandie,"* or *"beurre demi-sel." Demi-sel* is Brittany's lightly salted butter. Rarely used in cooking, it finds its place on the table. (While the bulk butters look good and fresh, beware, they sit all day absorbing the mingled odors of the cheeses and are not always terribly fresh.)

The French don't usually butter their bread, so whether or not butter appears on the home or restaurant table is really a matter of personal taste. Butter is always served with *charcuterie* (cold cuts), with radishes, anchovies, sardines, and with the rye bread that comes as part of any order of oysters or other shellfish. If you don't see butter on a restaurant table, it is perfectly proper to ask for it, though in more casual restaurants you may be charged a *supplément* of a few francs. Butter is usually included with the cheese course, and is used to soften the effect of strong and salty cheeses such as Roquefort.

it easily replaces butter; Tanatais goat cheese, much like a Charolais, dry and delicious with a bloomy crust; and a Petit-Suisse *"comme autrefois"* (like the old days), a fragile cheese that stays fresh just four or five days. Real, fresh *crème Chantilly* (sweetened *crème fraîche*) and Fontainebleau (a creamy dessert cheese) are sold here as well.

**FROMAGERIE
COURCELLES,**
79 Rue de Courcelles,
   Paris 17.
(622.22.36).
Métro: Courcelles.
Open 8:30 A.M. to 1 P.M.
   and 4 P.M. to 7:30 P.M.
   Closed Sunday, Monday
   morning, and the month
   of August.

A bright new renovation of a classic, quality *fromagerie*. There's always a line out the door at this tiny, spotless shop, where raw milk Camembert (the Grand Béron can be remarkable), Pyramide goat cheese, Alsatian Munster, Epoisses from Burgundy, and Roquefort are always in perfect form.

THE RIND

The million dollar question: Should you eat the rind or shouldn't you? Even the experts don't agree. According to *Larousse des Fromages,* the French cheese bible, it is all a question of personal taste. Larousse advises, however, not to leave a messy plate full of little bits of crust. Pierre Androuët, the dean of Paris cheese merchants, is more definite. Never eat the rind, he says, because it harbours all the cheese's developing molds and yeast and can emit an alkaline odour. The truth? It's really up to you, though let logic rule. The rinds of soft-ripened cheese such as Brie and Camembert are definitely edible, and when the cheese is perfectly ripe, the thin, bloomy *croûte* adds both flavour and texture. However, with another soft cheese, Vacherin, the rind is removed, and the creamy cheese is scooped out with a spoon. The rinds of semi-soft cheese, such as Reblochon, can have a very nutty flavour. I sometimes cut off the rind and eat it separately. The crust is always discarded when eating hard mountain cheeses, such as Emmenthal, Gruyère and Tête de Moine.

ALAIN DUBOIS,
80 Rue de Tocqueville,
   Paris 17.
(227.11.38).
Métro: Villiers.
Open 7:30 A.M. to 1 P.M.
   and 4 P.M. to 7:30 P.M.
   Closed Sunday
   afternoon, Monday, and
   the month of August.

Young Alain Dubois turned the family *crémerie* into a full-fledged *fromagerie* in the early 1970s. The shop is artfully and tastefully arranged, and Dubois is proudest of his Epoisses de Bourgogne, washed with *marc de Bourgogne* every day or so, and aged according to his own "secret" process; his Fribourg, a softer Swiss Gruyère, aged in cellars in the Jura region for at least two years; and his Swiss Vacherin Mont d'Or, still made in chalets and available from the end of fall into the early spring. Dubois offers some seventy varieties of goat cheese, according to the season. The current goal is to persuade restaurants to take the cheese course more seriously. He dines anonymously in restaurants, studies the cuisine, then approaches the chef with suggestions for a selection that fits the personality of the restaurant. Dubois is categorically opposed to aging certain cheese, such as Brie, Camembert, or Saint-Nectaire, in Paris *caves*. "Certain varieties must taste of the soil and air of the region in which they were made, and they can't be aged in small batches in the city," insists the smiling, outgoing Dubois. "For a truly great Brie, you need an enormous amount aged in the same spot." His argument is convincing, for his Camembert—aged in Normandy at the Cooperative d'Isigny—is creamy, refined, and delicious. Eighty percent of his cheese comes direct from the farm, since, as he puts it "farm cheese is what gave France its great reputation for cheese." He and his wife love visiting farms in search of good cheese, and are avid restaurant goers, feeling that one can't be a good *fromager* without being a dedicated *gastronome*. His cheese appears in more than a dozen Paris restaurants, including Jacques Cagna, Le Petit Bedon and Pavillon des Princes. .

CRÈME FRAÎCHE

Where would French cuisine be without crème fraîche, that thick and slightly tangy cream that lies somewhere between heavy cream and sour cream? Every crémerie in France sells crème fraîche in bulk, usually ladled out of giant round crockery bowls. It's versatile and nearly indispensable, showing up in hot and cold sauces, and is perfect for whipping with a touch of sugar to dab on a mound of fresh wild strawberries.

1 cup (250 ml) heavy cream (you cannot use ultra-pasteurized)
1 tablespoon cultured buttermilk

1. Mix the heavy cream and buttermilk together in a medium-size bowl. Cover loosely with plastic wrap and let stand at room temperature overnight, or until fairly thick.

2. Cover tightly and refrigerate for at least 4 hours, to thicken it even more. The cream may be stored for several days, as the tangy flavor continues to develop.

Yield: 1 cup (250 ml).

Chèvre in a multitude of forms.

*Inside the Fromagerie de Mont-
martre (see entry, page 184).*

FONTAINEBLEAU

This creamy, white, succulent dessert cheese is found, from time to time, in Paris fromageries. Usually sold in little white containers lined with cheesecloth, the fresh cheese takes its name from the town of Fontainebleau, south of Paris. Although Fontainebleau is far from rare, this elegant cheese is seen less and less frequently in Paris shops: It stays fresh for just twenty-four hours, and it is not economical for most cheese shops to handle. But since this appealing dessert is easy to make, there's no reason not to serve it often. In France, Fontainebleau is made at home with fromage blanc, sort of a "curdless" cottage cheese, but I found that yogurt is an excellent substitute. This version is similar to coeur à la crème, but since it is lightened with egg whites, Fontainebleau is less rich. It is an ideal dessert for a large group, because the recipe can easily be doubled or tripled. And, since it is made a day in advance, it takes no last minute preparation. Fontainebleau is particularly beautiful when made in a white ceramic coeur à la crème mould, but it can be formed in a strainer as well. I serve Fontainebleau with a fresh raspberry sauce and the little almond cakes, financiers (see recipe, page 145). It is also delicious with strawberries, fresh figs, or blueberries.

2 cups (500 ml) low-fat
  yogurt
1 cup (200 g) sugar
2 cups (500 ml) heavy
  cream (preferably not
  ultra-pasteurized) or
  crème fraîche (see recipe,
  opposite page)
3 egg whites

1. In a large mixing bowl, combine the yogurt and all but 2 tablespoons of the sugar.

2. In a second bowl, whip the cream or *crème fraîche* until stiff and fold into the yogurt mixture.

3. In yet another bowl, whip the egg whites until stiff, add the reserved 2 tablespoons of sugar, and whip until glossy, about another 20 seconds. Gently fold the egg whites into the yogurt-cream mixture.

4. Transfer mixture to a 6-cup (1.5-litre) cheesecloth-lined, perforated mould (or use two or more smaller moulds). Cover the mould, and place it in a bowl in the refrigerator. Refrigerate for 24 hours, draining off the liquid from time to time. The cheese should become fairly firm and dry, almost like a whipped cream cheese.

5. To serve, unmould the Fontainebleau onto a platter, unwrap, and surround with a colourful fresh fruit sauce or fresh berries. Serve immediately.

Yield: 8 to 10 servings.

MONTMARTRE
18th arrondissement

FROMAGERIE DE MONTMARTRE,
9 Rue du Poteau, Paris 18.
(606.26.03).
Métro: Jules-Joffrin.
Open 8:45 A.M. to 12:30
   P.M. and 4 P.M. to 7:30
   P.M. Closed Sunday and
   Monday.

If you just love looking at beautiful cheese displays, don't miss this spacious *fromagerie,* typical of the pretty food shops along Rue du Poteau. It offers a sparkling variety of farm-fresh, raw milk cheese from all over France, and the owner, Madame Delbey, is happy to let you "window shop" as you wander about the well-organized store, examining the flawless selection of cheese displayed on trays of straw and aged in her own cellars. Goat cheese is one of their best features—they offer more than forty different varieties. Outstanding cheese sampled here includes Ma Petite Clochette, the large, bell-shaped, smooth and creamy goat cheese from Poitou; Fougéru, a supple, tangy Coulommiers aged in fern fronds from the Ile de France region around Paris; and *crème Chantilly.* They sell their aged cheeses while still a bit young, and as a result some cheeses, such as Livarot and Munster, are milder and less pungent than normal.

"The Roquefort, with its blue and yellow marbling, looks diseased, like rich people who have eaten too many truffles."
—Emile Zola,
Le Ventre de Paris

DEGUSTATION

A favourite way to enjoy French cheese is to take a tour of France through a *dégustation* (tasting) of the country's more than 180 varieties of cheese. The following restaurants, most of which are also *fromageries* offer a *dégustation* of cheeses on their menus.

Androuët, 41 Rue d'Amsterdam, Paris 8. (874.26.93). (874.26.93). Métro: Liège. Restaurant open noon to 2:30 P.M. and 7 P.M. to 9:30 P.M. Closed Sunday. Credit cards: AE, DC, V. 120-franc *dégustation.* Reservations advised.

The most elaborate *dégustation* in France is found at Androuët, the mecca for cheese lovers in Paris. Their speciality is a seven-course meal consisting solely of cheese. All is carefully planned so you begin with the richest, mildest cheese, move on to the cooked and half-cooked varieties, dip into the goat cheeses, and end on a heady finale of blues. As each of the seven trays is presented, the waiter explains a little about each type of cheese, suggesting you try three or four small samples per tray. It pays to set aside an entire afternoon for the experience, so you can savour and compare varieties, spacing them with bits of a crusty *baguette* and sips of solid Bordeaux.

A selection of Cantal.

La Boutique à Sandwiches, 12 Rue du Colisée, Paris 8. Métro: Franklin Roosevelt. (359.56.69). Open noon to 4 P.M. and 6 P.M. to midnight. Closed Sunday and the month of August. About 75 francs.

For an unusual cheese experience, wander up to the first floor of this simple delicatessen to sample raclette, a hearty, filling Swiss dish that includes firm, buttery melted cheese, potatoes boiled in their skins, pickled onions, and cornichons. Huge wheels of several varieties of Swiss cheese are split in half, then the exposed portion is placed under a special raclette broiler. As the cheese melts, it is scraped off—crispy, bubbling brown crust and all—and brought to the table. You will hardly be able to finish the tangy melted cheese before the waiter is back, ready to scrape another serving onto your plate. With the raclette, savour the delicate white Apremont wine, from Savoie.

———

La Ferme Saint-Hubert, 21 Rue Vignon, Paris 8. (742.79.20). Métro: Madeleine. Restaurant open 11:30 A.M. to 3 P.M. and 6:45 P.M. to 10 P.M. Closed Sunday and Monday. 50-franc *dégustation.*

Next door to La Ferme Saint-Hubert *fromagerie* you'll find a tiny, casual little lunchroom serving abbreviated *dégustations* suited to cheese enthusiasts with limited time. Their most popular platter is made up of seven varieties, representing the seven major types of French cheese. At La Ferme Saint-Hubert, they are aged to the borderline of perfection, while reflecting the owner's preference for ripe, full-flavored cheese. Platters of goat cheese and salads are also available. There's a small wine selection, and little pots of pure white goat's milk butter are served with a fresh country loaf from baker Lionel Poilâne. The cheese is not labelled, so you'll have to make good mental notes, then slip into the shop next door after the meal to identify the cheese you have just tasted. Raclette is served every evening.

———

Ferme Sainte-Suzanne, 4 Rue des Fossés Saint-Jacques, Paris 5. (354.90.02). Métro: Luxembourg. Restaurant open noon to 2:30 P.M., Monday through Friday; 7 P.M. to 9:30 P.M., Thursday. Closed Saturday, Sunday, and the month of August. About 50 francs.

A lively, skylit neighbourhood lunch spot, with a simple, cheese-based menu featuring savory *crêpe tourtes;* salads that combine greens, goat cheese, and walnuts; and nicely labeled *dégustation* platters served with the fabulously crusty *baguettes* from the nearby Boulangerie Moderne. The melted Swiss Raclette cheese is served with tiny boiled potatoes and slices of delicious smoked ham. There's a small wine list, including an excellent Côtes-du-Rhône.

Charcuteries
PREPARED FOODS
TO GO

Decisions are easy, if you know what you want.

To lovers of all things earthy, hearty, rib-sticking, and aromatic, the Paris *charcuterie* is a touch of heaven. Literally meaning the shop where you buy *chair cuite*—cooked meat—the city has hundreds — some museumlike with carved marble counters and hanging brass racks, others modern and spotless with wares displayed like diamonds in a jeweller's window. There you can buy fragrant sausages and mosaic pâtés, salted and smoked hams, and strange-sounding *grattons, fritons, rillettes,* and *rillons.* Who else but the French could manage to make so much of the lowly pig? And where else but Paris can you find one shop with fifteen different kinds of *boudin* sausage made right on the premises; another with more than a dozen different kinds of hams; still others that sell not just pork products, but also caviar and *foie gras,* fresh country breads and smoked salmon, and even the vodka, Champagne, or Sauternes to go with them?

You need not go beyond Paris to sample the wonders of the French world of *charcuterie*—my favourite regional shops feature rustic products from the rugged Auvergne region in south-central France, and offer farm-fresh goat and sheep's milk cheese, a heady *bleu d'Auvergne,* dozens of kinds of hams, sausages, and pâtés of so many different names, colours, and shapes it makes the mind spin. There are also Alsatian-owned shops redolent with the pungent warmth of cooked sauerkraut, mounds of pork chops, and colourful assorted sausages, plus some of the finest farm Munster cheese, and romantic, heart-shaped gingerbread cookies.

Shops with a Breton accent are likely to feature Brittany's tangy cheese tart, known as *encalat,* while those from the Savoie region bordering Switzerland will offer mountain-cured hams and sausages, and local white wines, such as the pale, delicate Apremont or fizzy, light Crépy.

The size and selection available vary widely from shop to shop, neighbourhood to neighbourhood. Run-of-the-mill *charcuteries* make only a small portion of the products themselves (75 percent of the products sold in *charcuteries* nationwide are industrially produced), but the finest shops, such as those mentioned here, either produce most of their own sausages, hams, pâtés, and *terrines,* or buy them direct from independent farmers in various regions of France.

Many but not all Paris *charcuteries* also offer hot meals at lunch and dinnertime, a concept that to most of us seems essentially modern. It's not, for ever since *charcuteries* were first established in 1475, their very reason for existence was to sell cooked pork products. In days when a large percentage of Parisians lived without cooking facilities, the *charcuterie* served as a kitchen away from home, ready with hot, take away meals all week long.

Along with the hundreds of different meat products, most *charcuteries* also sell *escargots* (snails) ready for popping in the oven, a variety of pastry-topped pâtés or *terrines* to be eaten warm or cold, pizzas and *quiches,* and dozens of salads, ranging from those of ivory-coloured celery root or bright red beets to a julienne of carrots showered with vinaigrette. Condiments such as olives, pickles, and *cornichons* can almost always be found, along with many kinds of regional, packaged cakes, cookies, and pastries.

Today, the Parisian definition of *charcuterie* is a broad one, and major shops such as Fauchon, Lenôtre, Dalloyau, Hédiard, and Flo Prestige (all listed elsewhere in this guide) perform the services of *charcuterie* and caterer, offering as well pastries, breads, chocolates, wines, spirits, and condiments. What follows here, then, is a choice selection of the smaller shops, most of them family-run, with unique personalities all their own. In each case, a sampling of this, a slice of that, will help make a picnic lunch or snack a true Parisian feast.

TUILERIES
1st arrondissement

CHEDEVILLE,
12 Rue du Marché-Saint-
  Honoré, Paris 1.
(261.11.11).
Métro: Tuileries.
Open 8:30 A.M.to 1 P.M.
  and 3:30 P.M. to 7 P.M.
  Closed Sunday and
  Monday.
Credit card: V

One of the city's major *charcuteries,* famous for the pâtés, sausages, and hams which find their way into some of Paris's better restaurants. A place full of character, where you are welcome to watch the half dozen butchers hard at work preparing for the day's labours.

MARAIS, BASTILLE
4th and 11th arrondissements

**GALOCHE
D'AURILLAC,**
41 Rue de Lappe, Paris 11.
(700.77.15).
Métro: Bastille.
Open 10 A.M. to 2 A.M.
  Closed Sunday, Monday,
  and the month of
  August.

This out-of-the-way, fine, and friendly *charcuterie* is worth a detour. Perfectly aged Reblochon; fresh, smoked, and dried sausages right from the Savoie mountains; an admirable selection of Savoie wines and even a little bar at which to enjoy a few of these delicacies.

**MAISON SUBA/
PRODUITS
HONGROIS,**
11 Rue de Sévigné, Paris 4.
(887.46.06).
Métro: Saint-Paul.
Open 9 A.M. to 1 P.M. and
  3 P.M. to 7 P.M. Closed
  Sunday and Monday.

A tidy, tiny shop near the Place des Vosges, full of fresh, aromatic, and delicious Hungarian sausages. A special, spicy treat: the beef and pork sausage seasoned with hot peppers.

*Sausage and frites, at 49 Rue
Mazarine, Paris 6.*

LA SAVOYARDE,
39 Rue Popincourt,
Paris 11.
(No telephone).
Métro: Voltaire.
Open 9 A.M. to 8 P.M.
Closed Monday.

This always lively local bistro also sells regional hams, sausages, breads, cheese, and wine; a nice spot to know about late at night or at lunchtime, when other neighbourhood *charcuteries* tend to be closed.

ORDERING CHARCUTERIE

The best way to visit a Paris *charcuterie* is armed with a little knowledge and a hearty appetite. The following are some of the most commonly found products:

Andouille: cold smoked chitterling (tripe) sausage.

Andouillette: smaller chitterling (tripe) sausage, usually served grilled.

Ballotine: usually poultry, boned, stuffed, and rolled.

Boudin blanc: white sausage, of veal, chicken, or pork.

Boudin noir: pork blood sausage.

Cervelas: garlicky cured pork sausage.

Confit: duck, goose, or pork cooked and preserved in its own fat.

Cou d'oie farci: neck skin of goose, stuffed with meat and spices, much like a sausage.

Crépinette: small sausage patty wrapped in caul fat.

Fritons: coarse pork *rillettes,* or a minced spread, that includes organ meats.

Fromage de tête: head cheese, usually pork.

Galantine: cooked, boned poultry or meat stuffed and rolled, classically glazed with gelatin, and served cold.

Grattons: crisply fried pieces of pork, goose, or duck skin; cracklings.

Hure (de porc, or *de marcassin):* a head cheese prepared from the head of a pig or boar.

Jambon (ham)

    d'Auvergne: raw, dried, salt-cured smoked ham.

    de Bayonne: raw, dried, salt-cured ham.

    de Bourgogne: also *persillé;* cold cooked ham, cubed and preserved in parsleyed gelatin, usually sliced from a terrine.

    cru: any raw, cured ham.

    cuit: any cooked ham.

    fumé: any smoked ham.

    de montagne: any mountain ham.

    à l'os: ham with the bone in.

de Paris: pale, lightly salted, cooked ham.

de Parme: Italian *prosciutto* from Parma.

du pays: any country ham.

persillé: also *de Bourgogne;* cold cooked ham, cubed and preserved in parsleyed gelatin, usually sliced from a terrine.

sec: any dried ham.

de Westphalie: German Westphalian ham, raw-cured and smoked.

de York: smoked English-style ham, usually poached.

Jambonneau: cured ham shank or pork knuckle.

Jésus: pork sausage from the Franche-Comté.

Lard: bacon.

Lardons: cubes of bacon.

Merguez: small spicy sausage.

Museau de porc: vinegared pork muzzle.

Oreilles de porc: cooked pig's ears, served grilled, with a coating of egg and bread crumbs.

Pâté (minced meat that is moulded, spiced, baked, and served hot or cold)

de campagne: coarse country-style.

de canard: with duck.

de chevreuil: with venison.

en croûte: baked in pastry.

de foie: with liver.

de grive: with thrush, or songbird.

de lapin: with rabbit.

de lièvre: with wild hare.

maison: in the style of the house or *charcuterie.*

d'oie: with goose.

Pied (foot)

de cochon: pig's foot.

de mouton: sheep's foot

de porc: pig's foot.

Poitrine fumée: smoked bacon.

Poitrine d'oie fumée: smoked goose breast.

Rillettes (d'oie): minced spread of pork (goose); also can be made with duck, fish, or rabbit.

Rillons: pork belly, cut up and cooked until crisp, then drained of fat; can also be made of duck, goose, or rabbit.

Rosette (de boeuf): dried pork (or beef) sausage, usually from Beaujolais.

Saucisse (most often, small fresh sausage, which is cooked in liquid and/or broiled, and eaten warm)

　　chaude: warm sausage.

　　de Francfort: hot dog.

　　de Strasbourg: red-skinned hot dog.

　　de Toulouse: mild, country-style pork sausage.

Saucisson (most often, a large, air-dried sausage, such as salami, eaten sliced as a cold cut. When fresh, usually called *saucisson chaud*—hot sausage)

　　à l'ail: garlic sausage, usually to be cooked and served warm.

　　d'Arles: dried, salami-type sausage.

　　de campagne: any country-style sausage.

　　en croûte: sausage cooked in pastry crust.

　　de Lyon: air-dried pork sausage, flavoured with garlic and pepper, and studded with chunks of pork fat.

　　sec: any dried sausage, or salami.

Terrine (actually the earthenware container used for cooking meat, game, fish, or vegetable mixtures. It also refers to the pâté served in the vessel. It differs from a pâté proper in that the *terrine* is actually sliced out of the vessel, while a pâté has been removed from the terrine)

　　d'anguille: eel.

　　de caille: quail.

　　de campagne: country-style.

　　de canard: of duck.

　　du chef: in the chef's special style.

　　de faisan: of pheasant.

　　de foie: of liver.

　　de foies de volaille: of chicken liver.

　　de grives: of thrush, or songbird.

　　maison: in style of the *charcuterie* or house.

　　de perdreau: of partridge.

　　de volaille: of chicken.

"*D*rink wine when you eat ham.

Soup is for ordinary hunger; roasts make a meal festive.

Venison pâté is too good for disobedient children."

　—Lesson from a 17th-century French schoolbook.

CHEZ TEIL,
6 Rue de Lappe, Paris 11.
(700.41.28).
Métro: Bastille.
Open 9 A.M. to 1 P.M. and
  3 P.M. to 8 P.M.
  Tuesday through
  Saturday, 9 A.M. to 1
  P.M. Sunday. Closed
  Monday and the month
  of August.

Is there an earthier, more authentically old-fashioned street in all of Paris than Rue de Lappe? Dance halls for tangos; neighbourhood bistros for dining; and *charcuterie* after *charcuterie* for sausages, cheese, country bread, and *foie gras*. This tiny shop is a treasure not to be missed.

**A LA VILLE
D'AURILLAC,**
34 Rue de Lappe, Paris 11.
(805.94.85).
Métro: Bastille.
Open 8 A.M. to 8 P.M.
  Monday through
  Saturday, 9 A.M. to
  1 P.M. Sunday. Closed
  Monday.

Be prepared to take a deep, deep breath when you enter this modest Auvergnat *charcuterie,* filled with the heady, mingling aromas of well-seasoned sausages, fine, aged hams, plus honest Saint-Nectaire and mountain fresh Cantal cheese. The friendly Bonal family also sells walnut oil, and shiny patent *galoches,* the wooden shoes with leather uppers, direct from the country.

**A LA VILLE
DE RODEZ,**
22 Rue Vieille-du-Temple,
  Paris 4.
(887.79.36).
Métro: Saint-Paul.
Open 8 A.M. to 1 P.M. and
  3 P.M. to 7:30 P.M.
  Closed Sunday, Monday,
  and July 14 to
  September 1.

The long, hearty loaves of country bread come up from Aurillac in south-central France four times a week, while the fragrant sausages and hams that hang from the rafters of this spotless shop all have the wholesome Auvergnat stamp. You will also find buckwheat flour for earthy *crêpes; fouace* (an extra-buttery regional *brioche* studded with candied fruits); *boudin noir* (blood sausage); rough red regional wines; and that delicate, straw-yellow, Cantal-like cheese, Laguiole. You can select an entire picnic or a simple snack, then buy a handmade wicker basket in which to carry your treasures.

**AUX VRAIS PRODUITS
D'AUVERGNE ET
DE BRETAGNE,**
98 Rue de la Roquette,
  Paris 11.
(379.70.28).
Métro: Bastille or Voltaire.
Open 8:45 A.M. to 12:45
  P.M. and 3 P.M. to 7:45
  P.M. Closed Sunday and
  the month of August.

Walking into this well-stocked regional *charcuterie* is like walking into a catch-all country store: Shall it be lightly salted butter from Brittany or hams from Bayonne or the Savoie? Why not a fine farm Reblochon or a fresh, mild Saint-Marcellin? There are also country breads, cakes, sausages, and tarts, all to be enjoyed with an old Cahors wine or a fresh and fruity white from the Savoie.

ODEON
6th arrondissement

**CHARCUTERIE
COESNON,**
30 Rue Dauphine, Paris 6.
(326.56.39).
Métro: Odéon.
Open 8:30 A.M. to 1 P.M.
and 3 P.M. to 7:30 P.M.
Tuesday through Friday,
8:30 A.M. to 7:30 P.M.
Saturday. Closed Sunday,
Monday, and the month
of August.

One of the city's most respected family *charcuteries,* run by the friendly Coesnon family, who came to Paris from Normandy nearly thirty years ago. Their specialities include homemade French sausages, with more than fifteen different varieties of *boudin noir* (blood sausage), some filled with raisins, chestnuts, apples, or herbs; and *boudin blanc* (pork and veal sausage); along with *andouillettes* (chitterling sausages). In the winter months, the *boudin* is made fresh each Tuesday and Thursday. Also game terrines, home-smoked bacon, and *foie gras cru* (fresh fattened goose and duck liver), all year round.

PORTE D'ORLEANS
14th arrondissement

**DUCREUX PRODUITS
REGIONAUX,**
5 Rue Sarrette, Paris 14.
(327.06.05).
Métro: Alésia.
Open 8 A.M. to 1 P.M. and
4 P.M. to 8 P.M.
Tuesday through
Saturday, 8 A.M. to
1 P.M. Sunday. Closed
Monday and the month
of August.

Walking into this shop is like being transported to a family farm in Brittany. This rather funky, spotless *charcuterie* is filled with the salty aroma of fresh-cured hams, while regional cheese tarts (*encalats*) and the local prune-filled *far breton* compete for your palate's attention.

Oh là là!

Coils of boudin.

FOIE GRAS

═══

*F**oie gras*—a crown jewel of French gastronomy—is the smooth and buttery liver from a fattened duck or goose. Seasoned lightly with salt and pepper, then cooked gently in a white porcelain terrine, this highly perishable delicacy demands no further embellishment than a slice of freshly toasted country bread and a glass of chilled, sweet Sauternes. At its best, *foie gras* is one of the world's most satisfying foods. Earthy and elegant, a single morsel of it melts slowly on the palate, invading one's senses with an aroma and flavour that's gracefully soothing, supple, and rich, with a lingering, almost organic aftertaste. Depending on its origin and length of cooking time, the colour of *foie gras* ranges from a slightly golden brown to a peach-blushed rose. Rich in calories (about 450 for each 3-ounce, or 90-gram slice) *foie gras* is best enjoyed slowly, and parsimoniously. It is also expensive: that 3-ounce slice will cost you about 90 francs.

Which is better, goose or duck liver? It is purely a matter of preference. Fattened goose liver (*foie gras d'oie*) is less common and more expensive than fattened duck liver (*foie gras de canard*) because its production requires more intensive care and feeding. Geese are very susceptible to disease or perturbation in their daily routine, so the casualty rate is high. Ducks are more hardy and less demanding, and during the past twenty years the fattened duck liver has gained popularity, as French restaurateurs and consumers have also developed a strong appetite for the breast of the fattened duck, the *magret de canard*. As for taste, goose liver is slightly subtle and mild, duck liver more forward-tasting and a bit more acidic.

What does one look for in *foie gras?* Ideally, a slice of *foie gras* should be the same colour throughout, a sign that it is from the same liver, and has been carefully and uniformly cooked. It should always have a fresh, appealing, liverlike aroma.

Serve *foie gras* slightly chilled, but not too cold. If possible, remove it from the refrigerator fifteen to twenty minutes before serving. When too cold, flavours are masked. When too warm, *foie gras* can turn mushy, losing its seductive charm.

Legally, any product labeled *foie gras* must contain actual pieces of fattened duck or goose liver, with a 10 to 15 percent allowance for veal, pork, or chicken meat added. Additionally, the label of all liver products must clearly list ingredients. The best contain nothing but *foie gras,* and salt and pepper, but today even many respectable firms insist on adding nitrites and other preservatives.

The following are the legal French definitions and preparations for *foie gras*. When purchasing it preserved, look for products packed in terrines or glass jars, rather than tins, so you can see exactly what you are buying. The best *foie gras* has a fresh colour, slices neatly, is generally free of blood vessels, and is not heavily surrounded with fat. Many shops also sell *foie gras* by the slice, cut from a larger terrine. This should be refrigerated, and is best eaten within a few hours. *Foie gras* that can legally enter the United States must have been sterilized—cooked at a temperature of 230°F (110° C)—and is generally marked *foie gras de conserve*.

Foie gras cru: Raw liver. If of good quality, this is the ultimate in *foie gras*. Usually found only at select Paris *charcuteries* around the end of the year, it is delicious sliced raw and spread on warm, toasted bread; it can also be preserved in a terrine at home. Often sold vacuum-packed. The best are the smallest, a little over 1 pound (500 to 600 grams) for goose, a little under 1 pound (400 grams) for duck. Lobes should be supple, round, smooth rather than granular, and without spots. Usually a good buy, but only when purchased from a reputable merchant.

Foie gras mi-cuit or nature: The lightly cooked preserved *foie gras* of connoisseurs, and the best way to sample *foie gras* for the first time. Ideally, only the highest quality livers are preserved in this manner. The terms *mi-cuit* and *nature* are used interchangeably with *foie gras frais*, denoting that the livers have been pasteurized at 175 to 200° F (80 to 90° C). Next to raw, this is the best way to enjoy *foie gras*, for it is barely cooked, retaining its pure, agreeably rich flavour. Sold in terrines; vacuum packed; in aluminum foil-wrapped rolls; in a can or jar; it requires refrigeration. Depending on packaging, it will last several days to several months.

Today's specials.

Foie gras entier: Entire lobes of the fattened liver, lightly seasoned and generally cooked in a terrine or glass jar. If the container is large, additional pieces of another liver may be added to fill it in. Sold fresh (*frais*), which requires refrigeration, and must be consumed within a few weeks or months (depending on length of cooking time); and *en conserve*, which requires no refrigeration, and will last several years.

Foie gras en conserve: Fattened livers, whole or in pieces, that have been seasoned, then sterilized in a jar or can, at 230 to 240° F (108 to 115° C). Requires no refrigeration. Carefully conserved, high-quality *foie gras* will actually ripen and improve with age. It should be stored in a cool, dry place and turned from time to time, and could be kept for up to ten years. A good buy when purchased from a reputable merchant.

Bloc de foie gras: By law, composed of either 50 percent fattened duck liver or 35 percent goose liver that must be obviously present in chunks, held together by *foie gras* that has been mechanically blended. Not the best buy, for there is also a 10 percent allowance for pork barding fat.

Foie gras truffé: Foie gras with at least 3 percent truffles. A bad buy, for the flavor and essence of the expensive truffle is totally lost, the price greatly inflated.

Foie gras parfait: A mechanically mixed blend of usually mediocre quality *foie gras* surrounded with stuffing of pork, veal, or chicken meat, then wrapped in barding fat. A bad buy.

Foie gras pâté, galantine, or *purée:* Various products with a base of *foie gras.* Usually composed of lowest quality livers mixed with pork, chicken, or veal, surrounded by barding fat. The word *gras* may be missing, but the mixtures must contain a minimum of 50 percent *foie gras,* with added stuffing mixture and pork barding fat. A bad buy.

VICTOR-HUGO, ARC DE TRIOMPHE, VILLIERS
16th and 17th arrondissements

CORDIER,
129 Avenue Victor-Hugo, Paris 16.
(727.97.74).
Métro: Victor-Hugo.
Open 8:30 A.M. to 1:15 P.M. and 3:30 P.M. to 7:45 P.M. Closed Sunday.

A solid, traditional, neighbourhood *charcuterie,* with a touch of luxury. Fine smoked salmon, and fresh, raw fattened duck and goose liver (*foie gras*) at holiday time.

AUX FERMES D'AUVERGNE,
13 Rue Poncelet, Paris 17.
(622.50.45).
Métro: Ternes.
Open 9 A.M. to 1 P.M. and 4 P.M. to 7:30 P.M. Tuesday through Friday, 9 A.M. to 1 P.M. and 3:30 P.M. to 7:30 P.M. Saturday, 9 A.M. to 1 P.M. Sunday. Closed Monday and the months of July and August.

My favourite *charcuterie* in Paris; a spotless, active little shop where you can find more than a dozen varieties of ham, homemade sausages, a superb and always fresh assortment of farm cheeses. These include a variety of Cantals, mild Saint-Marcellin, nicely aged *brebis* from sheep's milk, and crottin goat cheese.

Carefully slicing into a terrine at Aux Fermes d'Auvergne.

**JEAN-CLAUDE
ET NANOU,**
46 Rue Legendre, Paris 17.
(227.15.08).
Métro: Malesherbes.
Open 8:30 A.M. to 1 P.M.
and 4:15 P.M. to 8 P.M.
Tuesday through
Saturday, 8:30 A.M. to
1 P.M. Sunday. Closed
Monday and the month
of August.

Chic, friendly, and outgoing, the young Jean-Claude and Nanou run a tidy family *charcuterie,* filled with impeccably fresh sausages and hams, pâtés and *foie gras* shipped up from the Auvergne region every few days. A respectable assortment of regional cheeses and extraordinary dried and smoked sausages can be bought here as well.

MAISON POU,
16 Avenue des Ternes,
Paris 17.
(380.19.24).
Métro: Ternes.
Open 9:30 A.M. to 1:15
P.M. and 3:15 P.M. to
7:15 P.M. Tuesday
through Friday and
Sunday, 9:30 A.M. to
2:45 P.M. Saturday.
Closed Monday.
Credit cards: AE, DC, V.

A "press-your-nose-against-the-window" shop: elegant, upscale, and spotless, filled with fragrant sausages, steaming sauerkraut, pâtés and hams, not to mention a wide selection of wines, cheeses, wild mushrooms and truffles.

SCHMID,
41 Rue Legendre, Paris 17.
(763.31.04).
Métro: Villiers.
Open 9:30 A.M. to 1 P.M.
and 4 P.M. to 7 P.M.
Closed Sunday and
holidays.

Almost as good as a trip to Alsace: windows filled with heart-shaped Alsatian spice cookies; golden farm-aged Munster; sausages for slicing or poaching; plus wines, liqueurs, and *foie gras* from the region.

Chocolateries
CHOCOLATE SHOPS

The allure of chocolate.

The way the French fuss over chocolate, you might think they had invented it. They didn't, but as in so many matters gastronomic, they inspire envy. The French have refined the art of chocolate making, carefully coaxing and coddling their bonbons into existence, working until they've produced some of the smoothest, strongest, richest, most intoxicating and flavourful to be found anywhere in the world.

The French chocolate-buying public is discriminating, and the *chocolatiers*, or chocolate makers, are fortunate to have a clientele willing to pay a premium price for confections made from the finest South American cocoa beans, the best Madagascar vanilla, the freshest Sicilian pistachios, the most expensive Dutch cocoa butter.

Before there was chocolate as we know it today—in bars and bonbons, taken as a snack or dessert—chocolate was prepared as a drink: a combination of roasted ground cocoa beans, sugar, cinnamon, and perhaps vanilla. As the brew became popular in Europe during the 17th century, it also became the subject of dispute. Was chocolate healthy? Was it lethal? Was it a dangerous aphrodisiac? The famous Madame de Sévigné wrote her daughter at the time: "It flatters you for awhile, it warms you for an instant; then it kindles a mortal fever in you." But when her daughter moved from Paris, she worried about how she could "get along" without a *chocolatière*, or chocolate pot.

Paris's first chocolate shop—situated on Rue de l'Arbre-Sec in what is now the 1st *arrondissement*—was opened in 1659, when Louis XIV gave one of Queen Anne's officers the exclusive privilege to sell chocolate.

Chocolate soon became the rage of the French courts. It was served at least three times a week at Versailles, and it is said that Napoleon preferred chocolate to coffee as a morning pick-me-up. In Voltaire's later years, he consumed twelve cups a day, always between five in the morning and three in the afternoon. He lived to be eighty-four years old. Brillat-Savarin put it most concisely: "Chocolate is health."

And it was to that point that in the early 1800s two very clever Parisians figured a way around the still raging dispute concerning the wholesomeness of chocolate. They sold it as medicine. A certain Monsieur Debauve, a *chocolatier*, and a Monsieur Gallais, a pharmacist, teamed up and opened an elegant shop at 30 Rue des Saints-Pères, just off the Boulevard Saint-Germain. Soon the nervous, the sickly, the thin, the obese, were going to Debauve & Gallais for "the chocolate treatment." It's no surprise to find that the chocolate preparations became bigger business than other pharmaceuticals, and Debauve & Gallais—still selling chocolates on the same spot today—soon became the most important chocolate shop in Paris.

Today in France, chocolate remains synonymous with *gourmandise* and comfort. But the French display a great deal of discipline when it comes to their beloved bonbons. They actually eat much less chocolate than their neighbours–the French consume about eleven pounds of chocolate per person per year, compared to twenty-two for the Swiss, and fifteen for the Belgians (the Americans consume about nine pounds). But when they eat chocolate, they want plenty of it: 80 percent of all the chocolate sold in Paris is sold during the last three weeks of December!

BASTILLE
3rd and 11th arrondissements

CLICHY,
5 Boulevard Beaumarchais,
Paris 3.
(887.89.88).
Métro: Bastille.
Open 9 A.M. to 6:30 P.M.
Closed Monday and the
month of August.

Just a few steps from the Bastille, this popular, old-fashioned pastry and chocolate shop also has a little tea salon in the back, for sampling their better-than-average *croissants* and *pains au chocolat*, or their chocolates, with a cup of rich, black *express*. The chocolates to try here are the chunky, wonderful *mendiants*, palm-sized rounds of bittersweet chocolate filled with walnuts, hazelnuts, and gigantic raisins. At Eastertime, the whole neighbourhood comes to admire chef Paul Bugat's windows, artfully arranged with hand-moulded chocolate eggs and fish. Also, there are *marrons glacés* (candied chestnuts) in the fall and spectacular displays of *pâtes de fruits,* or jellied fruit, all year long.

LA PETITE FABRIQUE,
19 Rue Daval, Paris 11.
(805.82.02).
Métro: Bréguet-Sabin.
Open 10 A.M. to 12:30
  P.M. and 3 P.M. to 7:30
  P.M. Closed Sunday and
  Wednesday.

A bright pink neon sign leads you to the door, and the rich, alluring aroma of chocolate calls you inside. This is a tiny shop offering a small, artisanal selection of good quality chocolates. Try the huge *palet d'or*, deep, dark chocolate filled with cream and more chocolate; the satisfying praline-filled *rocher*, and the sweet, hearty *bûche*, a cute little log of dark chocolate filled with bright green almond paste.

SEVRES-BABYLONE, ECOLE MILITAIRE
6th and 7th arrondissements

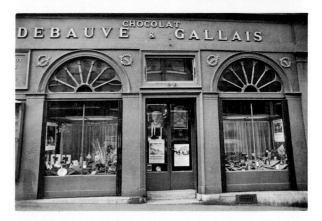

DEBAUVE & GALLAIS,
30 Rue des Saints-Pères,
  Paris 6.
(548.54.67).
Métro: Sèvres-Babylone.
Open 10 A.M. to 1 P.M.
  and 2 P.M. to 7 P.M.
  Closed Sunday, Monday,
  the month of August,
  and the first week of
  September.

A little jewel—begun as a pharmacy that also dispensed chocolate—this shop has barely changed in 150 years. The sturdy pharmacy counter is now covered with glass amphoras filled with hazelnut pralines and chocolate truffles dusted with cocoa. The pharmacy shelves, flanking a huge mirror, now hold colourful tin containers filled with coffee and tea, both dispensed without prescription. And when the sun shines, it still cuts its way through the elegant *cosse d'orange* windows, arranged to form an elegant orange wedge. Like all Paris chocolate shops, Debauve & Gallais handle their wares like diamonds, wrapping each order, no matter how small, in bags decorated with gold seals and silver ribbons. Their chocolates are dark, intense, strong, and masculine. Here, flavour's the thing, not texture, for some chocolates are a bit grainy and sugary.

LENOTRE,
44 Rue du Bac, Paris 7.
(222.39.39).
Métro: Rue du Bac.
Open 9:45 A.M. to 7:30 P.M. Monday through Saturday, 9:45 A.M. to 1 P.M. Sunday. Closed Sunday and Monday in August.

Some of the most beautiful and ethereal chocolates in town. Ask for a 100-gram assortment and you'll find ten different chocolates, wonderfully aromatic, with a smooth and even texture. There's a good, strong burst of real chocolate flavour on the palate. The *palet d'or* and little triangles of *noisettes* (hazelnuts) are exceptional. (See also Pâtisseries.)

PUYRICARD,
27 Avenue Rapp, Paris 7.
(705.59.47).
Métro: Ecole Militaire.
Open 9:30 A.M. to 1 P.M. and 2 P.M. to 7 P.M. Closed Monday morning and all day Sunday.

A sober, old-fashioned shop selling handmade chocolates from Aix-en-Provence—rich and creamy, with the intensity of good South American chocolate.

MADELEINE, ROND-POINT, ARC DE TRIOMPHE
8th and 9th arrondissements

DALLOYAU,
101 Rue du Faubourg Saint-Honoré, Paris 8.
(359.18.10).
Métro: Saint-Philippe-du-Roule.
Open 9:30 A.M. to 7 P.M. Monday through Saturday, 9:30 A.M. to 1 P.M. and 3 P.M. to 6:30 P.M. Sunday.

Classic and creamy chocolates, all made in an impeccable workshop near the Opéra. The best are the cinnamon and praline-filled "El Dorado" and the smooth, bittersweet chocolate-covered caramels. This shop is old and traditional: Neighbourhood matrons settle into cosy, upholstered chairs while they wait for their pastries and boxes of chocolates to be wrapped. (See also Pâtisseries.)

LA MAISON DU CHOCOLAT,
225 Rue du Faubourg Saint-Honoré, Paris 8.
(227.39.44).
Métro: Ternes.
Open 9:30 A.M. to 7 P.M. Closed Sunday and Monday.

A chocolate-lover's dream: chocolate-coloured facade, chocolate-coloured blinds, even the *chocolatier* Robert Linxe in a chocolate-coloured apron. You feel as though you'll gain a pound or two just walking into the shop. Monsieur Linxe is the undisputed king of chocolate in Paris, selling a sophisticated, handmade assortment made in the neat little basement workshop of this former wine and spirits shop. He's rightly proud of his *framboise* (raspberry-flavored chocolate), and his creamy *palet d'or* melts in your mouth. There's also a good selection of wines, a fine and inexpensive house Champagne, and a remarkable choice of Armagnacs. (See also Vin, Bière, Alcool.)

Robert Linxe, chocolatier at La Maison du Chocolat.

MARQUISE DE SEVIGNE,
32 Place de la Madeleine, Paris 8.
(265.19.47).
Métro: Madeleine.
Open 9:45 A.M. to 7 P.M. Closed Sunday.

With a name like this, who could go wrong? A portrait of the famous Marquise de Sévigné—in all her abundance—appears on the chocolate box lids and on the gold-foil wrappers that envelop the shop's delicious pralines. Also sample the *coeur de Paris*, an almost solid heart of chocolate filled with a hazelnut and a touch of praline; and the fresh and creamy *palet*, dark chocolate filled with cream and chocolate.

MEURISSE,
49 bis Avenue Franklin-D.-
Roosevelt, Paris 8.
(225.06.04).
Métro: Franklin-D.-
Roosevelt.
Open 9:30 A.M. to 7 P.M.
(10 A.M. to noon and
12:30 P.M. to 7 P.M. in
summer months).
Closed Saturday, Sunday,
and the month of
August.

A sparkling, old-fashioned shop with bold, cocoa-buttery chocolates. Try *turinos*, chocolate covered rounds filled with chestnut cream and rum, or *brunas*, almonds coated with dark, bitter chocolate.

CHOCOLATE FOR ALL SEASONS

In Paris, chocolate is always in fashion. Throughout the year, the sparkling windows of the city's chocolate shops serve as a calendar, announcing each season, each holiday, beginning with Valentine's Day when thousands of chocolate hearts are broken.

Spring is ushered in as shop windows are aswim with chocolate fish in anticipation of *Poisson d'Avril,* April Fool's Day. Large fish with bows around their tails are filled with schools of *fritures,* tiny chocolate minnows. And little metal boxes filled with milk chocolate "sardines," appear everywhere.

At Eastertime chocolate bunnies, chicks, ducks, and puppies frolic in displays. They are surrounded by chocolate eggs wrapped with silvery, glittery, magical paper. On the Place de la Madeleine, Fauchon's huge, lacy chocolate egg sits in regal splendour, stopping pedestrian traffic for weeks.

Easter has hardly passed when tiny chocolate pots of *muguets,* lilies of the valley, appear as the traditional French symbol for the first of May. They keep company with the hearts and flowers that burst forth for *Fête des Mères,* Mother's Day.

Although the summer heat signals a slowdown for chocolates in Paris, chocolate shops refuse to give up. Windows are full of summer symbols, all nicely moulded in chocolate—pails and shovels for playing in the sand, starfish, and shells.

Fall comes in with blustery days and sudden rainstorms, announcing the season for chocolate mushrooms and luscious, creamy truffles. All of this is a fanfare to Christmas, when chocolate shops split their attention between the candied chestnuts known as *marrons glacés* and *bûches de Noël,* or Christmas log cakes, homey reminders of times past, when guests offered their hosts a real log to keep the fire burning.

SPECIALITES DE FRANCE,
44 Avenue Montaigne,
Paris 8.
(720.99.63).
Métro: Franklin-D.-
Roosevelt.
Open 9:30 A.M. to 6:30
P.M. Closed Sunday.
Credit cards: AE, DC, V.

A bright, neatly organized shop that carries regional specialties from all over France: sophisticated chocolates; little packages of hard candy wrapped like bundles of twigs; fabric bags filled with assorted candies. Try the *chocolat au Calvados*, from Le Havre, or the *palet Cognac de Meaux*, from France's Brie capital, along with the cocoa-covered almonds, *amandas* from Montargis. The shop is happy to make up a gift assortment. (See also Spécialités Gastronomique.)

TANRADE,
18 Rue Vignon,
    Paris 9.
(742.26.99).
Métro: Madeleine.
Open 9:15 A.M. to noon
    and 1:30 P.M. to 6:30
    P.M. Closed Sunday,
    Monday, and the month
    of August.

A venerable establishment on Rue Vignon, Tanrade has been in business since 1820, and at its present location, just around the corner from Fauchon's and the Place de la Madeleine food shops, for more than sixty years. (This is why we have included it in the 8th *arrondissement* listing.) There, in the shop's carefully preserved *Art Déco* interior, Pierre Tanrade makes chocolates exactly as generations of Tanrades have before him. The best are the *rochers*, little rounds of toasted almonds covered with chocolate. This firm is also known throughout the world for its *marrons glacés*, marvelous candied chestnuts, available only from November through February. Tanrade also specializes in *confitures*, or jams and jellies, which are made by hand in tiny batches in the same unlined copper basins they use to make their candied chestnuts. When visiting the shop, be sure to notice the frosted glass and black wrought iron chandeliers: Pierre Tanrade's grandmother designed them herself, working the outline of the Tanrade confiture pot into the design. (See also Spécialités Gastronomiques.)

TRINITE, NOTRE-DAME-DE-LORETTE, GARE SAINT-LAZARE
9th arrondissement

**BONBONNIERE
DE LA TRINITE,**
4 Place d'Estienne-d'Orves,
    Paris 9.
(874.23.38).
Métro: Trinité.
Open 10 A.M. to 7 P.M.
    Monday through
    Saturday. Closed Sunday,
    and Saturday and
    Sunday in August.

LENOTRE,
5 Rue du Havre, Paris 9.
(522.22.59).
Métro: Saint-Lazare.
Open 9 A.M. to 7:30 P.M.
    Tuesday to Friday, 9:45
    A.M. to 7:45 P.M.
    Saturday and Monday.
    Closed Sunday.
See Lenôtre, 6th
    arrondissement, page 201.

A father-to-son operation since 1925, this cosy neighborhood shop offers fresh-flavoured, intense chocolates, some decorated with dainty candied violets. The shop also offers dozens of varieties of teas, flavored honey, and tins of regional cakes and cookies.

CANDIED CHESTNUTS

C andied chestnuts, *marrons glacés,* are fall and winter specialities sold at most of the better chocolate shops in town. They appear around the beginning of November, when the first fresh chestnuts begin arriving from the Ardèche, in southeast France. They generally disappear at the close of the season, around the middle of January. The process of turning fresh raw chestnuts into little candied jewels is painstakingly slow, and requires immense patience.

The fresh chestnuts are first boiled several times to free them from their shells and skins. If any bits of skin remain, they are removed by hand. The chestnuts are then wrapped in cheesecloth to prevent them from falling apart during the next process—a three to seven hour stint in a pressure cooker. Next, they are cooked again, this time for 48 hours in a vanilla sugar syrup over very low heat. The chestnuts are often delivered to shops in this form, conserved in syrup. They are then glazed in small quantities by sprinkling them with water and baking them, a process which gives the chestnuts their characteristic sugary appearance. Finally they are wrapped in the traditional shiny gold foil paper.

A LA MERE DE FAMILLE,
35 Rue du Faubourg Montmartre, Paris 9.
(770.83.69).
Métro: Notre-Dame-de-Lorette.
Open 9:30 A.M. to 1:30 P.M. and 3 P.M. to 7 P.M. Closed Sunday, Monday, the month of August, and the first week of September.

This shop comes right out of a fairy tale. Stop in at three in the afternoon, as the children are getting out of school, and watch Suzanne and Albert Brethonneau spoil the entire neighbourhood with their incredible variety of sweets from all parts of France. In the chocolate department, sample the little *barquettes* of dark chocolate filled with *cassis* (black currant) or *framboise* (raspberry).(See also Spécialités Gastronomiques.)

VICTOR-HUGO
16th arrondissement

BOISSIER,
184 Avenue Victor-Hugo, Paris 16.
(504.24.43).
Métro: Victor-Hugo.
Open 9:30 A.M. to 1 P.M. and 2:30 P.M. to 7 P.M. Closed Sunday.

LENOTRE,
49 Avenue Victor-Hugo, Paris 16.
(501.71.71).
Métro: Victor-Hugo.
Open 9:30 A.M. to 7:15 P.M. Tuesday to Saturday, 9 A.M. to 1 P.M. Sunday. Closed Monday.
See Lenôtre, 6th *arrondissement,* page 201.

The discreet exterior suggests this is a bank, not a chocolate shop. Once inside, you know differently. Wander into Boissier, if only to admire the marble counter set with little trays of cakes and chocolates, looking as if someone is getting ready for a very exclusive bake sale. Many wealthy families in the neighbourhood may have full-time cooks, but the woman of the house still comes in, personally, to carefully select the evening's dessert. The chocolates themselves are not terrific.

Fine chocolates listed in a fine handwriting.

**MARQUISE DE
SEVIGNE,**
1 Place Victor-Hugo,
    Paris 16.
(500.89.68).
Métro: Victor-Hugo.
Open 9 A.M. to 6:45 P.M.
    Closed Sunday.
See Marquise de Sévigné,
    8th *arrondissement,* page
    202.

*Luscious bonbons to suit any
palate.*

MACARONS CREOLES
CHOCOLATE MACAROONS

One day I was exhausted and a friend suggested that what I needed was chocolate. Not just any chocolate, but something special from La Maison du Chocolat, one of the best chocolate shops in Paris. Fortunately, it just happens to be at the end of my street. I bought a chocolate-filled chocolate macaroon and was instantly cured. In gratitude and greed, I created this recipe the very next day, and have never found anyone who'd turn them down.

Macaroons:
3½ ounces (100 g)
    bittersweet chocolate
    (preferably Lindt or
    Tobler brand)
1 teaspoon vanilla
2 large egg whites (2½
    ounces; 70 g)
1 cup (140 g) almonds,
    toasted and ground to
    a fine powder
¾ cup (150 g) sugar
1 tablespoon unsalted
    butter, for buttering
    the baking sheet

Filling:
1¾ ounces (50 g)
    bittersweet chocolate
2 tablespoons *crème fraîche*
    (see recipe, page 182)
    or heavy cream
    (preferably not ultra-
    pasteurized)

1. Preheat the oven to 275° F (135° C).

2. In a small saucepan, over very low heat, melt 3½ ounces (100 g) of chocolate with the vanilla.

3. In the bowl of an electric mixer on slow speed, mix the egg whites, almonds, and sugar until well blended. With the machine still running, add the melted chocolate mixture, and continue beating until thoroughly mixed.

4. Butter a baking sheet (or line with cooking parchment, then butter the paper). Spoon the batter onto the baking sheet, allowing 1 heaping tablespoon of batter for each macaroon.

5. Bake for about 15 to 18 minutes, or just until the macaroons are set. They should be slightly firm but not dry. Transfer the macaroons to a rack to cool.

6. Meanwhile, prepare the filling. In a small saucepan, over very low heat, melt the 1¾ ounces (50 g) chocolate. Add the *crème fraîche* or heavy cream and stir until well blended. Set aside to cool.

7. When the macaroons and the filling have cooled, spread a heaping teaspoonful of the filling on half the macaroons, and cover each with a second macaroon, making a sort of sandwich. The macaroons may be served immediately, and, preferably within a few hours.

Yield: 10 to 12 filled macaroons.

Spécialités Gastronomiques
SPECIALITY SHOPS

The exotic world of Izraël (see entry, page 210).

The speciality shops of Paris, ranging from old-fashioned, family-owned sweet and spice shops to slick and rambling food emporiums, offer a potpourri of good things at your finger-tips. Whether you're looking for the best caviar or the freshest black truffle; whether you plan to indulge in thirty different kinds of honey or would like to sample a peanut-flavoured mustard; or whether you just want to purchase a little sack of licorice as you wander about Paris, the following should offer some guidance. From the exotic to the commonplace, here is a hint of the things of which dreams are made.

PALAIS-ROYAL, LES HALLES, BOURSE, OPERA
1st and 2nd arrondissements

PAUL CORCELLET,
46 Rue des Petits-Champs,
   Paris 2. (296.51.82).
Métro: Pyramides.
Open 9:30 A.M. to 7 P.M.
   Closed Sunday and
   Monday.
Credit cards: AE, V.

SPECIALITIES:
Tea, honey, vinegar, mustard,
syrups, and spices.

Imagine, sixty varieties of tea, fifteen kinds of honey, twenty-five varieties of vinegar, and more than twenty-five different mustards (even a peanut-flavoured version inspired by former President Carter). Along with all this you get Paul Corcellet himself—robust, rotund, and indefatigable. He'll probably introduce his friendly wife, invite you to sample a drink in the shop, then share with you his latest discovery, be it a new cocktail or a new mustard. Corcellet remains faithful to exotic fare: He first opened in 1934, specializing in North African spices and produce, and still sells a wide assortment of exotic syrups and spices. Many products are available in miniature containers, handy for sampling and for travelling.

FLO PRESTIGE,
42 Place du Marché-Saint-
Honoré, Paris 1.
(261.45.46).
Métro: Pyramides.
Open daily, 7 A.M. to
midnight.
Credit cards: AE, DC, V.

SPECIALITIES:
Carry-out foods perfect for picnickers.

One of Paris's newest carry-out food shops, offering a bright and fresh selection of raw milk cheeses, beautiful smoked salmon, assorted *charcuterie, foie gras,* and salads. Everything can be purchased in individual portions (there's even bread by the slice), so put together a picnic and head for the Tuileries Gardens. Wine and pastries are also available.

GARGANTUA,
284 Rue Saint-Honoré,
Paris 1.
(260.63.38).
Métro: Tuileries.
Open 8 A.M. to 7:30 P.M.
Closed Sunday.
Credit cards: AE, V.

SPECIALITIES:
Large-size pastry and carry-out charcuterie.

As the name suggests, everything here is king-size. Enjoy quality *croissants, pains au chocolat,* and oversize puff pastry *palmiers,* all big enough to feed a family of four, at the small counter tucked in back of the shop. The place is casual and colourful, with a wide selection of *charcuterie,* wines, spirits, and salads, ready to take home, on a picnic, or on a plane.

LUCIEN LEGRAND,
1 Rue de la Banque,
Paris 2.
(260.07.12).
Métro: Bourse.
Open 8:30 A.M. to 7:30
P.M. Tuesday through
Friday, 8:30 A.M. to
1 P.M. and 3 P.M.
to 7 P.M. Saturday.
Closed Sunday, Monday,
and last two weeks in
August.

SPECIALITIES:
Wonderful selection of wines, spices, and candies.

There have been no cosmetic changes here since 1890, when this combination wine shop and *épicerie* (grocery) began selling mustard and lentils, wine

by the barrel, lamp oil, and the dozens upon dozens
of multi-coloured sweets and bonbons now displayed
outdoors in huge glass containers. Today, the beautiful
Belle Epoque facade remains, while inside Legrand serves
as one of the city's better wine shops, with more than
a touch of character and history. Monsieur Legrand is
a born storyteller, a source of wisdom about old Paris
as well as wine. English spoken.

PETIT QUENAULT,
56 Rue Jean-Jacques-
    Rousseau, Paris 1.
(233.46.85).
Métro: Les Halles.
Open 8 A.M. to 12:30 P.M.
    and 1:30 P.M. to 7:30
    P.M. Closed Saturday
    afternoon, all day
    Sunday, and Monday
    morning.

SPECIALITIES:
*Wild mushrooms, chocolate,
and spices in bulk.*

Petit Quenault is a simple, matter-of-fact restaurant
supply house, selling everything from Heinz cat-
sup to bouillon cubes. But the shop is also open to
individuals, and this is the place to go to stock up on
quantities of dried wild mushrooms, including *cèpes*
and *morilles*. Their prices are among the lowest in
town. Also try the Le Pecq baking chocolate, the
brand preferred by many of Paris's pastry chefs.

**TETREL EPICERIE/
CONFISERIE,**
44 Rue des Petits-Champs,
    Paris 2.
(296.59.58).
Métro: Pyramides.
Open 9 A.M. to 7 P.M.
    Closed Sunday.

SPECIALITIES:
Old-fashioned sweets.

A pristine little shop for fine foodstuffs, the polished
wood counters and sparkling windows all
crowded with tins of sweets, *confit,* and sardines. This
is a good place to experience old Paris and pick up
some old-fashioned sweets or a small gift reminiscent
of the 19th century.

VERLET,
256 Rue Saint-Honoré,
    Paris 1.
(260.67.39).

Métro: Palais-Royal.
Open 9 A.M. to 7 P.M.
    Closed Sunday, Monday,
    and the month of
    August.

SPECIALITIES:
*A fine selection of unusual
coffees and teas.*

For common and uncommon coffees and teas, fresh
from the world over. Stop in after a walk along the
Rue de Rivoli for a pick-me-up in the homey, aromatic
little lunch room. They serve a good *croque-monsieur*
and fine, fresh desserts. (See also Salons de Thé).

MARAIS, ILE SAINT-LOUIS
4th arrondissement

IZRAEL,
30 Rue François-Miron,
  Paris 4.
(272.66.23).
Métro: Saint-Paul.
Open 9:30 A.M. to 1 P.M.
  and 2:30 P.M. to 7 P.M.
  Tuesday through Friday,
  9:30 A.M. to 7 P.M.
  Saturday. Closed Sunday
  and Monday.
Credit card: V.

SPECIALITIES:
North African products and
also foods imported from
throughout the world.

Some years ago, a friendly, robust man named Israel married a woman named Izraël, hence the name of the shop. That doesn't quite make him Israel Izraël, but he does have a great sense of humour about it. The shop opened more than forty-five years ago, specializing in North African products. Today, the cluttered, delicious-smelling store features more than 3,000 products from all over the world, everything from guava paste to Fritos, delicious Polish buckwheat to woven African baskets. There's a marvellous assortment of grains, rice, flours, dried fruits, and nuts, sold out of giant sacks.

It's a pleasure to breathe the
air, redolent with spices, at
Izraël.

A L'OLIVIER,
77 Rue Saint-Louis-en-l'Ile,
  Paris 4.
(329.58.32).
Métro: Pont-Marie.
Open 9:30 A.M. to 12:30
  P.M. and 2:30 P.M. to
  7:30 P.M. Closed
  Sunday and Monday.
Credit card: V.

SPECIALITIES:
Oils of all kinds and for all
purposes.

This bright and newly situated shop along one of the main streets of l'Ile Saint-Louis offers every kind of oil imaginable, from olive, walnut, and hazelnut for the table to palm oil for frying and almond oil for massages. Although the quality of the oil is not extraordinary, the nicely packaged products make fine gifts.

LATIN QUARTER, SAINT-GERMAIN, SEVRES-BABYLONE, INVALIDES
5th, 6th, and 7th arrondissements

HEDIARD,
126 Rue du Bac,
  Paris 6.
(544.01.98).
Métro: Sèvres-Babylone.
Open 9:15 A.M. to 7:30
  P.M. Closed Sunday.
Credit cards: AE, EC, V.
See Hédiard, 8th
  arrondissement.

SARDINES

Decades ago, most self-respecting French gourmands tucked tins of fine and delicate Brittany sardines away in their *caves* (cellars), sometimes aging the tender little fish for a decade or more. Vintage, or *millésime*, sardines are again the rage in Paris, where most fine speciality shops offer a mixed assortment, tinned and carefully dated. Once they're taken home, the tins must be stored in a cool spot, and turned every three or four months. As the unctuous, chewy sardines age, they become softer, more refined and delicate, ready to be consumed with a slice of crusty bread.

Sardines destined for *millésime* stardom bear no resemblance to the cheap, garden variety canned fish. Vintage sardines are always preserved fresh, while most ordinary sardines are frozen, then fried and processed. To prepare vintage sardines for processing, the fish are usually washed, grilled, and quickly deep-fried before being packed, by hand, into small oval tins. Generally the head, skin, and central backbone are removed from sardines packed for aging. Oil—usually the finest virgin olive oil—is added, perhaps a touch of spice or simply salt, then the tins are sealed and stored. They are turned regularly to ensure even aging, then put on the market one to two years after processing.

Many tins of vintage sardines include the words *première catégorie* or *extra* on the label, assuring that the sardines were prepared fresh, not frozen. Check for the processing date stamped into the bottom of the tin, so you know how long to keep them. Years ago, the tins were thick and solid enough to withstand decades of aging, but today very lightweight tin is used, and experts recommend the sardines be kept no more than four years.

The following are just a few of the shops offering vintage sardines. The tin or wrapper will bear the processing date.

Hédiard, 21 Place de la Madeleine, Paris 8. (266.44.36).

Fauchon, 26 Place de la Madeleine, Paris 8. (742.60.11).

Au Soleil de Provence, 6 Rue du Cherche-Midi, Paris 6. (548.15.02).

Au Verger de la Madeleine, 4 Boulevard Malesherbes, Paris 8. (265.51.99).

MAISON WOERLI,
36 Rue Saint-André-des-
  Arts, Paris 6.
(326.89.49).
Métro: Saint-Michel.
Open 8:30 A.M. to 6:30
  P.M. Closed Sunday
  afternoon and the month
  of August.

SPECIALITIES:
Assorted sweets.

An authentic, old-fashioned neighborhood *épicerie* (grocery), with dozens of glass jars lined up outside, filled with mysterious sweets. Even if your purchase of licorice amounts to three or four francs, the friendly shop owner will carefully select each piece with little tongs, as though you were buying diamonds. Sweet shops such as Woerli are disappearing, so go before this remnant of Paris's past is no more.

PETROSSIAN,
18 Boulevard La Tour-
  Maubourg, Paris 7.
(551.59.73).
Métro: Invalides.
Open 9 A.M. to 1 P.M. and
  2:30 P.M. to 7 P.M.
  Tuesday through Friday,
  9:30 A.M. to 7:30 P.M.
  Saturday. Closed Sunday
  and Monday.

SPECIALITIES:
The finest Russian caviar, plus
high-quality smoked salmon,
foie gras, and truffles.

As Christian Petrossian says, "We sell dreams." And dreams are made of Russian caviar, smoked salmon, *foie gras,* truffles, and Sauternes. Everything here is of high quality, but the prices are competitive. I wouldn't buy caviar anywhere else in Paris—Christian himself makes regular trips to the Caspian Sea to monitor its processing. Other specialities in this elegant, well-appointed shop include Russian pastries, fresh blinis, assorted herring, vodka, and delicious black Georgian tea, along with Petrossian's own line of French products from the Périgord.

A la Mère de Famille (see entry, page 205).

SOLEIL DE PROVENCE,
6 Rue du Cherche-Midi,
  Paris 6.
(548.15.02).
Métro: Sèvres-Babylone.
Open 9:45 A.M. to 7 P.M.
  Closed Sunday, Monday,
  and the month of
  August.

SPECIALITIES:
Olives, olive oil, honey, herbs,
and soap.

Make a special detour and come here for the first-rate olives, olive oil, and honey shipped direct from Paul Tardieu's organic farm in Provence. The olives are the best cured black olives France has to offer, and the light, fruity oil is first pressed, virgin. Just ask for Monsieur Tardieu's products under his name. The shop also sells a variety of oils out of giant metal vats, along with dried Provençal herbs and refreshing soaps.

THAN BINH,
25 Rue Galande, 18 Rue
Lagrange, and 29 Place
Maubert, Paris 5.
(354.03.34, 354.66.11,
325.81.65).
Métro: Maubert-Mutualité.
Open 8:30 A.M. to 7:30
P.M. Monday through
Saturday, 9 A.M. to
7:30 P.M. Sunday.

SPECIALITIES:
Vietnamese products.

Take a quick trip to Asia via the three tiny Than Binh shops scattered about the Left Bank. The Vietnamese produce is fresh and beautiful, and wandering through the cluttered shops is like paying a visit to an exotic food museum. Very little French and no English is spoken, so you're on your own.

CHAMPS-ELYSEES, MADELEINE, NOTRE-DAME-DE-LORETTE
8th and 9th arrondissements

CAVIAR KASPIA,
17 Place de la Madeleine,
Paris 8.
(265.33.52).
Métro: Madeleine.
Open 9 A.M. to midnight.
Closed Sunday.
Credit cards: AE, DC, V.

SPECIALITIES:
Caviar, smoked salmon, blinis.

A neat, simple little boutique on the Place de la Madeleine, offering well-priced pressed caviar (about 185 francs for about 3 ounces, or 100 grams), superb smoked salmon, and delightfully fresh blinis to take with you. There is also a nice, informal restaurant upstairs, where you can sample the house specialities on the spot. (See also Restaurants.)

A jumble of good things fills the windows.

FAUCHON,
26 Place de la Madeleine,
  Paris 8.
(742.60.11).
Métro: Madeleine.
Open 9:40 A.M. to 6:30
  P.M. Closed Sunday.
  (Only the pastry shop is
  open Monday, 9:40 A.M.
  to 6:30 P.M.)
Credit cards: AE, DC, V.

SPECIALITIES:
International selection of over
20,000 products including
imported, exotic fruits and
vegetables.

A visit to Fauchon is better than going to the theatre. Many even find their two shops on the Place de la Madeleine more fascinating than the Louvre. Fauchon's pristine glass windows, filled with expensive and exotic fruits and vegetables from every corner of the world, still stop traffic. Even the most jaded palates are tempted by the sheer quantity of food: more than 20,000 products including pastries, chocolates, a mammoth international selection of fresh and packaged goods, coffee, tea, spices, and a complete *charcuterie*. The famous pastry shop—with little tables for stand-up snacking—is always bustling. Certainly the best known food shop in town, but not always the friendliest, nor always the best.

FLORA DANICA,
142 Avenue des Champs-
  Elysées, Paris 8.
(359.20.41).
Métro: Charles-de-Gaulle-
  Etoile.
Open daily, noon to
  midnight.

SPECIALITIES:
Danish foods.

A tiny, popular lunchroom and boutique offering fresh Danish specialties for taking with you or sampling there: pastries, cured salmon, smoked salmon, eel and halibut, pickled herring, hearty rye bread, and Danish beer. (See also Restaurants.)

HEDIARD,
21 Place de la Madeleine,
  Paris 8.
(266.44.36).
Métro: Madeleine.
Open 9:15 A.M. to 7:30
  P.M. Closed Sunday.

SPECIALITIES:
Hédiard brand spices, oils,
vinegars, teas, and coffees.

Tea, spice, everything nice, and more. A new facade, restaurant, and expanded wine shop make Hédiard one of the best shows in town, with one-stop shopping for everything from their famous spices to exotic blends of vinegar or oil. Many visitors make annual visits just to stock up on a few of Hédiard's thirty varieties of tea; also, their freshly roasted coffee beans are top quality. The wine cellar offers an extensive selection of Bordeaux at high prices.

LA MAISON DU MIEL,
24 Rue Vignon, Paris 9.
(742.26.70).
Métro: Madeleine.
Open 9:30 A.M. to 7 P.M.
  Closed Sunday.

SPECIALITIES:
Unique varieties of honey
(miel) and honey products.

Even if you're not passionate about honey, put this shop on your list. The "House of Honey" is one of the few stores in the world devoted totally to honey and honey products, and it's been at Rue Vignon since 1908. The fantasylike tile decor—buzzing with bees and colourful hives—has not changed since then, nor has the founding family, the Gallands. They tend their own hives throughout France and buy selectively around the world. They sell some fifty-three tons of honey a year, producing about one-fourth of it themselves. Personal favourites include the hearty, rust-toned heather *(bruyère)*, and the delicate, mellow linden tree blossom *(tilleul)*. Sample tastings are offered in the shop, and most varieties are available in miniature jars, allowing one to sample several. Unfortunately, service can be cold and unfriendly. Honey-based soaps and health products are also sold.

RAGOUT D'HUITRES ET DE NOIX DE SAINT-JACQUES AU CAVIAR JAMIN
JAMIN'S RAGOUT OF OYSTERS AND SCALLOPS WITH CAVIAR

For about a six-month period one spring, I sampled this dish every few weeks at one of my favourite Paris restaurants, Jamin (see Restaurants, page 64). It's one nouvelle cuisine dish that can be prepared rather easily at home, served as either a first course at dinner or as a main luncheon dish. The spinach and scallop moulds can be prepared several hours in advance, then cooked at the last minute. The caviar is a lavish addition, but not essential.

2 dozen oysters, with
  their liquor
6 tablespoons unsalted
  butter, melted
12 sea scallops or 10½
  ounces (295 g) bay
  scallops, finely minced
Salt and freshly ground
  black pepper
16 to 20 large, fresh
  spinach leaves,
  deveined
1 small fennel bulb,
  trimmed and finely
  minced
1 small onion, finely
  minced
½ cup (125 ml) dry white
  wine
1 cup (250 ml) *crème
  fraîche* (see recipe, page
  182) or heavy cream,
  preferably not ultra-
  pasteurized
Pinch of saffron (optional)
4 teaspoons caviar
  (optional)

1. Combine the oysters, their liquor, and 1 tablespoon butter in a small saucepan. Bring to a boil over high heat, then remove from the burner, and immediately strain the oysters, reserving the liquor. Set oysters aside in a covered, ovenproof container.

2. Season the minced scallops with salt and pepper and mix with 1 tablespoon butter. Set aside.

3. Blanch the spinach leaves in boiling water. Drain well and use the leaves to line four 1-cup (250-ml) molds (round, flat-bottomed porcelain terrines work well). Place the lighter side of the spinach leaves facing in and allow a part of the leaves to remain above the top of the mold. Fill each mold with minced scallops and cover the top by overlapping the leaves. Set aside.

4. Preheat the oven to 350° F (175° C).

5. In a small saucepan, combine the remaining 4 tablespoons butter with the fennel and onion, and cook over low heat for 10 minutes. Add the wine, oyster liquor, and *crème fraîche* or heavy cream, and cook for 2 to 3 minutes.

6. Strain the sauce through a sieve (discarding the fennel and onion), return the sauce to the saucepan, add the optional saffron, and cook the sauce over medium heat, until it is reduced by one-third, or until it is smooth and glossy. If preparing this in advance, keep the sauce warm in the top of a double boiler over low heat.

7. Place the moulds in the oven and cook for 15 minutes. Reheat the oysters for about 4 minutes in the oven, keeping them covered so they do not dry out.

8. Unmould each spinach and scallop mould onto the centre of a warm dinner plate, arrange 3 oysters on each plate, and cover the oysters with the sauce. If you are serving caviar, place 1 teaspoon on top of each mould, and serve immediately.

Yield: 4 servings.

**LA MAISON DE
LA TRUFFE,**
19 Place de la Madeleine,
   Paris 8. (265.53.22).
Métro: Madeleine.
Open 9 A.M. to 8 P.M.
   Closed Sunday.
Credit cards: AE, DC, V.

SPECIALITIES:
*Truffles (truffes), plus foie gras
and charcuterie.*

Ffrom November to March come for the best fresh truffles to be found in Paris. Year-round, there are preserved truffles, goose and duck *foie gras,* exotic fruit, smoked salmon, a variety of *charcuterie,* and a respected assortment of wines and liqueurs.

**A LA MERE DE
FAMILLE,**
35 Rue du Faubourg
   Montmartre,
   Paris 9. (770.83.69).
Métro: Rue Montmartre.
Open 7:30 A.M. to 1:30
   P.M. and 3 P.M. to
   7 P.M. Closed Sunday
   and Monday.

SPECIALITIES:
*A fine selection of sweets and
jams.*

Walking into this spotless, sparkling sweet shop is like wandering into the midst of a *naïf* painting. Suzanne and Albert Brethonneau—with their rosy cheeks, smooth complexions, and clean white smocks—are the third generation to tend this old-fashioned shop that dates back to 1791. The window display and exterior are worth a trip on their own: the colourful, decorative boxes of bonbons, sugar candies, biscuits, and jams change with the seasons, but there's always a sense of organized clutter, inside and out. You'll find products from all over France, including the famous Madeleines de Commercy and caramel-coated Pralines de Montargis. (See also Chocolateries.)

**SPECIALITES DE
FRANCE,**
44 Avenue Montaigne,
   Paris 8. (720.99.63).
Métro: Franklin-D.-
   Roosevelt.
Open 9:30 A.M. to 6:30
   P.M. Closed Sunday.
Credit cards: AE, DC, V.

SPECIALITIES:
Sweets of all kinds.

Whether or not you need to nourish a sweet tooth, this glistening little sweet shop off the Champs-Elysées is worth a visit. It's like going on a veritable *tour de France* of sweets, as the delightful, traditional confections from every region of the country are gathered here under one roof. (See also Chocolateries.)

TANRADE,
18 Rue Vignon,
   Paris 9. (742.26.99).
Métro: Madeleine.
Open 9:15 A.M. to noon
   and 1:30 P.M. to 6:30
   P.M. Closed Sunday,
   Monday, and the month
   of August.

SPECIALITIES:
*Candied chestnuts (marrons
glacés) and assorted sweets.*

A jewel of a shop, still run by the friendly, outgoing Tanrade family. From November to February lovers of *marrons glacés* stream out the door, as Tanrade offers some of the best and freshest candied chestnuts in Paris. There are also fifty kinds of bonbons, fine chocolates, and revered *confitures* (jams). (See also Chocolateries.)

Escalope de Saumon aux Truffes Le Bernardin
LE BERNARDIN'S SALMON WITH TRUFFLES

This is one of the ten best dishes I've sampled during the past few years. Chef Gilbert Le Coze of Le Bernardin (see Restaurants, page 67) outdid himself on this creation, irresistibly fragrant with fresh, black truffles, unctuously alive with salmon, a touch of cream, a bit of butter. Uncork a bottle of finely aged Meursault, and take a trip to heaven. If truffles don't fit into the budget, substitute either fresh or dried wild mushrooms, and you won't be disappointed. (If using dried mushrooms, soak them first for 20 minutes in boiling water, drain them in several thicknesses of cheesecloth and carefully pat them dry.)

2 cups (500 ml) *crème fraîche* (see recipe, page 182) or heavy cream, preferably not ultra-pasteurized.
1 to 1½ ounces (40 g) preserved black truffle, cut into julienne strips, or ½ ounce (15 g) dried mushrooms, prepared as per above. (If using truffle reserve the juice.)
⅔ cup (5 ounces; 140 g) unsalted butter, chilled
1 tablespoon lemon juice
Salt and freshly ground black pepper to taste
1¾ pounds (800 g) salmon, skinned and cut into 12 thin filets

1. Preheat the oven to 500° F (260° C).

2. In a medium-size saucepan over high heat combine the *crème fraîche* or heavy cream, truffles and truffle juice or dried mushrooms. As soon as the mixture comes to a boil, reduce the heat and cook just until the *crème fraîche* begins to thicken, about 3 or 4 minutes. Remove from the heat and whisk in the butter, tablespoon by tablespoon, until it is completely incorporated. Add the lemon juice and stir, then season to taste with salt and freshly ground black pepper.

3. Spoon half of the sauce on the bottom of four oven-proof plates. Place three filets of salmon side by side on each plate. The filets should not overlap. Spoon the rest of the sauce over the salmon.

4. Place the plates in the oven for 2 to 3 minutes, or just long enough to barely cook the salmon and heat the dish through. Be careful not to leave the plates in the oven too long, or the sauce will separate. Serve immediately.

Yield: 4 servings.

Arc de Triomphe, Trocadero
16th and 17th arrondissements

FLO PRESTIGE,
61 Avenue de la Grand-Armée, Paris 16.
(500.12.10).
Métro: Argentine.
Open daily, 7 A.M. to midnight.
Credit cards: AE, DC, V.
See Flo Prestige, 1st *arrondissement,* page 208.

Sweets and spice at Legrand (see entry, page 208).

HEDIARD,
70 Avenue Paul-Doumer,
   Paris 16.
(504.51.92).
Métro: Muette.
Open 9:15 A.M. to 7:30
   P.M. Closed Sunday.
Credit cards: AE, EC, V.
See Hédiard, 8th
   arrondissement, page 214.

HEDIARD,
106 Boulevard de
   Courcelles, Paris 17.
(763.32.14).
Métro: Courcelles.
Open 9:15 A.M. to 1 P.M.
   and 2:30 P.M. to 7:30
   P.M. Closed Sunday.
Credit cards (only for
   purchases over 100
   francs): AE, DC, V.
See Hédiard, 8th
   arrondissement, page 214.

TRUFFLES

Delicate, earthy, and increasingly rare, the prized black Périgord truffle symbolizes the grand gastronomic life of Paris, past and present. The writer Colette, who devoted one day each year to eating truffles, said it best: "If I can't have too many truffles, I'll do without truffles."

The Périgord truffle—in appearance a rather inelegant, wrinkled black nugget generally the size of a walnut, although it can be as small as a pea or as large as an orange—is perhaps the world's most mysterious food. A fungus with a capricious personality, it stubbornly refuses to be cultivated. (As one Frenchman observed, "Growing truffles is not farming, it's luck.") And its flavour is just as elusive. No one has succeeded in adequately describing the taste of a truffle. Some say it's licoricelike, others find a hint of black pepper. As with many highly aromatic foods, it is the truffle's rich, pungent, and pervasive aroma that makes its flavour so singular. Eating fresh truffles makes me think of a quiet walk in the autumn woods under a slow drizzle; of freshly upturned black earth; of hazelnuts; of luxury, and pleasure.

The traditional truffle comes primarily from the southwest of France, in the Quercy and Périgord regions east of Bordeaux, though in recent years the crop is slowly moving further south. Truffles are also found in the Tricastin area of the Rhône Valley, and a small quantity of the truffles processed in France come from Italy and Spain.

Truffles grow three inches to a foot underground, in stony, porous soil near the roots of scrub oak trees. Gathered from November to March by farmers using dogs or pigs trained to scent out and unearth the elusive tuber, the truffle reaches its peak of flavour toward the month of January. Truffles thrive on a rainy summer and autumn, and their presence can be spotted by the burned patch around the base of the tree—the truffle's way of ensuring enough air for itself by killing the undergrowth—or by the presence of a swarm of truffle flies that hover above where the tuber is growing.

Fresh truffles (*truffes fraîches*), are sold in Paris speciality shops from mid-November through March, selling for 900 to 1,200 francs per pound (or 1,800 to 2,400 francs per kilo). An average-size fresh truffle weighs about 3 ounces, or about 100 grams, and though one truffle can't be considered an avalanche, it's enough for a gastronomic adventure.

At Paris's La Maison de la Truffe, which sells more than 600 pounds (about 300 kilos) of fresh and preserved truffles each year, fresh truffles arrive every two or three days from November to April direct from the Périgord or Tricastin. Still encrusted with soil, the fragrant gems are placed unwrapped in small wicker baskets, so they can breathe during the four to five hour train ride. A fresh truffle will last only three or four days, losing about one-twentieth of its weight by evaporation each day after it is unearthed. Meanwhile, its flavour fades rapidly. Guy Monier, owner of La Maison de la Truffe, suggests that if a fresh truffle must be kept longer than three or four days, it should be buried in goose or duck fat and refrigerated; otherwise it is likely to mildew. It may be stored in fat for up to six months. A fresh truffle can also be refrigerated for two or three days locked tight in a glass jar with several raw eggs still in their shells. The pungent truffle aroma will permeate the eggs, which can then be used to prepare a truffle-laced omelet, perhaps the best way to first experience a truffle.

For most of the world, the only known truffle is a preserved one. Although fresh is best, well-preserved truffles are better than no truffles at all. What does one look for in buying a preserved truffle? First, only buy truffles in a glass container, so you can see what you are getting, and buy only:

Truffes brossées au naturel: truffles that have been sterilized in water and salt, with no alcohol or spices used to mask or heighten their flavour. For the closest thing to a fresh truffle, try the whole, preserved *truffe extra,* the top grade truffle that is uniformly black and firm. If available, ask for a truffle of *première ébullition,* that is, a truffle that has been brushed, salted, placed in its container, then sterilized. Since a truffle loses 25 percent of its weight during cooking, the weight of the *première ébullition* truffle cannot be verified on the label. Thus, processors are required to underestimate on the label the true weight of the truffle. Most common are truffles of *deuxième ébullition.* In this process the truffle is sterilized, removed from its container to verify its weight, then resterilized. All preserved truffles should be consumed within three years of processing.

The following are other truffle gradings and other truffle preparations found on the market:

Truffes premier choix: small, irregularly shaped truffles that are more like pieces than whole truffles, and are more or less black.

Truffes en morceaux: broken pieces of truffle that must be at least ¼-inch (5-mm) thick. Considered equal in quality to *premier choix,* and generally lower in price.

Truffes en pelures: truffle peelings or shavings. Generally not worth the price.

Truffes préparées: truffles sterilized in water and salt, with liquor, alcohol, or wine added. A bad buy.

Jus de truffe: truffle juice. Not worth the price.

RAFFI,
60 Avenue Paul-Doumer,
   Paris 16.
(503.10.90).
Métro: Muette.
Open 10 A.M. to 1:30 P.M.
   and 3:30 P.M. to 8 P.M.
   Closed Sunday, Monday,
   and one week in
   August.
Credit card: V.

SPECIALITIES:
International foods, including
Bulgarian and Middle
Eastern.

This welcoming, expansive exotic shop run by the chatty, outgoing Martine Raffi offers a trip around the world. Wander among the huge gunnysacks full of buckwheat, *couscous,* corn, and rice, select multi-spiced black and green olives from a dozen barrels, inhale the pungent Bulgarian sheep's milk cheese, and take out a sampling of Middle Eastern snacks: fresh *tarama, hummous,* and pastries. The natural, unfermented Lucques d'Oc brand of green *olives de Mireille,* are firm, flavorful, and delicious.

CORNICHONS
TINY TART PICKLES

The cornichon, a tiny tart pickle, is ubiquitous in France. Cornichons arrive at the table in squat white crocks, ready to be served with pâtés, rillettes, slices of salty country ham, or with pot-au-feu. The first time I made cornichons was in New York City. Picking through a bin full of garden fresh cucumbers at the farmer's market on Union Square, I was able to come up with enough tiny cucumbers to make one precious quart. Now, frankly, I'm spoiled, for each August, the fresh cucumbers appear in abundance in Paris's open-air markets, ready for "putting up" with tiny white onions and plenty of fresh tarragon. I like them spicy and hot, so I add plenty of garlic and hot peppers.

60 to 70 2-inch (5-cm)
   pickling cucumbers
   (about 2 pounds;
   900g)
¼ cup (65 g) coarse
   (kosher) salt
1 quart (1 litre) cold
   water, plus an
   additional 1½ cups
   (375 ml)
3 cups (750 ml) best-
   quality white wine
   vinegar
1 tablespoon sugar
12 small white pickling
   onions, peeled but
   with ends intact
4 large sprigs fresh
   tarragon
6 cloves garlic, peeled
8 small hot red peppers
   (fresh or dried)
½ teaspoon whole black
   peppercorns
2 bay leaves

1. Trim off stem ends of the cucumbers, then rinse and drain. In a large bowl combine the salt with 1 quart (1 litre) water. Stir until the salt is dissolved, add the cucumbers, and let stand in a cool place for 6 hours.

2. Scald two 1-quart (1 litre) canning jars, lids, and rings with boiling water and drain well.

3. Drain the cucumbers.

4. In a medium-size saucepan over medium heat combine the vinegar, 1½ cups (375 ml) water, and the sugar, and bring to a boil.

5. Layer the jars with the drained cucumbers, the onions, herbs and spices, making sure to divide the ingredients evenly between the jars.

6. Pour the boiling vinegar, water, and sugar mixture into the jars, letting a bit of the liquid overflow the jars; this helps seal the lids well. Wipe the rim of each jar and seal. Let stand until cool. Store in a cool place for at least three weeks before serving. Refrigerate after opening.

Yield: 2 quarts (2 litres) *cornichons.*

Vin, Bière, Alcool
WINE, BEER, AND SPIRITS

Wine, an indispensable part of a meal.

In Paris, wine and spirits shops are not designed for popping in and out of quickly. Like most everything gastronomic in France, wine is selected with care, after conversation and contemplation. Wine shop owners are much like restaurant *sommeliers*. Passionate about their chosen field, they love to discuss, to advise, to help clients select a perfect little wine for a perfect little meal. Many of the shops listed here are small and specialized reflecting the personal tastes of their owners.

PALAIS-ROYAL, LES HALLES, OPERA, BOURSE
1st and 2nd arrondissements

JEAN DANFLOU,
36 Rue du Mont-Thabor,
Paris 1. (261.51.09).
Métro: Concorde.
Open 8 A.M. to noon and 2 P.M. to 6 P.M. Open Saturday morning during last two weeks in December, otherwise closed Saturday and Sunday.
Credit card: DC.

Set aside a long and languid afternoon for sampling the wide assortment of Jean Danflou's fine fruit-based liqueurs, Calvados, Armagnac, and Cognac. This is a wine and spirits shop, yes, but also an elegant, friendly tasting salon set in a tiny apartment just off the Rue de Rivoli. Jean Danflou, nephew of the man who founded the Paris-based company in 1925, is warm and welcoming, offering sample after sample of his exquisite, clear *eaux-de-vie,* including a fine Poire William, made only from the freshest Rhône Valley pears. (More than sixteen pounds of fruit go into preparing each bottle of Danflou's Poire William.) Sample, too, the raspberry (*framboise*), cherry (*kirsch*), yellow plum (*mirabelle*), and purple plum (*quetsch*) liqueurs, all distilled east of Paris, in the Vosges. Along with the tasting, you will learn some history (President Eisenhower stocked Danflou Cognac at the White House) and take a lesson in *eau-de-vie* etiquette (drink it at room temperature, not chilled, but from a chilled glass). Call or stop by for an appointment. English spoken.

LA GALERIE DES VINS,
201 Rue Saint-Honoré,
　Paris 1.
(261.81.20).
Métro: Palais-Royal.
Open 10 A.M. to 7 P.M.
　Closed Sunday.
Credit cards: AE, V.

An eclectic assortment of new and old vintages, particularly red Bordeaux, in everything from half-bottles to magnums and double magnums. Worth a stop if you're in the neighbourhood. English spoken.

GAMBRINUS,
13-15 Rue des Blancs-
　Manteaux, Paris 4.
(887.81.92).
Métro: Rambuteau.
Open 11 A.M. to 1:30 P.M.
　and 3 P.M. to 8 P.M.,
　open until 9 P.M.
　Wednesday. Opens at 9
　A.M. Saturday. Closed
　Sunday.
Credit card: V.

More than 300 brands of beer from thirty-four different countries, for collectors, connoisseurs, or those just interested in a frothy bottle of beer.

THE QUINTESSENTIAL WINE GLASS

Getting the most out of a good wine involves more than just uncorking the bottle and pouring it into a glass. If the wine is good enough to merit attention, it merits a special wine glass for tasting. The Institut National des Appellations d'Origine (I.N.A.O.) in Paris responded to this need by designing what it considers the perfect tasting glass, as complementary to the wine as it is agreeable to the taster.

The glass has a wide base, a short stem, and an elongated egg-shaped cup that embraces the wine, carefully guarding its bouquet. Made of lead crystal, it is simple and undecorated, holding 1 cup (25 cl).

What are the qualities of a good wine glass? It should allow the wine to breathe without losing its strength; to develop without becoming faint; and it must permit the wine to show its deep, rich colors with no cuttings or etchings to interfere. The stem should be long enough to allow the wine to be swirled without being warmed by one's hand, and the bowl itself should be longer than it is wide, so the bouquet is gently contained.

The I.N.A.O. glass is available in Paris at L'Esprit et Le Vin, 65 Boulevard Malesherbes, Paris 8 (522.60.40) and at Simon, 36 Rue Etienne-Marcel, Paris 2 (233.71.65).

LUCIEN LEGRAND,
1 Rue de la Banque,
  Paris 2.
(260.07.12).
Métro: Bourse.
Open 8:30 A.M. to 7:30
  P.M. Tuesday through
  Friday, 8:30 A.M. to 1
  P.M. and 3 P.M. to 7
  P.M. Saturday. Closed
  Sunday, Monday, last
  two weeks in August.

**LUCIEN LEGRAND
FILLES ET FILS,**
12 Galerie Vivienne,
  Paris 2.
(260.07.12).
Métro: Bourse.
Open 9 A.M. to 12:30 P.M.
  and 2 P.M. to 7 P.M.
  Tuesday through Friday,
  9 A.M. to 1 P.M. and 3
  P.M. to 7 P.M. Saturday.
  Closed Sunday, Monday,
  and the last two weeks
  in August.

There are at least two reasons to go out of your way to visit this lovely, well-stocked wine shop. One reason, of course, is the carefully chosen selection of French wines (many from small, independent growers) and alcohols. The other is to examine the perfectly retained decor of this 19th-century *épicerie fine,* packed to the ceiling with candies, coffees, teas, and chocolates. Monsieur Legrand's selection of Laberdolive brand Armagnac is remarkable. English spoken. (See also Spécialités Gastronomiques.)

While family members tend to the front of the shop, the outgoing, chatty Lucien Legrand manages the back, offering a select assortment of French wines by the case: The choice is small, but prices are fair. Many wines can be tasted on the spot. English spoken.

LATIN QUARTER, SEVRES-BABYLONE, ECOLE MILITAIRE
5th, 6th, and 7th arrondissements

**JEAN-BAPTISTE
BESSE,**
48 Rue de la Montagne
  Sainte-Geneviève,
  Paris 5.
(325.35.80).
Métro: Maubert-Mutualité.
Open 10 A.M. to 1 P.M.
  and 4:30 P.M. to 8:30
  P.M. Tuesday through
  Saturday, 11 A.M. to
  1:30 P.M. Sunday.
  Closed Monday and the
  month of August.

Jean-Baptiste Besse, who has been at this tumbledown corner grocery since 1932, is a charming, modest little man with a permanent smile and most humble carriage. If he has time, he'll talk your head off about Cognac and Armagnac, perhaps even about Bordeaux. Come here when you've plenty of time to chat or wait in line, or look on as he stumbles about the store in search of your request. (Treasures here are not always obvious.) Monsieur Besse can be trusted. You won't be sorry when you buy the Château de Bréat Bas Armagnac. (He advises the 1943 or 1947, saying "anything older is more symbolic than good.")

KING HENRY,
44 Rue des Boulangers,
  Paris 5.
(354.54.37).
Métro: Jussieu.
Open 10 A.M. to 8 P.M.
  Closed Sunday.

The king of beer in Paris offers more than 500 different brands of beer, 200 kinds of whisky, and an assortment of other alcohols and liqueurs.

**LA MAISON DU
WHISKY,**
48 Avenue de Saxe, Paris 7.
(783.66.21).
Métro: Ségur.
Open 9 A.M. to 12:30 P.M.
  and 1:30 P.M. to 7:30
  P.M. Monday through
  Friday. 9 A.M. to 12:30
  P.M. Saturday. Closed
  Sunday and the month
  of August.
Credit card: V.

It's hard to imagine a larger selection, even in Scotland or Ireland. The little shop offers dozens of brands and vintages of unblended single malt Scotch whisky (including the superb Macallan, and earthy Lagavulin), some prestige vintages (single malts from the 1930s and 1940s) as well as blended Scotch, Irish whiskey, bourbon, and Canadian whisky, and rye.

PETIT BACCHUS,
13 Rue du Cherche-Midi,
  Paris 6.
(544.01.07).
Métro: Sèvres-Babylone.
Open 9:30 A.M. to 7:30
  P.M. Closed Sunday,
  Monday, and the month
  of August.

A small and friendly combination wine bar and wine shop, featuring little-known, less expensive French regional wines. Jean-Marie Picard travels constantly, in search of good wines and good buys. (See also Bistros á Vin.)

CHAMPS-ELYSEES, MADELEINE, GRANDS BOULEVARDS
8th arrondissement

AUGE,
116 Boulevard Haussmann,
  Paris 8.
(522.16.97).
Métro: Miromesnil.
Open 8:30 A.M. to 12:30
  P.M. and 2:30 P.M. to
  7:30 P.M. Monday
  through Friday, 8:30
  A.M. to 12:30 P.M. and
  3 P.M. to 7:30 P.M.
  Saturday. Closed Sunday
  and the month of
  August.
Credit cards: AE, EC, V.

An elegant, classic *épicerie fine,* offering not just fruits and wines, but a fine assortment of vintage and non-vintage Port, Cognac, Armagnac, and Champagne.

**LA CAVE DE
GEORGES DUBOEUF,**
9 Rue Marbeuf, Paris 8.
(720.71.23).
Métro: Alma-Marceau.
Open 9 A.M. to 1 P.M. and
3:30 P.M. to 7:30 P.M.
Closed Sunday, Monday,
and the month of
August.

Georges Duboeuf is perhaps the most respected name in Beaujolais, and his small shop off the Champs-Elysées offers Beaujolais as well as a fine selection of Burgundies.

PARISIAN VINEYARDS

Vineyards in Paris? Their history dates back to the Middle Ages, when abbey vineyards dotted the city and the wine they produced found their way to the noblest tables. (It was, in fact, the white claret from the suburb of Suresnes that François I said was "as light as a tear in the eye.")

Today the heritage continues as each year a few hundred bottles of authentic Parisian wine are carefully, ceremoniously bottled.

Tucked away in the hills of Montmartre, hidden among the narrow houses and overparked sidewalks, rests a minuscule vineyard that annually produces just 500 bottles of a red wine simply labeled "Clos Montmartre." The harvest *fête,* a traditional celebration full of pageantry, takes place the first Saturday of October. For the harvest itself, the basement of the 18th *arrondissement mairie* (town hall), is turned into a wine cellar, and later, some 200 bottles are sold there for about 150 francs each. The remainder is sold at auction. The wine does not lay claims to greatness: It is more of an historical amusement than a gustatory treasure.

A second vineyard lies in the suburban community of Suresnes, west of Paris. Once considered the best in the Ile-de-France, the Suresnes vineyard was replanted in 1965. Now the local rugby team turns out to harvest the grapes and the community celebrates the event on the first Sunday of October. The 2,000 or so bottles of Clos du Pas-Saint-Maurice are sold on the last Saturday of September and the first Sunday of October for about 30 francs each at the Suresnes city hall.

In 1983, in an apparent effort to revive its illustrious wine heritage, the city planted another 800 vines of Loire Valley wine grapes on the south side of Georges-Brassens Square, in the 15th *arrondissement* park built on the site of the former stockyards of Paris.

For more information about the harvests and wine sales, contact:

Montmartre, *Mairie* of the 18th *arrondissement,* 1 Rue Jules-Joffrin, Paris 18. (252.42.00). Métro: Jules-Joffrin.

Suresnes, *Mairie* of Suresnes, 28 Rue Melrin-de-Thionville, 92150 Suresnes. (506.32.10). Accessible via the No. 244 bus from Porte Maillot, the No. 144 bus from Pont de Neuilly, or the suburban train from Gare Saint-Lazare. The stop is Suresnes Mont Valérien.

FAUCHON,
26 Place de la Madeleine,
Paris 8.
(742.60.11).
Métro: Madeleine.
Open 9:40 A.M. to 6:30
P.M. Closed Sunday and
Monday.
Credit cards: AE, DC, V.

A well-stocked *cave,* particularly if you're shopping for a fine Armagnac or Cognac. Prices are on the high side. (See also Spécialités Gastronomiques.)

LA CAVE D'HEDIARD,
21 Place de la Madeleine,
Paris 8.
(266.44.38).
Métro: Madeleine.
Open 9:15 A.M. to 7 P.M.
Closed Sunday.
Credit cards: AE, DC, V.

A newly enlarged *cave* with an expanded assortment, offering perhaps the largest selection of Bordeaux wines in Paris. Also a large selection of Armagnac, Calvados, and Cognac. Prices are on the high side. (See also Spécialités Gastronomiques.)

LA MAISON DU WHISKY,
20 Rue d'Anjou, Paris 8.
(265.03.16).
Métro: Madeleine.
Open 9 A.M. to 7 P.M.
Monday through Friday,
9 A.M. to 12:30 P.M.
Saturday. Closed Sunday
and the month of
August.
Credit card: V.
See La Maison du Whisky,
7th *arrondissement,* page
224.

CURNONSKY

C urnonsky, the 20th-century French food critic named "prince of gastronomes" by his peers, classed the five best white wines in France, perhaps the world:

Château d'Yquem: "The matchless sweet wine; true liquid gold."

Château-Chalon: "The prince of the Jura yellow wines, full-bodied, with the penetrating bouquet of walnuts."

Château-Grillet: "The legendary wine of the Côtes-du-Rhône, with a stunning aroma of violets and wild flowers; as changing as a pretty woman."

Montrachet: "The splendid lord of Burgundy, which Alexander Dumas counselled to drink, bare-headed, while kneeling."

Savennières Coulées de Serrant: "The dazzling dry wine from the vineyards of the Loire."

**STEVEN SPURRIER/
CAVES DE LA
MADELEINE,**
25 Rue Royale (Cité
Berryer; enter between
23 and 25 Rue Royale),
Paris 8.
(265.92.40).
Métro: Madeleine.
Open 9 A.M. to 7 P.M.
Monday through Friday,
10 A.M. to 2 P.M.
Saturday. (Open
Saturdays in December,
from 10 A.M. to 6 P.M.)
Closed Sunday.

T he Englishman Steven Spurrier has made his mark on Paris, offering one of the largest selections of both little-known and well-known Burgundies and Bordeaux, along with a fine assortment of wines from France's southwest, Provence, Languedoc, the Loire and Rhône valleys, the Jura and Corsica—even Spain and Italy. There's also a fine selection of Cognac, Armagnac, and Calvados. Try the *eau-de-vie de framboise sauvage* (wild raspberry) from J. P. Mette in Ribeauville.

**AU VERGER DE
LA MADELEINE,**
4 Boulevard Malesherbes,
  Paris 8.
(265.51.99).
Métro: Madeleine.
Open 9:45 A.M. to 1:15
  P.M. and 3 P.M. to 8
  P.M. Closed Sunday.

Need an 1820 Cognac, an 1893 Sauternes, or a 1922 Lafite-Rothschild? Maurice and Jean-Pierre Legras will be happy to oblige. Since 1937, the Legras family has operated one of Paris's grand *épiceries fines,* and today they specialize in old bottles, odd bottles, new bottles, little bottles. Just give them a special date—birthday, anniversary, wedding—from within the last 150 years and they should come up with an appropriate bottle to help you celebrate. Effervescent Jean-Pierre is crazy about wine, and loves digging up dust-covered relics from the spacious underground *caves.* He's proud of their collection of Sauternes old and new (especially the 1934 Château d'Yquem), of the fine and rare white Nuits-Saint-Georges from Henri Gouges, the straw-colored *vin de paille* of the Jura, and the Rhône's famous white Château-Grillet, not to mention his exclusive right to sell wine from Liechtenstein, or his small stock of the famous Paris red from the vineyards at Montmartre. The family also offers a vast collection of Armagnacs, Cognacs, and Port.

NATION
11th and 12th arrondissements

**L'ARBRE A VIN,
CAVES RETROU,**
4 Rue du Rendez-Vous,
  Paris 12.
(346.81.10).
Métro: Nation.
Open 8:30 A.M. to 12:30
  P.M. and 4 P.M. to 7:40
  P.M. Tuesday through
  Saturday, 8:30 A.M. to
  12:30 P.M. Sunday.
  Closed Monday.
Credit card: V.

A funky sort of wine depot-supermarket, offering a wide variety of seldom-found, inexpensive, often regional wines. Included are some fine Côtes-du-Rhône and Madiran, and lesser known, amusing wines such as the Basque Irouléguy. Be sure to take a stroll around the Place de la Nation, with dozens of chic and lovely shops.

L'OENOPHILE,
30 Boulevard Voltaire,
  Paris 11.
(700.69.45).
Métro: Nation.
Open 9 A.M. to 1 P.M. and
  3 P.M. to 8 P.M.
  Tuesday through
  Saturday, 9 A.M. to 1
  P.M. Sunday. Closed
  Monday and the month
  of August.

L'Oenophile is Michel Renaud's second shop, run by his wife, Dominique, offering the same products as the main listing on page 228.

CAVE MICHEL RENAUD,
12 Place de la Nation, Paris 12.
(307.98.93).
Métro: Nation.
Open 9 A.M. to 1 P.M. and 3 P.M. to 8 P.M. Tuesday through Saturday, 9 A.M. to 1 P.M. Sunday, 3 P.M. to 8 P.M. Monday.

This picturesque, elegant wine shop is neat as a pin, and so is its genteel owner, Michel Renaud. His carefully and personally stocked shop reflects a passion for wine: He even has an interest in a Portuguese cork-producing firm. Monsieur Renaud spends a good deal of time searching out the good little wines of France, but offers as well some better-known Bordeaux, the fine Hermitage of Gérarud Chave, and a wonderful, well-priced Bas Armagnac.

ARC DE TRIOMPHE
17th arrondissement

LA MAISON DU WHISKY,
24 Rue de Tilsitt, Paris 17.
(380.27.63).
Métro: Charles-de-Gaulle-Etoile.
Open 9 A.M. to 7 P.M. Monday through Friday, 9 A.M. to 12:30 P.M. Saturday. Closed Sunday and month of August.
Credit card: V.
See La Maison du Whisky, 7th *arrondissement,* page 224.

PETRISSANS,
30 bis Avenue Niel, Paris 17.
(227.83.84).
Métro: Ternes.
Open 9:30 A.M. to 1:30 P.M. and 3 P.M. to 8 P.M. Tuesday to Friday, 9:30 A.M. to 1:30 P.M. Monday and Saturday. Closed Sunday.

A small, old-fashioned family operation, offering fine selections of Burgundy and Bordeaux. A small wine bar adjoins the shop, if you should decide to sample on the spot. (See also Bistros à Vin.)

La Maison du Chocolat for fine champagne as well as chocolate (see Chocolateries, page 201).

Librairies Spécialisées: Gastronomie
FOOD AND WINE BOOK SHOPS

Almost every bookstore and department store in Paris has a section devoted to *cuisine*. The following are just a few suggestions for finding old and new cookbooks, guidebooks, and historical, food-related volumes.

LES HALLES, BOURSE, OPERA
1st, 2nd, and 4th arrondissements

AU BAIN MARIE,
2 Rue du Mail, Paris 2.
(260.94.55).
Métro: Bourse.
Open 9:30 A.M. to 7 P.M.
　Closed Sunday.
Credit cards: AE, V.

A lovely little shop, devoted to food books and cookbooks, old and new, in French and in English, along with an assortment of old cooking magazines. Also take time to visit Aude Clément's other Au Bain Marie (nearby at 20 Rue Hérold—see Kitchen and Tableware chapter, 1st and 2nd *arrondissements*) devoted to old and new items for the kitchen and the table.

BAZAR DE L'HOTEL DE VILLE (B.H.V.),
55 Rue de la Verrerie,
　Paris 4.
(274.90.00).
Métro: Hôtel-de-Ville.
Open 9 A.M. to 6:30 P.M.,
　Wednesday until 10
　P.M., Saturday until 7
　P.M. Closed Sunday.
Credit card: V.

This giant and often confusing department store offers an extensive cookbook selection, particularly good if you're looking for books the French housewife might use. Sales tables can offer some terrific bargains. (See also Pour la Maison.)

BRENTANO'S,
37 Avenue de l'Opéra,
　Paris 2.
(261.52.50).
Métro: Opéra.
Open 10 A.M. to 7 P.M.
　Closed Sunday.

This English-language book shop offers a rather extensive selection of cookbooks, most of them British. A good place to go for food- and wine-related guidebooks.

COOKING AND WINE SCHOOLS

The following are the most popular cooking and wine schools in Paris. If you plan to visit any of the schools, write or call for a brochure first, so you know what to expect. In many cases, custom-tailored courses can be arranged for groups of ten or more.

L'Académie du Vin, 25 Rue Royale (Cité Berryer; enter between 23 and 25 Rue Royale), Paris 8. (265.09.82). Métro: Madeleine.

A popular wine school, with classes in English or French, run by an Englishman, Steven Spurrier, and an American, Patricia Gallagher. L'Académie du Vin offers beginning, intermediate, and advanced wine classes, including theory, history, and tastings of at least six wines during each class. Each Friday, the school offers a combination wine tasting and cold buffet.

Le Cordon Bleu, 24 Rue du Champ-de-Mars, Paris 7. (555.02.77). Métro: Ecole Militaire.

This famous, classic French school has been instructing students in French cooking and pastry since 1895. Visitors may reserve a few days ahead for a single afternoon demonstration; and menus are available in advance for each month's program. Courses are ongoing, in French, and the number of students varies according to the program.

Découverte du Vin/Alain Segelle, 45 Rue Liancourt, Paris 14. (327.67.21). Métro: Gaité.

Alain Segelle is an outgoing young Frenchman with a passion for wine. His classes are serious affairs, in which he discusses in depth a variety of wine subjects. Eighteen different courses are offered, ranging from a beginner's on the principles of wine tasting, to more specific classes on wines from the most important wine regions in France. Courses are in French, and the makeup of students is international. Students sample and discuss three or four wines during each session.

Ecole de Cuisine la Varenne, 34 Rue Saint-Dominique, Paris 7. (705.10.16). Métro: Invalides.

This popular, American-oriented cooking school was founded by Anne Willan, the English cookbook writer, journalist, and food historian. Situated in small but well-equipped quarters near the Invalides, the school offers both participation and demonstration courses in French cuisine. Students can stop in for a single afternoon demonstration, or stay on for as long as a year, working toward a *grand diplôme*. Week-long courses are also offered in regional cooking, summer cooking, *nouvelle cuisine,* and classic French cuisine. Classes, taught by a staff of French chefs and local visiting chefs, are offered year round, although the school is generally closed during part of August and on French holidays. For daily demonstrations, limited to about fifty stu-

Ecole de Cuisine La Varenne.

dents, reserve a few days in advance. For longer courses, register several months in advance. Classes are in French, and though English translations are provided, an understanding of French is most helpful.

Ecole Lenôtre, Hameau des Gâtines, 78370 Plaisir. (055.81.12). Accessible by car or train from the Montparnasse station.

This is where the best pastry chefs of France go for "refresher" courses. Gaston Lenôtre is one of the most respected and successful pastry chefs in France, and his school in the suburbs of Paris is open to professionals only. Ongoing, full-participation courses are offered in pastry, chocolate, bread-baking, ice cream, *charcuterie*, and catering. A knowledge of French is essential.

Marie-Blanche de Broglie Cooking School, 18 Avenue de la Motte-Picquet, Paris 7. (551.36.34). Métro: Ecole Militaire.

Marie-Blanche de Broglie is an outgoing, enthusiastic woman offering a number of courses in her well-appointed Paris apartment as well as in her Normandy château. In Paris, she offers demonstration courses in the harmony of wine and foods, pastry, and French regional cooking. In her Normandy château, she offers weekend and week-long demonstration and participation classes for groups of five to fifteen. These include regional tours, wine tastings, and a visit to a Calvados distillery. Courses may be arranged in English, French, or Spanish, with translations where necessary.

Paris en Cuisine, 78 Rue de La Croix-Nivert, Paris 15. (250.04.23). Métro: Cambronne.

Robert Noah, a friendly, well-informed American in Paris, offers a variety of food-related tours of Paris. He arranges private or group visits to the Rungis wholesale market; tours of top restaurant kitchens; wine or cheese tastings; visits to Paris *charcuteries*, pastry, or bread shops; and even longer excursions into the countryside of France. The tours are useful for those who do not speak French, for groups are kept to a maximum of ten, and Mr. Noah is a clear and careful translator.

DELAMAIN,
155 Rue Saint-Honoré,
  Paris 1.
(261.48.78).
Métro: Palais-Royal.
Open 10 A.M. to 7 P.M.
  Monday through Friday,
  10 A.M. to 6:45 P.M.
  Saturday. Closed Sunday.

A serious but friendly old bookshop, with a good selection of French cookbooks devoted to regional cuisine.

FNAC,
Forum Les Halles Shopping
  Mall, 1 Rue Pierre
  Lescot, Paris 1.
(261.81.18).
Métro: Les Halles.
Open 1 P.M. to 7 P.M.
  Monday, 10 A.M. to 7
  P.M. Tuesday through
  Saturday. Closed Sunday.

This mammoth stereo/record/camera/bookshop includes a large book section, with one of the city's best and most up-to-date selections of French books on food and wine. Usually, the lowest price in town.

M.O.R.A.,
13 Rue Montmartre,
  Paris 1.
(508.19.24).
Métro: Les Halles.
Open 8:30 A.M. to noon
  and 1:30 P.M. to 5:30
  P.M. Monday through
  Friday, 8:30 A.M. to
  noon Saturday. Closed
  Sunday.

A cookware shop, featuring a small but complete assortment of professional books devoted to breads, pastry, general cooking, and hotel and restaurant cooking. (See also Pour la Maison.)

W. H. SMITH,
248 Rue de Rivoli, Paris 1.
(260.37.97).
Métro: Concorde.
Open 9 A.M. to 6:30 P.M.
  Monday through
  Thursday, 9 A.M. to
  6:30 P.M. Friday and
  Saturday. Closed Sunday.

W.H. Smith offers the city's most extensive selection of English language books on food and wine, most of them British. Also a good selection of food- and wine-related guidebooks.

Browsing at M. G. Bardon.

SAINT-MICHEL, LUXEMBOURG
5th arrondissement

M. G. BARDON,
Bookseller at Box 11, Quai
   de Montebello, Paris 5.
(260.27.50).
Métro: Saint-Michel.
Flexible hours, generally
   open 11 A.M. to 7:30
   P.M. Closed Sunday and
   Monday.

The friendly, outgoing Madame Bardon is herself a passionate collector of old French cookbooks, and many of them find their way into her little wooden stall along the *quai*. A fine place for book browsing in the shadow of Notre-Dame.

GIBERT JEUNE,
5 Place Saint-Michel,
   Paris 5.
(325.70.07).
Métro: Saint-Michel.
Open 10 A.M. to 7:30 P.M.
   Closed Sunday.

This is one of Paris's largest bookshops, offering an extensive assortment of food-related books (most in French, a few in English), scattered about the second and third floors.

**LE VERRE ET
L'ASSIETTE,**
1 Rue du Val-de-Grâce,
   Paris 5.
(633.45.96).
Métro: Port-Royal.
Open 10 A.M. to 12:30
   P.M. and 2:30 P.M. to 7
   P.M. Closed Sunday.
Credit cards: AE, DC, V.

If you've time to visit only one cookbook shop, this is it. You'll find a vast and esoteric collection of French (and some English) books devoted to food and wine, along with an assortment of wine-related paraphernalia: corkscrews, wine glasses, vineyard maps, and thermometers. To keep up-to-date on wine and food happenings in Paris, subscribe to their chatty monthly newsletter. Current rates are 65 francs per year for residents of France, 85 francs for subscribers outside France.

BOULEVARD SAINT-GERMAIN, MONTPARNASSE
6th and 7th arrondissements

LIBRAIRIE ELBE,
23 bis Boulevard Saint-
   Germain, Paris 7.
(548.77.97).
Métro: Rue du Bac.
Open 10 A.M. to noon and
   2 P.M. to 7 P.M. Closed
   Saturday, Sunday, and
   the month of August.

Librairie Elbe offers maps, charts, posters, and old books, including a small, eclectic collection that is food-related. Some fine offbeat finds from time to time.

FNAC,
136 Rue de Rennes,
    Paris 6.
(544.39.12).
Métro: Montparnasse-
    Bienvenüe.
Open 10 A.M. to 7:30 P.M.
    Closed Sunday and
    Monday.
See FNAC, 1st
    arrondissement, page 232.

EDGAR SOETE,
5 Quai Voltaire, Paris 7.
(260.72.41).
Métro: Rue du Bac.
Open 10 A.M. to noon and
    2 P.M. to 6:30 P.M.
    Closed Saturday, Sunday,
    and the month of
    August.

A sober and serious shop which devotes itself to cookbooks, some new, some old, some rare. Until they decide you're a serious shopper, the welcome can be stiff and cool.

ARC DE TRIOMPHE, PLACE VICTOR-HUGO
16th and 17th arrondissements

FNAC,
26 Avenue de Wagram,
    Paris 17.
(766.52.50).
Métro: Charles-de-Gaulle-
    Etoile.
Open 10 A.M. to 7 P.M.
    Closed Sunday and
    Monday. See FNAC, 1st
    arrondissement, page 232.

**LIBRAIRIE FONTAINE
VICTOR HUGO,**
95 Avenue Victor-Hugo,
    Paris 16.
(553.76.72).
Métro: Victor-Hugo.
Open 10 A.M. to 7:30 P.M.
    Closed Sunday.
Credit card: V.

An extensive *cuisine* section, largely new releases.

Pour la Maison
KITCHEN AND TABLEWARE SHOPS

Papeterie Moderne for any sign you desire (see entry, page 237).

If you have been searching for long-wearing cotton chefs' uniforms, odd-size baking tins, antique Champagne glasses, or functional white laboratory pitchers for storing wooden utensils, you need look no more. These, plus lovely pastel-toned, turn-of-the-century oyster or asparagus plates; sparkling, contemporary glassware; and sturdy copper pots are just a few of the hundreds of particularly French kitchen and table items found in the following shops. Note that some are small and sometimes casually run, so that opening and closing hours may not always be followed to the letter.

LES HALLES, PALAIS-ROYAL, PLACE DES VICTOIRES
1st and 2nd arrondissements

AU BAIN MARIE,
20 Rue Hérold, Paris 1.
(260.94.55).
Métro: Bourse.
Open 9:30 A.M. to 7 P.M.
   Closed Sunday.
Credit cards: AE, V.

Thanks to the good taste and energy of Aude Clément, Au Bain Marie is the city's most beautiful, most eclectic shop for the kitchen and table. A mouthwatering selection of antique and modern silver, porcelain and china, including a large and lovely collection of antique *barbotines,* asparagus, artichoke, and oyster plates. There's a fine assortment of silver, porcelain, and china from the famous ship the Normandie, exquisite crystal carafes, expensive but incredibly outfitted wicker picnic baskets, plus amusing knife rests, asparagus tongs, occasional posters, and odd and enviable food-related collector's items. Upstairs there is a fine selection of elegant, handmade table and bed linens in silk, cotton, and pure linen.

LA BOVIDA,
36 Rue Montmartre,
  Paris 1.
(236.09.99).
Métro: Les Halles.
Open 6:30 A.M. to 6 P.M.
  Monday through Friday,
  7 A.M. to 11:45 A.M.
  Saturday. Closed
  Saturday afternoon and
  Sunday.

A kitchen equipment shop for professionals, La Bovida has an impressive inventory of stainless steel, copper, porcelain, and earthenware, as well as serving platters, a variety of spices in bulk, and paper doilies in more than a dozen shapes and sizes. Service can be cool indeed.

CENTRAL UNION,
28 Rue de la Grande
  Truanderie, Paris 1.
(261.55.30).
Métro: Les Halles.
Open 11 A.M. to 1 P.M.
  and 2 P.M. to 7:30 P.M.
  Tuesday through
  Saturday, 2 P.M. to 7:30
  P.M. Monday. Closed
  Sunday.

This shop specializes in "punk" art objects and whimsical items such as their 1950s teapots, some winged, some shaped like houses, and others sporting the Rolls-Royce insignia and hood ornament, certain to have you pouring tea with a smile. They have geometric-design coffee cups and reproductions of old canisters.

CHRISTOFLE,
31 Boulevard des Italiens,
  Paris 2.
(265.62.43).
Métro: Richelieu-Drouot.
Open 9:30 A.M. to 7 P.M.
  Closed Sunday and
  Monday (open Monday
  in December).
Credit cards: AE, DC,
  EC, V.

Gleaming with opulence, this popular boutique is one of Paris's better-known addresses for silver, china, crystal, and giftware.

E. DEHILLERIN,
18-20 Rue Coquillière,
  Paris 1.
(236.53.13).
Métro: Les Halles.
Open 8 A.M. to 12:30 P.M.
  and 2 P.M. to 6 P.M.
  Closed Sunday.

A fascinating, though often overwhelming, clutter of professional cookware covering every inch of available wall, floor, and ceiling space. The selection of copper cookware, baking pans, and unusual kitchen tools is remarkable. Professional-size kitchenware is found in the basement. Some English is spoken by the helpful, if gruff, salespeople, and merchandise catalogs are available. They're experts at retinning copper, though plan on waiting two to three weeks. The store will mail purchases.

DUTHILLEUL ET MINART,
13 and 15 Rue Turbigo,
Paris 1.
(233.44.36).
Métro: Les Halles.
Open 9 A.M. to 12:30 P.M. and 2 P.M. to 6 P.M.
Closed Saturday, Sunday, and the month of August.

Artisan's uniforms since 1850, natural fibre work clothes, café waiters' vests, shirts, and ties, along with jewellers' smocks, meat deliverers' hooded robes, animal purveyors' *blouses* in red, black, and tan, and professional chef outfits, tailored to fit. They also have an extensive selection of professional-quality cotton and linen dish towels.

LE LOUVRE DES ANTIQUAIRES,
2 Place du Palais-Royal,
Paris 1.
(297.27.00).
Métro: Palais-Royal.
Open 11 A.M. to 7 P.M.
Closed Monday.
Some merchants accept credit cards.

More than 250 antique dealers, right across from the Louvre. There are few bargains, but one can easily spend several hours here wandering through the sparkling shops, in search of antique china and silver, folkloric wooden objects for the kitchen and table, as well as crystal, artwork, and furniture. There is a special shipping department for mailing purchases.

M.O.R.A.,
13 Rue Montmartre,
Paris 1.
(508.19.24, 508.11.47).
Métro: Les Halles.
Open 8:30 A.M. to noon and 1:30 P.M. to 5:30 P.M. Monday through Friday, 8:30 A.M. to noon Saturday. Closed Sunday.
Credit card: V.

Another in the group of cookware shops near Les Halles, still frequented by professionals. M.O.R.A. has a large assortment of tools, baking tins (including several sizes of *pain de mie* moulds), large *baguette* pans, and cake moulds. (Be sure to come with dimensions of your oven: Many objects are oversize, made to fit large professional ovens.) They also have a good professional cookbook selection. (See Librairies Spécialisées: Gastronomie.)

PAPETERIE MODERNE,
12 Rue de la Ferronnerie,
Paris 1.
(236.21.72).
Métro: Châtelet/Les Halles.
Open 7:30 A.M. to noon and 1 P.M. to 7 P.M.
Closed Sunday, and two weeks in August.

When you see this simple shop, unchanged for decades, you'll know the source of all the city's myriad signs. They're everywhere—all the signs you have ever dreamed of—stashed into corners, piled on counters, hanging from the wall and the ceiling, on nails and thumbtacks. There are signs for cheese, butter, sausages, beef tongue, or head cheese, along with café menus, bakery price lists, requests for people to stop smoking or spitting, even French "beware of dog" and "post no bills" warnings. Signs can be made to order and take about ten days.

**PORCELAINE
BLANCHE,**
108 Rue Saint-Honoré,
    Paris 1.
(236.90.73).
Métro: Louvre.
Open 10 A.M. to 7:15 P.M.
    Closed Sunday.
Credit card: V.

This is one of a chain of shops specializing in simple, solid-white porcelain, including bistro plates, *café au lait* bowls, terrines, coffee and tea pots, vases, and vinegar jars. Also, some basketry, cutlery, and glassware, all at prices 15 to 30 percent lower than most other shops.

QUATRE SAISONS,
2-6 Rue du Jour, Paris 1.
(508.56.56).
Métro: Les Halles.
Open 10:30 A.M. to 7 P.M.
    Tuesday through
    Saturday, 1 P.M. to 7
    P.M. Monday. Closed
    Sunday.
Credit card: V.

A huge selection of handmade baskets hang from the rafters of this light, airy shop, built nearly on top of the Saint-Eustache church, which incidentally has a sentimental monument inside it, dedicated to the vendors at the old Les Halles market. Quatre Saisons also sells bright, striped cotton and cotton/linen blend fabric for making tea towels; Alsatian cookie stamps; wooden furniture; and some bathroom accessories.

AU TEMPS RETROUVE,
6 Rue Vauvilliers, Paris 1.
(233.66.17).
Métro: Les Halles.
Open 12:30 P.M. to 7 P.M.
    Closed Sunday.

This tiny, old-fashioned shop near the old Les Halles market offers complete services of antique Limoges, Vieux Paris, Creil, Choisy, and Gien porcelain, as well as individual plates, crystal, table linens, and other treasures.

SIMON,
36 Rue Etienne-Marcel,
    Paris 2.
(233.71.65).
Métro: Les Halles.
Open 8:30 A.M. to 6:30
    P.M. Closed Sunday.

This sedate establishment has professional serving dishes, porcelain, crystal and china, salt and pepper grinders, mustard jars, lovely white terrines, a wide variety of paper doilies, wicker cheese trays, and bread baskets. At their annex across the street (go through the courtyard at 33 Rue Montmartre), there's

*Beautiful tableware at Au
Bain Marie (see entry,
page 229).*

professional cookware from copper pots to baking molds, and scales to cookie cutters, along with the attractive, marble-base Roquefort cheese cutters used in the best restaurants. Very helpful salespeople.

MARAIS, ILE SAINT-LOUIS, BASTILLE
4th and 11th arrondissements

L'ARLEQUIN,
13 Rue des Francs-
  Bourgeois, Paris 4.
(278.77.00).
Métro: Saint-Paul.
Open 11:30 A.M. to 7 P.M.
  Closed Sunday, Monday,
  and the month of August.

Ancient and beautiful glassware on dusty shelves that reach from floor to ceiling. Liqueur glasses, champagne *coupes,* wine glasses, water glasses, juice glasses. The perfect place to compose your own mixed or matched set. A few vases as well.

**BAZAR DE L'HOTEL
DE VILLE (B.H.V.),**
55 Rue de la Verrerie,
  Paris 4.
(274.90.00).
Métro: Hôtel-de-Ville.
Open 9 A.M. to 6:30 P.M.,
  Wednesday until 10
  P.M., Saturday until 7
  P.M. Closed Sunday.
Credit card: V.

Almost every contemporary kitchen tool or piece of equipment ever invented is available on the third floor of this enormous, catch-all department store, as well as china and crystal, baskets, table linens, and everyday kitchen products. (See also Librairies Spécialisées: gastronomie.)

COEURS D'ALSACE,
33, Quai de Bourbon,
  Paris 4.
(633.14.03).
Métro: Pont-Marie.
Open 10:30 A.M. to 7 P.M.
  Closed Wednesday from
  12:30 P.M. to 2:30
  P.M., Sunday, Monday,
  and the month of July.

Like a trip to the old world, this colourful shop has *anis* cookie stamps, pottery, heart-shaped earthenware cake molds, painted furniture, and cookbooks, all direct from the Alsace region in eastern France.

**LESCEN
DURA-EUROCAVE,**
63 Rue de la Verrerie,
  Paris 4.
(272.08.74).
Métro: Hôtel-de-Ville.
Open 9 A.M. to 12:30 P.M.
  and 1:35 P.M. to 6:30
  P.M. Closed Sunday and
  two weeks in August.

If it is winter, warm your hands at the old woodstove that may well have been in this shop since it was founded in 1875, then peruse the supply of absolutely everything for the winemaker and wine drinker— bottles and corks, small grape presses, beautiful pre-printed wine labels along with those to inscribe yourself for your own house vintage. There are brass-bound, wooden measuring containers; casks for aging wine (or making vinegar), along with a variety of corkscrews; tasting cups; and other table accessories.

The shop offers a large selection of glassware, from a special French wine tasting glass (ask for the one approved by I.N.A.O.) to small Riesling glasses with deep green stems. You can also find *express* coffee machines, and pocket knives of every price and description. The staff is not terribly eager to serve.

PARIS CARTES POSTALES,
45 Rue de la Roquette, Paris 11.
(806.40.21).
Métro: Bastille.
Open 2 P.M. to 7 P.M.
  Closed Sunday and the month of July.

"Rummage around, look for yourself," insists the proprietor of this musty, jam-packed, sure-to-yield-a-treasure shop. Eccentric but fascinating, there are old postcards, menus, labels, posters, and literary oddities to please every interest.

LA POUSSIERE D'OR,
10 Rue du Pont Louis-Philippe, Paris 4.
(274.57.68).
Métro: Pont-Marie.
Open noon to 6:30 P.M.
  Tuesday through Friday, 2:30 P.M. to 6:30 P.M.
  Saturday. Closed Sunday, Monday, and the month of August.

Lovely, delicate, turn-of-the-century linens, china, crystal, tea and coffee services, little wooden and leather boxes. Everything is of the finest quality, hand-picked and carefully cleaned and restored by the friendly owner.

LAURENCE ROQUE, LE COMPTOIR DES ETOFFES,
69 Rue Saint-Martin, Paris 4.
(272.22.12).
Métro: Hôtel-de-Ville.
Open 11 A.M. to 7 P.M. Tuesday through Saturday, 2 P.M. to 7 P.M. Monday. Closed Sunday and the month of August.

A charming shop for do-it-yourself decorators: beautiful embroidery and needlepoint patterns; lace; jaunty-patterned fabrics for edging kitchen shelves; upholstery patterns and fabrics; and a small but select collection of antique teapots.

LATIN QUARTER, SEVRES-BABYLONE
5th, 6th, and 7th arrondissements

CULINARION,
99 Rue de Rennes, Paris 6.
(548.94.76).
Métro: Saint-Sulpice.
Open 10 A.M. to 7 P.M. Closed Sunday. (In August, also closed Monday.)
Credit card: V.

Offering the usual and the unusual for the kitchen and the table. *Madeleine* tins, *financier* moulds, a small roaster for home-roasted coffee beans, egg-shaped timers, and colourful cast iron cookware at reasonable prices.

DINERS EN VILLE,
27 Rue de Varenne, Paris 7.
(222.78.33).
Métro: Rue du Bac.
Open 11 A.M. to 7 P.M. Tuesday through Saturday, 2 P.M. to 7 P.M. Monday. Closed Sunday and two weeks in August.
Credit cards: V.

An elegant shop that specializes in both useful and frivolous accessories and objects for home and table, stocking a wide variety of 19th- and 20th-century silver sets of dishes, coffee pots, teapots and cups, serving dishes, and some fabrics.

HELENE FOURNIER-GUERIN,
25 Rue des Saints-Pères, Paris 6.
(260.21.81).
Métro: Saint-Germain-des-Prés.
Open 10:30 A.M. to 12:30 P.M. and 2:30 P.M. to 7 P.M. Tuesday through Saturday, 2:30 P.M. to 7 P.M. Monday. Closed Sunday and the month of August.

Eighteenth-century faïence (earthenware china), and porcelain from Strasbourg, Rouen, Sceaux, and Moustiers; lovely serving dishes and 18th-century Delft tiles, all displayed like crown jewels.

**GALERIE
MICHEL SONKIN,**
10 Rue de Beaune, Paris 7.
(261.27.87).
Métro: Rue du Bac.
Open 2:30 P.M. to 7 P.M.
  Closed Sunday and the
  month of August.
Credit cards: AE, V.

As much a cosy museum as antique shop, Galerie Michel Sonkin is filled with lovingly restored folk objects, most of them in golden, gleaming wood. Monsieur and Madame Sonkin have searched throughout Europe to find their treasures, and are particularly proud of their intricately carved, initialled bread stamps, dating from the days when villagers depended on communal ovens for baking. Each loaf was stamped with the family seal or initials, so the baker could tell loaves apart. Also wooden butter moulds, milk filters and carved spoons, porcelain cheese moulds, some solid antique chests and pieces of furniture.

LEFEBVRE FILS,
24 Rue du Bac, Paris 7.
(261.18.40).
Métro: Rue du Bac.
Open 10:30 A.M. to noon
  and 2:30 P.M. to 6 P.M.
  Closed Sunday and the
  month of August.

Georges Lefèbvre offers an exclusive collection of faïence (earthenware china), with a penchant for 18th-century *trompe l'oeil* serving dishes shaped like boar's heads, cabbages, a plate of olives. Hours are variable, so call before a visit, to be certain the shop is open.

MAZOT MEYER,
32 Rue de Verneuil,
  Paris 7.
(261.08.39).
Métro: Rue du Bac.
Open 3 P.M. to 7 P.M.
  Closed Sunday and
  Monday.

An incredible collection of *barbotines*—1900s asparagus and artichoke plates, sauce pitchers, serving platters—most in excellent condition, displayed in every corner of this cluttered shop. The friendly owner, who also has tea sets, vases, some paintings, and other valuable treasures, is passionate about antiques, and shares her knowledge with inquisitive customers.

**NEWMAN &
NEWMAN,**
40 Rue de Verneuil,
  Paris 7.
(296.39.75).
Métro: Rue du Bac.
Open 1 P.M. to 7 P.M.
  Closed Sunday, Monday,
  and two weeks in
  August.

A plush little shop filled with exquisite silver—sets of coffee or tea spoons, table menu holders, some serving dishes—all carefully labelled with dates and history. Some crystal and table linens, all willingly shown by the owner.

PORCELAINE,
22 Rue de Verneuil,
  Paris 7.
(260.94.36).
Métro: Rue du Bac.
Open 11 A.M. to 7 P.M.
  Closed Sunday, Monday,
  and the month of
  August.
Credit cards: AE, DC, V.

High-quality Pillivuyt dishes in dozens of attractive patterns and colors, stainless steel and bronze flatware with colourful handles, tablecloths, napkins, trays and table mats. Also complete cheese-making and candy-making kits.

**PORCELAINE
BLANCHE,**
25 Avenue de la Motte-
Picquet, Paris 7.
(705.94.28).
Métro: Ecole Militaire.
Open 10 A.M. to 7:30 P.M.
Closed Sunday.
Credit card: V.
See Porcelaine Blanche, 1st
arrondissement, page 238.

**PORCELAINE
BLANCHE,**
119 Rue Monge, Paris 5.
(331.93.93).
Métro: Censier-Daubenton.
Open 10:30 A.M. to 7:30
P.M. Closed Sunday.
See Porcelaine Blanche, 1st
arrondissement, page 238.

**PORCELAINE
BLANCHE,**
112 bis Rue de Rennes,
Paris 6.
(549.06.52).
Métro: Saint-Sulpice.
Open 10 A.M. to 7 P.M.
Closed Sunday.
See Porcelaine Blanche, 1st
arrondissement, page 238.

PROSCIENCES,
44 Rue des Ecoles, Paris 5.
(633.33.00).
Métro: Maubert-Mutualité.
Open 8:30 A.M. to 6:30
P.M. Closed Sunday and
the month of August.

FLORENCE ROUSSEAU,
9 Rue de Luynes, Paris 7.
(548.04.71).
Métro: Rue du Bac.
Open 2 P.M. to 6:30 P.M.
Closed Sunday, Monday,
and the month of
August.

This store looks like it is stocked strictly for equip-
ping classrooms or science laboratories, but their
functional white porcelain measuring pitchers are great
for the kitchen, handy for measuring or storing wooden
utensils. Also kitchen scales, mortars and pestles, porcelain spoons, and clear glass jugs with handy spouts.

A limited but very high-quality selection of tabletop
furnishings, including *barbotines*—artichoke,
oyster, and asparagus plates and serving dishes—turn-
of-the-century vases with grandiose patterns, unusual
serving platters, silver sugar tongs and spoons. The
door of this small shop is locked, so be sure to knock
to be let in.

SURFACE,
16 Rue Saint-Simon,
Paris 7.
(222.30.08).
Métro: Rue du Bac.
Open 9 A.M. to 6 P.M.
Monday through Friday,
10 A.M. to 1 P.M. and 2
P.M. to 5 P.M. Saturday.
Closed Sunday.

A vast selection of Italian decorator tiles in a multitude of contemporary designs and colours for mixed, matched, and creative personalized decors. Many are handpainted. The shop will ship individual orders.

THAT SPECIAL DISH

Y ou can take them with you—The dishes, at least. Two of Paris's most famous landmarks, the restaurant Tour D'Argent and the brasserie La Coupole, sell place settings from their well-known tables. The classic blue and white Tour d'Argent dinner plates are sold at the restaurant, 15-17 Quai de la Tournelle, Paris 5 (354.23.31), from noon to 4 P.M. and from 7 P.M. to 11 P.M. every day but Monday. La Coupole, 102 Boulevard Montparnasse, Paris 14 (320.14.20), sells its signature Limoges porcelain plates and demi-tasse cups in the afternoon after 3 P.M..

TIANY CHAMBARD,
32 Rue Jacob, Paris 6.
(329.73.15).
Métro: Saint-Germain-des-Prés.
Open noon to 7 P.M.
Closed Sunday, Monday,
and the month of
August.

A tiny shop with tiny things like old, colourful, beautifully designed fruit and liqueur labels from obsolete canneries and distilleries, perfect for framing and hanging in the kitchen or in the bar.

LA TUILE A LOUP,
35 Rue Daubenton, Paris 5.
(707.28.90).
Métro: Censier-Daubenton.
Open 10:30 A.M. to 1 P.M.
and 3 P.M. to 7:30 P.M.
Tuesday through
Saturday, 11 A.M. to 1
P.M. Sunday. Closed
Monday.

A rustic little shop specializing in French regional arts and crafts, pottery dishes in rich green and blue glazes, beautiful handmade wooden bowls, baskets and candles, and a wide selection of books on the folklore and customs of regional France.

MADELEINE, ARC DE TRIOMPHE
8th arrondissement

LA BOUTIQUE DANOISE,
42 Avenue de Friedland,
Paris 8. (227.02.92).
Métro: Charles-de-Gaulle-Etoile.
Open 9:45 A.M. to 7 P.M.
Closed Sunday.
Credit cards: AE, DC, V.

A ll the sleek modern lines of Danish design are here in wood, glass, and stainless steel furniture and lamps, heavy crystal table accessories and vases, and some porcelain and cutlery. There are wall hangings, rugs, and clothes in rich, subdued colours and natural fibres.

LA CARPE,
14 Rue Tronchet, Paris 8.
(742.73.25).
Métro: Madeleine.
Open 9:30 A.M. to 6:45
P.M. Tuesday through
Saturday, 1:30 P.M. to
6:45 P.M. Monday.
Closed Sunday and the
month of August.

Located just off the Place de la Madeleine, this is where to find items you didn't know you needed: several different kinds of oyster knives; cherry and peach pitters; an espresso machine that works off a car battery; and many more. The staff is very friendly and helpful.

CHRISTOFLE,
12 Rue Royale, Paris 8.
(260.34.07).
Métro: Madeleine.
Open 9:30 A.M. to 7 P.M.
Closed Sunday.
Credit cards: AE, DC,
EC, V.
See Christofle, 2nd
arrondissement, page 236.

KITCHEN BAZAAR,
17 Boulevard de Courcelles,
Paris 8.
(563.79.66).
Métro: Villiers.
Open 10 A.M. to 7 P.M.
Tuesday through
Saturday, 12:30 P.M. to
7 P.M. Monday. Closed
Sunday and the month
of August.

Everything for the kitchen, from timers on strings to Italian-designed balancing scales, tiny chocolate molds and citrus fruit peelers, zesters, curlers, all of good quality. Some baking dishes and a small collection of cookbooks.

PETER,
191 Rue du Faubourg
Saint-Honoré, Paris 8.
(563.88.00).
Métro: Saint-Philippe-du-
Roule.
Open 10 A.M. to 1 P.M.
and 1:30 P.M. to 7 P.M.
Tuesday through
Saturday, 2 P.M. to
7 P.M. Monday. Closed
Sunday and the month
of August.

Elegant, modern, refined: a shop featuring silverware, crystal, china, and giftware along with professional cutlery and cutting boards.

PUIFORCAT,
131 Boulevard Haussmann,
Paris 8.
(563.10.10).
Métro: Miromesnil.
Open 9:30 A.M. to 6:30
P.M. Closed Sunday.
Credit cards: AE, DC.

My favourite Paris shop for superbly designed silver cups—*timbales* (monogrammed, they make perfect baby gifts, ready for use much later in life as brandy or Cognac snifters); elegant silver wine and champagne buckets; fine reproductions of antique china and exquisite Puiforcat silver patterns from the 1920s and 1930s. The salesladies are always accommodating.

RUE DE PARADIS, GARE DE L'EST
10th arrondissement

ARTS CERAMIQUES,
15 Rue de Paradis,
Paris 10.
(824.83.70).
Métro: Château d'Eau
Open 9:45 A.M. to 6:45
  P.M. Tuesday through
  Saturday, 2:30 P.M. to
  6:45 P.M. Monday.
  Closed Sunday.
Credit cards: AE, V.

This shop has a large selection of reproduction Rouen, Quimper, and Marseilles faïence (earthenware china), all hand-painted in true, vivid colours. There is also a selection of pewter tea and coffee pots, plates, and accessories.

EDITIONS PARADIS,
29 Rue de Paradis,
Paris 10.
(523.05.34).
Métro: Château d'Eau.
Open 10 A.M. to 6:30 P.M.
  Closed Sunday.
Credit cards: AE, DC,
  EC, V.

A shop filled with hundreds of pieces of glittering crystal and fragile china. Their most unique item: a silverplate milk pot and tiny gas burner, a replica of one used by the French poet the Countess of Noailles in her travels, perfect for heating milk in a hotel room! Also available here are the silverplate *clochettes* (bell-shaped domes) like those used to present exquisite dishes in grand restaurants throughout the world.

LIMOGES UNIC,
12 Rue de Paradis,
Paris 10.
(770.54.49 and
  523.31.44).
Métro: Chateau d'Eau.
Open 9:45 A.M. to 6:45
  P.M. Closed Sunday.
Credit cards: AE, V.

Limoges porcelain everywhere: tea pots and chocolate services, and simple, classic sets of dishes in every colour. Also Meissen teapots, Baccarat, Saint-Louis, Daum, and Lalique crystal, and Christofle and Têtard silver.

LE SERVICE DE TABLE,
56 Rue de Paradis,
Paris 10.
(770.26.65).
Open 10 A.M. to 1 P.M.
  and 2 P.M. to 6:45 P.M.
Credit cards: AE, DC, V.

An elegant, backlit showroom of contemporary designer vases, dishes, and other tabletop accessories from France, Denmark, and Germany.

LA TISANERIE,
35 Rue de Paradis,
Paris 10.
(770.40.49).
Open 10 A.M. to 7 P.M.
  Closed Sunday and
  Monday.
Credit card: V.

Almost all white porcelain, including simple Pillivuyt bowls, plates, cups, coffee and tea pots, all of which can be personalized with your initials or a design of your choice, applied and baked on in the stone oven right in the shop. Personalization might take a few days, depending on how many pieces you request. Also available here are tart pans, serving plates, and platters, all at reasonable prices.

MONTPARNASSE
14th and 15th arrondissements

**ATELIER
FRANÇOISE CATRY,**
16 Rue Ernest Cresson,
  Paris 14.
(545.91.39).
Métro: Denfert-Rochereau.
Open 9 A.M. to 12:30 P.M.
  and 2 P.M. to 6:30 P.M.
  Closed Sunday and
  Monday.

The objects in this bright-white shop window are so beautiful people can't help but stop and look. The artist and proprietor, Mademoiselle Catry, specializes in painting exact replicas of 17th-century and 18th-century patterns on porcelain and earthenware. Her work is rare and beautiful, from the intricate, vividly coloured border designs to the gold leaf she applies with painstaking care, producing pieces that seem to belong in a historical museum. She also loves to do contemporary designs, in subtle but cheerful colour. Specializing in fruit and flower motifs, she paints on porcelain that is hand-thrown to her own specifications. Working right in her shop, Mademoiselle Catry will personalize dishes with names, dates, or initials, or reproduce a faithful copy of a china pattern.

KITCHEN BAZAAR,
11 Avenue du Maine,
  Paris 15.
(222.91.17).
Métro: Montparnasse.
Open 10 A.M. to 7 P.M.
  Closed Sunday, Monday,
  and the month of
  August.
Credit card: V.
See Kitchen Bazaar, 8th
  arrondissement, page 245.

**PORCELAINE
BLANCHE,**
135 Rue d'Alésia, Paris 14.
(543.78.95).
Métro: Alésia.
Open 10 A.M. to 7 P.M.
  Closed Sunday and the
  month of August.
Credit card: V.
See Porcelaine Blanche, 1st
  arrondissement, page 238.

Copper pots in all shapes, to suit every need.

QUATRE SAISONS,
88 Avenue du Maine,
  Paris 14.
(321.28.99).
Métro: Gaîté.
Open 10:30 A.M. to 1:30
  P.M. and 2:30 P.M. to
  7 P.M. Tuesday through
  Friday, 10:30 A.M. to
  7 P.M. Saturday. Closed
  Sunday and Monday.
See Quatre Saisons, 1st
  arrondissement, page 238.

QUATRE SAISONS,
20 Boulevard de Grenelle,
  Paris 15.
(577.46.39).
Métro: Bir-Hakeim.
Open 10:30 A.M. to 1 P.M.
  and 2 P.M. to 7 P.M.
  Closed Sunday, Monday,
  and the month of
  August.
Credit card: V.
See Quatre Saisons, 1st
  arrondissement, page 238.

BUTTES-CHAUMONT
19th arrondissement

**COMPTOIR DE LA
MOSAIQUE ET DU
CARRELAGE,**
53 Rue du Général-Brunet,
  Paris 19.
(208.90.80).
Métro: Danube.
Open 8 A.M. to noon and 2
  P.M. to 6 P.M. Monday
  through Friday, 8 A.M.
  to noon Saturday. Closed
  Sunday.

It's a long way out to this builder and home decorator's warehouse, filled with tiles for every room in the house. They specialise in unique, folkloric, painted tiles, including a series of French Revolution tiles with crowing cock and guillotine, busy bakers and pastry chefs baking in wood-fired ovens, and *montgolfière* hot-air balloon tiles that are miniature works of art. There are miniature Toulouse-Lautrec posters on tiles; individual scenes with Paris's old-time street criers; tiles that, when put together, make a pretty ocean scene; along with tiles of the seasons, of herbs, flowers, and vegetables. The staff is most helpful, and will sell tiles by the piece or by the metre. Orders can be shipped, but because of fragility and time delays, they advise against it.

French/English Food Glossary

What's on the menu?

Even for the French, the local restaurant menu can be confusing. For instance, the average Frenchman would be hard pressed to tell you exactly what goes into a sauce Albuféra (it's a bechamel with sweet peppers) or how a *canard de Barbarie* differs from a *canard de Nantes* (the latter duck is smaller and more delicate).

The following is a brief glossary of common menu terms—words, phrases, and preparations that you are likely to find on a French menu. In all cases, I have tried to offer brief explanations, limiting entries to those diners are most likely to need when dining in Paris.

A

A.A.A.A.A.: the Association Amicale des Authentiques Amateurs d'Andouillettes gives this label only to the best *andouillettes,* or chitterling sausages.

A point: medium rare.

Abats: organ meats.

Abricot: apricot.

Acidulé: acidic.

Addition: bill.

Affiné(e): aged or refined.

Agneau (de lait): lamb (young, milk fed).

Agrumes: citrus fruits.

Aiglefin, églefin: haddock.

Aigre: sour.

Aigre-doux: sweet and sour.

Aigrelette (sauce): a sour or tart sauce.

Aiguillettes: thin slivers, usually of duck breast.

Ail: garlic.

Aile: wing of poultry or game bird.

Aile et cuisse: used to describe white breast meat (aile) and dark thigh meat (cuisse), usually of chicken.

Aileron: wing tip.

Aïoli: garlicky blend of eggs and olive oil.

Airelles: wild cranberries.

Albuféra: bechamel sauce with sweet peppers.

Algues: edible seaweed.

Aligot: mashed potatoes with fresh Cantal cheese and garlic.

Allumettes: puff pastry strips; also fried matchstick potatoes.

Alose: shad.

Alouette: lark.

Aloyau: loin area of beef.

Alsacienne (à l'): Alsace style; often including sauerkraut, sausage, or *foie gras.*

Amandes: almonds.

Amande de mer: smooth-shelled shellfish, like a small clam, with a sweet, almost hazelnut flavour.

Amer(ère): bitter; as in un-sweetened chocolate.

Amertume: bitterness.

Amourettes: spinal bone marrow of calf or ox.

Amuse-bouche (gueule): literally, "amuse the mouth"; appetizer.

Ananas: pineapple.

Anchoïade: purée of anchovies, olive oil, and vinegar.

Anchois: anchovy.

Ancienne (à l'): in the old style.

Andouille: cold smoked chitterling (tripe) sausage.

Andouillette: smaller chitterling (tripe) sausage, usually served grilled.

Aneth: dill.

Anguille: eel.

Anis: aniseed.

Arachide (huile d'): peanut (oil).

Araignée de mer: spider crab.

Ardennaise (à l'): Ardennes style; often with juniper berries.

Ardoise: literally, slate; usually refers to day's specialities.

Arêtes: fish bones.

Argenteuil: usually asparagus-flavoured soup, named for the Paris suburb that once was the asparagus capital.

Aromates: spices and herbs.

Artichaut (violet): artichoke (small purple).

Asperge: asparagus.

Assiette: plate.

Assiette de pêcheur: assorted fish platter.

Assorti(e): assorted.

Aubergine: eggplant.

Aumônière: literally, beggar's purse; thin *crêpe,* filled, and wrapped like a bundle.

Aurore: tomato and cream sauce.

Automne: autumn.

Auvergnat(e): Auvergne style; often with cabbage, sausage, and bacon.

Avocat: avocado.

B

Baba au rhum: sponge cake with rum-flavoured syrup.

Baguette: classic long, thin loaf of bread.

Baies: berries.

Baies roses: pink peppercorns.

Baigné: bathed.

Ballotine: usually poultry, boned, stuffed, and rolled.

Banane: banana.

Bar: Mediterranean fish, also known as *loup,* similar to striped bass.

Barbarie (canard de): Barbary breed of duck (see *Canard de Barbarie).*

Barbue: brill, a Mediterranean flatfish related to turbot.

Baron: hindquarters and legs of lamb.

Baron de lapereau: baron (hindquarters and legs) of young rabbit.

Barquette: small pastry shaped like a boat.

Basilic: basil.

Basquaise: Basque style; usually with ham or tomatoes or red peppers.

Bavaroise: cold dessert; a rich custard made with cream and gelatin.

Bavette: skirt steak.

Béarnaise: tarragon-flavored sauce of egg yolks, butter, shallots, white wine, vinegar, and other herbs.

Béatilles: dish combining various organ meats.

Bécasse: woodcock.

Béchamel: white sauce made with butter, flour, and milk, usually flavored with onion, bay leaf, pepper, and nutmeg.

Beignet: fritter or doughnut.

Belon: prized, flat-shelled *plate* oyster.

Bercy: fish stock-based sauce thickened with flour and butter and flavoured with white wine and shallots.

Berrichonne: garnish of braised cabbage, glazed baby onions, chestnuts, and lean bacon.

Betterave: beet.

Beurre: butter.

Beurre blanc: reduced sauce of vinegar, white wine, shallots, and butter.

Beurre noir: sauce of browned butter, lemon juice or vinegar, parsley, and sometimes capers.

Beurre noisette: lightly browned butter.

Biche: female deer.

Bien cuit(e): well done.

Bifteck: steak.

Bigarade: orange sauce.

Bigarreau: red, firm-fleshed variety of cherry.

Bigorneaux: periwinkles, tiny sea snails.

Billy Bi, Billy By: cream of mussel soup.

Biscuits à la cuillère: ladyfingers.

Bisque: shellfish soup.

Blanc (de poireau): white portion (of leek).

Blanc (de volaille): usually breast of chicken.

FRICASSEE DE COQUILLAGES LE BERNARDIN
LE BERNARDIN'S SHELLFISH STEW

This is the very first dish I ever sampled at Le Bernardin, and it is one of the restaurant's most popular. A colourful blend of eight different shellfish, the fricassée is really a rich and elegant soup with a sea-scented broth enlivened with herbs, tomatoes, butter, and cream. In France, the fantastic abundance of clams—including the 'clam,' 'praire,' 'amande, 'vénus' and 'coque'—give this dish remarkable depth and texture. In preparing it at home, use whatever combination of the freshest mussels, clams, and scallops available, and you are certain to be pleased with the results. Serve the fricassée with plenty of fresh, crusty bread for soaking up the golden, saucelike broth.

¾ cup (6 ounces; 170 g) unsalted butter

1¼ cup (310 ml) *crème fraîche* or heavy cream, preferably not ultra-pasteurized

4 medium-size tomatoes, peeled, seeded, and chopped

1 clove garlic, finely minced

1 shallot, finely minced

1 bunch parsley, finely minced

1 tablespoon Cognac

Freshly ground black pepper to taste

12 large chowder or razor clams, thoroughly scrubbed in several changes of water

1½ pounds or 1 quart (1 litre) mussels, thoroughly scrubbed in several changes of water, and bearded

1½ pounds or 1 quart (1 litre) small cherrystone or littleneck clams, thoroughly scrubbed in several changes of water

1 pound (450 g) shelled bay or sea scallops (if using sea scallops, cut them in half)

4 freshly opened oysters, in the shell

1. Preheat the oven to 200°F (90°C).

2. In a very large skillet or casserole combine the butter, *crème fraîche* or heavy cream, tomatoes, garlic, shallot, and parsley and stir over high heat until melted. Add the Cognac and pepper. When the mixture comes to a boil, add the large clams, cover, and cook just until they begin to open (about 5 minutes). Add the mussels, cover, and cook until all the shellfish are open (another 3 or 4 minutes).

3. Transfer all the opened shellfish to a warmed bowl, cover, and place the bowl in the oven to keep warm. Leave any unopened shellfish in the sauce to cook further. Add the smallest clams to the sauce, cover, and cook until they begin to open (another 3 or 4 minutes), then add the scallops. Cook covered, for an additional 4 minutes.

4. Keep the broth boiling as you remove all the shellfish with a slotted spoon. Discard any that remain unopened. Divide the shellfish, including the ones keeping warm in the oven, among four large, warmed soup bowls. Set a raw oyster, still in its shell, in each bowl. Spoon equal amounts of broth into each bowl, and serve immediately, with empty side dishes for the discarded shells.

Yield: 4 servings.

Blanquette: veal, lamb, chicken, or seafood stew with egg and cream enriched white sauce.

Blette: Swiss chard.

Bleu: blood rare, usually for steak.

Blinis: small, thick pancakes.

Boeuf à la mode: beef marinated and braised in red wine, served with carrots, mushrooms, onions, and turnips.

Boeuf au gros sel: boiled beef, served with vegetables and coarse salt.

Boissons (non) comprises: drinks (not) included.

Bombe: moulded, layered ice cream dessert.

Bonne femme (cuisine): home-style cooking; also a meat garnish of bacon, potatoes, mushrooms, and onions; a fish garnish of shallots, parsley, mushrooms and potatoes; or a white wine sauce with shallots, mushrooms, and lemon juice.

Bordelaise: Bordeaux style; also refers to a brown sauce of shallots, red wine, and bone marrow.

Bouchée: a tiny mouthful; may refer to a bite-size pastry or to a *vol-au-vent*.

Boudin: technically a meat sausage, but generically any sausage-shaped mixture.

Boudin blanc: white sausage, of veal, chicken, or pork.

Boudin noir: pork blood sausage.

Bouillabaisse: Mediterranean fish and shellfish soup.

Bouillon: a light soup or broth.

Boulette: meatball or fishball.

Bouquet: large reddish shrimp (see also *crevettes roses*).

Bourdaloue: hot poached fruit, sometimes wrapped in pastry.

Bourguignonne: Burgundy style; often with red wine, onions, mushrooms, and bacon.

Bouribot: spicy, red wine duck stew.

Bourride: egg-based Mediterranean fish and shellfish soup served with *aïoli*.

Braise: live coals.

Braiser: to braise; to cook meat by browning in fat, then simmering in covered dish with small amount of liquid.

Brandade (de morue): warm garlicky purée of salt cod, milk or cream or oil, and sometimes mashed potatoes.

Brebis (fromage de): sheep (sheep's milk cheese).

Bretonne: in the style of Brittany; a dish served with white beans; or may refer to a white wine sauce with carrots, leeks and celery.

Brioche: buttery, egg-enriched yeast bread.

Broche (à la): spit-roasted.

Brochet: pike.

Brochette: cubes of meat or fish and vegetables on a skewer.

Brouillé(es): scrambled, usually eggs.

Brûlé: literally, burned; usually refers to dark caramelization.

Brunoise: tiny diced vegetables.

Buffet froid: variety of dishes, served cold, sometimes from a buffet.

Buccin: (see *Bulot*).

Bugnes: sweet fried doughnuts or fritters, originally from Lyons.

Buisson: literally, a bush; generally a dish including vegetables arranged like a bush; classically, a crayfish presentation.

Bulot: large sea snail, also called *buccin*.

C

Cabécou: small, round goat cheese.

Cabillaud: fresh cod.

Cacahuètes: peanuts.

Caen (à la mode de): named after the Normandy town; usually a dish cooked in Calvados and white wine and/or cider.

Café: coffee, as well as a type of eating place where coffee is served.

Café au lait: coffee with milk.

Café crème: coffee with milk.

Café déca: decaffeinated coffee.

Café liégeois: iced coffee served with ice cream (optional) and whipped cream.

Café noir: black coffee.

Cagouille: small *petit-gris* land snail, found in the Saintonge province of western France.

Caille: quail.

Calmar: small squid, similar to *encornet*, with interior cartilage instead of a bone.

Campagne (à la): country-style.

Canapé: triangular pieces of toasted bread, usually served with game; also, an appetizer with a bread base, garnished with a variety of savoury mixtures.

Canard: duck.

Canard à la presse: roast duck served with sauce of juices obtained from pressing the carcass, combined with red wine and Cognac.

Canard de Barbarie: Barbary breed of duck raised in southwest France, with strong-flavoured flesh; generally used for braising.

Canard de Nantes: also called *canard de Challans;* very delicate-flavored small duck.

Canard de Rouen: cross between domestic and wild duck; classically, Rouen ducks are smothered and not bled, giving a special taste to the meat.

Canard sauvage: wild duck.

Caneton: young male duck.

Canette: young female duck.

Cannelle: cinnamon.

Caprice: (literally, a whim) usually a dessert.

Carafe d'eau: pitcher of tap water.

Carbonnade: a Belgian braised beef stew prepared with beer and onions; also refers to a cut of beef.

Cardon: cardoon; large, celerylike vegetable in the artichoke family.

Carré d'agneau: rack (ribs) or loin of lamb.

Carré de porc: rack (ribs) or loin of pork.

Carré de veau: rack (ribs) or loin of veal.

Carrelet: summer flounder or plaice.

Carte: menu.

Carvi: caraway seeds.

Casse-croûte: (literally, breaking bread) slang for snack.

Casse-pierre: edible seaweed.

Cassis: black currant; also black currant liqueur.

Cassolette: usually a dish presented in a small casserole.

Cassoulet: casserole of white beans, including various combinations of sausages, duck, pork, lamb, mutton, and goose.

Caviar d'aubergine: cold eggplant purée.

Céleri: celery.

Céleri-rave: celeriac.

Cèpe: large, meaty wild boletus mushroom.

Cerfeuil: chervil.

Cerise: cherry.

Cerise noire: black cherry.

Cerneau: walnut meat; also refers to unripe walnut.

Cervelas: garlicky cured pork sausage; also refers to fish and seafood sausage.

Cervelles: brains, of calf or lamb.

Chair: the fleshy portion of either poultry or meat.

Champêtre: rustic; describes a simple presentation of a variety of ingredients.

Champignon: mushroom.
de bois: wild mushroom, from the woods.
de Paris: cultivated mushroom.
sauvage: wild mushroom.

Champignons à la grecque: tiny cultivated mushrooms cooked in water, lemon juice, olive oil, and spices, served as a cold appetizer.

Chanterelle: pale, curly-capped wild mushroom.

Chantilly: sweetened whipped cream.

Chapon: capon, or castrated chicken.

Chapon de mer: Mediterranean fish, in the *rascasse*

or scorpion fish family.

Charcuterie: cold cuts, sausages, *terrines, pâtés;* also, shop selling such products.

Chariot (de desserts): rolling cart, usually carrying varied desserts.

Charlotte: moulded dessert with lady-fingers and custard filling, served cold; or fruit compote baked with buttered white bread, served hot.

Charolais: light-coloured cow which produces high-quality beef.

Chartreuse: a dish of braised partridge and cabbage; also herb and spiced-based liqueur made by the Chartreux monks.

Chasse: the hunt.

Chasseur: hunter; also sauce with white wine, mushrooms, shallots, tomatoes, and herbs.

Châtaigne: chestnut, smaller than *marrons,* with multiple nut meats.

Chateaubriand: thick filet steak, traditionally served with sautéed potatoes and a sauce of white wine, dark beef stock, butter, shallots, and herbs, or with a *béarnaise* sauce.

Chaud(e): hot or warm.

Chaud-froid: poultry dish served cold, usually covered with a cooked sauce, then with aspic.

Chaudrée: fish stew, sometimes with potatoes.

Chausson: a filled pastry turnover, sweet or savory.

Chemise (en): wrapped with pastry.

Chèvre (fromage de): goat cheese.

Chevreau: young goat.

Chevreuil: young roe deer.

Chicorée: curly endive.

Chiffonnade: shredded herbs and vegetables, usually green.

Chinchard: saurel; ocean fish with bonelike cartilaginous plates along its backbone, generally used for soups.

Chipiron: Basque name for small squid or *encornet.*

Chocolat: chocolate.

Chocolat amer: bittersweet chocolate, with very little sugar.

Chocolat au lait: milk chocolate.

Chocolat mi-amer: bittersweet chocolate, with more sugar than *chocolat amer.*

Chocolat noir: used interchangeably with *chocolat amer* chocolate.

Choix (au): a choice; usually meaning one may choose freely from several offerings.

Choron (sauce): béarnaise sauce with tomatoes.

Chou: cabbage.

Chou-fleur: cauliflower.

Chou frisé: kale.

Chou rouge: red cabbage.

Chou vert: curly green Savoy cabbage.

Choucroute: sauerkraut; also main dish of sauerkraut, various sausages, bacon, and pork, served with potatoes.

Choux (pâte à): cream puff pastry.

Choux de Bruxelles: brussels sprouts.

Ciboulette: chives.

Cidre: cider, either apple or pear.

Citron: lemon.

Citron vert: lime.

Citronelle: lemon grass, an oriental herb.

Citrouille: pumpkin, gourd.

Civelles: spaghettilike baby eels, also called *piballes.*

Civet: a stew of game thickened with blood.

Civet de lièvre: jugged hare.

Clafoutis: traditional tart from the Limousin, made with a kind of *crêpe* batter and fruit, usually black cherries.

Claires: oysters; also a designation given to certain oysters to indicate they have been put in *claires,* or oyster beds in salt marshes, where they are fattened up for several months before going to market.

Clamart: Paris suburb once famous for its green peas; today a garnish of peas.

Clémentine: small tangerine, from Morocco or Spain.

Clouté: studded with.

Cochon (de lait): pig (suckling).

Cochonnailles: pork products; usually an assortment of sausages and/or pâtés served as a first course.

Cocotte: casserole or cooking pot.

Coeur: heart.

Coeur de filet: thickest (and best) part of beef filet, usually cut into chateaubriand steaks.

Coffret: literally, small box; usually presentation in a small rectangular pastry case.

Coing: quince.

Colin: hake.

Colvert: wild ("green collared") duck.

Compote: stewed fresh or dried fruit.

Concassé: coarsely chopped.

Concombre: cucumber.

Confit: duck, goose, or pork cooked and preserved in its own fat; also fruit or vegetables preserved in sugar, alcohol or vinegar.

Confiture: jam.

Confiture de vieux garçons: varied fresh fruits macerated in alcohol.

Congeler: to freeze.

Congre: conger eel; a large ocean fish resembling an eel, often used in fish stews.

Consommé: clear soup.

Contre-filet: cut of sirloin taken above the loin on either side of the backbone, tied for roasting or braising (can also be cut for grilling).

Convives (la totalité des): (all) those gathered at a single table.

Copeaux: literally, shavings, such as from chocolate or vegetables.

Coq (au vin): mature male chicken (stewed in wine sauce).

Coque: tiny, mild-flavoured, clamlike shellfish.

Coque (à la): soft-cooked egg, or anything served in a shell.

Coquelet: young male chicken.

Coquillages: shellfish.

Coquille: shell.

Coquille Saint-Jacques: sea scallop.

Corail: coral-colored egg sac, found in scallops, spiny lobster, or crayfish.

Corbeille (de fruits): basket (of fruit).

Coriandre: coriander, either the fresh herb or dried seeds.

Cornichon: tiny tart pickle.

Côte d'agneau: lamb chop.

Côte de boeuf: beef blade or rib steak.

Côte de veau: veal chop.

Côtelette: thin chop or cutlet.

Cotriade: fish stew from Brittany, which can include sardines, mackerel, and porgy, cooked with butter, potatoes, onions, and herbs.

Cou d'oie (canard) farci: neck skin of goose (sometimes also duck), stuffed with meat and spices, much like a sausage.

Coulibiac: a hot Russian pâté, usually filled with salmon and covered with *brioche.*

Coulis: purée of raw or cooked vegetables or fruit.

Coupe: cup; refers to dessert served in a goblet.

Courge: squash or gourd.

Courgette: zucchini.

Couronne: ring or circle, usually of bread.

Court-bouillon: broth, or aromatic poaching liquid.

Couscous: granules of semolina, or hard wheat flour; also refers to a complete Moroccan dish that includes the steamed grain, broth, vegetables, meats, hot sauce, and sometimes chick peas and raisins.

Couteau: knife.

Couvert: a place setting, including dishes, silver, glassware, and linen.

Crabe: crab.

Crapaudine: preparation of grilled poultry or game bird with backbone removed.

Crécy: a dish garnished with carrots.

Crème: cream.

Crème anglaise: custard sauce.

Crème brûlée: rich custard dessert with a top of caramelized sugar.

Crème chantilly: sweetened whipped cream.

Crème fouettée: whipped cream.

Crème fraîche: thick, sour, heavy cream.

Crème pâtissière: custard filling for pastries and cakes.

Crème plombières: custard filled with fresh fruits and egg whites.

Crêpe: thin pancake.

Crêpes Suzette: hot *crêpe* dessert flamed with orange liqueur.

Crépine: caul fat.

Crépinette: small sausage patty wrapped in caul fat.

Cresson(ade): watercress (watercress sauce).

Crête (de coq): cock's comb.

Creuse: elongated, crinkle-shelled oyster.

Crevette grise: tiny, soft-fleshed shrimp that turns gray when cooked.

Crevette rose: small, firm-fleshed shrimp that turns red when cooked; when large, called *bouquet.*

Criste marine: edible algae.

Croquant(e): crispy.

Croque-monsieur: toasted ham and cheese sandwich.

Croquette: ground meat, fish, fowl, or vegetables bound with eggs or sauce, shaped into various forms, usually coated in bread crumbs and deep fried.

Crottin (de Chavignol): firm goat cheese (from Chavignol).

Croustade: usually small, pastry-wrapped dish; also regional southwestern pastry filled with prunes and/or apples.

Croûte (en): in pastry.

Croûte de sel (en): in a salt crust.

Croûtons: small cubes of toasted or fried bread.

Cru: raw.

Crudités: raw vegetables.

Crustacés: crustaceans.

Cuillière (à la): to be eaten with a spoon.

Cuisse de poulet: chicken drumstick.

Cuisson: cooking.

Cuissot: haunch, of veal, venison, or wild boar.

Cuit(e): cooked.

Cul: haunch or rear, usually of red meat.

Culotte: rump (usually of beef).

Cure-dent: toothpick.

D

Dariole: usually a garnish in a cylindrical mould.

Darne: slice or steak from fish, often salmon.

Dattes: dates.

Daube: stew, usually meat.

Daurade: dorade or sea bream, similar to porgy.

Décaféiné: decaffeinated.

Decortiqué(e): shelled or peeled.

Dégustation: tasting or sampling.

Déjeuner: lunch.

Délice: delight, usually used to describe a dessert.

Demi: half; also refers to a 1-cup (25-cl) glass of beer.

Demi-deuil: (literally, in half mourning) poached (usually chicken) with truffles inserted under the skin; also, sweetbreads with a truffled white sauce.

Demi-glace: concentrated, beef-based sauce lightened with consommé, or a lighter brown sauce.

Demi-sel: lightly salted.

Désossé: boned.

Diable: method of preparing poultry, served with a peppery sauce, often mustard-based.

Dieppoise: Dieppe style; usually white wine, mussels, shrimp, mushrooms, and cream.

Dijonnaise: Dijon style; usually with mustard

Dinde: turkey hen.

Dindon (neau): turkey, in general (young turkey).

Dîner: dinner; to dine.

Discrétion (à la): on menu usually refers to wine, which may be consumed—without limit—at the customer's discretion.

Dodine: cold, boned stuffed duck.

Dos: back; also refers to meatiest portion of fish.

Dos et ventre: (literally, back and front) both sides (usually fish).

Douceurs: sweets or desserts.

Doux, douce: sweet.

Dugléré: white flour-based sauce with shallots, white wine, tomatoes, and parsley.

Duxelles: chopped mushrooms and shallots sautéed in butter then mixed with cream.

E

Eau du robinet: tap water.

Ecailler: to scale fish; also refers to an oyster opener, or seller.

Echalotes: shallots.

Echine: spare ribs.

Echiquier: checkered.

Ecrevisse: freshwater crayfish.

Effiloché: frayed, thinly sliced.

Eglefin, aiglefin: haddock.

Emincé: thin slice; usually of meat.

Encornet: small squid; in Basque region called *chipiron.*

Endive: chicory.

Entrecôte: beef rib steak.

Entrecôte maître d'hôtel: beef rib steak with herb butter.

Entrecôte marchand de vin: beef rib steak with sauce of red wine and shallots.

Entrée: first course.

Entremets: sweets.

Epaule: shoulder, of veal, lamb, mutton, or pork.

Eperlan: smelt of whitebait, usually fried.

Epices: spices.

Epinard: spinach.

Epi de maïs: ear of sweet corn.

Escabèche: a Provençal preparation of sardines or *rouget,* in which the fish are browned in oil, then marinated in vinegar and herbs and served very cold; also raw fish marinated in lemon or lime juice and herbs.

Escalope: thinly sliced meat or fish.

Escargot: land snail.

Escargot de Bourgogne: land snail prepared with butter, garlic, and parsley.

Escargot petit-gris: small land snail.

Espadon: swordfish.

Estofinado: fish stew from Auvergne, made with dried Atlantic cod, and cooked in walnut oil with eggs, garlic, and cream.

Estouffade: stew of beef, pork, onions, mushrooms, and red wine.

Estragon: tarragon.

Eté: summer.

Etrille: small crab.

Etuvé(e): cooked in ingredient's own juice;braised.

Eventail (en): fan-shaped; usually refers to shape vegetables or fish are cut in.

F

Façon (à ma): (my) way of preparing a dish.

Faisan(e): pheasant.

Farandole: rolling cart, usually of desserts or cheese.

Farci(e): stuffed.

Farine: flour.

Faux-filet: sirloin steak.

Fenouil: fennel.

Féra: salmonlike lake fish.

Ferme (fermier): farmfresh (farmer).

Fermé: closed.

Feu de bois (au): cooked over a wood fire.

Feuille de chêne: oak-leaf lettuce.

Feuille de vigne: vine leaf.

Feuilletage (en): (in) puff pastry.

Fèves: broad beans.

Ficelle (à la): tied with a string; also small, thin baguette of bread.

Figue: fig.

Financière: Madeira sauce with truffle juice.

Fines de claire: elongated, crinkle-shelled oysters that stay in fattening beds (*claires*) up to two months.

Fines herbes: mixture of herbs; usually parsley, chives, tarragon.

Flageolets: small, pale green kidney-shaped beans.

Flamande (à la): Flemish style; usually with stuffed cabbage leaves, carrots, turnips, potatoes, and bacon.

Flambé: flamed.

Flamiche: savoury tart with rich, bread dough crust.

Flan: sweet or savoury tart; sometimes refers to a crustless custard pie.

Flanchet (de veau): flank (of veal).

Flagnarde, flaugnarde: hot, fruit-filled, batter cake made with eggs, flour, milk, and butter, and sprinkled with sugar before serving.

Flétan: halibut.

Fleur: flower.

Fleurons: puff pastry crescents.

Florentine: with spinach.

Foie: liver.

Foie gras d'oie (canard): liver of fattened goose (or duck).

Foies blonds de volaille: chicken livers; also sometimes a chicken liver mousse.

Foin (dans le): cooked in hay.

Fond: cooking juices from meat, used to make sauces; also, bottom.

Fondant: (literally melting) refers to cooked, worked sugar that is flavoured, then used for icing cakes.

Fond d'artichaut: heart and base of an artichoke.

Fondu(e): melted.

Forestière: garnish of wild mushrooms, bacon, and potatoes.

Four (au): baked in oven.

Fourchette: fork.

Fourré: stuffed or filled.

Frais, fraîche: fresh or chilled.

Fraise: strawberry.

Fraise des bois: wild strawberry.

Framboise: raspberry.

Frangipane: almond custard filling.

Frappé: usually refers to a drink served very cold or with ice.

Frémis: quivering; often refers to barely cooked oysters.

Friandises: sweets, *petits fours.*

Fricadelles: fried minced meat patties.

Fricandeau: thinly sliced veal or a rump roast, braised with vegetables and white wine.

Fricassée: classically, ingredients braised in wine sauce or butter with cream added; currently denotes any mixture of ingredients—fish or meat—stewed or sautéed.

Frisé(e): curly; usually curly endive.

Frit(e): fried.

Frites: French fries.

Fritons: coarse pork rillettes, or a minced spread, that includes organ meats.

Fritot: small organ meat fritter, where meat is partially cooked, then marinated in oil, lemon juice, and herbs, dipped in batter and fried just before serving; also can refer to any small, fried piece of meat or fish.

Friture: frying; also refers to preparation of small fried fish, usually whitebait or smelt.

Froid(e): cold.

Fromage: cheese.

Fromage blanc: a smooth, low-fat cheese similar to cottage cheese.

Fromage maigre: low-fat cheese.

Fromage de tête: head cheese, usually pork.

Fruit de la passion: passion fruit.

Fruits confits: preserved fruits; generally refers to candied fruits.

Fruits de mer: seafood.

Fumé: smoked.

Fumet: fish stock.

G

Galantine: boned poultry or meat that is stuffed, rolled, cooked, glazed with gelatin, and served cold.

Galette: round, flat pastry, pancake, or cake; can also refer to pancakelike savoury preparations.

Gambas: large prawns.

Garbure: generally, a hearty soup of cabbage, beans, and salt pork.

Garni(e): garnished.

Garniture: garnish.

Gâteau: cake.

Gaufre: waffle.

Gayettes: small sausage patties made with pork liver and bacon wrapped in caul fat and bacon.

Gelée: aspic.

Genièvre: juniper berry.

Génoise: sponge cake.

Germiny: garnish of sorrel; sorrel and cream soup.

Gésier: gizzard.

Gibelotte: fricassee of rabbit in red or white wine.

Gibier: game.

Gigot: usually leg of lamb.

Gigot de mer: a preparation, usually of large pieces of monkfish (*lotte*), oven-roasted like a leg of lamb.

Gigue (de): haunch (of) certain game meats.

Gingembre: ginger.

Girofle: cloves.

Girolle: delicate, pale orange wild mushroom.

Glace: ice cream.

Glacé: iced, crystallized, or glazed.

Gougère: cheese flavoured *chou* pastry.

Goujonnettes: generally used to describe small slices of fish, such as sole, usually fried.

Goujons: small catfish; also often applied to any small fish; also a preparation in which the central part of a larger fish is coated with bread crumbs, then deep fried.

Haricot de Mouton Chez Rene
MUTTON WITH WHITE BEANS

This is the Thursday plat du jour—daily special—at the popular left bank bistro, Chez René (see entry, page 35). Haricot de mouton is a classic bistro dish, and one that French women prepare often at home, usually with either lamb or mutton shoulder. I prefer it with big, hearty chunks of lamb and lots and lots of white beans. If you have fresh herbs around, all the better. Although, today, haricot de mouton is quite naturally made with haricots, or beans, the dish name is actually a corruption of a 16th-century lamb stew called halicot mouton (halicoter being old French for "to cut"). The dish was first made with fava beans, then later turnips or potatoes. Haricot de mouton keeps well and tastes great the second or third day, so make a big batch.

Lamb or mutton:

3 tablespoons unsalted butter

3 tablespoons olive oil

3½ pounds (approximately 1.5 kg) lamb or mutton shoulder, cut into 2-inch (5-cm) chunks (a butcher can do this for you)

⅓ cup (45 g) unbleached flour

1 cup (250 ml) dry white wine

3 cups (750 ml) water

2 fresh tomatoes, cubed, or 2 tablespoons tomato paste

4 carrots, peeled and cut into 1-inch (2.5-cm) rounds

2 onions, halved

4 whole cloves

1 teaspoon dried thyme

3 bay leaves

3 tablespoons finely chopped fresh parsley

Salt and freshly ground black pepper to taste

Beans:

1 pound (450 g) dried white beans

2 bay leaves

6 whole cloves

2 teaspoons dried thyme

Salt

1. In a deep, 12-inch skillet, heat the butter and oil. When hot, begin browning the lamb. You may want to do this in batches. Do not crowd the pan, and be sure that each piece is thoroughly browned before turning.

2. When all the lamb is browned, sprinkle with the flour and mix well. Leaving the lamb in the skillet, add the white wine, then the 3 cups of water, and deglaze the pan, scraping up any browned bits. Add the tomatoes or tomato paste, vegetables, and herbs, and cook, covered, over medium heat for about 1 hour and 15 minutes. Add salt and pepper to taste.

3. While the lamb is cooking, prepare the beans. Rinse them well, put them in a large saucepan, and cover with cold water. Over high heat, bring to a boil. Once boiling, remove the pan from the heat, leave covered, and let rest for 40 minutes.

4. Drain the beans, discarding the cooking liquid (to help make the beans more digestible). Rinse the beans and cover again with cold water. Add the bay leaves, cloves, and thyme, and bring to a boil over medium heat. Cook, covered, over medium heat for about 40 minutes. The beans should be cooked through but still firm. Add salt to taste.

5. To serve, check the lamb and beans for seasoning, then arrange meat on a platter, surrounded by the white beans.

Yield: 6 servings.

Gourmandises: sweet-meats.
Gousse (d'ail): clove (of garlic).
Graine de moutarde: mustard seed.
Graisse: fat.
Graisserons: crisply fried pieces of duck or goose skin; cracklings.
Grand veneur: usually a brown sauce for game, with red currant jelly.
Granité: water ice.
Gras: fatty.
Gras-double: tripe baked with onions and white wine.
Gratin: crusty-topped dish that has been put under a broiler; also refers to a casserole.
Gratin dauphinois: baked casserole of sliced potatoes, usually with cream, milk, and sometimes cheese.
Gratin savoyard: baked casserole of sliced potatoes, usually with bouillon, cheese, and butter.
Gratiné(e): having a crusty, browned top.
Grattons: crisply fried pieces of pork, goose, or duck skin; cracklings.
Gratuit: free.
Grelot: small white bulb onion.
Grecque (à la): cold vegetables, usually mushrooms, cooked in seasoned mixture of oil, lemon juice, and water.
Grenade: pomegranate.
Grenadin: small veal scallop.
Grenouille (cuisses de): frog's legs.
Gribiche (sauce): mayonnaise with capers, *cornichons,* and herbs.
Grillade: grilled meat.
Grillé(e): grilled.
Griotte: shiny, slightly acidic, reddish black cherry.

Grive: thrush.
Grondin: gurnard or gurnet—spiked-head, bony ocean fish, used in fish stews such as *bouillabaisse.*
Gros sel: coarse salt.
Groseille: red currant.
Gruyère: hard, mild Swiss cheese.

H

Hachis: minced or chopped meat or fish preparation.
Hareng: herring.
Haricot: bean.
Haricot blanc: white bean, usually dried.
Haricot de mouton: stew of mutton and white beans.
Haricot rouge: red kidney bean; also, preparation of red beans in red wine.
Haricot vert: green bean, usually fresh.
Hiver: winter.
Hochepot: thick stew, usually of oxtail.
Hollandaise: sauce of butter, egg yolks, and lemon juice.
Homard: lobster.
Hongroise (à la): Hungarian style; usually with paprika and cream.
Hors d'oeuvre: appetizer; can also refer to a first course.
Huile: oil.
Huile d'arachide: peanut oil.
Huile de pépins de raisins: grapeseed oil.
Huître: oyster.
Hure de porc: head of pig or boar; usually refers to head cheese preparation.
Hure de saumon: a salmon "head cheese," or pâté, prepared with salmon meat, not actually the head.

I

Ile flottante: (literally "floating island") most commonly used interchangeably with *oeufs à la neige,* poached meringue floating in *crème anglaise;* classically, a layered cake covered with whipped cream and served with custard sauce.
Impératrice (à l'): usually rice pudding dessert with candied fruit.
Indienne (à l'): East Indian style, usually with curry powder.
Infusion: herb tea.

J

Jambon: ham; also refers to thigh or shoulder of meat, usually pork.
Jambon cru: usually salt-cured or smoked ham that has been aged but not cooked.
Jambon d'oie (or de canard): breast of fattened goose (or duck), smoked, or salted, or sugar-cured, and resembling ham in flavour.
Jambon de Bayonne: raw, dried, salt-cured ham.
Jambon de Paris: lightly salted, cooked ham, very pale in colour.
Jambon d'York: smoked English-style ham, usually poached.
Jambonneau: pork knuckle.
Jambonnette: boned and stuffed knuckle of ham or poultry.
Jardinière: garnish of fresh cooked vegetables.
Jarret de veau: stew of veal shin.

Jerez: refers to sherry.
Jésus de Morteau: pork sausage from the Franche-Comté.
Jeune: young.
Joue: cheek.
Julienne: slivered vegetables (sometimes meat).
Jus: juice.

K

Kir: an aperitif made with *crème de cassis* and most commonly white wine, but sometimes red wine.
Kir royal: a *kir,* made with champagne.
Kougelhopf, kougelhof, kouglof, kugelhopf: sweet, crown-shaped Alsatian breadlike yeast cake, with almonds and raisins.

L

Lait: milk.
Laitance: soft roe (often of herring), or eggs.
Laitue: lettuce.
Lamelle: very thin strip.
Lamproie: lamprey, eel-shaped fish, either fresh- or saltwater.
Langouste: clawless spiny lobster; sometimes called crawfish, and mistakenly, crayfish.
Langoustine: clawed crustacean, smaller than either *homard* or spiny lobster, with very delicate meat.
Languedocienne: garnish, usually of tomatoes, eggplant, and wild *cèpe* mushrooms.
Lapereau: young rabbit.
Lapin: rabbit.
Lapin de garenne: wild rabbit.

Lard: bacon.
Lardon: cube of bacon.
Larme: (literally, a teardrop) a very small portion of a liquid.
Lèche: thin slice of bread or meat.
Léger(ère): light.
Légume: vegetable.
Lieu (jaune): pollack, a prized small yellow saltwater fish.
Lièvre: hare.
Limande: solelike ocean fish, not as firm as sole.
Limande sole: lemon sole.
Lisette: small mackerel.
Lit: bed.
Lotte: monkfish or angler fish, a large, firm-fleshed ocean fish.
Lou magret: breast of fattened duck.
Loup (de mer): Mediterranean fish, also known as *bar,* similar to striped bass.
Lyonnaise (à la): in the style of Lyons, often garnished with onions.

M

Macédoine: diced mixed fruit or vegetables.
Macérer: to steep, pickle, or soak.
Mâche: lamb's lettuce, a tiny, dark green lettuce.
Madeleines: small tea cakes.
Madère: Madeira.
Magret de canard (d'oie): breast of fattened duck (goose).
Maigre: thin, non-fatty.
Maïs: corn.
Maison (de la): of the house, or restaurant.
Maître d'hôtel: head waiter; also, sauce of butter, parsley, and lemon.

Maltaise: orange-flavoured hollandaise sauce.
Mandarine: tangerine.
Mange-tout: (literally, "eat it all") a podless green runner bean; a snow pea; a type of apple.
Mangue: mango.
Manière (de): in the style of.
Maquereau: mackerel.
Maraîchère (à la): market-garden style, usually refers to a dish, or salad, including various greens.
Marbré(e): marbled.
Marc: distilled residue of grape skins or other fruits after they have been pressed.
Marcassin: young wild boar.
Marchand de vin: wine merchant; also a sauce made with red wine, meat stock, and chopped shallots.
Marché: market.
Marée (la): (literally, the tide) usually used to indicate that the seafood is fresh.
Marennes: flat-shelled, green-tinged *plate* oysters; also French coastal village where flat-shelled oysters are raised.
Mareyeur: wholesale fish merchant.
Mariné: marinated.
Marinière (moules): method of cooking mussels in white wine with onions, shallots, butter, and herbs.
Marjolaine: marjoram; also, multilayered chocolate and nut cake.
Marmite: small covered pot; also a dish cooked in a small casserole.
Marquise (au chocolat): mousselike (chocolate) cake.
Marron: large chestnut.

Matelote (d'anguilles): freshwater fish stew (or of eels).

Mauviette: wild meadow lark or skylark.

Médallion: round piece or slice.

Mélange: mixture or blend.

Méli-mélo: an assortment of fish and/or seafood, usually served in a salad.

Melon de Cavaillon: small, canteloupelike melon from Cavaillon, a town in Provence known for its wholesale produce market.

Ménagère (à la): (literally, in the style of a housewife) usually a simple preparation including onions, potatoes, and carrots.

Menthe: mint.

Menthe poivrée: peppermint.

Mer: sea.

Merguez: small spicy sausage.

Merlan: whiting.

Merle: blackbird.

Merveilles: hot, sugared doughnuts.

Mesclun, mesclum: mixture of at least seven multi-shaded salad greens.

Mets: dish or preparation.

Mets selon la saison: seasonal preparation; according to the season.

Meunière (à la): (literally, in the style of a miller's wife) refers to a fish that is seasoned, rolled in flour, fried in butter, and served with lemon, parsley, and hot melted butter.

Meurette: in, or with, a red wine sauce; also, a Burgundian fish stew.

Miel: honey.

Mignardises: synonym for *petits fours.*

Mignonette: small cubes, usually of beef; also refers to coarsely ground black or white peppercorns.

Mijoté(e) (plat): simmered (dish or preparation).

Mille-feuille: refers to puff pastry with many thin layers; usually a cream-filled rectangle of puff pastry, or a Napoleon.

Mimosa: garnish of chopped, hard-boiled egg yolks.

Minute (à la): prepared at the last minute.

Mirabeau: garnish of anchovies, pitted olives, tarragon, and anchovy butter.

Mirabelle: yellow plum.

Mirepoix: cubes of carrots and onions or mixed vegetables, usually used in braising to boost the flavour of a meat dish.

Miroton (de): slices (of); also stew of meats flavoured with onions.

Mitonnée: a simmered, souplike dish.

Mode (à la): in the style of.

Moelle: beef bone marrow.

Moka: refers to coffee, or coffee-flavored dish.

Montagne (de la): from the mountains.

Montmorency: garnished with cherries.

Morceau: piece or small portion.

Morille: wild morel mushroom, dark brown and conical-shaped.

Mornay: thickened, milk-based sauce including flour, butter, and egg yolks, with cheese added.

Morue: salted or dried codfish.

Mouclade: creamy mussel stew, sometimes flavored with curry.

Moule: mussel.

Moules d'Espagne: large, sharp-shelled mussels, often served raw, as part of a seafood platter.

Moules de bouchot: small, highly-prized cultivated mussels, raised on stakes driven into the sediment of shallow coastal beds.

Moules de Parques: Dutch, cultivated mussels, usually raised in fattening beds, or diverted ponds.

Moules marinière: mussels cooked in white wine with onions, shallots, butter, and herbs.

Mousse: light, airy mixture usually containing eggs and cream, either sweet or savoury.

Mousseline: refers to ingredients that are usually lightened with whipped cream or egg whites, as in sauces, or with butter, as in *brioche mousseline.*

Mousseron: tiny, delicate, wild mushroom.

Moutarde (à l'ancienne en graines): mustard (coarse-grained).

Mouton: mutton.

Mulet: mullet, a rustic-flavoured ocean fish.

Mûre: blackberry.

Muscade: nutmeg.

Museau de porc (de boeuf): vinegared pork (beef) muzzle.

Myrtilles: bilberries (bluish black European blueberries).

Mystère: cone-shaped ice cream dessert; also dessert of cooked meringue with ice cream and chocolate sauce.

N

Nage (à la): aromatic poaching liquid (served in).

Nantua: sauce of crayfish, butter, cream, and truffles; also garnish of crayfish.

Nappé: covered, as with a sauce.

Nature: refers to simple, unadorned preparations.

Navarin: lamb or mutton stew.

Navet: turnip.

Newburg: lobster preparation with Madeira, egg yolks, and cream.

Nid: nest.

Nivernaise: in the style of Nevers; with carrots and onions.

Noisette: hazelnut; also refers to small round piece (such as from a potato), generally the size of a hazelnut, lightly browned in butter; also, center cut of lamb chop; also, dessert flavored with hazelnut.

Noix: walnut; nut; nut-size.

Normande: in the style of Normandy; sauce of seafood, cream, and mushrooms; also refers to fish or meat cooked with apple cider or Calvados; or dessert with apples, usually served with cream.

Nouilles: noodles.

Nouveau, nouvelle: new or young.

Nouveauté: a new offering.

Noyau: stone or pit.

O

Oeuf à la coque: soft-boiled egg.

Oeuf brouillé: scrambled egg.

Oeuf dur: hard-cooked egg.

Oeuf en meurette: poached egg in red wine sauce.

Oeuf mollet: egg simmered in water for 6 minutes.

Oeuf poché: poached egg.

Oeuf sauté à la poêle, oeuf sur le plat: fried egg.

Oeufs à la neige: sweetened whipped egg whites poached in milk and served with vanilla custard sauce.

Offert: offered, free or given.

Oie: goose.

Oignon: onion.

Omble chevalier: freshwater char, a member of the trout family, with firm, flaky flesh varying from white to deep red.

Onglet: cut similar to beef flank steak; also cut of beef sold as *biftek* and *entrecôte;* technically a tough cut, but better than flank steak.

Oreilles (de porc): ears (of pig).

Orties: nettles.

Ortolan: tiny wild bird from southern France, Italy, Greece, and Spain, formerly very popular in French cuisine, now forbidden due to diminished supply.

Os: bone.

Oseille: sorrel.

Oursin: sea urchin.

Ouvert: open.

P

Paillard (de veau): thick slice (of veal).

Pailles (pommes): fried straw potatoes (finely shredded).

Paillettes: cheese straws, usually made with puff pastry and Parmesan cheese.

Pain: bread.

Paleron: shoulder of beef.

Paletot: (literally, coat) the skin, bone, and meat portion that remains of a fattened duck or goose once the liver is removed.

Palmier: palm-leaf-shaped cookie made of sugared puff pastry.

Palmier (coeurs de): palm hearts.

Palombe: wood or wild pigeon.

Palourde: prized, medium-size clam.

Pamplemousse: grapefruit.

Panaché: mixed; now liberally used menu term to denote any mixture.

Panade: panada, a thick mixture used to bind forcemeats and *quenelles,* usually flour and butter based, but can also contain fresh or toasted bread crumbs, rice, or potatoes; also refers to soup of bread, milk, and sometimes cheese.

Panais: parsnip.

Pané(e): breaded.

Panier: basket.

Pannequets: small, thick pancake, covered with either sweet or savoury mixture.

Papillote (en): cooked in parchment paper or foil wrapping.

Paquets (en): in packages or parcels.

Parfait: a dessert mousse; also mousse-like mixture of chicken, duck, or goose liver.

Parfum: flavor.

Parisienne (à la): varied vegetable garnish that always includes potato balls that have been fried and tossed in a meat glaze.

Parmentier: dish with potatoes.

Partager: to share.

Passe-pierre: edible seaweed.

Pastèque: watermelon.

Pastis: anise liqueur.

Pâte: pastry or dough.

Pâte à choux: cream puff pastry.

Pâte brisée: pie pastry.

Pâte sablée: sweeter, richer dough than *pâte sucrée,* sometimes leavened.

Pâte sucrée: sweet pie pastry.

Pâté: molded, spiced, minced meat, baked and served hot or cold.

Pâté (en croûte): pâté baked in a pastry crust.

Pâtes (fraîches): pasta (fresh).

Pâtisserie: pastry.

Pâtissier: pastry chef.

Patte: paw, foot, or leg of bird or animal.

Patte blanc: small crayfish no larger than 2 to 2½ ounces (60 to 75 g).

Patte rouge: large crayfish.

Paupiettes: thin slices of meat, usually beef or fish, filled, rolled, then wrapped.

Pavé: (literally, paving stone) usually a thick slice of boned beef or of calf's liver; also, a kind of pastry.

Paysan(ne) (à la): country style; also, garnish of carrots, turnips, onions, celery, and bacon.

Peau: skin.

Pêche: peach.

Pêche Melba: poached peach with vanilla ice cream and raspberry sauce.

Pêcheur: (literally, fisherman) usually refers to fish preparations.

Pelure: peelings, such as from truffles, often used for flavouring.

Perce-pierre: samphire, edible seaweed.

Perche: perch.

Perdreau: young partridge.

Perdrix: partridge.

Périgourdine (à la): sauce, usually with truffles and foie gras.

Persil: parsley.

Persillade: chopped parsley and garlic.

Petit déjeuner: breakfast.

Petit-gris: small land snail.

Petit-pois: small green pea.

Petits fours: tiny cakes and pastries.

Pétoncle: tiny scallop, similar to American bay scallop.

Pets de nonne: small, dainty fried pastry.

Piballes: small eels, also called *civelles.*

Pièce: portion, or piece.

Pied de mouton: meaty, cream-coloured wild mushroom; also, sheep's foot.

Pied de porc: pig's foot.

Pigeonneau: young pigeon or squab.

Pignons: pine nuts, or pignoli.

Pilau, pilaf: rice cooked with onions and broth.

Piment doux: sweet pepper.

Piment (poivre) de Jamaïque: allspice.

Pince: claw; also, tongs used when eating snails or seafood.

Pintade: guinea fowl.

Pintadeau: young guinea fowl.

Pipérade: Basque dish of scrambled eggs with pepper, onions, tomatoes, and ham.

Piquant(e): sharp or spicy tasting.

Piqué: larded; studded.

Pissaladière: a flat, open-face tart like a pizza, garnished with onions, olives, and anchovies.

Pissenlit: dandelion (leaves).

Pistil de safran: thread of saffron.

Pistache: pistachio nut.

Pistou: sauce of basil, garlic, and olive oil; also, a rich vegetable soup.

Pithiviers: classic round of puff pastry filled with almond cream.

Plat: a dish.

Plat principal: main dish.

Plates côtes: part of beef ribs usually used in pot-au-feu.

Plateau: platter.

Plateau de fruits de mer: seafood platter combining raw and cooked shellfish; usually includes oysters, clams, mussels, *langoustines,* periwinkles, crabs.

Pleurote: very soft-fleshed, feather-edged wild mushroom.

Plie franche: flounder; flat ocean fish; also known as *carrelet* (plaice).

Plombières: dessert of vanilla ice cream, candied fruit, kirsch, and sweetened whipped cream.

Pluches: leaves of herbs or plants, generally used for garnish.

Poché: poached.

Pochouse: freshwater fish stew prepared with white wine.

Poêlé: pan-fried.

Pointe (d'asperge): tip (of asparagus).

Poire: pear.

Poires Belle Hélène: poached pears served on vanilla ice cream with hot chocolate sauce.

Poireau: leek.

Pois: pea.

Poisson: fish.

Poitrine: breast (of meat or poultry).

Poitrine fumée: smoked slab bacon.

Poitrine demi-sel: unsmoked slab bacon.

Poivrade: a peppery brown sauce made with wine, vinegar, and cooked vegetables, that is strained before serving.

Poivre: pepper.
Poivre frais de Madagascar: green peppercorns.
Poivre noir: black peppercorns.
Poivre rose: pink peppercorns.
Poivre vert: green peppercorns.
Poivron (doux): sweet bell pepper.
Polenta: cooked dish of cornmeal and water, usually with added butter and cheese.
Pommade (en): usually refers to a thick, smooth paste.
Pomme: apple.
en l'air: caramelized apple slices, usually served with *boudin noir* (blood sausage).
Pommes (de terre): potatoes.
à l'anglaise: boiled.
allumettes: very thin fries, cut in ¼ × 2½ inch (½ cm × 6½ cm) slices.
boulangère: potatoes cooked with the meat they accompany; also, a potato gratin of sliced potatoes with onions and sometimes bacon and tomatoes.
dauphine: mashed potatoes mixed with *chou* pastry, shaped into small balls and fried.
dauphinoise: baked dish of sliced potatoes, milk, garlic, and cheese.
duchesse: mashed potatoes with butter, egg yolks and nutmeg, used for garnish.
frites: French fries.
gratinées: browned potatoes, often with cheese.
lyonnaise: sautéed potatoes, with onions.
paille: potatoes cut into julienne strips, then fried.

Pont-Neuf: classic fries, cut into ½ × 2½ inch (1 cm × 6½ cm) slices.
en robe de champs: potatoes cooked with skins on.
soufflées: small, thin slices of potato fried twice, causing them to inflate, so they look like little pillows.
vapeur: steamed or boiled potatoes.
Porc (carré de): pork (loin).
Porc (côte de): pork (chop).
Porcelet: young suckling pig.
Porto (au): (with) port.
Portugaises: elongated, crinkle-shell oysters.
Potage: soup.
Pot-au-feu: boiled beef prepared with vegetables, often served in two or more courses.
Pot-de-crème: individual custard or *mousse*-like dessert, often chocolate.
Potée: hearty soup of pork and vegetables, generally cabbage and potatoes.
Poularde: fatted hen.
Poule d'Inde: turkey hen.
Poule faisane: female pheasant.
Poulet (rôti): chicken (roast).
Poulet basquaise: Basque-style chicken; with tomatoes and sweet peppers.
Poulet de Bresse: high-quality, free-running, corn-fed chicken.
Poulet de grain: corn-fed chicken.
Poulet fermier: free-range chicken.
Poulpe: octopus.
Pousse-pierre: edible seaweed.
Poussin: baby chicken.
Praire: small clam.
Pralin: ground caramelized almonds.

Praline: caramelized almonds.
Primeur: refers to early fresh fruits and vegetables.
Printanière: garnish of a variety of spring vegetables; or vegetables cut into dice or balls.
Printemps: spring.
Prix fixe: fixed-price menu.
Prix net: service included.
Profiteroles: chou pastry dessert, usually filled with ice cream and topped with chocolate sauce.
Provençal(e): in the style of Provence; usually includes garlic, tomatoes, and/or olive oil.
Prune: fresh plum.
Pruneau: prune.

Q

Quenelle: dumpling; usually of veal, fish, or poultry.
Quetsch: small purple Damson plum.
Queue (de boeuf): tail (oxtail).

R

Râble de lièvre (lapin): saddle of hare (rabbit).
Raclette: rustic Swiss dish of melted cheese served with boiled potatoes, *cornichon* pickles, and pickled onions.
Radis: small red radish.
Radis noir: large black radish, often served with cream, as a salad.
Ragoût: stew; usually of meat.
Raie: skate (fish) or sting ray.
Raifort: horseradish.
Raisin: grape.

Ramequin: small individual casserole; also a small tart.

Râpé: grated or shredded.

Rascasse: scorpion fish.

Ratatouille: cooked dish of eggplant, zucchini, onions, tomatoes, peppers, garlic, and olive oil.

Rave: category of root vegetables, including celery, turnip, radish.

Ravigote: thick vinaigrette sauce with vinegar, white wine, shallots, herbs; also cold mayonnaise with capers, onions, and herbs.

Réchauffer: to reheat.

Reine-claude: greengage plum.

Reinette (reine de): fall and winter variety of apple.

Rémoulade: sauce of mayonnaise, capers, mustard, herbs, anchovies, and gherkins.

Repas: meal.

Rillettes (d'oie): minced spread of pork (goose); also can be made with duck, fish, or rabbit.

Rillons: usually pork belly, cut up and cooked until crisp, then drained of fat; can also be made of duck, goose, or rabbit.

Rince doigt: finger bowl.

Ris d'agneau: lamb sweetbreads.

Ris de veau: veal sweetbreads.

Rivière: river.

Riz: rice.

Riz à l'impératrice: cold rice pudding with candied fruit.

Riz complet: brown rice.

Riz sauvage: wild rice.

Rognonnade: veal loin with kidneys attached.

Rognons: kidneys.

Romarin: rosemary.

Rondelle: round slice.

Rosé: rare (meat).

Rosette (de boeuf): dried sausage (of beef), usually from Beaujolais.

Rôti: roast.

Rouelle (de): slice of meat or vegetable cut at an angle.

Rouget (rouget barbet): sweet, red-skinned fish commonly called red mullet; the smallest are most prized.

Rouille: thick, spicy, rust-coloured sauce, with olive oil, peppers, tomatoes, and garlic; usually served with fish soups.

Roulade: roll, often stuffed.

Roulé(e): rolled.

Roux: sauce base or thickening of flour and butter.

S

Sabayon: light sweet sauce of egg yolks, sugar, wine, and flavouring, which is whipped while being cooked in a water bath.

Sablé: shortbreadlike cookie.

Safran: saffron.

Saignant(e): very rare (for cooking meat).

Saint-Germain: with peas.

Saint-Hubert: sauce *poivrade* with chestnuts and bacon added.

Saint-Jacques (coquille): sea scallop.

Saint-Pierre: mild, flat, white ocean fish; in England, John Dory.

Saison (suivant la): according to the season.

Salade folle: mixed salad, usually including green beans and *foie gras*.

Salade panachée: mixed salad.

Salade verte: green salad.

Salé: salted.

Salicorne: edible algae, often pickled and eaten as a condiment.

Salmis: stewlike preparation of game birds or poultry, with sauce made from the pressed carcass.

Salpicon: diced vegetables, meat, and/or fish in a sauce.

Salsifis: salsify or oyster plant.

Sandre: perchlike freshwater fish.

Sang: blood.

Sanglier: wild boar.

Sarriette: summer savoury; also called *poivre d'âne*.

Saucisse: small fresh sausage.

Saucisson: large dried sausage.

Saucisson de Lyon: air-dried pork sausage, flavored with garlic and pepper, and studded with chunks of pork fat.

Sauge: sage.

Saumon (sauvage): salmon (literally, wild; a non-cultivated salmon).

Saumon d'Ecosse: Scotch salmon.

Saumon fumé: smoked salmon.

Saupiquet: classic aromatic wine sauce thickened with bread.

Sauté: browned in fat.

Sauvage: wild.

Savarin: yeast-leavened cake shaped like a ring, soaked in sweet syrup.

Savoyarde: usually flavoured with Gruyère cheese.

Scarole: escarole.

Seiche: large squid or cuttlefish.

Sel: salt.

Selle: saddle (of meat).

Selon arrivage: according to delivery or arrival.

Selon grosseur (S.G.): according to size.

Selon le marché: according to what is in season, and available.

Selon poids (S.P.): according to weight.

Serpolet: wild thyme.

Serviette: napkin.

Service (non) compris: service (not) included.

Service en sus: service not included.

Smitane: sauce of cream, onions, white wine, and lemon juice.

Soissons: dried or fresh white beans.

Sorbet: sherbet.

Soubise: onion sauce.

Soufflé: light sweet or savoury mixture served either hot or cold, the bulk of whose volume is egg whites.

Soupière: soup tureen.

Stockfish: flattened, dried cod.

Succès au pralin: cake flavoured with caramelized almonds and frosted with meringue and butter cream.

Sucre: sugar.

Suprême: a veal- or chicken-based white sauce thickened with flour and cream; a boneless breast of poultry or a filet of fish.

Surgelé: deep frozen.

T

Tablier de sapeur: tripe that is marinated, breaded, and grilled.

Tagine: spicy North African stew of veal, lamb, chicken, or pigeon with vegetables.

Tanche: tench, a freshwater fish with mild, delicate flavour; often an ingredient in *matelote,* freshwater fish stew.

Tapenade: blend of black olives, anchovies, capers, olive oil, and lemon juice, and sometimes tuna fish.

Tarama: mullet roe, often made into a spread (taramasalata) of the same name.

Tartare: chopped raw beef, seasoned and garnished with raw egg, capers, chopped onion, and parsley.

Tarte: tart; open-face pie or *flan,* usually sweet.

Tarte Tatin: caramelized, upside-down apple pie.

Tartine: open-face sandwich; buttered bread.

Tendre: tender.

Tendrons: cartilaginous meat cut from beef or veal ribs.

Terrine: earthenware container used for cooking meat, game, fish, or vegetable mixtures; also the mixture cooked in such a container.

Tête de veau (porc): head of veal (pork), usually used in head cheese.

Thé: tea.

Thon: tuna fish.

Thym: thyme.

Tian: earthenware gratin dish; also vegetable mixture cooked in such a dish.

Tiède: lukewarm.

Tilleul: lime, or linden tree, blossom (herb tea).

Timbale: round mould with straight or sloping sides; also, a mixture prepared in such a mould.

Topinambour: Jerusalem artichoke.

Torchon: dishcloth.

Tortue: turtle.

Toulousaine: Toulouse style; usually with truffles, or sweetbreads, cock's combs, mushrooms, or *quenelles.*

Tournebroche: spit, for grilling.

Tournedos: center portion of beef filet, usually grilled or sautéed.

Tournedos Rossini: sautéed *tournedos* garnished with *foie gras* and truffles.

Tourteau: large crab.

Tourtière: shallow cooking vessel; also, southwestern pastry dish filled with apples and/or prunes and sprinkled with Armagnac.

Tranche: slice.

Travers de porc: spare ribs.

Tripes à la mode de Caen: beef tripe, carrots, onions, leeks, and spices cooked in water, cider, and Calvados (apple brandy).

Tripoux: mutton tripe.

Trompettes de la mort: dark brown "horn of plenty" wild mushrooms.

Tronçon: cut of meat or fish resulting in a piece that is longer than it is wide; generally refers to slices from the largest part of a fish.

Truffe (truffé): truffle (with truffles).

Truite: trout.

Truite saumonée: salmon trout.

Tuile: (literally, tile) delicate almond-flavoured cookie.

Turban: usually mixture or combination of ingredients cooked in a ring mold.

Turbot(in): turbot (small turbot).

V

Vacherin: dessert of baked meringue, with ice cream and cream; also, strong, supple winter cheese; the best is Mont-d'Or.

Vallée d'Auge: region of Normandy; also, garnish of cooked apples and cream.

Vanille: vanilla.

Vapeur (à la): steamed.

Veau: veal.

Velouté: veal- or chicken-based sauce thickened with flour.

Venaison: venison.

Ventre: belly or stomach.

Vénus: American clam.

Verjus: juice from unripe grapes, once used in sauces instead of vinegar; now found primarily in French regional dishes.

Vernis: large, fleshy clam with small, red tongue and shiny, varnishlike shell.

Vert-pré: a watercress gar-nish, sometimes includes potatoes.

Verveine: lemon verbena (herb tea).

Vessie (en): cooked in a pig's bladder (usually a chicken).

Viande: meat.

Vichy: with glazed carrots; also a brand of mineral water.

Vichyssoise: cold, creamy leek and potato soup.

Vierge (beurre): whipped butter sauce with salt, pepper, and lemon juice.

Vierge (huile d'olive): virgin olive oil.

Vieux (vieille): old.

Vigneron: wine grower.

Vinaigre (vieux): vinegar (aged).

Vinaigre de xérès: sherry vinegar.

Vinaigrette: oil and vinegar dressing.

Vivant(e): living.

Vivier: fish tank.

Volaille: poultry.

Vol-au-vent: puff pastry shell.

Volonté (à): at the customer's discretion.

X

Xérès (vinaigre de): sherry (vinegar).

Y

Yaourt: yogurt.

Z

Zeste: peel of orange or lemon, with white pith removed.

Food Lover's Ready Reference

Aissa Fils (Chez), Paris 6

Albert (Chez), Paris 14

Allard, Paris 6

Ambassade d'Auvergne, Paris 3

Ambroisie (L'), Paris 5

Ami Louis (L'), Paris 3

Androuët, Paris 8

Anges (Chez les), Paris 7

Aquitaine (L'), Paris 15

Archestrate (L'), Paris 7

Artois (L'), Paris 8

Benoît, Paris 4

Bernardin (Le), Paris 17

Bofinger, Paris 4

Boutarde (La), Neuilly

Cartet, Paris 11

Caviar Kaspia, Paris 8

Cazaudehore, Saint-Germain-en-Laye

Chardenoux, Paris 11

Charlot, Le Roi des Coquillages, Paris 9

Charpentiers (Aux), Paris 6

Châteaubriant (Au), Paris 9

Chiberta, Paris 8

Cochon d'Or (Au), Paris 1

Cochon d'Or (Au), Paris 19

Copenhague, Paris 8

Coq de la Maison Blanche, Saint-Ouen

Coquille (La), Paris 17

Coupole (La), Paris 14

Diamantaires (Les), Paris 9

Divellec (Le), Paris 7

Dodin-Bouffant, Paris 5

Duc (Le), Paris 14

Duc d'Enghien, Enghien-les-Bains

Fénix (Jacqueline), Neuilly

Ferme Irlandaise (La), Paris 1

Flo (Brasserie), Paris 10

Flora Danica, Paris 8

Fontaine de Mars (La), Paris 7

Georges (Chez), Paris 2

Gérard, Paris 2

Glénan (Les), Paris 7

Globe d'Or (Le), Paris 1

Gourmets des Ternes (Les), Paris 17

Grand Véfour (Le), Paris 1

Ile Saint-Louis (Brasserie de l'), Paris 4

Isse, Paris 2

Jamin/Joël Robuchon, Paris 16

Jardin de la Paresse (Le), Paris 14

Jenny (Chez), Paris 3

Joséphine, Paris 6

Julien, Paris 10

Louis XIV, Paris 1

Lozère (La), Paris 6

Maître Paul (Chez), Paris 6

Marée (La), Paris 8

Mère-Grand, Paris 20

Moissonnier, Paris 5

Montecristo, Paris 4

Olympe (Restaurant l'), Paris 15

Pantagruel, Paris 7

Pauline (Chez), Paris 1

Petit Bedon (Le), Paris 16

Petit Marguery (Le), Paris 13

Petit Montmorency (Le), Paris 8

Petit Riche (Au), Paris 9

Pharamond, Paris 1

Philippe/Auberge Pyrénées-Cévennes (Chez), Paris 11

Pied de Cochon (Au), Paris 1

Pierre Traiteur, Paris 1

Pile on Face, Paris 2

Polidor, Paris 6

Porte Fausse (La), Paris 6

Poularde Landaise (La), Paris 8

Pré Catelan (Le), Paris 16

Pressoir (Au), Paris 12

Quai des Ormes (Au), Paris 4

Quai d'Orsay (Au), Paris 7

Relais des Pyrénées, Paris 20

René (Chez), Paris 5

Ritz-Espadon, Paris 1

Roi du Pot-au-Feu (Le), Paris 9

Rostang (Michel), Paris 17

Ruban Bleu (Le), Paris 1

Savoy (Guy), Paris 16

Sologne (La), Paris 7

Sousceyrac (A), Paris 11

Table de Jeannette (La), Paris 1

Taillevent, Paris 8

Terminus Nord, Paris 10

Tiepolo (Restaurant), Paris 5

Timgad (Le), Paris 17

Toison d'Or (La), Paris 15

Tour d'Argent (La), Paris 5

Toutoune (Chez), Paris 5

Train Bleu (Le), Paris 12

Trois Marches (Les), Versailles

Trois Piloux (Les), Paris 19

Trou Gascon (Au), Paris 12

Vaudeville, Paris 2

Vieille (Chez la), Paris 1

Vieux Berlin (Au), Paris 8

Villars Palace, Paris 5

RESTAURANTS LISTED BY ARRONDISSEMENTS

Palais-Royal, Les Halles, Opéra, Bourse
1st and 2nd arrondissements

Au Cochon d'Or

La Ferme Irlandaise

Chez Georges

Gérard

Le Globe d'Or

Le Grand Véfour

Isse

Louis XIV

Chez Pauline

Pharamond

Au Pied de Cochon

Pierre Traiteur

Pile ou Face

Ritz-Espadon

Le Ruban Bleu

La Table de Jeannette

Vaudeville

Chez la Vieille

République, Bastille, Les Halles, Ile Saint-Louis
3rd, 4th, and 11th arrondissements

Ambassade d'Auvergne

L'Ami Louis

Benoît

Bofinger

Cartet

Chardenoux

Brasserie de l'Ile Saint-Louis

Chez Jenny

Montecristo

Chez Philippe/Auberge Pyrénées-Cévennes

Au Quai des Ormes

A Sousceyrac

Latin Quarter, Luxembourg, Sèvres-Babylone
5th and 6th arrondissements

Chez Aissa Fils

Allard

L'Ambroisie

Aux Charpentiers

Dodin-Bouffant

Joséphine

La Lozère

Chez Maître Paul

Moissonnier

Polidor

La Porte Fausse

Chez René

Restaurant Tiepolo

La Tour d'Argent

Chez Toutoune

Villars Palace

Faubourg Saint-Germain, Invalides, Ecole Militaire
7th arrondissement

Chez les Anges

L'Archestrate

Le Divellec

La Fontaine de Mars

Les Glénan

Pantagruel

Au Quai d'Orsay

La Sologne

Madeleine, Saint-Lazare, Champs-Elysées
8th arrondissement

Androuët

L'Artois

Caviar Kaspia

Chiberta

Copenhague

Flora Danica

La Marée

Le Petit Montmorency

La Poularde Landaise

Taillevent

Au Vieux Berlin

Grands Boulevards, Place de Clichy, Gare du Nord
9th and 10th arrondissements

Charlot, Le Roi des Coquillages

Au Châteaubriant

Les Diamantaires

Brasserie Flo

Julien

Au Petit Riche

Le Roi du Pot-au-Feu

Terminus Nord

Gare de Lyon, Bois de Vincennes
12th arrondissement

Au Pressoir

Le Train Bleu

Au Trou Gascon

Gobelins, Vaugirard, Montparnasse, Grenelle, Denfert-Rochereau
13th, 14th, and 15th arrondissements

Chez Albert

L'Aquitaine

La Coupole

Le Duc

Le Jardin de la Paresse

Restaurant l'Olympe

Le Petit Marguery

La Toison d'Or

Arc de Triomphe, Trocadéro, Bois de Boulogne, Neuilly
16th arrondissement and Neuilly

La Boutarde

Jacqueline Fénix

Jamin/Joël Robuchon

Le Petit Bedon

Le Pré Catelan

Guy Savoy

Arc de Triomphe, Place des Ternes, Porte Maillot
17th arrondissement

Le Bernardin

La Coquille

Les Gourmets des Ternes

Michel Rostang

Le Timgad

Saint-Ouen, La Villette, Belleville, Père Lachaise
19th and 20th arrondissements and Saint-Ouen

Au Cochon d'Or

Coq de la Maison Blanche

Mère-Grand

Relais des Pyrénées

Les Trois Piloux

Paris Environs: Enghien-les-Bains, Saint-Germain-en-Laye, Versailles

Cazaudehore

Duc d'Enghien

Les Trois Marches

RESTAURANTS: BISTROS

Allard, Paris 6

L'Ami Louis, Paris 3

L'Artois, Paris 8

Benoît, Paris 4

La Boutarde, Neuilly

Cartet, Paris 11

Aux Charpentiers, Paris 6

Au Cochon d'Or, Paris 1

La Coquille, Paris 17

La Fontaine de Mars, Paris 7

Chez Georges, Paris 2

Gérard, Paris 2

Les Gourmets des Ternes, Paris 17

Joséphine, Paris 6

Louis XIV, Paris 1

Chez Maître Paul, Paris 6

Mère-Grand, Paris 20

Moissonnier, Paris 5

Chez Pauline, Paris 1

Le Petit Marguery, Paris 13

Le Petit Montmorency, Paris 8

Au Petit Riche, Paris 9

Chez Philippe/Auberge
Pyrénées-Cévennes,
Paris 11

Pierre Traiteur, Paris 1

Polidor, Paris 6

Au Quai d'Orsay, Paris 7

Relais des Pyrénées,
Paris 20

Chez René, Paris 5

Le Ruban Bleu, Paris 1

A Sousceyrac, Paris 11

Chez Toutoune, Paris 5

Les Trois Piloux, Paris 19

Chez la Vieille, Paris 1

RESTAURANTS: BRASSERIES

Bofinger, Paris 4

La Coupole, Paris 14

Brasserie Flo, Paris 10

Brasserie de l'Ile Saint-
Louis, Paris 4

Chez Jenny, Paris 3

Julien, Paris 10

Terminus Nord, Paris 10

Le Train Bleu, Paris 12

Vaudeville, Paris 2

RESTAURANTS OPEN AFTER 11 P.M.

The following restaurants keep later than normal hours. The time in parentheses notes the approximate time at which final orders will be taken. In all cases, reservations are advised.

Chez Aissa Fils (midnight),
Paris 6

Le Bernardin (11:30 P.M.),
Paris 17

Bofinger (1 A.M.),
Paris 4

Caviar Kaspia (11:30 P.M.),
Paris 8

Charlot, Le Roi des Coquillages (12:45 A.M.),
Paris 9

Aux Charpentiers (11:30
P.M.), Paris 6

La Coupole (1:30 A.M.),
Paris 14

Dodin-Bouffant (12:45
A.M.), Paris 5

Brasserie Flo (1:30 A.M.),
Paris 10

Brasserie de l'Ile Saint-Louis
(1:00 A.M.), Paris 4

Chez Jenny (1 A.M.),
Paris 3

Julien (1:30 A.M.), Paris 10

Restaurant l'Olympe (mid-
night), Paris 15

Au Petit Riche (12:45
A.M.), Paris 9

Au Pied de Cochon (open
24 hours), Paris 1

Terminus Nord (midnight),
Paris 10

Vaudeville (2 A.M.),
Paris 2

RESTAURANTS OPEN ON SATURDAY

Chez Aissa Fils (dinner),
Paris 6

Chez Albert, Paris 14

Ambassade d'Auvergne,
Paris 3

L'Ambroisie, Paris 5

L'Ami Louis, Paris 3

Androuët, Paris 8

Chez les Anges, Paris 7

L'Aquitaine, Paris 15

Le Bernardin, Paris 17

Bofinger, Paris 4

La Boutarde (dinner),
Neuilly

Brasserie Flo, Paris 10

Caviar Kaspia, Paris 8

Cazaudehore, Saint-
Germain-en-Laye

Charlot, Le Roi des Coquillages, Paris 9

Aux Charpentiers, Paris 6

Au Châteaubriant, Paris 9

Au Cochon d'Or (dinner),
Paris 1

Au Cochon d'Or, Paris 19

Copenhague, Paris 8

Coq de la Maison Blanche,
Saint-Ouen

La Coquille, Paris 17

La Coupole, Paris 14

Les Diamantaires, Paris 9

Le Divellec, Paris 7

Duc d'Enghien, Enghien-
les-Bains

La Ferme Irlandaise, Paris 1

Flora Danica, Paris 8

La Fontaine de Mars
(lunch), Paris 7

Chez Georges, Paris 2

Gérard (dinner), Paris 2

Le Grand Véfour, Paris 1

Brasserie de l'Ile Saint-
Louis, Paris 4

Isse, Paris 2

Le Jardin de la Paresse,
Paris 14

Chez Jenny, Paris 3

Julien, Paris 10

La Lozère, Paris 6

Chez Maître Paul, Paris 6

Mère-Grand, Paris 20

Moissonnier, Paris 5

Montecristo, Paris 4

Restaurant l'Olympe
(dinner), Paris 15

Pantagruel (dinner), Paris 7

Chez Pauline, Paris 1

Le Petit Marguery, Paris 13

Au Petit Riche, Paris 9

Pharamond, Paris 1

Au Pied de Cochon, Paris 1

Polidor, Paris 6

La Porte Fausse, Paris 6

Le Pré Catelan, Paris 16

Au Quai d'Orsay, Paris 7

Ritz-Espadon, Paris 1

Le Roi du Pot-au-Feu,
Paris 9

Michel Rostang (dinner,
October to March),
Paris 17

Terminus Nord, Paris 10

Restaurant Tiepolo, Paris 5

Le Timgad, Paris 17

La Toison d'Or, Paris 15

La Tour d'Argent, Paris 5

Chez Toutoune, Paris 5

Le Train Bleu, Paris 12

Les Trois Marches,
Versailles

Les Trois Piloux, Paris 19

Vaudeville, Paris 2

Villars Palace, Paris 5

RESTAURANTS OPEN ON SUNDAY

Chez Albert, Paris 14

L'Ambroisie (lunch), Paris 5

L'Ami Louis, Paris 3

Chez les Anges (lunch),
Paris 7

Bofinger, Paris 4

Cazaudehore, Saint-
Germain-en-Laye

Charlot, Le Roi des Coquillages, Paris 9

Au Cochon d'Or, Paris 19

Coq de la Maison Blanche
(lunch), Saint-Ouen

La Coupole, Paris 14

Les Diamantaires, Paris 9

Duc d'Enghien, Enghien-
les-Bains

La Ferme Irlandaise, Paris 1

Brasserie Flo, Paris 10

Flora Danica, Paris 8

Brasserie de l'Ile Saint-
Louis, Paris 4

Le Jardin de la Paresse
(lunch year round, din-
ner from May to Octo-
ber), Paris 14

Chez Jenny, Paris 3

Julien, Paris 10

Moissonnier (lunch), Paris 5

Restaurant l'Olympe (din-
ner), Paris 15

Le Petit Marguery, Paris 13

Au Pied de Cochon, Paris 1

Le Pré Catelan (lunch),
Paris 16

Relais des Pyrénées,
Paris 20

Ritz-Espadon, Paris 1

Terminus Nord, Paris 10

La Toison d'Or, Paris 15

La Tour d'Argent, Paris 5

Le Train Bleu, Paris 12

Vaudeville, Paris 2

Villars Palace, Paris 5

RESTAURANTS OPEN ON MONDAY

Allard, Paris 6

Ambassade d'Auvergne, Paris 3

Androuët, Paris 8

L'Archestrate, Paris 7

L'Artois, Paris 8

Benoît, Paris 4

Bofinger, Paris 4

La Boutarde, Neuilly

Cartet, Paris 11

Caviar Kaspia, Paris 8

Chardenoux, Paris 11

Charlot, Le Roi des Coquillages, Paris 9

Aux Charpentiers, Paris 6

Chiberta, Paris 8

Au Cochon d'Or, Paris 1

Au Cochon d'Or, Paris 19

Copenhague, Paris 8

Coq de la Maison Blanche, Saint-Ouen

La Coupole, Paris 14

Les Diamantaires (lunch), Paris 9

Dodin-Bouffant, Paris 5

Jacqueline Fénix, Neuilly

Brasserie Flo, Paris 10

Flora Danica, Paris 8

La Fontaine de Mars, Paris 7

Chez Georges, Paris 2

Gérard, Paris 2

Les Glénan, Paris 7

Le Globe d'Or, Paris 1

Les Gourmets des Ternes, Paris 17

Le Grand Véfour, Paris 1

Brasserie de l'Ile Saint-Louis, Paris 4

Jamin/Joël Robuchon, Paris 16

Le Jardin de la Paresse (May to October), Paris 14

Chez Jenny, Paris 3

Joséphine, Paris 6

Julien, Paris 10

Louis XIV, Paris 1

La Marée, Paris 8

Mère-Grand, Paris 20

Montecristo, Paris 4

Pantagruel, Paris 7

Chez Pauline, Paris 1

Le Petit Bedon, Paris 16

Le Petit Montmorency, Paris 8

Au Petit Riche, Paris 9

Chez Philippe/Auberge Pyrénées-Cévennes, Paris 11

Au Pied de Cochon, Paris 1

Pierre Traiteur, Paris 1

Pile ou Face, Paris 2

La Poularde Landaise, Paris 8

Au Pressoir, Paris 12

Au Quai des Ormes, Paris 4

Au Quai d'Orsay, Paris 7

Relais des Pyrénées, Paris 20

Chez René, Paris 5

Ritz-Espadon, Paris 1

Le Roi du Pot-au-Feu, Paris 9

Michel Rostang, Paris 17

Guy Savoy, Paris 16

La Sologne, Paris 7

A Sousceyrac, Paris 11

La Table de Jeannette, Paris 1

Taillevent, Paris 8

Terminus Nord, Paris 10

Restaurant Tiepolo, Paris 5

Le Timgad, Paris 17

La Toison d'Or, Paris 15

Le Train Bleu, Paris 12

Au Trou Gascon, Paris 12

Vaudeville, Paris 2

Chez la Vieille (lunch), Paris 1

Au Vieux Berlin, Paris 8

Villars Palace, Paris 5

RESTAURANTS OPEN IN AUGUST

Ambassade d'Auvergne, Paris 3

Androuët, Paris 8

Chez les Anges, Paris 7

L'Aquitaine, Paris 15

Bofinger, Paris 4

La Boutarde, Neuilly

Caviar Kaspia, Paris 8

Cazaudehore, Saint-Germain-en-Laye

Aux Charpentiers, Paris 6

Au Cochon d'Or, Paris 1

Au Cochon d'Or, Paris 19

Coq de la Maison Blanche, Saint-Ouen

Le Duc, Paris 14

Duc d'Enghien, Enghien-les-Bains

La Ferme Irlandaise, Paris 1

Brasserie Flo, Paris 10

Flora Danica, Paris 8

Chez Georges, Paris 2

Le Globe d'Or, Paris 1

Isse, Paris 2

Jamin/Joël Robuchon, Paris 16

Le Jardin de la Paresse, Paris 14

Chez Jenny, Paris 3

Joséphine, Paris 6

Julien, Paris 10

Mère-Grand, Paris 20

Chez Pauline, Paris 1

Le Petit Marguery, Paris 13

Pharamond, Paris 1

Au Pied de Cochon, Paris 1

La Poularde Landaise, Paris 8

Le Pré Catelan, Paris 16

Ritz-Espadon, Paris 1

Le Roi du Pot-au-Feu, Paris 9

Guy Savoy, Paris 16

Terminus Nord, Paris 10

Restaurant Tiepolo, Paris 5

La Tour d'Argent, Paris 5

Le Train Bleu, Paris 12

Les Trois Marches, Versailles

Au Trou Gascon, Paris 12

Vaudeville, Paris 2

Au Vieux Berlin, Paris 8

Villars Palace, Paris 5

RESTAURANTS WITH PRIVATE DINING ROOMS OR AREAS

The following restaurants provide private dining rooms or areas for groups. The maximum number of diners each can serve is noted in parentheses. In all cases, reserve in advance. In most cases, special menus can be arranged.

Chez Aissa Fils (25), Paris 6

Ambassade d'Auvergne (16), Paris 3

Androuët (24), Paris 8

Chez les Anges (15), Paris 7

L'Artois (12), Paris 8

Bofinger (250), Paris 4

Caviar Kaspia (20), Paris 8

Cazaudehore (30), Saint-Germain-en-Laye

Au Cochon d'Or (18), Paris 19

Le Divellec (15), Paris 7

Le Grand Véfour (14), Paris 1

Jamin/Joël Robuchon (24), Paris 16

Le Jardin de la Paresse (30), Paris 14

Chez Jenny (150), Paris 3

Louis XIV (10), Paris 1

Chez Maître Paul (25), Paris 6

La Marée (30), Paris 8

Montecristo (8), Paris 4

Chez Pauline (16), Paris 1

Le Petit Marguery (25), Paris 13

Au Petit Riche (45), Paris 9

Pharamond (18), Paris 1

Au Pied de Cochon (40), Paris 1

Polidor (only parties of 60), Paris 6

Le Pré Catelan (440), Paris 16

Au Pressoir (18), Paris 12

Au Quai des Ormes (30), Paris 4

Michel Rostang (20), Paris 17

La Sologne (24), Paris 7

Taillevent (32), Paris 8

Terminus Nord (10), Paris 10

La Tour d'Argent (40), Paris 5

Le Train Bleu (26), Paris 12

Les Trois Marches (40), Versailles

Au Vieux Berlin (40), Paris 8

Villars Palace (50), Paris 5

RESTAURANTS WITH PAVEMENT TABLES OR OUTDOOR TERRACE

L'Aquitaine, Paris 15

Bofinger, Paris 4

Dodin-Bouffant, Paris 5

Les Gourmets des Ternes, Paris 17

Louis XIV, Paris 1

Pharamond, Paris 1

Au Pied de Cochon, Paris 1

Pile ou Face, Paris 2

La Porte Fausse, Paris 6

Au Quai des Ormes, Paris 4

Au Quai d'Orsay, Paris 7

Le Roi du Pot-au-Feu, Paris 9

Terminus Nord, Paris 10

Chez Toutoune, Paris 5

Vaudeville, Paris 2

RESTAURANTS WITH GARDEN DINING

Cazaudehore, Saint-Germain-en-Laye

Duc d'Enghien, Enghien-les-Bains

Flora Danica, Paris 8

Le Jardin de la Paresse, Paris 14

Le Pré Catelan, Paris 16

Ritz-Espadon, Paris 1

AIR-CONDITIONED RESTAURANTS

Allard, Paris 6

Ambassade d'Auvergne, Paris 3

Chez les Anges, Paris 7

L'Archestrate, Paris 7

Charlot, Le Roi des Coquillages, Paris 9

Au Châteaubriant, Paris 9

Chiberta, Paris 8

Au Cochon d'Or, Paris 1

Au Cochon d'Or, Paris 19

La Coquille, Paris 17

Le Divellec, Paris 7

Dodin-Bouffant, Paris 5

Jacqueline Fénix, Neuilly

Le Grand Véfour, Paris 1

Isse, Paris 2

Jamin/Joël Robuchon, Paris 16

Restaurant l'Olympe, Paris 15

Chez Pauline, Paris 1

Le Petit Bedon, Paris 16

Chez Philippe/Auberge Pyrénées-Cévennes, Paris 11

Au Pressoir, Paris 2

Au Quai des Ormes, Paris 4

Au Quai d'Orsay, Paris 7

Michel Rostang, Paris 17

Guy Savoy, Paris 16

La Sologne, Paris 7

Taillevent, Paris 8

Terminus Nord, Paris 10

Le Timgad, Paris 17

Au Trou Gascon, Paris 12

Au Vieux Berlin, Paris 8

RESTAURANTS FEATURING FRENCH REGIONAL SPECIALITIES

ALSACE

Bofinger, Paris 4

Brasserie Flo, Paris 10

Brasserie de l'Ile Saint-Louis, Paris 4

Chez Jenny, Paris 3

AUVERGNE

Ambassade d'Auvergne, Paris 3

La Lozère, Paris 6

BURGUNDY/LYONS

Allard, Paris 6

Benoît, Paris 4

Cartet, Paris 11

Louis XIV, Paris 1

Moissonnier, Paris 5

Le Train Bleu, Paris 12

Chez la Vieille, Paris 1

JURA

Chez Maître Paul, Paris 6

Moissonnier, Paris 5

NORMANDY

Pharamond, Paris 1

PROVENCE

La Porte Fausse, Paris 6

Chez Toutoune, Paris 5

SOLOGNE

La Sologne, Paris 7

SOUTHWEST/ BORDEAUX

L'Aquitaine, Paris 15

Le Globe d'Or, Paris 1

Chez Philippe/Auberge Pyrénées-Cévennes, Paris 11

Poularde Landaise, Paris 8

Relais des Pyrénées, Paris 20

La Table de Jeannette, Paris 1

Les Trois Piloux, Paris 19

Au Trou Gascon, Paris 12

RESTAURANT SPECIALITIES

ANDOUILLETTE

Ambassade d'Auvergne, Paris 3

Benoît, Paris 4

La Coquille, Paris 17

Chez Georges, Paris 2

Au Pied de Cochon, Paris 1

BOUDIN

Ambassade d'Auvergne, Paris 3

Benoît, Paris 4

La Coquille, Paris 17

CASSOULET

Ambassade d'Auvergne, Paris 3

Benoît, Paris 4

Le Globe d'Or, Paris 1

Julien, Paris 10

Chez Philippe/Auberge Pyrénées-Cévennes, Paris 11

La Table de Jeannette, Paris 1

Au Trou Gascon, Paris 12

CHOUCROUTE

Bofinger, Paris 4

Brasserie Flo, Paris 10

Brasserie de l'Ile Saint-Louis, Paris 4

Chez Jenny, Paris 3

Terminus Nord, Paris 10

CONFIT

L'Aquitaine, Paris 15

L'Artois, Paris 8

Le Globe d'Or, Paris 1

Chez Philippe/Auberge Pyrénées-Cévennes, Paris 11

Pile ou Face, Paris 2

La Poularde Landaise, Paris 8

Relais des Pyrénées, Paris 20

Le Ruban Bleu, Paris 1

La Table de Jeannette, Paris 1

Au Trou Gascon, Paris 12

ESCARGOTS

Allard, Paris 6

L'Ami Louis, Paris 3

La Coquille, Paris 17

Polidor, Paris 6

FISH AND SHELLFISH

L'Aquitaine, Paris 15

Le Bernardin, Paris 17

Caviar Kaspia, Paris 8

Charlot, Le Roi des Coquillages, Paris 9

Copenhague, Paris 8

La Coquille, Paris 17

La Coupole, Paris 14

Le Divellec, Paris 7

Dodin-Bouffant, Paris 5

Le Duc, Paris 14

Brasserie Flo, Paris 10

Flora Danica, Paris 8

Les Glénan, Paris 7

Isse, Paris 2

La Marée, Paris 8

La Sologne, Paris 7

Terminus Nord, Paris 10

Villars Palace, Paris 5

FOIE GRAS

L'Ambroisie, Paris 5

L'Ami Louis, Paris 3

Jacqueline Fénix, Neuilly

Brasserie Flo, Paris 10

Joséphine, Paris 6

Julien, Paris 10

Restaurant l'Olympe, Paris 15

Chez Pauline, Paris 1

Le Petit Montmorency, Paris 8

Chez Philippe/Auberge Pyrénées-Cévennes, Paris 11

Pierre Traiteur, Paris 1

Relais des Pyrénées, Paris 20

A Sousceyrac, Paris 11

La Table de Jeannette, Paris 1

Terminus Nord, Paris 10

Au Trou Gascon, Paris 12

Vaudeville, Paris 2

GAME (November through January)

La Coquille, Paris 17

Jamin/Joël Robuchon, Paris 16

La Marée, Paris 8

Pantagruel, Paris 7

Le Petit Marguery, Paris 13

Le Pré Catelan, Paris 16

La Sologne, Paris 7

A Sousceyrac, Paris 11

Au Trou Gascon, Paris 12

GRILLED MEATS

Au Cochon d'Or, Paris 1

Au Cochon d'Or, Paris 19

La Coupole, Paris 14

Gérard, Paris 2

Les Gourmets des Ternes, Paris 17

La Sologne, Paris 7

Au Pied de Cochon, Paris 1

OYSTERS YEAR ROUND

Le Bernardin, Paris 17

Le Divellec, Paris 7

Dodin-Bouffant, Paris 5

Le Duc, Paris 14

Brasserie Flo, Paris 10

Au Pied de Cochon, Paris 1

Terminus Nord, Paris 10

Vaudeville, Paris 2

WINE LISTS WORTH NOTING

Le Grand Véfour, Paris 1

Joséphine, Paris 6

La Marée, Paris 8

Au Pressoir, Paris 12

Taillevent, Paris 8

La Tour d'Argent, Paris 5

Les Trois Marches, Versailles

Au Trou Gascon, Paris 12

FOREIGN RESTAURANTS

GERMAN

Au Vieux Berlin, Paris 8

GREEK

Les Diamantaires, Paris 9

IRISH

La Ferme Irlandaise, Paris 1

ITALIAN

Au Châteaubriant, Paris 9

Montecristo, Paris 4

Restaurant Tiepolo, Paris 5

JAPANESE

Isse, Paris 2

MOROCCAN

Chez Aissa Fils, Paris 6

Le Timgad, Paris 17

RUSSIAN

Caviar Kaspia, Paris 8

La Toison d'Or, Paris 15

SCANDINAVIAN

Copenhague, Paris 8

Flora Danica, Paris 8

OTHER ESTABLISHMENTS OPEN ON SUNDAY

Check individual entries for more complete details regarding business hours.

BISTROS A VIN
WINE BARS

L'Ecluse (noon to 2 A.M.),
Paris 8

Ma Bourgogne (7 A.M. to
8:30 P.M.), Paris 8

La Tartine (7:30 A.M. to
10 P.M.), Paris 4

PATISSERIES
PASTRY SHOPS

Boudin (6:30 A.M. to
8 P.M.), Paris 6

C. Brocard (8 A.M. to
7:30 P.M.), Paris 16

Christian Constant (8 A.M.
to 8 P.M.), Paris 7

Coquelin Aîné (9 A.M. to
1 P.M.), Paris 16

Dalloyau (9:30 A.M. to
1:30 P.M./3 P.M. to
6:30 P.M.), Paris 8

Finkelsztajn (9 A.M. to
1:30 P.M./2:30 P.M. to
7:30 P.M.), Paris 4

Ganachaud (7:30 A.M. to
1:30 P.M.), Paris 20

Hellegouarch (8:30 A.M. to
7:30 P.M.), Paris 15

Hellegouarch/Pâtisserie
Montmartre (9 A.M. to
7:30 P.M.), Paris 18

Lenôtre (9:45 A.M. to
1 P.M.), Paris 7; (9:15
A.M. to 7:15 P.M.), Rue
d'Auteuil, Paris 16;
(9 A.M. to 1 P.M.),
Avenue Victor-Hugo,
Paris 16; (9 A.M. to
1 P.M.), Paris 17.

Lerch (8 A.M. to
1:15 P.M./3:15 P.M. to
7 P.M.), Paris 5

Millet (9 A.M. to 1 P.M.),
Paris 7

Le Moule à Gâteau (9 A.M.
to 1:30 P.M.), Paris 5
and Paris 17

Peltier (9:30 A.M. to
6:30 P.M.), Paris 7

Saffray (7:30 A.M. to
7 P.M.), Paris 7

Pâtisserie Saint-Paul
(8 A.M. to 1:30 P.M./
3 P.M. to 7:30 P.M.),
Paris 4

Stohrer (7:30 A.M. to
8 P.M.), Paris 2

Vaudron (7:30 A.M. to
1 P.M./2 P.M. to
7:15 P.M.), Paris 17

BOULANGERIES
BAKERIES

Aux Armes de Niel
(6:30 A.M. to 8 P.M.),
Paris 17

J. M. Callede (7:30 A.M. to
8 P.M.), Paris 18

Ganachaud (7:30 A.M. to
1:30 P.M.), Paris 20

La Hacquinière (8:30 A.M.
to 1:30 P.M./3:30 P.M.
to 8:30 P.M.), Paris 17

Lenôtre (9:15 A.M. to
7:15 P.M.), Rue d'Au-
teuil, Paris 16; (9 A.M.
to 1 P.M.), Avenue
Victor-Hugo, Paris 16;
(9 A.M. to 1 P.M.),
Paris 17.

Les Panetons (10 A.M. to
2 P.M./4 P.M. to 8
P.M.), Paris 4; (7:30
A.M. to 1 P.M.),
Paris 5

Place Monge Market, Stall
61 (7 A.M. to 1 P.M.),
Paris 5

Lionel Poilâne (7 A.M. to
8 P.M.), Paris 15

Boulangerie Quentin
(7 A.M. to 1:30 P.M./
4 P.M. to 8 P.M.),
Paris 17

Rouillon (7:30 A.M. to
8:30 P.M.), Paris 13

Boulangerie Vacher
(7 A.M. to 8 P.M.),
Paris 17

CHARCUTERIES
PREPARED FOODS
TO GO

Ducreux Régionaux
(8 A.M. to 1 P.M.),
Paris 14

Aux Fermes d'Auvergne
(9 A.M. to 1 P.M.),
Paris 17

Jean-Claude et Nanou
(8:30 A.M. to 12:45
P.M.), Paris 17

Maison Pou (9:30 A.M. to
2:45 P.M.), Paris 17

Aux Produits de Gers
(8 A.M. to 12:30 P.M./
1 P.M. to 8 P.M.),
Paris 16

La Savoyarde (9 A.M. to
8 P.M.), Paris 11

Chez Teil (9 A.M. to
1 P.M.), Paris 11

A la Ville de Rodez
(8 A.M. to 1 P.M.),
Paris 4

A la Ville d'Aurillac
(9 A.M. to 1 P.M.),
Paris 11

Aux Vrais Produits d'Auvergne (8:30 A.M. to 12:30 P.M.), Paris 11

SPECIALITES GASTRONOMIQUES
SPECIALITY SHOPS

Flo Prestige (7 A.M. to midnight), Paris 1

Flora Danica (noon to midnight), Paris 8

Maison Woerli (8:30 A.M. to noon), Paris 6

Than Binh (8:30 A.M. to 7:30 P.M.), Paris 5

VIN, BIÈRE, ALCOOL
WINE, BEER, AND SPIRITS

L'Arbre à Vin/Caves Retrou (8:30 A.M. to 12:30 P.M.), Paris 12

Jean-Baptiste Besse (11 A.M. to 1:30 P.M.), Paris 5

L'Oenophile (8:30 A.M. to 1 P.M.), Paris 11

Cave Michel Renaud (9 A.M. to 1 P.M.), Paris 12

Index

W

Recipe Index

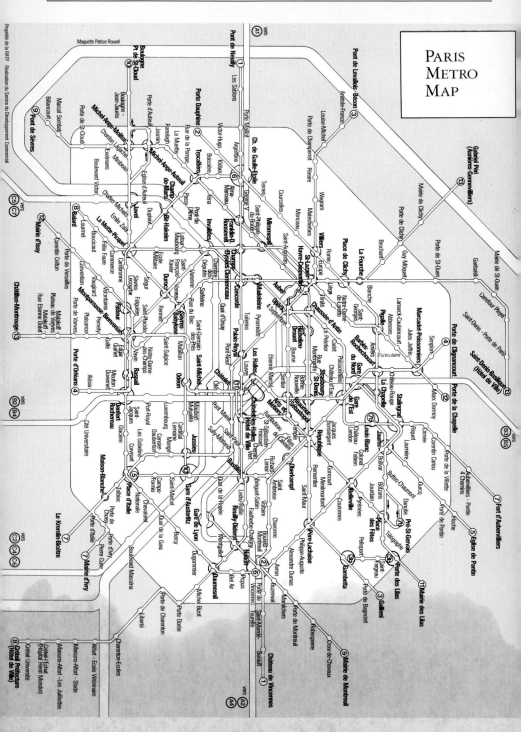

PARIS
METRO
MAP

Paris Notes

Paris Notes

Paris Notes

Paris Notes

Paris Notes

Paris Notes

Paris Notes